CHILDREN'S WORK IN AFRICAN AGRICULTURE

The Harmful and the Harmless

Edited by
James Sumberg and Rachel Sabates-Wheeler

With a Foreword by
Michael Bourdillon

BRISTOL
UNIVERSITY
PRESS

First published in Great Britain in 2023 by

Bristol University Press
University of Bristol
1–9 Old Park Hill
Bristol
BS2 8BB
UK
t: +44 (0)117 374 6645
e: bup-info@bristol.ac.uk

Details of international sales and distribution partners are available at bristoluniversitypress.co.uk

British Library Cataloguing in Publication Data
A catalogue record for this book is available from the British Library

ISBN 978-1-5292-2605-8 paperback
ISBN 978-1-5292-2606-5 ePub
ISBN 978-1-5292-2607-2 ePdf

Cover design: Lyn Davies Design
Front cover image: Getty / SEAN GLADWELL
Bristol University Press use environmentally responsible print partners.
Printed and bound in Great Britain by CPI Group (UK) Ltd, Croydon, CR0 4YY

FSC
www.fsc.org
MIX
Paper | Supporting responsible forestry
FSC® C013604

Contents

List of Figures, Tables and Boxes

Figures

Tables

Boxes

List of Abbreviations

ACRWC	African Charter on the Rights and Welfare of the Child
AGRA	Alliance for a Green Revolution in Africa
AOCC	African Orphan Crops Consortium
BCC	behaviour change communication
BDH	*Bono de Desarrollo Humano*
CAADP	Comprehensive African Agricultural Development Programme
CCT	conditional case transfer
CGP	Child Grants Programme (Lesotho)
CHW	children's harmful work
CLMRS	Child Labour Monitoring and Remediation System
CLU	Child Labour Unit
COCOBOD	Ghana Cocoa Board
CRC	Convention on the Rights of the Child
CRPD	Convention on the Rights of Persons with Disabilities
CSG	Child Support Grant (South Africa)
CSR	corporate social responsibility
CVB	Cocoa Verification Board
DHS	Demographic and Health Survey
EFA	Education for All
EMIS	Education Management Information System
FAO	Food and Agriculture Organization
FCUBE	Free Compulsory Universal Basic Education
FSC	Forest Stewardship Council
GAGE	Gender and Adolescence Global Evidence
GBDN	Global Business Disability Network
GCLMS	Ghana Child Labour Monitoring System
GES	Ghana Education Service
GFD	Ghana Federation of Disability Organisations
GLSS	Ghana Living Standards Survey
GNCC	Ghana National Commission on Children
GoG	Government of Ghana
GSS	Ghana Statistical Service

GVC	global value chain
HCDA	Horticultural Crops Development Authority (Kenya)
ICESCR	International Covenant on Economic, Social and Cultural Rights
ICF	International Classification of Functioning, Disability and Health
ICI	International Cocoa Initiative
ICLS	International Conference of Labour Statisticians
ICS	Internal Control System
IITA	International Institute of Tropical Agriculture
ILO	International Labour Organization
IMF	International Monetary Fund
INGO	international non-governmental organization
IPEC	International Programme for the Elimination of Child Labour
ISEAL	International Social and Environmental Accreditation and Labelling
LEAP	Livelihood Empowerment Against Poverty
LFS	Labour Force Survey
LID	living income differential
LSMS	Living Standards Measurement Survey
MDG	Millennium Development Goal
MESW	Ministry of Employment and Social Welfare
MGNREGS	Mahatma Gandhi National Rural Employment Guarantee Scheme
MICS	Multiple Indicator Cluster Survey
MPI	multidimensional poverty index
MSP	multi-stakeholder platform/multi-stakeholder partnership
NCLS	National Child Labour Survey
NGO	non-governmental organization
NORC	National Opinion Research Center at the University of Chicago
NPA1	National Plan of Action for the Elimination of the Worst Forms of Child Labour (first phase)
NPA2	National Plan of Action for the Elimination of the Worst Forms of Child Labour (second phase)
NPAHT	The National Plan of Action for the Elimination of Human Trafficking in Ghana
ODI	Overseas Development Institute
OECD	Organisation for Economic Co-operation and Development
OOSC	out-of-school children
OPD	organization of people with disabilities

OVC-CT	Cash Transfer for Orphans and Vulnerable Children (Kenya)
PABRA	Pan-Africa Bean Research Alliance
PSNP	Productive Safety Net Programme (Ethiopia)
PSSN	Productive Social Safety Net (Tanzania)
PTA	parent teacher association
PWs	public work programmes
RCT	randomized control trial
RPS	*Red de Protección Social*
SAFL	Southern Africa Food Lab
SAN	Sustainable Agriculture Network
SCTP	Social Cash Transfer Programme (Malawi)
SDG	Sustainable Development Goals
SFP	school feeding programme
SIMPOC	Statistical Information & Monitoring Programme on Child Labour
SNV	Netherlands Development Organization
SSA	sub-Saharan Africa
SWTS	School to Work Transition Survey
TUC	Trade Union Congress
UCT	unconditional cash transfer
UCW	Understanding Child Work programme
UNDP	United Nations Development Programme
UNESCO	United Nations Educational Science and Cultural Organization
UNFPA	United Nations Population Fund
USAID	United States Agency for International Development
USDoL	United States Department of Labor
V4CP	Voice for Change Partnership
WACAP	West Africa Cocoa and Commercial Agriculture Project
WASH	Water, Sanitation and Hygiene
WFP	World Food Programme
WHO	World Health Organization

Notes on Contributors

Abdulai Abubakari is Senior Research Fellow and Director of the Institute for Interdisciplinary Research (IIR), University for Development Studies (UDS), Tamale, Ghana. He is a sociologist by training and has experience in community development, farmer–herder conflicts, the impact of climate change on livestock and civil society participation in education. His current research focus is on farmer–herder relations, the role of non-state actors in basic education service delivery, chieftaincy and traditional institutions in northern Ghana.

Felix Ankomah Asante is Professor in the Institute of Statistical, Social and Economic Research (ISSER) and currently Pro-Vice-Chancellor in charge of Research, Innovation and Development at the University of Ghana. He was the Director of ISSER from August 2013 to July 2019. His research focuses on a broad range of themes in development economics relating to household food security, decentralization and provision of public goods and services, health issues and climate change.

Inka Barnett is Research Fellow at the Institute of Development Studies (IDS). She is a behavioural epidemiologist and nutritionist with experience in international child health and nutrition research. Inka is specialized in the application of mixed methods approaches to address complex health and nutrition challenges in low-and-middle income countries. She is also Health Research Associate for the Young Lives Study at the Oxford Department of International Development (ODID), University of Oxford.

Imogen Bellwood-Howard is Research Fellow at the Institute of Development Studies (IDS). Her research focuses on sustainable agriculture and food systems in rural and urban West Africa. In previous roles, she has focused on social embeddedness of agricultural markets and city-region food systems, and sustainable soil management. Imogen draws on environmental geography, agroecology, socioecological systems thinking, science and technology studies, political ecology and practice theory.

Rosilin Bock is a technical advisor in the field of gender and children's rights in development and humanitarian settings. She is a political scientist by training and has worked for government agencies, NGOs and faith-based organizations, often in cooperation with UN institutions. Rosilin is based in Berlin and recently finished her Master's degree in Children's Rights Studies at the University of Geneva.

Máiréad Dunne is Professor of the Sociology of Education and former Director of the Centre for International Education at the University of Sussex. Her research has attended to the links between educational and social inequalities in the Global South. In particular, she has focused on gender and sexuality; identities and difference; and youth and citizenship in contexts of poverty, inequality and conflict.

Irene Egyir is Associate Professor in the Department of Agricultural Economics and Agribusiness at the University of Ghana. Her research focuses primarily on sustainable agricultural intensification, gender studies and farmer cooperation. Her key concerns have been inclusivity and sustainability of farming systems.

Emmanuel Frimpong Boamah is Associate Professor with the Department of Urban and Regional Planning and the Community for Global Health Equity at the State University of New York, Buffalo. As an interdisciplinary scholar, he deploys multiple theoretical and methodological lenses to unpack the impacts of institutional arrangements on the governance of social-ecological systems (SES) in sub-Saharan Africa and the United States.

Neil Howard is Lecturer in International Development at the University of Bath. His research focuses on the governance of exploitative and so-called 'unfree' labour and in particular its various forms targeted for eradication by the Sustainable Development Goals. He conducts ethnographic and participatory action research with people defined as victims of trafficking, slavery, child labour and forced labour, and political anthropological research on the institutions that seek to protect them.

Sara Humphreys is a freelance researcher and Visiting Research Fellow at the Centre for International Education, University of Sussex. She has lived and worked in education in Africa, South America and Europe and is currently based in the Caribbean. Her research interests include issues surrounding gender, identity and social inequalities, and the micro-processes of schooling, particularly in sub-Saharan Africa.

Vicky Johnson is Professor of Childhood, Youth and Sustainability and Director for the Centre for Remote and Sustainable Communities at the University of the Highlands and Islands (UHI) and an Honorary Associate at the Institute of Development Studies (IDS). She has over 20 years of experience leading international teams as a Principal Investigator, complemented by engagement in the international NGO sector. Research interests include understanding how marginalized people can be supported as agents of change in rapidly changing environmental, political and cultural contexts.

Tessa Lewin is Research Fellow in the Participation, Inclusion and Social Change cluster at the Institute of Development Studies (IDS), where she co-convenes the MA in Gender and Development. Her work involves creative, visual and participatory research, teaching and communication. Her recent research has focused on gender politics, sexuality, visual activism and child rights. Her doctoral research investigated the nature of queer visual activism in South Africa.

Roy Maconachie is Professor of Natural Resources and Development in the Department of Social and Policy Sciences at the University of Bath. Roy's research in sub-Saharan Africa explores the social, political and economic aspects of food production and natural resource management, and their relationships to wider societal change. Much of his recent work has been concerned with the politics of natural resource management in West Africa, with a particular focus on the extractive industries, livelihood change and social conflict.

Rebecca Mitchell is Senior Research Officer and Programme Manager at the Institute of Development Studies (IDS). Her recent research concentrates on the lives of vulnerable migrants and refugees, including exploring experiences of accessing healthcare in the UK. Rebecca also works as part of a global team investigating the different economies that operate in protracted displacement affected communities in five international contexts. She is also the Programme Manager for the FCDO funded Better Assistance in Crises (BASIC) Research Programme, exploring how social protection operates in contexts experiencing crises.

Samuel Okyere is Senior Lecturer at the University of Bristol. He is primarily interested in the interplay between human and child rights, power, class, ethnicity, (un)freedom, inequality, the legacies of slave trade and colonization under conditions of globalization, mainly but not exclusively in African contexts. Over the last decade, he has explored these issues through field research on child and youth labour (primarily in agriculture, mining, fishing and other precarious sectors) migration, artisanal mining, sex work, forced labour, trafficking and other phenomena popularly labelled as 'modern slavery'.

Keetie Roelen is Research Fellow in the Rural Futures cluster at the Institute of Development Studies (IDS), and Co-Director of the Centre for Social Protection. Her research focuses on (child) poverty and wellbeing, social protection and anti-poverty interventions in relation to children, and women and psychosocial wellbeing, predominantly using mixed methods approaches. She has worked on projects in Southern and Eastern Africa, Asia, Central and Eastern Europe and Haiti.

Rachel Sabates-Wheeler is Professorial Fellow at the Institute of Development Studies (IDS). She is a Development Economist with extensive experience in rural development, institutional analysis, migration and social protection. Much of her research in the last 20 years has focussed on the lives and livelihoods of the most poor and vulnerable in many countries of sub-Saharan Africa. She is founder and Co-Director of the Centre for Social Protection at IDS.

James Sumberg is Emeritus Research Fellow at the Institute of Development Studies (IDS). He has spent most of his career studying small-scale agriculture in sub-Saharan Africa, and particularly West Africa. Since 2009 his research has focused largely on young people in rural Africa.

Carolina Szyp is Research Officer at the Institute of Development Studies (IDS). She is currently working on the FCDO-funded Better Assistance in Crises (BASIC) Research programme. Her research experience and interests include children's and youth livelihoods, decent work, education and social protection.

Jodie Thorpe is Research Fellow in the Business, Markets & State Cluster and Business and Development Centre at the Institute of Development Studies (IDS). Her work explores the relationships between market actors, and between the market and the state, to understand what drives business investment that is more or less inclusive and how these relationships impact development outcomes. Jodie is interested in the governance processes and institutional structures that mediate state–business interactions, both formal arrangements and informal networks.

Dorte Thorsen is Research Fellow at the Institute of Development Studies (IDS). With a particular interest in rural West Africa, her research has focused on gendered and generational dimensions of labour migration and the intersection with social and cultural transformations. A prominent part of her work has explored adolescents' 'independent' migration for work and education in Burkina Faso, Senegal and Ghana.

Giel Ton is Research Fellow at the Institute of Development Studies (IDS) and Director of the Centre for Development Impact (CDI). His research interest is the institutional arrangements that support collective action and coordination in agricultural value chains, including the design challenges to impact evaluations in agricultural value chains and private-sector development. He promotes Contribution Analysis as an overarching approach of theory-based evaluation and critical reflection in the mixing of methods for appropriate evaluation design.

Amy Warmington is Project Manager at the Institute of Development Studies. As part of the Better Assistance in Crises (BASIC) Research Programme, Amy supported senior researchers in their investigation of how to strengthen social assistance in the most difficult protracted crisis settings and for the populations that are the hardest to reach. Currently, at the International Centre for Tax and Development, she manages more than 30 research projects across 14 countries in Africa and South Asia. The projects seek to improve the quality of tax policy and administration in lower-income countries through collaborative, policy-oriented research.

Mary Wickenden is Research Fellow at the Institute of Development Studies (IDS) and leads the Disability Research team within the Participation, Inclusion and Social Change Cluster. She is a social/medical anthropologist and is interested in the perceptions and experiences of people with disabilities in high-income, middle-income and low-income settings. She has a particular interest in exploring the lives of children with disabilities and their families, and has worked on developing inclusive methodologies for participatory research, mainly in low-resource settings in the global South. Her regional experience is mainly in South Asia, southern Africa and East Africa. Her current research interests include community understandings of disability; the relationship between disability and poverty; participatory evaluation of disability programmes; sexuality/sexual abuse of disabled people; the wellbeing of carers; and the mainstreaming of disability components into broader research agendas. Mary is passionate about developing better dialogue across disciplines and with other actors such as governments, non-governmental organizations (NGOs) and organizations of people with disabilities (OPDs), working with disabled children and adults, their families and allies.

Thomas Yeboah is Research Fellow with the Bureau of Integrated Rural Development, College of Agriculture and Natural Resources, Kwame Nkrumah University of Science and Technology, Kumasi, Ghana. Thomas' research focuses on youth and children's mobilities including migration journeys, decision-making, working lives and lived experiences in the realm of spatial and social mobilities. He is also interested in young people's imagined futures, and the challenges of youth and employment in Africa, particularly how young people engage with the rural economy.

Acknowledgements

This book is based on work undertaken during the inception phase of the Action on Children's Harmful Work in African Agriculture (ACHA) programme. ACHA was funded by the UK government through the Department for International Development (now part of the Foreign, Commonwealth and Development Office [FCDO]) and led by Rachel Sabates-Wheeler and James Sumberg at the Institute for Development Studies (IDS). The views expressed are those of the authors and do not represent the views of the UK government.

Foreword

Michael Bourdillon

As the planet on which we live continues to deteriorate under pressure from a variety of human activities, it is clear that children will bear the brunt of the future cost in declining opportunities and standards of living. Indeed, many children, especially in marginal deprived communities, are already having their lives disrupted. Their situation has recently been exacerbated by the economic and social effects of the COVID-19 pandemic, and now by food shortages following the war in Ukraine. It becomes more than ever important to eliminate, or at least to mitigate, harm to children without diminishing what benefits they have. This is no time for well-wishing persons and organizations to impose policies based on ideals of childhood derived from prosperous societies in prosperous ages; such policies, ignoring the cultural and social diversity in which children grow up, all too often can further damage fragile lives.

In sub-Saharan Africa, young people dominate the population, which still has a large rural base. Agriculture, particularly family-based agriculture, is important not only for the large rural population, but also to sustain the growing urban populations. There is good reason for the United Nations to declare 2019–28 to be the Decade of Family Farming. Children invariably have a role in small-scale family farming; and apart from contributing to family sustenance, children's work in agriculture has a role in their development, embedding them socially in their societies and providing them with skills and knowledge needed for agriculture. The introduction to this volume points to a consequent problem: on the one hand, family-based production is encouraged as a way to keep populations sustained; on the other, there is pressure to eliminate child labour, and particularly to keep children out of the production and marketing chains of certain goods with international value. The failure of the Action Plan for the Decade of Family Farming to mention the role of children underlines the importance of this book.

The studies behind this volume were intended to be a prelude to field research. Although the research was sadly abandoned in the face of the COVID-19 pandemic and subsequent financial constraints, this publication makes the evidence-based insights from a wide range of data across several disciplines available to other researchers and indeed to all who are concerned about the predicaments facing a large number of children now and in the future.

The coherent approach adopted by the team has a number of striking features that provide understanding often missed in discourse on child labour. First, children's work is not presented simply as an uncomfortable phenomenon that we can eliminate from our experience; rather it is recognized as an activity in the lives of young people. Rather than perceiving working children as passive victims to be rescued, their work is understood as a component in their strategies and responses to the changing situations in which they live. Simply to eliminate their work, even harmful work, therefore means some disruption. To effectively eliminate or mitigate harm accruing to children through their work requires an understanding of the place of work in their lives and a careful identification of the harm to be eliminated, two themes that persist through this volume.

In particular, the relationship between work and education is examined. Child labour discourse commonly presents work as opposed to education (often assumed to be synonymous with schooling) and presents an ideal of replacing children's work with schooling. Throughout the volume, learning and developmental benefits of work are recognized, making appropriate work a component of education understood in the fullest sense. Chapters 3 and 4 focus on the complex relationships between work, school and education, and demand a critical examination of schooling as well as of work.

The emphasis in this volume on understanding work in the contexts of children's lives is extended to understanding children's lives in the contexts of the communities in which they live. Children's activities, including their work – both productive and other kinds – are imbedded in their relations with those around them. Their work therefore is relational and affects their standing in their communities as they mature.

In this way, the approach in this volume diverges from the strange individualism that dominates so much of Western thinking, assuming that societies can be understood as collections of autonomous units interacting with each other in pursuance of their individual interests and rights. In contrast, many African cultures see people as existing precisely in relation to each other, sometimes elaborated in the African philosophical concept of *Ubuntu*. This relational way of thinking resonates with certain trends in scientific thinking. Whereas in the past, science has broken the world down into ever smaller particles considered atomically and then sub-atomically, now these particles are understood as existing in relation to each other rather than independently, as do the larger conglomerations of them. Life is seen now as systems of interdependent forms feeding into and on each other. Human consciousness develops in relation to the various, and now interconnected, cultural contexts in which it grows. While philosophical discussion of such issues lies outside the domain of the current volume, its relational approach to children and their work resonates better with contemporary appreciation of the complexities of reality than does a naïve assumption that activities like work and labour can be isolated and eliminated.

The different contexts in which children develop result in different childhoods, another theme that runs through the volume. This contrasts with widespread assumptions about the universality of childhood, based largely on childhood in well-resourced sectors of society that have no need for children to take on any responsibility, and to which all other societies are assumed to aspire. In the real world, societies respond to the varied situations in which they live with different ideals in rearing children. We are learning about the importance for a healthy planet of diversity in many areas; a diversity in childhoods is needed for flourishing in the diverse and changing situations in which children find themselves. In particular, some form of productive work is normal for many children – including disabled children (see Chapter 5).

This approach requires detailed observations of the diversity in children's lives, which largely escape statistical analyses of large data sets. A strength of this volume is its assemblage of data from across disciplines, including qualitative research. Chapter 3 explicitly reviews different methods that are used for assessing harmful work in agriculture.

A pervasive problem in the discourse on child labour arises from confusing and often misleading uses of the term, and blurredness in understanding the harm from which children should be protected. Much literature follows the lead of the International Labour Organization, which offers a common definition of 'child labour' as work that is in some way harmful or hazardous to children, and assumes thereafter that activities classified as 'child labour' using different criteria are always harmful (see Chapter 7). The editors of this collection are refreshingly careful about the terminology used. Two chapters (2 and 3) scrutinize notions of harm with respect to children's work; the focus throughout the book is on work in which actual harm is experienced.

Much discussion of children's work concerns protecting children from exploitation and harm. Child protection suffers a fundamental problem resulting from the instinctive human aversion to risk: behavioural psychology has established that people are more strongly influenced by the fear of harm or loss than they are by considerations of gain; this bias can result in restrictive protective policies that impede opportunities for learning and development. When children are exploited or harmed in work, the need for protective action readily overrides consideration of retaining any benefits of work. This volume gives consistent attention to how children's work is implicated in their relationships and their development, shifting the object of policy and intervention towards identifying and removing harm without disrupting childhood and the family agriculture on which children depend.

Such a nuanced approach to protection is costly in terms of the time and effort needed to examine diverse situations of children. For those who are really concerned about protecting children and who do not have time and resources for this kind of study, perhaps it would be more useful to focus on areas where the cause of harm is evident and widespread – such as global warming. But it is easier for policy makers and activists to adopt simple generalized principles for protection: the cost of such questionable protection can be heavy in disruption and lost opportunities, but these costs are born by children and their families and are easily ignored by those in power. James C. Scott, in *Seeing Like a State*, points to disastrous results when planners and politicians rely on abstract and simplified generalizations derived from the analysis of limited variables; he recommends instead more flexible planning that utilizes localized knowledge derived from the experience and ingenuity of people adapting to their local conditions. Similarly, if we are to genuinely benefit children who need support and protection, our understanding of their work should pay attention to how children and families find ways to live their lives in difficult situations. We can hope that this volume will contribute to such understanding.

It remains for me to congratulate and thank the teams of authors for producing this volume, and especially the editors, James Sumberg and Rachel Sabates-Wheeler, for bringing it together coherently and for their clear and informative introduction.

1

Children's Work in African Agriculture: An Introduction

Rachel Sabates-Wheeler and James Sumberg

Introduction

The United Nations declared 2019–28 to be the Decade of Family Farming, with a focus on 'all types of family-based production models in agriculture, fishery, forestry, pastoral and aquaculture, and include peasants, indigenous peoples, traditional communities, fisher folks, mountain farmers, forest users and pastoralists' (FAO and IFAD, 2019, p 8). Children are integral to most families – and to the very notion of family – so it follows that agriculture production that excludes children could hardly be considered 'family-based'. Yet, the Global Action Plan for the Decade of Family Farming makes no mention of children's roles in family farming, and neither child labour nor children's work is flagged as an issue to be addressed. This might suggest a desire to side-step the political landmine that is child labour; an understanding that, in many contexts, children make a positive contribution to family farming, and an implicit assumption that they will continue to do so; the perception that family farming makes a positive contribution to children's lives, skill set and future; or an assumption that no harm can arise when work occurs within the family.

While it is not evident from the Decade of Family Farming Action Plan, there is considerable pressure on (and by) international agencies (including those that sing the praises of family farming), governments, companies and others to eliminate child labour, and children more broadly, from some agricultural value chains. Under the closest scrutiny are value chains involving a handful of important internationally traded commodities – including cocoa, tea, sugar, coffee and tobacco – produced on many thousands of small-scale, 'family farms' in sub-Saharan Africa

(SSA). After all, if anything could instantaneously flatten the milk foam of an expensive cappuccino in Tokyo, Cape Town, London or New York, it is the idea that the coffee beans were produced with child labour. Much less attention is paid to value chains for local food crops, from staple grains to vegetables, to which the vast majority of children's work on farms in SSA is devoted. Unusually, a report by the Understanding Children's Work (UCW) programme focuses on children's work across the whole of Ghana's agricultural sector (UCW, 2017).

This apparent tension – between the celebration of family farming on the one hand and the desire to eliminate child labour from agricultural value chains on the other – is at the heart of this book.

Children's welfare and development, from nutrition and health to education and protection, are core concerns of social policy. And with the creation of the International Labour Organization (ILO) in 1919, the abolition of children's economic activity – framed as 'child labour' – became a central, if contested and politicized, plank of the emerging framework of global social policy (Meerkerk, 2008; Liebel and Invernizzi, 2019; Maul, 2019; van Daalen and Hanson, 2019). It remains so today, supported by a complex, multi-layered infrastructure of international conventions, declarations, resolutions and definitions, and national laws and regulations.

If the commitment to end child labour remained largely unchanged over the last century, during this same period SSA experienced significant change in a number of critically important domains. The 1950s, 1960s and 1970s saw most countries become independent politically (if not economically). There have been improvements in health, significant population growth – from 227 million in 1960 to an estimated 1.1 billion in 2020[1] – and urbanization. Africans and African economies have been drawn into the era of globalization through petroleum and mineral extraction, expanding telecommunication and domestic, intra-continental and global labour migration (Akokpari, 2000). There has been dramatic growth in indicators of modernization such as the provision of tertiary education[2] and access to mobile phones.[3]

African agriculture, through traditional 'tropical commodities' including cocoa, coffee, tea and cotton and new exports like vegetables, flowers and cashews, is increasingly tied to highly coordinated, global value chains (Balié et al, 2019). These work to new quality standards and seek to project multiple extrinsic attributes, from fair trading relations and environmental stewardship to production systems free of child labour. In terms of development agendas and activities in SSA (and elsewhere), these have been increasingly shaped by international initiatives such as structural adjustment, the Millennium Development Goals (MDGs), the Sustainable Development Goals (SDGs) and the push for an African Green Revolution (for example, Adesina, 2010; D'Alessandro and Zulu, 2017).

At the same time, poverty remains a fact of life for people throughout rural SSA. For example, using a multidimensional poverty index (MPI) that captures simultaneous deprivations through ten indicators related to education, health and living standards, OPHI and UNDP (2020) estimated that 69.8 per cent of 654 million rural people in 41 African countries are MPI poor. Across all African countries, 82.1 per cent of all MPI poor people are in rural areas. Provision of education, health and other public services is patchy and too often of poor quality; and while engagement in the non-farm economy is increasing, such work is largely informal and insecure (Sumberg, 2021). The agricultural sector, which most households rely on to some extent, is dominated by small-scale family farming with generally low levels of productivity (Jayne and Sanchez, 2021). This is the context within which the tension around children's contribution to family farming and their involvement in agricultural value chains now plays itself out.

The intellectual framework supporting the global commitment to abolish child labour is also shifting. For example, the system of assumptions that underpins much child-oriented global social policy is increasingly being challenged. Southern academics and others argue that these assumptions run rough-shod over the diversity of local norms and expectations about children in families and society, about the very nature of childhood and about what constitutes appropriate parenting (for example, Abebe and Ofosu-Kusi, 2016; Twum-Danso Imoh et al, 2018; Botchway et al, 2019; Thum-Danso Imoh, 2019). The implication is that the image of a 'universal child' (Nieuwenhuys, 1998; Smith, 2010) living a childhood in which school and play are the primary points of reference, is inappropriate as a basis for either global or locally adapted policy.

Also, beginning in the 1980s, a series of publications began to change understanding of the economic activity of children in the developing world and of the opportunities (and pitfalls) for policy. Publications such as *Children, Work and Child Labor: Changing Responses to the Employment of Children* (White, 1994), *What Works for Working Children?* (Boyden and Ling, 1998), *Enfants travailleurs, repenser l'enfance* (*Working Children, Rethinking Childhood*) (Bonnet et al, 2006) and *Rights and Wrongs of Children's Work* (Bourdillon et al, 2010), and an associated body of scholarship, sought to reframe the debate by demonstrating the importance of seeing children's economic activity in context. In its simplest form, this reframing entails a shift away from the singular focus on the elimination of child labour, with nearly all economic activity by children being assumed to be abusive or harmful, and the children themselves assumed to be without agency and therefore vulnerable and in need of protection. The alternative framing portrays agentive children who engage in work, within and outside the home, for a variety of economic, social, cultural and personal reasons. There is no suggestion that those children who are exploited, harmed or forced to work to their detriment do not deserve protection. Neither is it suggested that simply because children are seen to be active (choosing to work) that their lives are without struggle or deprivation. Rather, the argument is that mainstream child labour discourse and its associated regulatory instruments and interventions do not recognize the economic necessity for poor children to work, the trade-offs being negotiated, or the real (economic, social and educational) benefits that can accrue to working children and their families (for an alternative view see Weber and Abbasi, 2022).

Children's work in African agriculture: the harmful and the harmless

This book is about the millions of rural children, throughout the sub-continent, who hoe, dig, plant, tend livestock, cook, scrub and undertake many other farm and domestic tasks. Most of this work takes place on the farms of parents or relatives, some is for wages, some is on the children's own plots, and some is forced and/or results in harm. In many situations, the contributions made by children through their work are important for family welfare, and learning to work is also seen as an important part of both growing up and responsible parenting. Many rural children combine school and work.

The problem that the book addresses is that at all levels of social policy, and in high-level public discourse, children's engagement in economic activity is frequently conflated with 'child labour', despite an acknowledgement that children also engage in 'benign' work. This conflation results in a strong emphasis on exploitation and harm. This is particularly problematic in Africa for three reasons: many rural children work at least some of the time as part of a normal rural childhood, to contribute to food security and school expenses, and to demonstrate allegiance to the family; much of this work is not harmful;[4] and the negative framing creates pressure within international value chains to 'eliminate' child labour. Unfortunately, few such 'elimination' initiatives are sufficiently nuanced to distinguish between economic activity that is harmful and that which is not, and as a consequence, these initiatives themselves have the potential to generate harm by curtailing income streams for poor households, thereby undermining their food security and livelihood possibilities.

The aims of the book are threefold. First, to help shift current policy debate and public discourse around children's economic activities in rural Africa. Second, to fill a gap in the literature by putting forward a coherent account of children's work in African agriculture. This account explores the notions of 'harm' and 'harmful work' in the context of the lives and livelihoods of rural households and the children within them, and the agricultural value chains within which much children's work is situated. And, finally, to provide new insights on the kinds of interventions that might better address harmful children's work within agricultural value chains.

The book puts the notions of 'harm' and 'harmful work' at centre stage, and argues that in most cases the work children do on farms does not result in harm. This is the first book to directly and singularly address children's work in African agriculture. It seeks to re-frame the debate about children's work and harm in rural Africa, with the aim of shifting research, public discourse and policy so that they better serve the varied interests of rural children and their families. It also seeks to increase understanding of rural children's lives and the multiple contingencies in their contexts that influence when, where and how they work.

Children's Work in African Agriculture makes an original contribution to thinking and debates around children's work and child labour. While others have argued the case for a broader view of children's economic activity (for example, White, 1994; Boyden and Ling, 1998; Bonnet et al, 2006; Bourdillon et al, 2010), this is the first book that uses a multi-disciplinary perspective to address this challenge specifically in relation to agriculture in Africa. This focus is particularly timely because of the potential for negative unintended consequences from efforts to address child labour in a handful of global agricultural value chains, with the cocoa to chocolate chain being the most prominent.

The book is organized around both themes and cases. The themes, including harm, education, disability, value chains, social protection and research methods are relevant across rural SSA. The case chapters, however, are all drawn from Ghana and include politics and policy, cocoa, the Lake Volta fishery and shallot production on the Keta peninsula. Ghana is particularly interesting because over the past three decades successive governments have committed themselves to all relevant international instruments and enacted a plethora of laws, policies and programmes aimed at defining, prohibiting or regulating particular forms of children's work. In effect, Ghana has been in the eye of the international storm around child labour because it is the world's second largest producer of cocoa beans. While we make no claim that Ghana in any way represents the diversity of agriculture or state engagement with the issue of child labour across SSA, we do argue that other countries and other crop-based value chains are, in the future, likely to experience similar pressure to act in order to protect agricultural export markets.

Although child trafficking and forced labour have been linked to both the cocoa (Minderoo Foundation, 2018; USDoL, 2020) and Lake Volta fishery (Adeyemi et al, 2016; CNN, 2019) cases, these phenomena are not a central focus of the book. The reason for this is that available evidence suggests that the vast majority of children who work in rural SSA – including in Ghana's cocoa areas and around Lake Volta – live with one or both parents or with a relative (ILO-IPEC, 2013a; Sadhu et al, 2020). Trafficking and forced labour are clearly social phenomena that must be addressed, but the overly simplistic narratives around these phenomena should not be allowed to drive either our understanding of children's economic activity or policy responses to it (see Hashim and Thorsen, 2011; Okyere, 2017; Koomson et al, 2022).

The remainder of this chapter consists of four main sections. The next three sections address in greater detail the agricultural context, changing perspectives on children and childhoods, and changing perspectives on children's work. The fourth section provides a brief chapter-by-chapter summary of the rest of the book.

Family farming in sub-Saharan Africa: change and continuity

In total, 59 per cent of the population of SSA continue to live in rural areas (ranging from 86 per cent in Burundi to 10 per cent in Gabon).[5] And, rural residents are almost three times as likely to be multidimensionally poor than those living in urban areas (OPHI and UNDP, 2020). They are also likely to be older: the share of 15–24 year olds in the rural population (19 per cent) is around 10 percentage points lower than in 'main cities' (Stecklov and Menashe-Oren, 2019).

Many rural residents are engaged in agriculture (including farming, livestock production and fishing) in one way or another, and to one degree or another (Abay et al, 2020). As a consequence, there are few rural households that do not rely on agriculture – ranging from gardening and farming to feed the family, to fully commercial production – for at least some of their livelihood. However, it is a mistake to frame this engagement as full-time farming: for many, farming is only one of a number of economic activities. Forms of engagement with, and the relative importance of, agriculture vary significantly depending on economic geography as well as household and individual characteristics and resources. The diversity in ways that people engage with farming has important implications for technological change, for the allocation of family labour, the rhythms of family life and for children's involvement in farm work.

Of course, this general picture is rooted in colonial regimes' push to produce export crops – oil palm, cotton, groundnut, cocoa, tea, coffee, tobacco, sugar and others – in order to fuel industrial expansion and satisfy consumer demand in Europe. It is against this legacy that at the beginning of the 1980s, the World Bank issued its report 'Accelerated Development in sub-Saharan Africa: An Agenda for Action' (Berg et al, 1981). This report, and the two decades of structural adjustment that followed, focused the minds of international financial institutions and development partners, and thus African governments, on 'agricultural sector reform'. Key objectives were to reduce the role of the state in the provision of agricultural inputs and the marketing of agricultural outputs, to expand 'non-traditional' agricultural exports and to re-orient and strengthen agricultural research (Commander, 1988; Cheru, 1992). The idea was that these reforms would incentivize farmers to engage more readily with input and output markets, to invest in technology and to start to see farming 'as a business.' It is in this context that the notion of 'the value chain' (see Chapter 6, this volume) became pervasive in discussions of agricultural and rural development in SSA.

As tolerance for structural adjustment waned across SSA, the agricultural development agenda focused on stimulating private-sector provision of seeds, fertilizer and rural financial services. A number of high-profile initiatives including the Comprehensive Africa Agriculture Development Programme (CAADP) (Brüntrup, 2011) and Alliance for a Green Revolution in Africa (AGRA) (Toenniessen et al, 2008; Kerr, 2012) sought to transform SSA's small-scale farming by investing in and promoting, for example, the adoption of agricultural and digital technology, mechanization, youth entrepreneurship, post-harvest transformation and policy reform – all couched in the language of increased productivity, closing yield gaps and value chains. While not fully embraced by the mainstream across SSA, there has, nevertheless, also been interest in alternative models of agricultural and rural development including, for example, agroecology and food sovereignty (Altieri et al, 2012).

It is undoubtedly the case that there have been significant changes in agriculture and livelihoods in rural SSA. And there is evidence of new trends including the growth in medium-sized farms (Jayne et al, 2019) and the development of land rental markets (Jayne et al, 2021) that have potential to alter agrarian relations in some areas. But it is also the case that much of the sub-region's agriculture remains largely reliant on family labour (that is, 'family farming'), makes limited use of new technology, is mixed in terms of its orientation (that is, toward both markets and household-provisioning) and is generally characterized by low levels of productivity. Despite some evidence of growth and 'rural transformation' (Barrett et al, 2017; Jayne et al, 2018), as indicated earlier, rural areas are still characterized by very high levels of multidimensional poverty.

This, then, is the complex and extremely diverse context within which children are integrated into family farming in SSA. One critically important axis of diversity relates to the characteristics of different agricultural value chains (Chapter 6, this volume; Barrett et al, 2020; Feyaerts et al, 2020; de Brauw and Bulte, 2021). For example, does a value chain respond to local or international demand; depend on global or domestic capital and firms; need to protect a retail brand and minimize the reputation risk of key corporate actors; and/or integrate independently monitored standards? This range of possibilities might include, at one extreme, cocoa produced to stringent fair trade and environmental standards and destined for luxury chocolate brands with global reach, and at the other, maize (or rice, cowpeas or any number of other food crops) produced with no reference to formal standards for own-consumption or domestic and regional markets.

Many family farms simultaneously participate in value chains having some characteristics of both of these stylized extremes: a child may carry cocoa pods one day and hoe maize destined for the family pot on another; or one sibling may help with the cocoa while another helps with the maize, works on their own tomato plot or facilitates the value chain work of other household members by undertaking domestic work. Similarly, within a village there will likely be some households that engage with international value chains and others that do not. Nevertheless, it is critically important to note that even though engagement with global value chains is only a small part of all children's work in rural SSA, the imperatives of these chains dominate and drive public discourse primarily because they serve northern consumers and carry significant reputational risk for corporate actors and brands (Sabates-Wheeler and Sumberg, 2022). The suggestion is not that a much greater share of children's work on family farms (or domestic work) should be brought into a child labour framing and marked for elimination (although this might be the result of 'area-based' as opposed to crop-based approaches to the elimination of child labour [for example, ILO-IPEC, 2013b, 2013c]). Quite the opposite: the argument that runs through the chapters of this book is that a more nuanced and contextualized understanding of the benefits and the harms arising from children's work can inform more appropriate approaches across all children's work domains and over the diversity of agricultural value chains.

Children and childhood: evolving perspectives

What defined the now century-old movement to establish a global approach to core social policy issues, like the regulation of work, is its universal ambition (de Castro, 2020). The idea, for example, that all members of identified social groups, be they working people, working children or people living in poverty or with disabilities – no matter who they are or where they live – could benefit from an overarching policy approach is nothing less than intoxicating. The assumption is that there is sufficient commonality across contexts to mean that much can be gained by a common approach, for example in the identification of priority areas, the setting of objectives and approaches to policy. Ironically, the universal ambition is also a weakness as it generates its own homogenizing dynamics. In other words, at the heart of the idea of global social policy and 'roll out' is a potential slippery slope – universal, universalizing, uniform, decontextualized.

Within development studies, the global or universal approach to children and childhood (Heinze, 2000; Smith, 2010) has been critiqued since at least the early 1990s, with, for example, Boyden (1990) arguing that it emerged from the historical and cultural ideals of Europe and the United States. She posited that purity and sanctity ideals attributed to the safe and happy child are products of a Judaeo-Christian culture that went hand-in-hand with the rise of capitalism. On this basis, Boyden argued that such ideals are historically and culturally bound rather than universal, and they are not appropriate to other contexts, regions, cultures or historical periods.

Others, including a growing cohort of Southern scholars, have expanded and deepened this critique (Smith, 2010; Abebe and Ofosu-Kusi, 2016; Twum-Danso Imoh, 2016; Botchway et al, 2019). In fact, the decolonial turn in social and political sciences is encouraging a discussion of assumptions underpinning the dominant portrayal of globalization processes, and in doing so, problematizing the concept of the universal child. Twum-Danso Imoh (2016) makes the point that there has been an overstatement and overemphasis on the marginalized childhood of the South, too easily characterized by lack, deprivation and constraint. As argued previously by Boyden, she suggests that this is likely due to 'a desire to demonstrate the dissonance between the global hegemonic ideal, with its roots in the North, and the local realities of a significant number of children in many contexts in the South' (p 457). The local is consistently posed in contrast with the ideal. This 'othering' means real-life dimensions and experiences of childhood that are culturally or contextually specific – such as child-headed households, children's sexualities, marriage and work expectations – are never revealed or explored as valid or meaningful. Along similar lines, Abebe and Ofusu-Kusi (2016) argue that local childhoods in the South cannot simply be reduced to backward or traditional, deviant or lacking. They emphasize the need to re-appraise difference and diversity in childhoods as a way of critiquing universalisms of knowledge and ideals, and making space for alternative conceptions.[6]

The problematic link between a defined 'ideal' child and children's rights is identified by a number of authors, with Heinze (2000) observing that 'to universalise children's rights is to universalise a culturally specific idea of childhood' (p 1), which works against heterogeneity across contexts and households. He further suggests that 'as definitions of what is acceptable become narrower, reactions to lifestyles that differ become harsher, leading even to the criminalisation of certain working class practices' (p 11). This is precisely what is seen with respect to children's economic activity, where international conventions that are mirrored in national legislation have defined as harmful (and at times criminalized) the everyday activities and experience of millions of children.

One implication of a move towards more local understandings is the challenge it poses to the definition of childhood based on chronological age. Article 1 of the Convention on the Rights of the Child (CRC) defines children exclusively in chronological terms (that is, as human beings below the age of 18). Similarly, the African Charter on the Rights and Welfare of the Child (ACRWC) defines children to include 'every human being below the age of eighteen years' (Organisation of African Unity, 1990). However, grounded research shows that independent of age, cultural and socio-economic contexts play a critical role in determining what constitutes childhood. Seniority, tradition, expectations, gender and household circumstances are key to the meaning of childhood, and when and how a child transitions to adulthood (White, 2002; Clemensen, 2016; Phiri and Abebe, 2016; Smørholm, 2016). In fact, in African rural communities, chronological age is rarely a culturally or socially accepted way to delineate the bounds of childhood. Ruddick (2003, p 357) notes how there are 'vastly different understandings of what it is to be young' and the irony of promoting the West's ideals of childhood in settings where they are alien, and where people generally lack the socio-economic resources needed to realize them.

The tension between formal definitions and local understandings of children and childhood has implications far beyond academic debate. When chronological age is used to define who is and is not a child, and capabilities within the category children, it also determines the hours and kinds of work that are acceptable, hazardous and so on. Formalizing an age-based definition in law delineates what is 'right' or 'wrong', what is 'criminal' or 'acceptable', regardless of local conditions, gender differences and traditions. Imposed constructions of childhood, in part, help explain why initiatives to address child labour may either be ineffective or have unintended consequences that negatively affect the wellbeing and life opportunities of children and their families.

The implications of the changing perspectives outlined in this section for the understanding of children's economic activity, and more specifically the links between children's work and harm, are profound. It is no longer defensible to impose a universalizing frame: local understandings, norms and experiences can no longer be simply dismissed as deviant or deficient (Chapter 8, this volume). However, this recognition does not necessarily mean that all is well, that all children's work is good work or that rural children's outcomes could not be improved.

Children's work

As the universal ambition of global social policy works its way through complex, multi-level political and bureaucratic processes, it runs the risk of being rendered into a story of decontextualization, homogenization and devaluation of the diversity of local histories, cultures, social traditions and norms within which rural people live. This is despite the acknowledged need for adaptation to suit local circumstances.

A girl child in Nigeria's Benue State spends the afternoon hoeing weeds on her family's maize plot. This could be seen to represent: (1) an afternoon of hazardous and/or harmful activity; exploitation; a childhood denied; infringement of international instruments and national legislation and regulation; or alternatively, (2) a contribution to household welfare; an expression of the child's desire to be seen as respectful, serious and dutiful; an opportunity for her to enhance her self-esteem; a lesson in individual responsibility; an opportunity to learn and practise a rural skill; an opportunity to earn money; an expression of a social or cultural norm.

One's perspective on the girl's afternoon of hoeing might depend on whether she should or could have been in school; the contribution that hoeing makes to her physical and/or psychological wellbeing; how she came to be hoeing, whether she had a choice; the nature of the tools she uses; the length of time she hoes; whether hoeing is an occasional or frequent activity; whether the tasks and work rate set for her are reasonable; whether she is supervised, can take breaks or is paid; whether she is exposed to hazards (for example, from unwanted advances from men or boys, or to agricultural chemicals and excessive heat) while moving between home and the plot, and/or while hoeing; whether she suffers harm as a result of any such exposure; and her age.

The point of this example is not to create or reinforce a dichotomy between economic activity that is 'bad' (child labour) and economic activity that is 'good' (children's work). Indeed, what separates the two perspectives is much more than a list of criteria to be ticked off and added up, and from which one can conclude that, because of her hoeing, she is either 'in child labour' (or hazardous child labour, or another of the 'worst forms' of child labour) (perspective 1), or working on the family farm as a normal and everyday part of a rural childhood (perspective 2).

The inescapable fact is that all over the world, children work. Girls and boys; poor and middle class; in the Global South and the Global North; rural and urban; at home, in schools, on farms and in myriad other locations – children work. Their economic activity is, by and large, neither infrequent nor deviant, and as the ILO itself makes clear, it should not necessarily be seen as problematic:

> The participation of children or adolescents above the minimum age for admission to employment in work that does not affect their health and personal development or interfere with their schooling, is generally regarded as being something positive. This includes activities such as assisting in a family business or earning pocket money outside school hours and during school holidays. These kinds of activities contribute to children's development and to the welfare of their families; they provide them with skills and experience, and help to prepare them to be productive members of society during their adult life.[7]

The two key provisos here are that the child is 'above the minimum age for employment' (which is set out in the Minimum Age Convention, 1973, No. 138, but can vary by country and type of work) and that 'the work does not affect their health and personal development or interfere with their schooling'. According to ILO, work that contravenes either of these provisos is considered as child labour and 'is to be targeted for elimination':

> The term 'child labour' is often defined as work that deprives children of their childhood, their potential and their dignity, and that is harmful to physical and mental development. It refers to work that:
>
> - is mentally, physically, socially or morally dangerous and harmful to children; and/or
> - interferes with their schooling by: depriving them of the opportunity to attend school; obliging them to leave school prematurely; or requiring them to attempt to combine school attendance with excessively long and heavy work.[8]

This approach shaped the context within which Goddard and White (1982, and the associated special issue of the journal *Development and Change*), White (1994), Boyden and Ling (1998), Bonnet et al (2006), Bourdillion et al (2010) and others sought to re-think and re-frame the discussion of children's economic activity. Despite these efforts, with its focus on danger and harm on the one hand and interference with schooling on the other, the ILO approach continues to directly inform current concerns about, and efforts to eliminate, child labour from some high-profile agricultural value chains in SSA.

At the heart of the movement to re-think child labour is a context sensitive, sociological perspective on children and families. As outlined in the previous section, this perspective challenges the narrative that children, by definition, are vulnerable and in need of protection; that the only acceptable childhood is one that prioritizes school and play; that clear lines can be drawn between work that is acceptable and work that is not, and between economic and non-economic work (and that these categories are independent); that school is always better than work; and that abolition or elimination is the only acceptable policy response to children's involvement in work that is hazardous or harmful.[9]

The alternative is not simply another high-level narrative that skates lightly over the diversity within the category children, the diversity of family social and economic situations, of the factors motivating children's economic activity, and of the cultural and social traditions and norms within which children's experiences take shape. Rather, it is in acknowledging this diversity that a more nuanced and relational picture is developed. Instead of an exclusive focus on individual children as vulnerable, as victims, their social milieu and agency are also highlighted. This opens important new ground: with children (and their families) seen to be navigating (local norms and institutions), adapting (to changing economic circumstance) and actively assessing trade-offs (for example, between school and work, or studying and household food production). It also draws attention to working children's efforts to organize and militate for better conditions (Liebel, 2013; Taft, 2013; Liebel and Invernizzi, 2019), although it is not clear how much impact these have had in rural SSA (Terenzio, 2007; and for some earlier examples of collective action by young agricultural workers in Ghana see Van Hear, 1982).

Bourdillon et al (2010) devote a chapter of their landmark book to the challenge of 'Assessing Harm Against Benefits', and this challenge is also central to *Children's Work in African Agriculture.* A difficulty arises because of the complex terminology and formalized definitions that have become integral to discourses around child labour. In order to avoid getting lost in this terminology the book will follow the scheme set out by Sabates-Wheeler and Sumberg (2022) (Box 1.1), which makes a clear distinction between hazard and harm, and reserves the term 'children's harmful work' for 'the actual experience of harm resulting from work' (also see Chapter 2, this volume).

Introduction to the chapters

The argument that runs through the chapters of this book is that a more nuanced and contextualized understanding of the benefits and the harms arising from children's work can inform more appropriate approaches across all children's work domains and over the diversity of agricultural value chains. The next six chapters explore themes, including harm, education, disability, value chains, social protection and research methods that are relevant across rural SSA. The following case chapters, however, are all drawn from Ghana and include politics and policy, cocoa, the Lake Volta fishery, and shallot production on the Keta peninsula. Here we provide a review of these chapters.

In Chapter 2, Roy Maconachie, Neil Howard and Rosilin Bock introduce the concept of 'harm' that is foundational to understanding what has been termed the 'rights and wrongs of children's work'. They explain how the concept remains a site of contestation, pushing us to re-examine formal, institutional understandings of harm, such as that put forward by the ILO. Their analysis, drawing from a review of the theorization of harm in various academic disciplines, points towards the need for a holistic approach to harm across academic research and policy, which seeks to incorporate grounded and more subjective dimensions, with wellbeing as a central focus. That said, children's work and any associated harm is notoriously difficult to

Box 1.1: Hazards, hazardous work, harm and children's harmful work

A **hazard** is a danger that is inherent to a task or job, or an aspect or feature of a work environment.

Hazard management refers to efforts by society at large, the state, local institutions, employers, parents and working children themselves to reduce children's exposure to workplace hazards, and/or help them navigate exposure to a hazard without being harmed.

The notion of **hazardous work** is rooted in an acknowledgement that every work task and work environment exposes workers to one or more hazards. However, because the nature of these hazards varies significantly, as does the level and effectiveness of hazard management, jobs and work environments can be considered to sit along a continuum from minimally to extremely hazardous.

Harm is an identifiable negative impact on an individual or household arising from a specific workplace hazard. Harm might be physical, psycho-social (including stress and anxiety), harm to development (for example, lost opportunities for schooling) and/or financial (that is, lost income).

Children's harmful work refers to any work that children undertake that results in harm to the child and/or their household. The emphasis here is on the actual experience of harm resulting from work, as opposed to the potential to be harmed or the risk of being harmed.

Source: Sabates-Wheeler and Sumberg (2022)

identify, assess and understand. In Chapter 3, Keetie Roelen, Inka Barnett, Vicky Johnson, Tessa Lewin, Dorte Thorsen and Giel Ton detail the merits and challenges of a range of quantitative, qualitative, participation and certification methods that have been variously used to measure and evaluate the extent and impact of children's work and child labour. The authors propose a set of research design principles for studying children's work and call for the use of new and innovative methods, highlighting the need for truly integrated mixed methods as well as more exploratory qualitative, participatory and emergent methodologies.

Chapter 4 situates children's work within a grounded and holistic understanding of where work and harm actually occur across the domains of children's lives: household, work and school. Máiréad Dunne, Sara Humphreys and Carolina Szyp introduce a relational, analytical edu-workscape within which they explore children's lives in rural SSA as they relate to schooling, work and harm. Through an exploration of key tensions between schooling and work – tensions mediated, for example, by gender, age and ability – the chapter highlights issues that are highly pertinent to policy interventions aimed both at increasing educational participation and addressing children's harmful work. As a conceptual framework, the eduworkscape focuses on the social geographies of children's lives as they move across different domains. It is a framework referenced throughout this book and has multiple implications for how we explore and address children's harmful work.

The shift towards a more nuanced understanding of children's lives makes visible the ways these are highly gendered and intersected by socioeconomic status, ethnicity, location, migration and other markers of social identity. One such marker is disability, a topic that is the focus of Chapter 5 and in which Mary Wickenden convincingly argues that as children with disabilities make up a large minority of all children, ignoring how they are involved with harmful work, and the extent of work they do, is not an option. Faced with a dearth of data on the nature and extent of work that disabled children do, Wickenden draws on what is available and in-depth knowledge of the subject to expound the complex relationships between work and disability, with harmful outcomes often being gendered and also exacerbated for children with disabilities. Children with disabilities face particular vulnerabilities and, therefore, challenges with regard to work in agriculture – challenges that are not addressed appropriately by current social policy initiatives that aim to improve the wellbeing of children. Two such initiatives – value chain interventions and social protection – are discussed in the following two chapters.

Through an exposition of the range of governance modalities found in agricultural value chains, in Chapter 6, Giel Ton, Jodie Thorpe, Irene Egyir and Carolina Szyp explain how the vast majority of work, including children's work, in African agricultural is integrally bound up with domestic and/or international value chains. These chains link processes of production, trade, processing and distribution, and determine how costs, benefits and risks are distributed. Therefore, children's work can never be seen as simply a local-level phenomenon, isolated from the broader web of economic and social relations, institutions and politics. In fact, children's work, on, for example, cocoa or sugar farms, links them to some of the world's largest markets and most powerful corporations. Through a deeper understanding of value chain governance, the authors are able to identify entry points for research on children's work and for interventions to address harmful work.

Social protection interventions, intended to help families and children make the 'right' choices to reduce children's harmful work, have become popular as an alternative to more punitive, legal measures. Drawing on a comprehensive review of evaluations of social assistance schemes, in Chapter 7 Rachel Sabates-Wheeler, Keetie Roelen, Rebecca Mitchell and Amy Warmington show that the behavioural rationale underpinning social protection is overly simplistic. The actual design and delivery of the interventions do not account for the nuanced role of work in children's lives, and current interventions are therefore ill-equipped to tackle children's harmful work. Few studies look beyond prevalence or intensity of work, resulting in a substantial knowledge gap about the extent to which, and how, social assistance may reduce harm through work, if at all. The authors propose a range of policy levers that can be useful in changing the likelihood of harm associated with specific hazardscapes in which children live and work.

Chapters 8 through 11 provide case examples, specific to Ghana, of how children's work and harm is portrayed in the development of policies and politics, and in relation to specific agricultural sectors and products.

In Chapter 8, Samuel Okyere, Emmanuel Frimpong Boamah, Felix Ankomah Asante and Thomas Yeboah explore policy and legislation aimed at preventing, regulating and abolishing harmful children's work in Ghana. The Ghanaian government aligns itself with mainstream development partners and the UN in viewing harmful children's work as a breach of the dignity, wellbeing and fundamental human rights of the child. Preventative and abolitionist campaigns, laws and policies have been put in place against such work. Despite this, the number of children involved in prohibited work and those combining such work with schooling have risen rather than decreased. The authors emphasize that the ineffectiveness of policies raises questions about the compatibility of the policies and programmes with the country's historical, socio-cultural, economic, and political realities. The chapter concludes that legislation and interventions aimed at preventing children's hazardous or harmful work should draw on both the formal legislative rights and the informal, traditional rights discourses if they are to help advance children's development, rights and best interests. They make the important point that child rights, and initiatives to address them, are intrinsically political.

Despite high levels of awareness of child labour and work in public and policy discourse in Ghana, in Chapter 9, Thomas Yeboah and Irene Egyir reveal that there is little to no evidence or policy attention given to the substantial level of children's work engagement in shallot and vegetable production more generally. Historically, the centuries-old intensive irrigated shallot production on the Keta Peninsula has relied on household labour, and continues to do so. Children have always been an integral part of this system, and depending on gender, age and abilities, they perform various task such as land preparation, planting and watering, harvesting, transportation, bagging and marketing of shallots at the local market. The authors conclude with a reflection that perhaps the limited attention to children's work on the Keta Peninsula is indicative of the cultural acceptability of children working to support the household and local community. In this regard, it might be better for policy makers and researchers to start with a framing of 'benefit' associated with children' work in shallot production rather than the simplistic assumption of 'harm' that arises when children engage in productive work.

Of course, in stark contrast to the lack of evidence and attention to the substantial roles of children's work in local, domestic and cross-border vegetable value chains, we see the excessive global interest in (and monitoring of) the incidence and nature of children's involvement in internationally traded crops, such as cocoa. In Chapter 10, Dorte Thorsen and Roy Maconachie explain that as the world's second largest cocoa producer, Ghana has signed up to the US-led Harkin–Engel Protocol, signalling their commitment to end the worst forms of child labour in cocoa production. The authors highlight the tension between those who view all children's work as 'harmful' and unacceptable (the 'abolitionists'), and those who locate children's work on a wider canvas, where cocoa production is embedded within indigenous social institutions and family relations. The chapter provides a synthesis of recent academic and policy debates in relation to children's work in cocoa production. In doing so, the authors develop a more dynamic assessment of children's work in the West African cocoa sector, a prerequisite for more tangible, empirically grounded, pro-poor child protection policies and interventions.

In Chapter 11, Imogen Bellwood-Howard and Abdulai Abubakari introduce the fascinating, yet largely unexplored, case of the Lake Volta fishery. Children's work in the area has a long history, takes various forms and provokes significant controversy. Drawing on historical and descriptive evidence from the fishery, they question the overly simplistic trafficking narratives around children's economic activity in the sector. They convincingly argue that this discourse obscures other dimensions of children's work, including motivations and trade-offs, and the exposure of migrant and home-working children to hazards and harm. Lack of evidence and robust research about this sector means that sensationalist stories around trafficking drive perceptions of children's relationship to the fishery. The authors call for more nuanced research into the nature of children's work in and along the fishery value chain so that policies are appropriate and supportive of the wellbeing of children and their families whose lives are woven through this sector.

And finally, in Chapter 12 James Sumberg and Rachel Sabates-Wheeler focus on ways forward, and particularly the need to think again about how to address harm experienced by children in rural Africa. They argue that the time has now come for fundamental change in the organizations, frameworks, strategies, programmes and interventions that seek to tackle children's harmful work, and they suggest ways that this can be done.

Notes

1 https://data.worldbank.org/indicator/SP.POP.TOTL?locations=ZG

2 Enrolment in tertiary education was estimated to be fewer than 200,000 in 1970, 4.5 million in 2008 and 9 million in 2018 (UNESCO-UIS, 2010; The World Bank, 2020).

3 In 2020 there were estimated to be 495 unique mobile subscribers in SSA, equivalent to 46 per cent of the population (GSMA, 2021).

4 The case of children who work in the production of tobacco leaf and suffer from 'green tobacco sickness' is an important exception (see, for example, McKnight and Spiller, 2005).

5 And for the six largest countries in SSA the rural population as a share of total population is as follows: Nigeria (48 per cent), Ethiopia (78 per cent), DR Congo (54 per cent), South Africa (33 per cent), Tanzania (65 per cent) and Kenya (72 per cent) (https://data.worldbank.org/indicator/SP.RUR.TOTL.ZS?locations=ZG&most_recent_value_desc=true)

6 Studies of childhood by South American scholars raise parallel concerns. De Castro (2020) argues that globalization processes have set up a research agenda in Childhood Studies whose scientific interests, from the late 1990s onwards, began to focus on issues associated with the process of 'becoming a global child' and/or 'the emergence of the global child' (p 48). He argues for 'critical evaluations of the present claim for "a global child in a global world" which stipulates a univocal trajectory for children and nations' (p 49). Local childhoods are seen as those that are not yet where they should be – providing space for developmentalism and associated policies and programmes. Instead, he advocates for a theory of childhood based explicitly on the 'politics of the local.'

7 'What is child labour?': https://www.ilo.org/ipec/facts/lang--en/index.htm, accessed 20 January 2022.

8 'What is child labour?': https://www.ilo.org/ipec/facts/lang--en/index.htm, accessed 20 January 2022.

9 See van Daalen and Hanson (2019) for a fascinating analysis of how at certain points in its history the ILO adopted a dual approach to child labour that included abolition 'in the long run combined with transitional measures aimed at improving the working conditions of children' (p 1). Such transitional measures are not currently being promoted.

Acknowledgements

We are very grateful to Máiréad Dunne, Keetie Roelen, Sara Humphries and Dorte Thorsen for insightful comments on an earlier draft.

References

Abay, K.A., Asnake, W., Ayalew, H., Chamberlin, J. and Sumberg, J. (2020) 'Landscapes of opportunity: patterns of young people's engagement with the rural economy in sub-Saharan Africa', *The Journal of Development Studies*, 57(4), pp 594–613.

Abebe, T. and Ofosu-Kusi, Y. (2016) 'Beyond pluralizing African childhoods: introduction', *Childhood*, 23(3), pp 303–16.

Adesina, A.A. (2010) 'Solving the food crisis in Africa: achieving an African green revolution', in Karapinar, B. and Häberli, C. (eds) *Food Crises and the WTO: World Trade Forum*. Cambridge: Cambridge University Press, pp 81–108.

Adeyemi, A. et al (2016) *Child Trafficking into Forced Labor on Lake Volta, Ghana*. Washington, DC: International Justice Mission.

Akokpari, J.K. (2000) 'Globalisation and migration in Africa', *African Sociological Review/Revue Africaine de Sociologie*, 4(2), pp 72–92.

Altieri, M.A., Funes-Monzote, F.R. and Petersen, P. (2012) 'Agroecologically efficient agricultural systems for smallholder farmers: contributions to food sovereignty', *Agronomy for Sustainable Development*, 32(1), pp 1–13.

Balié, J. et al (2019) 'Food and agriculture global value chains: new evidence from sub-Saharan Africa', in Elhiraika, A.B., Ibrahim, G. and Davis, W. (eds) *Governance for Structural Transformation in Africa*. Cham: Springer International Publishing, pp 251–76.

Barrett, C.B. et al (2017) 'On the structural transformation of rural Africa', *Journal of African Economies*, 26(1), pp i11–i35.

Barrett, C.B. et al (2020) 'Agri-food value chain revolutions in low-and middle-income countries', *Journal of Economic Literature*, 58, pp 1–67.

Berg, E. et al (1981) *Accelerated Development in Sub-Saharan Africa: An Agenda for Action*. Washington, DC: The World Bank.

Bonnet, M. et al (eds) (2006) *Enfants travailleurs, repenser l'enfance*. Lausanne: Editions Page deux.

Botchway, D.V.N., Sarpong, A. and Quist-Adade, C. (eds) (2019) *New Perspectives on African Childhood: Constructions, Histories, Representations and Understandings*. Wilmington, DE: Vernon Press.

Bourdillon, M. et al (2010) *Rights and Wrongs of Children's Work*. New Brunswick, New Jersey and London: Rutgers University Press.

Boyden, J. (1990) 'Childhood and the policy makers: a comparative perspective on the globalization of childhood', in James, A. and Prout, A. (eds) *Constructing and Reconstructing Childhood: Contemporary Issues in the Sociological Study of Childhood*. London: Falmer Press, pp 184–215.

Boyden, J. and Ling, B. (1998) *What Works for Working Children?* Florence: Innocenti Publications International Child Development Centre and Rädda Barnen.

de Brauw, A. and Bulte, E. (2021) *African Farmers, Value Chains and Agricultural Development: An Economic and Institutional Perspective*. Cham, Switzerland: Palgrave MacMillan.

Brüntrup, M. (2011) 'The comprehensive Africa agriculture development programme (CAADP): an assessment of a Pan-African attempt to revitalise agriculture', *Quarterly Journal of International Agriculture*, 50(1), pp 79–106.

de Castro, L.R. (2020) 'Why global? Children and childhood from a decolonial perspective', *Childhood*, 27(1), pp 48–62.

Cheru, F. (1992) 'Structural adjustment, primary resource trade and sustainable development in sub-Saharan Africa', *World Development*, 20(4), pp 497–512.

Clemensen, N. (2016) 'Exploring ambiguous realms: access, exposure and agency in the interactions of rural Zambian children', *Childhood*, 23(3), pp 317–32.

CNN (2019) CNN Exposes Child Slavery on Ghana's Lake Volta. Available at: https://www.youtube.com/watch?v=mRcVU678UPs (Accessed 13 February 2020).

Commander, S. (1988) 'Structural adjustment policies and agricultural growth in Africa', *Economic and Political Weekly*. Economic and Political Weekly, 23(39), pp A98–105.

van Daalen, E. and Hanson, K. (2019) 'The ILO's shifts in child labour policy: regulation and abolition', *International Development Policy, Revue internationale de politique de développement*, 11, pp 133–50.

D'Alessandro, C. and Zulu, L.C. (2017) 'From the Millennium Development Goals (MDGs) to the Sustainable Development Goals (SDGs): Africa in the post-2015 development Agenda. A geographical perspective', *African Geographical Review*, 36(1), pp 1–18.

FAO and IFAD (2019) *United Nations Decade of Family Farming 2019–2028. Global Action Plan*. Rome: FAO & IFAD.

Feyaerts, H., Broeck, G.V. den and Maertens, M. (2020) 'Global and local food value chains in Africa: a review', *Agricultural Economics*, 51(1), pp 143–57.

Goddard, V. and White, B. (1982) 'Child workers and capitalist development: an introductory note and bibliography', *Development and Change*, 13(4), pp 465–77.

GSMA (2021) *The Mobile Economy Sub-Saharan Africa, 2021*. London: GSMA.

Hashim, I. and Thorsen, D. (2011) *Child Migrants in Africa*. London: Zed Books.

Heinze, E. (2000) 'A universal child?', in Heinze, E. and O'Donovan, K. (eds) *Of Innocence and Autonomy: Children, Sex and Human Rights*. Aldershot: Ashgate, pp 3–25.

ILO-IPEC (2013a) *Analytical Study on Child Labour in Volta Lake fishing in Ghana*. Geneva: International Labour Organization – IPEC.

ILO-IPEC (2013b) *Integrated Area-Based Approach as a Strategy for Laying Foundations for Child Labour-Free Zones: A Case of Busia, Kilifi and Kitui Districts in Kenya*. Dar es Salaam: International Labour Organization.

ILO-IPEC (2013c) *Promoting Child Labour Free Zones (CLFZs) through an Integrated Area-Based Approach (IABA). IPEC Briefing Note*. Geneva: International Labour Organization.

Jayne, T.S. et al (2019) 'Are medium-scale farms driving agricultural transformation in sub-Saharan Africa?', *Agricultural Economics*, 50(S1), pp 75–95.

Jayne, T.S. et al (2021) 'Rising land commodification in sub-Saharan Africa: reconciling the diverse narratives', *Global Food Security*, 30, Article 100565. doi: 10.1016/j.gfs.2021.100565

Jayne, T.S., Chamberlin, J. and Benfica, R. (2018) 'Africa's unfolding economic transformation', *The Journal of Development Studies*, 54(5), pp 777–87.

Jayne, T.S. and Sanchez, P.A. (2021) 'Agricultural productivity must improve in sub-Saharan Africa', *Science*, 372(6546), pp 1045–7.

Kerr, R.B. (2012) 'Lessons from the old Green Revolution for the new: social, environmental and nutritional issues for agricultural change in Africa', *Progress in Development Studies*, 12(2–3), pp 213–29.

Koomson, B. et al (2022) 'I agreed to go because … examining the agency of children within a phenomenon conceptualised as trafficking in Ghana', *Children & Society*, 36(1), pp 101–17.

Liebel, M. (2013) 'Do children have a right to work? Working children's movements in the struggle for social justice', in Hanson, K. and Nieuwenhuys, O. (eds) *Reconceptualizing Children's Rights in International Development: Living Rights, Social Justice, Translations*. Cambridge: Cambridge University Press, pp 225–49.

Liebel, M. and Invernizzi, A. (2019) 'The movements of working children and the International Labour Organization: a lesson on enforced silence', *Children & Society*, 33(2), pp 142–53.

Maul, D. (2019) *The International Labour Organization 100: Years of Global Social Policy*. Berlin: Walter de Gruyter GmbH.

McKnight, R.H. and Spiller, H.A. (2005) 'Green tobacco sickness in children and adolescents', *Public Health Reports*, 120(6), pp 6025.

Meerkerk, E. (2008) 'The negotiable child: the ILO Child Labour Campaign 1919–1973', *International Review of Social History*, 53, pp 320–2.

Minderoo Foundation (2018) *Global Slavery Index: Cocoa*. Nedlands, Western Australia: Minderoo Foundation.

Nieuwenhuys, O. (1998) 'Global childhood and the politics of contempt', *Alternatives*, 23, pp 267–89.

Okyere, S. (2017) '"Shock and Awe": A critique of the Ghana-centric child trafficking discourse', *Anti-Trafficking Review*, (9), pp 92–105.

OPHI and UNDP (2020) *Charting Pathways Out of Multidimensional Poverty: Achieving the SDG*. Oxford: Oxford Poverty & Human Development Initiative and UNDP.

Organisation of African Unity (1990) African Charter on the Rights and Welfare of the Child in Africa. OAU Doc. CAB/LEG/24.9/49.

Phiri, D.T. and Abebe, T. (2016) 'Suffering and thriving: children's perspectives and interpretations of poverty and well-being in rural Zambia', *Childhood*, 23(3), pp 378–93.

Ruddick, S. (2003) 'The politics of aging: globalization and the restructuring of youth and childhood', *Antipode*, 35, pp 334–62.

Sabates-Wheeler, R. and Sumberg, J. (2022) 'Breaking out of the policy enclave approach to child labour in sub-Saharan African agriculture', *Global Social Policy*, 22(1), pp 46–66.

Sadhu, S. et al (2020) *Assessing Progress in Reducing Child Labor in Cocoa Production in Cocoa Growing Areas of Côte d'Ivoire and Ghana.* Chicago: NORC, University of Chicago.

Smith, R.S. (2010) *A Universal Child?* Basingstoke: Palgrave Macmillan.

Smørholm, S. (2016) 'Pure as the angels, wise as the dead: perceptions of infants' agency in a Zambian community', *Childhood*, 23(3), pp 348–61.

Stecklov, G. and Menashe-Oren, A. (2019) *The Demography of Rural Youth in Developing Countries. Ifad Research Series 41.* Rome: International Fund for Agricultural Development (IFAD).

Sumberg, J. (ed) (2021) *Youth and the Rural Economy in Africa: Hard Work and Hazard.* Wallingford, Oxfordshire: CABI.

Taft, J.K. (ed) (2013) *Nothing About Us, Without Us: Critiques of the International Labor Organization's Approach to Child Labor from the Movements of Working Children.* Lima: IFEJANT.

Terenzio, F. (2007) 'The African Movement of Working Children and Youth', *Development*, 50(1), pp 68–71.

The World Bank (2020) *The COVID-19 Crisis Response: Supporting Tertiary Education for Continuity, Adaptation, and Innovation.* Washington, DC: The World Bank.

Thum-Danso Imoh, A. (2019) 'Terminating childhood: dissonance and synergy between global children's rights norms and local discourses about the transition from childhood to adulthood in Ghana', *Human Rights Quarterly*, 4(1), pp 160–82.

Toenniessen, G., Adesina, A. and DevRies, J. (2008) 'Building an alliance for a green revolution in Africa', *Annals of the New York Academy of Sciences*, 1136, pp 233–42.

Twum-Danso Imoh, A. (2016) 'From the singular to the plural: exploring diversities in contemporary childhoods in sub-Saharan Africa', *Childhood*, 23(3), pp 455–68.

Twum-Danso Imoh, A., Bourdillon, M. and Meichsner, S. (2018) 'Introduction: exploring children's lives beyond the binary of the global north and global south', in Twum-Danso Imoh, A., Bourdillon, M. and Meichsner, S. (eds) *Global Childhoods Beyond the North-South Divide.* Cham, Switzerland: Springer Nature, pp 1–10.

UCW (2017) *Not Just Cocoa: Child Labour in the Agricultural Sector in Ghana.* Rome, Italy: Understanding Children's Work Project.

UNDP and OPHI (2021) *Global Multidimensional Poverty Index 2021: Unmasking Disparities by Ethnicity, Caste and Gender.* Oxford: United Nations Development Programme (UNDP) and Oxford Poverty & Human Development Initiative.

UNESCO-UIS (2010) *Trends in Tertiary Education in Sub-Saharan Africa. UIS Fact Sheet No. 10*. Montreal: UNESCO Institute for Statistics.

USDoL (2020) *2020 Findings on the Worst Forms of Child Labor*. Washington, DC: Office of Child Labor, Forced Labor, and Human Trafficking, United States Department of Labor.

Van Hear, N. (1982) 'Child labour and the development of capitalist agriculture in Ghana', *Development and Change*, 13(4), pp 499–514.

Weber, H. and Abbasi, A. (2022) 'Poverty is not "another culture": against a right of children to work to live', *Review of International Studies*. doi: 10.1017/S026021052200002X

White, B. (1994) 'Children, work and child labor: changing responses to the employment of children', *Development and Change*, 25(4), pp 849–78.

White, S.C. (2002) 'From the politics of poverty to the politics of identity? Child rights and working children in Bangladesh', *Journal of International Development*, 14(6), pp 725–35.

2

Theorizing 'Harm' in Relation to Children's Work

Roy Maconachie, Neil Howard and Rosilin Bock

Introduction

The International Labour Organization (ILO) estimates that, globally, 152 million children are in 'child labour'. Of these, almost 75 million are said to labour in conditions or circumstances that are hazardous. The ILO has made it an international political priority to eradicate all such labour by 2025, and this objective is enshrined as Target 8.7 of the Sustainable Development Goals (SDGs). To that end, hundreds of millions of pounds are being invested by governments, non-governmental organizations (NGOs), and international agencies in support of the development and roll-out of policies and project interventions. In this, they build on a now century-long tradition of political, legal and diplomatic efforts (van Daalen and Hanson, 2019).

Undoubtedly, this points to an established political and institutional consensus. But a significant body of evidence suggests that there are major problems within that consensus. The dominant approach, at its heart, involves preventing children from working in conditions deemed unacceptable and where prevention has failed, removing them from those conditions. Yet, researchers from all continents and across a number of disciplines, as well as movements of working children themselves, claim that this approach often fails and at times even makes life worse for the children it is supposed to be serving. This is largely because the process by which unacceptability is defined is non-participatory and thus fails to consider either the subjective or contextual realities of working children's lives. With this observation, critics identify a fault line among actors working on child labour – between those who are understood as 'abolitionists' (because they seek blanket bans on types of work) and those who favour a more nuanced, regulatory approach that is based on a contextual understanding of, and response to, work in children's lives.

A central concept in these debates is harm. The ILO formally defines child labour as work that is mentally, physically, socially or morally harmful to children. It also includes in this category work that interferes with children's schooling because this is understood as harmful to future economic prospects. Critics of this approach also frequently use the concept of harm, typically arguing two things. First, that the ILO approach is mistaken and overly simplistic in its identification of harm and, second, that this over-simplification can, paradoxically, harm the children thought to need protection. Nevertheless, even the critics are hard pressed to offer a formal definition of harm.

So, what is harm, and how should we understand it? This foundational concept is integral to understanding what have aptly been termed the 'rights and wrongs of children's work' (Bourdillon et al, 2010) and, evidently, it is a site of contestation. This chapter seeks to move the debate forwards by sketching out some possible answers to the questions of what harm is and how it may be identified in the context of children's work. It begins by outlining the formal, institutional understanding of harm as put forward by the ILO. It then examines how other major institutions address harm in the context of children's work and how this differs from the ILO approach. Next, the paper reviews literature from a variety of academic disciplines to assess how harm and related concepts are understood and theorized. The analysis presented here is further supported by interviews conducted by the authors with expert figures across a number of disciplines. Third, the chapter synthesizes the foregoing discussion and points towards a more holistic approach to harm, which seeks to incorporate both 'subjective' and 'objective' dimensions. Here the focus shifts to the desired state that preventing harm seeks to achieve – wellbeing. The chapter concludes with a discussion of some implications for future research and policy action.

The mainstream picture of harm

As the guardian of the world's labour standards, the ILO has the international mandate to define and differentiate acceptable from unacceptable work. It does this through tripartite negotiations between governments, representatives of employer associations and representatives of organized labour. The definitions arrived at via these negotiations are formalized in conventions, which become the benchmarks for categorizing different kinds of work. In relation to children, the two key conventions are 138 and 182, the *Minimum Age* and *Worst Forms of Child Labour* conventions respectively (ILO, 1973, 1999). These are supplemented by Recommendation 190

(ILO, 1999). In essence, these three texts plus the ILO's many clarifying publications break children's economic activity down into four categories:

1. ***Children's work***, which is often described as 'a non-technical term for economic activities of children', where these activities are acceptable because they fall outside any of the following categories (see ILO-IPEC, 2012, p 31).
2. ***Child labour***, which is typically framed as 'work that deprives children of their childhood, their potential and their dignity, and that is harmful to physical and mental development'. More specifically, the term 'refers to work that is mentally, physically, socially or morally dangerous and harmful to children; and/or interferes with their schooling'. Child labour is also determined by age, with legitimate activities for younger children including 'helping their parents around the home, assisting in a family business or earning pocket money outside school hours and during school holidays'.
3. ***The worst forms of child labour***, identified in particular by Convention 182, include categories such as slavery, serfdom, trafficking, and forced labour, alongside prostitution, pornography and illicit activities. Importantly, the worst forms are also understood to comprise 'work which, by its nature or the circumstances in which it is carried out, is likely to harm the health, safety or morals of children', which is in also the definition of hazardous child labour.
4. ***Hazardous child labour***, as a worst form, is a primary target for eradication. In concretely identifying it, governments are urged to look in particular at 'work which exposes children to physical, psychological or sexual abuse; work underground, under water, at dangerous heights or in confined spaces; work with dangerous machinery, equipment and tools, or which involves the manual handling or transport of heavy loads; work in an unhealthy environment which may, for example, expose children to hazardous substances, agents or processes, or to temperatures, noise levels, or vibrations damaging to their health; work under particularly difficult conditions such as work for long hours or during the night or work where the child is unreasonably confined to the premises of the employer'.

Embedded within these categories are the concepts of 'hazard' and 'risk'. The ILO explains that 'a "hazard" is anything with the potential to do harm', while 'a "risk" is the likelihood of potential harm from that hazard being realised'.[1] Hazards can be physical, chemical, biological, environmental, ergonomic and so on. Risks depend on the mechanisms put in place to mitigate or manage hazards. Importantly, ILO literature recognizes that work can be hazardous and risks must be managed for adults as well as children, but it consistently makes a strong scientific case that children are different in important respects and are thus more vulnerable.

The ILO urges all governments to collaboratively elaborate lists of types of work and working conditions that constitute hazardous child labour. Its handbook, *Determining Hazardous Child Labour* (ILO-IPEC, 2012), suggests that this process should be led by relevant government agencies and take the form of a committee pulling together representatives of all key stakeholders, in particular the ILO's tripartite core. It further suggests that committees consult with key social actors including child workers and their parents, so as to avoid the wholesale transposition of external norms onto local realities, as was the case during the period following formal decolonization (ILO-IPEC, 2012, p 15). However, despite the positive intentions these processes tend to be limited – consultations often take place over a few hours and largely at national or regional level,[2] which makes them far removed from the actual sites of most children's work and thus the lived contexts in which this work takes place.

In addition, and perhaps somewhat surprisingly, the ILO has itself never formally defined 'harm'. This means that harm tends to be implicitly constructed throughout ILO and related mainstream literature as a negative impact that may be physical, psycho-social or economic. In turn, this implicitly posits that harm is morally 'bad' or 'undesirable', with its absence correspondingly 'good' and therefore desirable. Yet the actual content of this 'good' is itself never analysed or theorized. As we will discuss, this is far too simplistic as a basis for developing well-grounded policies and interventions.

In short, despite the extensive thinking and research that has taken place, there is a pressing need for deeper understanding of children's involvement in work that harms them. A more dynamic and holistic picture of what harm entails and whether, when and how one should intervene to prevent it must be located within a variety of perspectives and disciplines, in particular those which are sensitive to local realities.

In the next section, we explore in greater detail how harm is referred to and understood, explicitly and implicitly, through different literatures on children's work. While a universal definition of harm in relation to children's work does not exist, the social sciences can provide valuable insight – particularly with respect to concepts, tools and analytical processes – because of their solidly empirical foundations which address real people in real contexts (Bourdillon et al, 2010, p 94).

Key literatures

Childhood studies

Childhood studies is an inter-disciplinary field that brings together scholars from a wide range of disciplines. Its foundations are often traced to the seminal work of Allison James and Alan Prout, and especially their book *Constructing and Reconstructing Childhood* (1997). However, preceding this, during the early 1990s, various academic institutions in the US and UK had already begun to demonstrate an interest in the field, establishing children's studies programmes with an emphasis on an interdisciplinary approach. Given these origins, its central and foundational premise is that childhood is a complex social phenomenon that is constructed, contested and partially stabilized as an ongoing artefact of social practice. In this, the field rejects essentialism and argues that any given experience of childhood or of being a child can only ever be meaningfully understood in relation to the many intertwined contexts and structures the child encounters. This, in turn, repudiates the idea that there is such a thing as a 'normal childhood' or indeed that any given practice of childhood is universal.

Although this may at first appear to be an unnecessary theoretical detour, it is in fact critical for understanding the social science pushback against the political consensus that 'child labour deprives children of their childhood', that certain kinds of work are inherently harmful and that children should thus be protected by being removed from that work. For if childhood is a social construct that is never fully fixed and always contextually variable, then it is impossible to be certain that any particular work activity will always and everywhere have the same outcome or that this outcome will be one of harm. This social science principle lies at the root of the anthropological and sociological critique, and is found in work from psychology, politics and law.

Anthropology and sociology

A primary focus of the extensive anthropological literature looking at child labour and children's work has been on the negative side-effects caused by abolitionist interventions seeking to protect children from harm. One of the seminal studies in this tradition is that by Boyden and Myers (1995), which documented the tragic case of children working in the Bangladeshi garment sector. In the early 1990s, as a result of a bill proposed by US Senator Tom Harkin to ban textile imports from Bangladesh unless employers could demonstrate that they were 'child-labour free', thousands of child workers found themselves unemployed overnight. As a consequence, many ended up in demonstrably worse conditions, driven to the streets, to sex work or to factories operating under the radar. The anthropologist Ali Khan tells a similar story of football stitchers in Sialkot, Pakistan (Khan, 2007). Before international pressure came to bear on major sports firms importing footballs from Pakistan, stitching was an important cottage industry around Sialkot. Poor families would work on balls in their own homes, and children, when not at school, would help out under the supervision of parents. So, what happened when this changed? Omar, a 14-year-old boy interviewed by Khan, said, 'We used to be able to stitch footballs when we needed to. Now there are no footballs coming to the homes for stitching. Why have they stopped our *rozi-roti* [means of living]? … They must hate us' (Khan, 2007, p 53). Similar examples abound from rural settings, with a number of alarming examples documented by Michael Bourdillon in Zimbabwe (see, for example, Bourdillon 1999; Bourdillon et al 2010).

At the heart of these studies is the idea of harm, and specifically that removing children from work that is difficult, dangerous, and at times even damaging, may not in fact be in their best interests because removal causes them even more harm. Primarily, this harm is understood in terms of children being unable to access the resources that they and their families need to get by. This point has been forcefully underscored by scholars working in contexts as different as West Africa and South America. In research with young migrant workers from Benin, for example, children who were removed from, or denied access to, work opportunities furiously accused those responsible of making their lives worse (Howard, 2017).

In South America, the anger of working children's movements towards the ILO has been documented (Liebel, 2004; Taft, 2013). These authors express concern for the 'collateral damage of interventions that seek to eradicate child labour on the surface but create more harm by criminalising it'.[3] Misguided interventions designed to address harmful children's work are thus widely critiqued within the anthropological literature, with some claiming that they violate the core humanitarian principle of 'do no harm' (see Hart, 2021). Others note that smaller child advocacy groups face significant pressure to conform to the stance of powerful organizations such as the ILO, given their financial resources and international clout. This has the tragic effect of ensuring that damaging policy tends to be recreated, with feedback and learning loops insufficiently powerful to affect meaningful change (Howard, 2017; Bourdillon and Myers, 2021). The situation is succinctly summarized by Bourdillon:

> It seems to me that the focus on work that harms children in formal project documentation derives from attempts to justify policies devised and publicised by institutions with little interest or competence in the development of children. The focus is determined by sources of funding rather than an understanding of children's lives and what they need to grow and develop. If the project is going to improve understanding necessary to develop interventions that have a good chance of improving lives, the examination of harm needs to be placed firmly in the context of children's needs to live and grow up in their respective societies.[4]

Inside this and related critiques of child labour abolitionism is also a well-grounded and now widespread assessment that work can be, and often is, directly beneficial for children. In their recent overview of the literature on the links between children's work and wellbeing, Aufseeser et al (2018) demonstrate that work has been shown to contribute to children's wellbeing in at least the following ways:

1. by sustaining them and their families materially;
2. by enabling them to continue their schooling or other education as a result of their earnings;
3. by providing them with skills, including those which may offer them a future livelihood;
4. by fostering a sense of competence and self-esteem;
5. by developing their social skills and relations;
6. by enabling their socialization into maturity and collective responsibility;
7. by enabling their social transition into adulthood, including through providing the resources necessary for marriage.

Point (1) has been addressed already so there is no need to repeat it, other than to note that the literature here is very large. Point (2) is interesting and, from a mainstream policy perspective, often counter-intuitive. A common assumption by policy makers is that children's work sits within an 'either/or' relationship with education. Yet a large body of ethnographic data shows that, in many cases, children are able to prolong their schooling in contexts where it carries hidden or heavy opportunity costs, *precisely by working*, including in circumstances deemed harmful. Okyere (2017a) has demonstrated this in Ghana with a compelling case study of children working in quarries. His findings are echoed by Maconachie and Hilson (2016) in the context of artisanal mining in Sierra Leone, as well as in case studies from across the African continent assembled by Thorsen and Hashim (2011). These trade-offs between education and work are also discussed in Chapter 4 (this volume). With regards to point (3), it is important to bear in mind that much formal education in the Global South is of poor quality, and very few formal employment opportunities may exist following schooling. As such, school is not always a guarantee of better future employment, which makes learning practical, marketable skills attractive for children and parents alike (for example Chapter 4, this volume; Morrow and Boyden, 2018)

In relation to points (4) to (7), it is worth remembering that the United Nations Convention on the Rights of the Child (CRC) understands education broadly as being about developing 'the child's personality, talents and mental and physical abilities to their fullest potential', a view to support the growth and flourishing of children into citizens able to partake fully in the human community (UNCRC, Article 29 (1)a). Much of the anthropological literature on children's work suggests that it can be beneficial for them in precisely this way. Data from every continent suggest that many young workers feel proud and experience heightened self-esteem when they are able to contribute to their families' wellbeing through their labour (see examples from the Young Lives study, Crivello et al, 2012). This, in turn, gives them confidence and indeed fosters resilience – which are vital in contexts of socio-economic vulnerability and can only be obtained through exposure to hazards that one then learns to manage (Boyden and Mann 2005; Liborio and Ungar 2010). Likewise, we know that work offers children a chance to develop their social skills and through these to accumulate social capital. Studies of children living and working on the streets have made this point especially clear (for example, Invernizzi, 2003), though findings of this nature are far from restricted to street-connected children (for example, Howard, 2008).

A key point is that work is understood and experienced in much of the world as a pathway through which children attain maturity and social responsibility, before becoming adults. The present authors have found this extensively in their own research in West Africa (Howard, 2014, 2017; Maconachie and Hilson, 2016; Okyere, 2017a), and it has been documented widely elsewhere. Heissler (2012), for example, found female migrant labourers in Bangladesh to increase their respect and status amid their families as a result of their work. Pankhurst et al (2015) note that in contexts across East Africa, children's work is regarded and experienced positively both by children and adults as a mechanism through which they can become integrated into the fabric of family and community life.

Embedded within the foregoing analyses, and indeed in literature across anthropology and sociology, is the idea that wellbeing is the benchmark by which we should evaluate the pros and cons of children's work, and, by extension, the policies that seek to limit it. Although rarely made explicit by most writers, wellbeing is implicit in almost all commentary, while Bourdillon et al (2010) stand out in making it the centrepiece of their analysis. Indeed, in the concluding chapter, they argue that policy makers should ground their efforts in a rigorous, social scientific attempt to understand and then advance child wellbeing (which they see as the cornerstone of decisions around what the UNCRC calls 'the best interests of the child'). For them, although any individual experience of harm will necessarily diminish aggregate wellbeing, the assessment as to how that harm should be navigated can only be made contextually and with reference to the overall bundle of inputs contributing to a child's wellbeing or illbeing. Naturally, this points to a different policymaking approach to harm and its place in children's working lives than is presently the norm. We return to this in the next section.[5]

Human geography

Scholarship within the discipline of human geography also makes a valuable contribution to understanding how harmful children's work is conceptualized, most notably by shedding light on the importance of locating 'harm' on a broader spatial canvas. Such an approach offers a useful lens for exploring variations on the notion of harm, as they are defined and redefined in the shifting landscapes of children's work. Situating knowledge and practice about children's work in time and space can reveal the geographically and culturally specific nature of what may be considered harmful work, and what may not be considered so.

Drawing inspiration from anthropology, many geographers have undertaken valuable studies of non-Western childhoods, challenging Eurocentric ideas of childhood, work and harm (for example, see Cindi Katz's [1991, 1993] work in rural Sudan, or Samantha Punch's [2000, 2002] studies of village children in Bolivia). Indeed, the study of the diverse conditions under which children live in non-Western contexts is an important sub-area of research, revealing the impacts of changing landscapes for children and work around the world in response to a wide range of drivers, including globalization, neo-liberalization and economic restructuring (see, for example, Abebe] [2007], Ansell and van Blerk [2004] and Robson [2004]).

By locating children at the centre of the analysis, rather than at the periphery, and situating their perspectives and experiences within the contours of a broader landscape that surrounds their work, geographers have contributed to rethinking the process of uneven development and the way in which global capitalism has bearing on local realities (see Dobson and Stillwell, 2000; Dyson, 2008; Bessell, 2011). Such grounded studies that document and analyse multi-scalar processes have been important, particularly in addressing generalizations about children and the work they do that underpin the mainstream view and the policy it generates (McKinney, 2015).

A further important focus that is relevant to the present discussion concerns the issue of representation and how perceptions are shaped by the construction of knowledge. Olga Nieuwenhuys (1996) reminds us that the concepts of child labour (and by extension, harmful children's work) are socially constructed – they embody a set of generalized representations of childhood (that are often founded in the Global North) that have strong political and moral undertones. Many children's geographers have expressed concern about the widespread tendency for academics and policy makers to generalize experiences and to naturalize constructions of childhood, both of which are common in orthodox framings of child labour. Such constructions can play a role in both excluding and marginalizing children and denying their agency (Holt and Holloway, 2006).

In sum, research by geographers underscores the significance of the work that children do, their importance as social actors and their agency within studies of globalized production (Punch, 2002, 2007; Robson, 2004). As Robson (2004) clearly demonstrates, children at work are active social and economic agents, making real contributions in rural societies. What is considered harmful, and what is not, must be seen in this context. Grounded geographies of working children in a globalized world demand an understanding of the contexts within which they work, the origins of framings of childhood and work, and the voices of children as they are incorporated into the global economy.

Political science

The political science literature concerned with harm in relation to children's work can be broken down into two strands. First, that which studies working children's movements and perspectives and thus repudiates abolitionist efforts to protect children from harm by preventing them from working. The work of Liebel and Taft is especially powerful, with both authors documenting at length the many positive benefits that organized working children claim to derive from their work and their organizing around it (for example, Liebel, 2004; Taft, 2013). In particular, Taft has discussed the concept of *Protagonismo*, which refers to the enactment of individual and collective agency and power. 'For the movement of working children', she notes, 'this has meant discussing how children are an oppressed social group that has been excluded from power, often with paternalistic justifications' (Taft, 2021). In turn, this sees children organizing their collective power in ways that enhance their self-esteem, confidence, life skills, and relationships – each of which is evidently beneficial.

Importantly, neither Liebel, Taft nor working children themselves suggest that 'anything goes' in relation to children's work or work conditions. Working children's movements in Latin America, Africa and South Asia all strongly advocate for 'dignified work' and for a definition of 'harm' that is neither exclusively age- or activity-based but instead takes account of 'exploitation, violence or abuse'.[6] Crucially, each of these concepts is inherently relational and deeply tied to the meta-concept of wellbeing, which points to the importance of relational experiences in children's conceptualizations of what is or is not acceptable and unacceptable work.

The second strand of political science literature echoes the first and emphasizes children's right to participate in conversations about their wellbeing. This strand is heavily influenced by anthropological and feminist thinking around participation as a question of substantive citizenship, and sees children as full rather than partial citizens whose preferences and perspectives must be taken seriously as their democratic right. As may be expected, writers in this tradition (for example, Swift 1997) are especially concerned with children's exclusion from conversations over how to define harm done to them, arguing that such exclusion is itself a power-based form of harm.[7]

Legal studies

The legal literature on harm in children's work is relatively limited and primarily centres on re-interpreting and challenging the hegemony of the ILO's foundational texts, as a way to contest the abolitionist approach to children's work (for example, Cullen, 2007; van Daalen and Hanson, 2019). The key concept in this effort is that of 'living rights', developed primarily by Hanson and Nieuwenhuys (2012). According to them, the idea of 'living rights' denotes that, far from being abstract or universally concrete, rights can be, and in practice always are, operationalized in different ways and in different settings. For instance, although 'the right to quality education' may always be written using the same words in the same order, what actually comprises 'quality' or 'education' and how practically to deliver either will necessarily vary. 'Living rights' thus attempts both to inject dynamism into the textual stasis of law by emphasizing the importance of paying close attention to the contexts in which children live and grow, as well as to those children themselves. These legal arguments are heavily influenced by work in the various disciplines discussed earlier and by debates over what actually harms children and how.

A second, related strand of legal work focuses on the CRC and the extent to which it either supersedes the ILO framework or can be used to challenge it. As mentioned previously, the ILO framework is built around Conventions 138 and 182. These texts have been interpreted as pushing for the complete exclusion of children from certain economic sectors or tasks, even where such exclusion goes against the preferences of children themselves and may, arguably, go against their interests. Certain scholars have therefore called for international agencies to give primacy to the CRC and in particular its Article 3, which states that all decisions related to children must be aimed at advancing their best interests and wellbeing (Bourdillon et al, 2010). In addition, others have called for greater attention to Article 12, which states that authorities must give 'the child who is capable of forming his or her own views the right to express those views freely in all matters affecting the child', and ensure that those views are 'given due weight' in eventual decisions concerning them (Hanson, 2012; Hanson et al, 2015; Myers, 2017).

The debate as to whether the CRC or ILO Conventions have primacy appears unlikely to have much impact, since the Committee on the Rights of the Child (which assesses implementation of the CRC) has consistently sought to avoid conflict by interpreting the two texts as complementary. This, in itself, is unsurprising, since the drafters of the CRC built heavily on the international legal tradition. In order to move beyond any deadlock, therefore, Hanson points to Recommendation 146 that accompanies Convention 138. It contains a detailed list of measures that should be taken 'to ensure that the conditions in which children and young persons under the age of 18 years are employed or work reach and are maintained at a satisfactory standard'.[8] In his view, 'this could provide an interpretation of children's rights law regarding child labour that allows (and even calls) to regulate child labour much more vigorously than has been done until now'.[9] This, in turn, would operationalize children's 'living right to work', the central underlying assumption of which is that if children are recognized as legal subjects, then their work-related rights of the International Covenant on Economic, Social and Cultural Rights (ICESCR) also have to be acknowledged and enforced, in the same contextually relevant way as for adults (Hanson and Vandaele, 2013). Implicit in this effort is the notion that abolitionism can harm children and their interests, while contextually relevant regulation would help.

Economics

The economics literature on children's work and child labour is extensive, though it generally does not interrogate either the concept of harm or the existing, mainstream approaches to it. The discipline tends to work with datasets built on the back of ILO estimates of child labour, hazardous child labour and so on, often within the context of national surveys. From there, regressions are conducted to examine the interaction between, say, labour and poverty (for example, de Hoop and Rosati, 2014; Del Carpio et al, 2016; Sarkar and Sarkar, 2016) or labour and education (for example, Edmonds, 2008). But, by exploring children's work exclusively using the data and proxies that are established by the ILO, much is missed. For example, it is impossible to assess the overall impact that any specific work activity may have on wellbeing or illbeing. Likewise, although some economics research does explore the potential income and non-income related benefits of children's work, such as the development of skills (Basu, 1999) or ability to combine work and schooling (Edmonds, 2008), often studies tend to view child development narrowly in terms of how income enhances measurable variables that contribute to national economic development (for example, levels of education or health, see Bourdillon et al, 2010). This is evidently limited.

There is one sub-field within the discipline of economics that has shed considerable light on the concept and experience of harm – feminist economics and particularly its focus on unpaid care.[10] Although this focus has little that is directly empirically relevant to SSA, it nevertheless contributes theoretically. Importantly, it underlines how the notion of 'care' as understood by society is intertwined with structures of inequality, gender, race, ethnicity and social class. Worldwide, austerity measures and neoliberal reforms, beginning in the 1980s, exacerbated a growing gender bias in unpaid care work, with particular impacts especially for girl children. As formal and informal pre-neoliberal structures performing a social protection function (such as common access to productive resources including land or fuel subsidies) were eroded under the impact of structural adjustment (Cornia et al, 1987; LeBaron and Ayers, 2013), increasing numbers of poor mothers in the Global South were compelled to enter the workforce to survive on poverty wages. This led more and more girls to take on the social reproductive burden, with impacts on wellbeing and human capital formation (Anderson, 2000; Folbre, 2006). Relatedly, a key consequence of the neoliberal turn in the Global North was the emergence of global care chains involving women and adolescent girls from the Global South moving to richer parts of the world to provide care services that the women of the North could no longer provide. This too led to care deficits in the migrants' home communities, again to be filled by young girls (Anderson, 2000; Folbre, 2006; Razavi, 2007). From the perspective of harm, these structural dynamics matter because evidence suggests both that care work is routinely under-valued and that it can take place in circumstances that are severely abusive. Considerable evidence suggests that girls, in particular, can suffer from physical and verbal abuse, isolation, seclusion, less time for school and are vulnerable to sex abuse in care work in the home and domestic work outside of it (Murray et al, 2004; Sturrock and Hodes, 2016). As will be explored later in the chapter, such exploitative working conditions also lead to severe harmful psychological impacts on (mostly female) children.

Feminist economists thus remind us both that the gendered nature of the global division of caring labour has political economic roots and that its impacts are not equally shared. Given this inequitable burden, it seems reasonable to assert, with Nieuwenhuys (2007) and others, that children, especially in the Global South, represent a reservoir of cheap and flexible labour that contributes towards circuits of global capital. Specifically, Nieuwenhuys argues that 'Children's everyday work that is done unpaid is even more "for free" than women's and can therefore be tapped into ad libitum' (2020, p 130), and this means that children, particularly girls, provide essential yet un-remunerated 'services' that produce the value that drives local and global economic growth. The fact that this labour, like most caring labour, is unpaid makes it arguably a form of structural, economic harm.

Importantly, ILO regulations are clear as to the potentially harmful impacts of unpaid care, with Convention 189, The Convention on Domestic Workers, establishing guidelines for what is and is not acceptable. But in reality, the core of the ILO and mainstream approach to children's work centres around Conventions 138 and 182, both of which focus primarily on paid work outside a domestic context, typically done by boys, which arguably reproduces gender bias by drawing attention away from girl children's vital and at times damaging work (Cullen, 2007, p 156).

Developmental psychology

Beyond the social sciences, the two disciplines with most to say about harm and how it can be understood are developmental psychology and health. We address each in turn.

Developmental psychology focuses on processes through which individuals grow and develop, cognitively, emotionally and socially. In particular, studies emphasize the importance of human relationships in advancing children's wellbeing (or illbeing), while a number have offered valuable longitudinal analyses, providing a picture of how children's lives are impacted over time. Such research is valuable in assessing both the cumulative impacts of 'invisible' harms and how the harm/benefit balance may shift over time due to changing conditions. While children themselves may place greater emphasis on harm that is experienced in the short term, where there are immediate consequences, it is also vital to understand the long-term effects of work activities.

The effect of work on children's psychological functioning was first raised as an issue by the World Health Organization (WHO) in 1972. In the 1980s, a joint ILO/WHO Committee on Occupational Health commissioned the first series of studies on the psychological factors associated with child work in four occupational sectors. However, little further research was carried out in the decades prior to 2000 (Gunn et al, 2015). One of the main reasons for this was the lack of appropriate tools (Dorman, 2008). In addition, the impacts of psychological harm, including mental illness, addiction and stress, can be slow to manifest as they are often 'invisible', making them difficult to identify (ILO, 2011). The effects of psychological harm on working children are still therefore largely under-recorded (Fassa et al, 2010; Fekadu et al, 2010; Sturrock and Hodes, 2016). While a burgeoning literature does exist, especially in societies of the Global North, generalizing this to the study of child work in the Global South is not straightforward. The export of observational, attitudinal and other diagnostic instruments is especially problematic unless their content is thoroughly revised to ensure local relevance (Woodhead, 2004).

In the psychological literature, harmful work is most often associated with the sister concept of 'abuse' (Fekadu et al, 2010), a pairing that is also evident in WHO literature (Woodhead, 2004, p 340). Children's experiences of abuse are known to be strongly affected by their gender, in terms of the likelihood of boys and girls becoming victims of sexual, physical and emotional abuse. Girls, in particular, are vulnerable to sexual abuse at work, with the impacts of this made worse when associated with shame and stigma (Woodhead, 2004).[11] However, both boys and girls may equally suffer emotional abuse at work, which can be manifested through unreasonable expectations of work productivity and work standards; lack of encouragement and support to ensure children are able to complete a task; scolding and punishment for failures, including ridicule and humiliation, harassment, or shaming; and isolating the child and denying their needs or requests for help (Woodhead, 2004).

Most occupation-specific psychological studies that have been undertaken have focused on the relatively small proportion of child workers engaged in sex-related occupations and in armed conflict (ILO-IPEC, 2014). Domestic work outside of a child's home has also been a focus. Findings suggest that, although potentially benign, this work can be rendered harmful by the conditions and social relations in which it takes place (Bourdillon et al, 2010). Some research suggests that domestic work under poor working conditions can be among the most harmful types of work (Sturrock and Hodes, 2016). In such situations, girls in particular can suffer physical and verbal abuse, isolation, seclusion, less time for school and are vulnerable to sexual abuse (Murray et al, 2004). It is therefore equally important to factor in the issue of gender-based violence when defining and assessing harm. Gender-based violence not only occurs in the context of domestic work, but also within the family or inside educational institutions (see Chapter 4, this volume). Knowledge and understanding of violence in schools has only recently emerged. Although normally considered to be a safe space, there is growing evidence to suggest that 'gender violence [has] become institutionalized and accepted as part of the landscape of schooling' (Dunne et al, 2006; also see Fassa et al, 2010; Fekadu et al, 2010; Sheth and Buhr, 2012; Sturrock and Hodes, 2016). The abuse of power by school authorities also increases the occurrence of transactional sex between adolescent girls and school authorities, which in sub-Saharan Africa is linked with high infection rates of HIV (UNESCO, 2006; Ijumba, 2011).

Martin Woodhead and Barbara Rogoff are perhaps the most celebrated psychologists looking at the relationship between children's work, development and harm. An important observation made by Woodhead (2004) is that well-recognized physical hazards can have strong psycho-social consequences. Such hazards may include:

- Toxic substances, which may impact on the developing nervous system and in turn on children's psychosocial functioning, as for example with lead.
- Unhealthy, noisy, poorly lit and ventilated environments, which can affect children's general health and increase stress, fatigue and cause demoralization. If children find it difficult to work in these circumstances, stress levels may increase.
- Dangerous tools, which without adequate safety precautions may induce stress and fear of accidents. Children may be traumatized by suffering or witnessing serious incidents, and those working in extreme conditions, (for example mining, fishing) are especially vulnerable.
- If children do suffer an accident in which they are disfigured or disabled, this may increase the risk of social rejection, isolation and stigmatization.

However, Woodhead's work also strongly suggests that whether or not work is considered harmful is more closely connected to its social context and the relationships in which it takes place, than to the nature of the work itself. His six-country comparative field study (Woodhead, 1998) is supported by a variety of further studies that emphasize that cultural meaning-scapes are vital for understanding how any given experience can be understood and processed by the individual in question as harmful or beneficial (Korbin, 2002; Rogoff et al, 2017). In turn, Woodhead suggests that children often value their work because it provides them with a sense of self-esteem and pride, and because it can play an important role in their personal development by helping them build a sense of efficacy. As Jo Boyden remarks, 'children prefer to work in factories instead of home: they earn more money and at home, parents have more power over them'.[12]

Likewise, Rogoff (2014)[13] suggests that work situations may provide developmental benefits to children's competence in more specific, culturally valued cognitive skills such as alertness, collaboration, perspective-taking, self-regulation and planning, in addition to their gaining of information and skills. As mentioned earlier, numerous anthropological studies have confirmed these observations, with some also showing how the personal value that children attach to their work can foster a sense of resilience (Werner and Smith, 1992; Boyden and Mann, 2005).

In short, this literature suggests that studies that build in an appreciation of culture and an understanding of its context are necessary for any analysis in relation to psychosocial child maltreatment, harm, and work. Psychological harm in children's working lives must be assessed in relation to the many other influences in their lives, and placed within a broader picture of the different contexts in which it occurs and the aggregate wellbeing or illbeing to which it contributes. This should be carried out at different levels, to include individual/micro systems (for example, family, school), mesosystems (for example, neighbourhoods) and macrosystems (for example, religious institutions) (ILO-IPEC, 2014).

Health

Within both the academic and institutional literatures on health and child labour, harm is most often understood in relation to injury or illness. The ILO sees children's occupational health as an area of analysis at the interface between: (1) work and child illnesses/injuries; (2) work and children's psychological functioning; and (3) work and children's physical or emotional development (ILO, 2011). The WHO's definition of 'child health', on the other hand, encompasses the 'complete physical, mental and social wellbeing of a child and not merely the absence of disease or infirmity' (White and Blackmore, 2016, p 20). However, in both cases, the ILO and WHO do not use the term 'harm' but rather focus on hazards. So, once again, we are confronted with the challenge of coming to terms with harm in relation to children's health and wellbeing.

From a health perspective, one might assume that the identification of the forms of child labour that are potentially the most harmful would appear to be straightforward. Children working under appalling conditions in construction, mining and manufacturing can face immediate and obvious threats to their health. However, evidence on the health consequences of children's work activity can be both limited and misleading. Indeed, the vast majority of studies focus on the injuries and illnesses that *could* occur, basing their assessments on general observations or on known risks to adults (ILO, 2011). These assessments estimate the risk of illness or injury by sector of employment, but in the absence of comparison with a 'no work' counterfactual, they do not provide an effective basis for evaluating the impact of work on health (O'Donnell et al, 2002).

In addition, from a health perspective, the definition of hazard as stated in the ILO Convention 182 becomes both challenging and complex. Interpretation of all current estimates of the relationship between child labour and health is difficult given the absence of analyses that account for the potential endogeneity of child work activity to health outcomes. For example, if individuals born with a predisposition to poor health are also those who are most likely to engage in work as a child, correlations between children's work and health will overstate the impact of the former on the latter. Due to the potential intergenerational effects of toxic substances, some children who work may also begin their life with lower intelligence or neurocognitive impairments (Ide and Parker, 2005). On the other hand, if healthy individuals work early as children, the true health impact of their work will be understated. Additionally, comparisons between the growth rates of working and non-working children in rural settings provide mixed results (O'Donnell et al, 2002).

Despite an absence of rigorous research focusing on the impact of work on the health of children in the Global South, over the past decade there has been some progress with child labour data becoming more comprehensive and accurate (Fassa et al, 2010). However, there is a pressing need for a clearer understanding of how child work relates to health, and how the notion of harm fits into this equation. Without the availability of larger, longitudinal studies, which use contextually meaningful indicators, the long-term health implications and potential gender disparities of children's work – except for missed school days – cannot be accurately characterized. Many recent studies on the health of child workers are poor methodologically, lack gender disaggregation and do not build intersectionality into their research designs. In such cases, sub-Saharan Africa is particularly under researched (Kuimi et al, 2018) with little analysis of the relationship between child labour and wider contextual factors such as high tuberculosis and HIV rates. This is surprising given that AIDS orphans are one of the most vulnerable groups that rely on work to survive (Hurst, 2007).

Consequently, the overall global health burden of illness or injury related to children's work may remain underestimated, and is certainly poorly understood (Ide and Parker, 2005; Fassa et al, 2010; Shendell et al, 2016; Kuimi et al, 2018). ILO publications (for example, ILO, 2011) rely on data from studies undertaken in developed countries – mostly from work-related injuries of children and young people in the US and Canada where routine data collection is much more complete (Fassa et al, 2010). However, these data cannot fully reflect the situation in non-industrialized countries (ILO-IPEC, 2014). To date, there is no pattern across countries in the raw correlations between child work and reported health problems (O'Donnell et al, 2002). Until the literature considers wider family and community effects, the work and health story will remain incomplete (Fassa et al, 2010).

In short, it is clear that a more systematic and situated focus on health among child workers is necessary. Harm is most often seen solely in relation to injury or illness that could occur, with very little research being carried out on actual harm or links between work-related harm and children's emotional and relational wellbeing.

Towards a re-conceptualization of children's work and harm

From the preceding discussion, it is clear that the concept of harm in the context of children's work is understood and theorized in diverse ways. At the heart of the critical literatures reviewed is the idea that harm is ambiguous, relative and contextual, and it may be unhelpful (and even problematic) to present harm as an 'objective' concept that can be defined, measured and assessed with discrete criteria. This literature underscores that there is a poor understanding of the contours of this broader 'harm-scape', and the relative importance of children's work within it. The potential for harm arises from a complex combination of factors, including: the situation of the child; the specific nature of the work; and the conditions or social relations that surround the work being undertaken. Also, very apparent in the anthropological critique is the position that removing children from work that is arduous, dangerous or potentially harmful, may not always be the best option for them.

In many respects, it is misleading to discuss the notion of harm in isolation, without some consideration of the related benefits that may also be derived, or the wider context. In relation to children's work in agriculture, the hazards, risks and benefits are often intermingled. Judgements about harm, and thus acceptability, therefore, require weighing up both costs and benefits in a situated context, while making some comparison with the realistic alternatives that exist. Such judgements must involve subjective and cultural values being combined with objective criteria. Here, there are undoubtedly lessons that can be learned from the literature on relational wellbeing, since wellbeing remains arguably the implicit benchmark for any discussion of harm or work that is harmful to children. Although the concept is itself the subject of much debate (for example, Doyal and Gough, 1991; Gough et al, 2007), the growing body of research on relational wellbeing could be vital, since it recognizes the importance of context (White, 2015). It will also help to prioritize the need for children to be appreciated as subjects rather than objects, refocusing the analysis on understanding their lifeworlds in their own terms (de Berry et al, 2003). This contrasts with most mainstream approaches to understanding harmful children's work, which tend to take a more positivist and objective stance, and fail to appreciate the social and relational aspects of what is or is not harmful, to whom, when and why, and which alternative states are possible and worth considering. At its heart, as noted by Atkinson et al (2012), relational wellbeing holds that notions of wellbeing and illbeing are socially and culturally constructed, and are rooted in a particular time and place. Shifting the focus to locate harm on a continuum of wellbeing and illbeing may prove to be a more appropriate and coherent way of understanding why children work, including in harmful situations, which situations are actually experienced as harmful, and how this varies across different contexts.

Without a more holistic outlook, a dominating fear of harm can result in policies that are so precautionary that the damage they do to children is greater than the harm they have been designed to avert, in the process unjustly over-riding children's perceptions, goals and wishes.[14] In short, a more balanced and conceptually sophisticated approach to policymaking is needed – one that also considers the impact of work on a child's development, wellbeing and needs from a multiplicity of perspectives. This position is well summarized by Richard Carothers, founder of the Children and Work Network, which brings together scholars and activists, including working children themselves, from over 100 countries and includes many of the most recognized scholarly authorities on children's work:

> I think an important step in dealing with 'harmful work' is the idea that we are trying to get rid of 'harm' and not necessarily get rid of work. The definition of harm will vary with situation and context and it may be possible to eliminate the harm within work or help children move from harmful work to less harmful work. In doing this, businesses and business support programs can play a useful role and the Occupational Health and Safety program of the ILO can become an ally with a different approach and contribution than the IPEC people.[15]

The belief that children's work can be dichotomized into typologies of 'acceptable and unacceptable' or 'good and bad' is highly problematic, and this in turn problematizes administrative categories like 'child labour' or 'harmful child labour', since these tend to be equated with good and bad and abstracted from all context or relationality. The distinction between harm and benefit can be fuzzy and variable, depending on the specific situation. It can also change over time. Studies have demonstrated that work which many observers would consider to be benign can be harmful due to the social relations and conditions that surround it. Alternatively, potentially harmful work can be beneficial to children if the social conditions are supportive. Ultimately, this all needs to be analysed in relation to the benchmark concept of wellbeing.

It may therefore be more useful to think of children's work as lying on a spectrum of harm and benefit. In assessing harm, we suggest that a variety of factors must be taken into consideration, including the temporal nature of harm (for example, the cumulative or 'invisible') and the trade-offs that must be assessed to determine if potential benefits outweigh potential risks. A set of key questions thus arise: Who is assessing the relative nature of harm, and how does this sit with other perspectives? How are different perspectives on harm reconciled? Likewise, is one instance of a hazardous activity enough to describe the entire work experience as 'harmful'? And, how does all of this relate to wellbeing?

Models designed to explore different children's work-environment scenarios, such as the state-and-transition model proposed by Sabates-Wheeler and Sumberg (2020), remain useful for assessing different points on the spectrum, but we must still come to grips with what harm actually entails and when and how it needs addressing. A definition of harmful children's work remains challenging, even if Woodhead (2004) provides an excellent starting point, at least for examining its subjective dimensions. On balance, the evidence suggests that it is incredibly difficult, and probably of little value, to develop a clear-cut, 'one-size-fits-all' set of criteria to distinguish between harmful and harmless children's work. Legal scholars continue to stress the need for an alternative translation of international labour law that is compatible with children's rights and the 'living right to work'. Work needs to be understood as bringing both benefits and (potential) harm to children, and it is necessary to balance benefits against harm, including in policy formulation and implementation.

While the extreme aspects of harmful children's work may be relatively unambiguous, this is not the case in less extreme situations. The risk of harm associated with work, and the actual experience of harm through work, will vary significantly among children. A starting point for understanding different contexts and getting the policies right involves participatory consultative processes that prioritize the perspectives and voices of children themselves, as well as their communities. Such accounts must take account of both physical and psychosocial factors, while also drawing on the extensive literature from health and related sciences about the impacts of specific activities or substances. Grounding policies more solidly in properly researched evidence, and less in conventional wisdom, unfounded assumptions and institutional traditions, will thus be key. At the same time, international institutions must work at scale, and for this they seek metrics or processes that can function across contexts. This, therefore, is as much a political as a conceptual–theoretical tension, and means that diplomatic endeavours may be as impactful as scholarly pursuit. For such endeavours to be successful, they will need to find a common ground that can integrate both the best of contemporary research *and* the major institutional imperatives. This is not impossible, but it is a challenge that must now be confronted.

Notes

1 https://www.ilo.org/ipec/facts/WorstFormsofChildLabour/Hazardouschildlabour/lang--en/index.htm
2 This was confirmed in interviews with scholars who have worked at length with the ILO.
3 Personal communication with Manfred Liebel, 26 March 2020
4 Personal communication with Michael Bourdillon, 19 February 2020.
5 There is an entire strand of primarily anthropological and sociological literature that echoes the critiques discussed in this section of the abolitionist approach to child labour within the field of Migration Studies. Interested readers might wish to consult these important texts for further information: (Hashim and Thorsen, 2011; Huijsmans and Baker, 2012; Thorsen, 2014; Howard and Okyere, 2015; Howard, 2017; Okyere, 2017b).
6 See, for example: https://www.opendemocracy.net/en/beyond-trafficking-and-slavery/secretariat-of-movement-of-latin-american-and-caribbean-working-children-and-adolescen/
7 As Jo Boyden said, 'Decent work is about rights and working children are a group that do not possess rights'. Telephone interview with Jo Boyden, March 2020.
8 Personal communication with Karl Hanson, April 2020.
9 Personal communication with Karl Hanson, April 2020.
10 Unpaid care work is work done primarily by women and children to care for family members: cooking, cleaning and shopping, as well as care of children, the sick and the elderly. It can also encompass growing food for personal consumption and collecting water and fuel – jobs that are categorized as productive activities (Razavi, 2007, p 186).
11 Personal communication with Jo Boyden, telephone interview, March 2020.
12 Personal communication with Jo Boyden, 4 March 2020.
13 Postcolonial scholars from Africa go even further in this line of argument. Building on the work of Frantz Fanon and Aimé Césaire, they advocate for overcoming the psychological effects of centuries of slavery and colonialization. In doing so, they deconstruct the dominant system of global capitalism and its objective of individual wealth accumulation. Grounded in indigenous cosmologies and modes of knowledge, postcolonial scholars define labour not only as an economic category but as a cultural artefact that forms a bridge between culture, society, spirituality, politics and the economy, and thus as something that the individual worker, including the child worker, must experience as a means of weaving connection with wider life (for example Sarr, 2016).
14 Personal communication with Michael Bourdillon, February 2020.
15 Personal communication with Richard Carothers, 18 February 2020.

References

Abebe, T. (2007) 'Changing livelihoods, changing childhoods: patterns of children's work in rural southern Ethiopia', *Children's Geographies*, 5(1,2), pp 77–93.

Anderson, B. (2000) *Doing the Dirty Work: The Politics of Domestic Labour.* London: Zed Books.

Ansell, N. and Van Blerk, L. (2004) 'Children's migration as a household/family strategy: coping with AIDS in Lesotho and Malawi', *Journal of Southern African Studies*, 30(3), pp 673–90.

Atkinson, S., Fuller, S. and Painter, J. (eds) (2012) *Wellbeing and Place.* Farnham: Ashgate Publishing.

Aufseeser, D. et al (2018) 'Children's work and children's well-being: implications for policy', *Development Policy Review*, 36(2), pp 241–61.

Basu, K. (1999) 'Child labor: cause, consequence, and cure, with remarks on international labor standards', *Journal of Economic Literature*, 37(3), pp 1083–119.

de Berry, J. et al (2003) *The Children of Kabul: Discussions with Afghan Families.* Kabul: Save the Children and UNICEF.

Bessell, S. (2011) 'Influencing international child labour policy: the potential and limits of children-centred research', *Children and Youth Services Review*, 33(4), pp 564–68.

Bourdillon, M. (1999) *Earn-and-Learn: Work for Education in the Eastern Highlands of Zimbabwe.* Unpublished paper.

Bourdillon, M. et al (2010) *Rights and Wrongs of Children's Work.* New Brunswick, New Jersey and London: Rutgers University Press.

Bourdillon, M. and Myers, B. (2021) 'Illusions in the protection of working children', in Okyere, S. and Howard, N. (eds) *International Child Protection: Towards Politics and Participation.* Basingstoke: Palgrave Macmillan, pp 77–100.

Boyden, J. and Mann, G. (2005) 'Children's risk, resilience, and coping in extreme situations', in Ungar, M. (ed) *Handbook for Working with Children and Youth: Pathways to Resilience Across Cultures and Contexts.* Thousand Oaks, CA: SAGE Publications, pp 3–26.

Boyden, J. and Myers, W. (1995) *Exploring Alternative Approaches to Combatting Child Labour: Case Studies from Developing Countries.* Innocenti Occasional Papers. Florence: UNICEF Office of Research.

Cornia, G.A., Jolly, R. and Stewart, F. (eds) (1987) *Adjustment with a Human Face.* Oxford: Clarendon Press.

Crivello, G., Vennam, U. and Komanduri, A. (2012) '"Ridiculed for not having anything": children's views on poverty and inequality in rural India', in Boyden, J. and Bourdillon, M. (eds) *Childhood Poverty: Multidisciplinary Approaches.* London: Palgrave Macmillan UK, pp 218–36.

Cullen, H. (2007) *The Role of International Law in the Elimination of Child Labor*. Leiden and Boston: Martinus Nijhoff.

van Daalen, E. and Hanson, K. (2019) 'The ILO's shifts in child labour policy: regulation and abolition', *International Development Policy, Revue internationale de politique de développement*, 11, pp 133–50.

Del Carpio, X.V., Loayza, N.V. and Wada, T. (2016) 'The impact of conditional cash transfers on the amount and type of child labor', *World Development*, 80, pp 33–47.

Dobson, J. and Stillwell, J. (2000) 'Changing home, changing school: towards a research agenda on child migration', *Area*, 32(4), pp 395–401.

Dorman, P. (2008) *Child Labour, Education and Health: A Review of the Literature*. Geneva: International Labour Office.

Doyal, L. and Gough, I. (1991) *A Theory of Human Need*. Basingstoke: Palgrave Macmillan.

Dunne, M., Humphreys, S. and Leach, F. (2006) 'Gender violence in schools in the developing world', *Gender and Education*, 18(1), pp 75–98.

Dyson, J. (2008) 'Harvesting identities: youth, work, and gender in the Indian Himalayas', *Annals of the Association of American Geographers*, 98(1), pp 160–179.

Edmonds, E.V. (2008) *Defining Child Labour: A Review of the Definitions of Child Labour in Policy Research*. Geneva: International Labour Office.

Fassa, A.G., Parker, D.L. and Scanlon, T.J. (2010) 'Child labour and health: changing the future', in Fassa, A.G., Parker, D.L., and Scanlon, T. (eds) *Child Labour: A Public Health Perspective*. Oxford: Oxford University Press. Available at: https://www.universitypressscholarship.com/view/10.1093/acprof:oso/9780199558582.001.0001/acprof-9780199558582-chapter-022 (Accessed 24 April 2020).

Fekadu, D., Hagglof, B. and Alem, A. (2010) 'Review of child labor with emphasis on mental health', *Current Psychiatry Reviews*, 6(3), pp 176–83.

Folbre, N. (2006) 'Measuring care: gender, empowerment, and the care economy', *Journal of Human Development*, 7(2), pp 183–99.

Gough, I., McGregor, J.A. and Camfield, L. (2007) 'Theorising need in international development', in Gough, I. and McGregor, I.A., J. A. (eds) *Wellbeing in Developing Countries: From Theory to Research*. Cambridge: Cambridge University Press, pp 3–44.

Gunn, S. et al (2015) *Development of an instrument for the psychosocial assessment of child workers*. Geneva: International Labour Office.

Hanson, K. (2012) 'Schools of thought in children's rights', in Liebel, M. et al (eds) *Children's Rights from Below: Cross-Cultural Perspectives*. London: Palgrave Macmillan UK, pp 63–79.

Hanson, K. and Nieuwenhuys, O. (eds) (2012) *Reconceptualizing Children's Rights in International Development: Living Rights, Social Justice, Translations*. Cambridge: Cambridge University Press.

Hanson, K. and Vandaele, A. (2013) 'Translating working children's rights into international labour law', in Hanson, K. and Nieuwenhuys, O. (eds) *Reconceptualizing Children's Rights in International Development: Living Rights, Social Justice, Translations*. Cambridge: Cambridge University Press, pp 250–72.

Hanson, K., Volonakis, D. and Al-Rozzi, M. (2015) 'Child labour, working children and children's rights', in Vandenhole, W. et al (eds) *International Handbook of Children's Rights Studies*. London: Routledge, pp 332–46.

Hart, J. (2021) 'Child protection in Palestine and Jordan: from rights to principles?', in Okyere, S. and Howard, N. (eds) *International Child Protection: Towards Politics and Participation*. Basingstoke: Palgrave MacMillan, pp 189–212.

Hashim, I. and Thorsen, D. (2011) *Child Migrants in Africa*. London: Zed Books.

Heissler, K. (2012) 'Children's migration for work in Bangladesh: the policy implications of intra-household relations', *Development in Practice*, 22(4), pp 498–509.

Holt, L. and Holloway, S.L. (2006) 'Editorial: theorising other childhoods in a globalised world', *Children's Geographies*, 4(2), pp 135–42.

de Hoop, J. and Rosati, F. (2014) *Cash Transfers and Child Labour*. Rome: Understanding Children's Work Project.

Howard, N. (2008) *Independent Child Migration in Southern Benin: An Ethnographic Challenge to the 'Pathological' Paradigm*. Saarbrucken: VDM Verlag. Available at: https://researchportal.bath.ac.uk/en/publications/independent-child-migration-in-southern-benin-an-ethnographic-cha (Accessed 24 April 2020).

Howard, N. (2014) 'Teenage labor migration and antitrafficking policy in west Africa', *Annals of the American Academy of Political and Social Science*, 653(1), pp 124–40.

Howard, N. (2017) *Child Trafficking, Youth Labour Mobility, and the Politics of Protection*. Basingstoke: Palgrave Macmillan.

Howard, N. and Okyere, S. (eds) (2015) *Childhood and Youth. Beyond Trafficking and Slavery Short Course*, Vol. 7. OpenDemocracy. Available at: https://drive.google.com/file/d/0B2lN4rGTopsaNjJNaDA1MFd3Qlk/view?resourcekey=0-f2hBZ85IdMVaNAYz38_RdA (Accessed 26 November 2022).

Huijsmans, R. and Baker, S. (2012) 'Child trafficking: "worst form" of child labour, or worst approach to young migrants?', *Development and Change*, 43(4), pp 919–46.

Hurst, P. (2007) 'Health and child labor in agriculture', *Food and Nutrition Bulletin*, 28(2 supplement), pp S364–71.

Ide, L.S.R. and Parker, D.L. (2005) 'Hazardous child labor: lead and neurocognitive development', Public Health Reports, 120(6), pp 607–12.

Ijumba, N. (2011) Impact of HIV/AIDS on Education and Poverty. South Africa: UN Chronicle. Available at: https://www.un.org/en/chronicle/article/impact-hivaids-education-and-poverty (Accessed 26 November 2022).
ILO (1973) *Convention C138: Minimum Age Convention, 1973 (No. 138).* Available at: https://www.ilo.org/dyn/normlex/en/f?p=NORMLEXPUB:12100:0::NO::P12100_ILO_CODE:C138 (Accessed 29 April 2020).
ILO (1999) *Convention C182: Worst Forms of Child Labour Convention, 1999 (No. 182).* Available at: https://www.ilo.org/dyn/normlex/en/f?p=NORMLEXPUB:12100:0::NO::P12100_ILO_CODE:C182 (Accessed 28 April 2020).
ILO (2011) *Children in Hazardous Work: What We Know, What We Need to Do.* Geneva: International Labour Organization.
ILO-IPEC (2012) *The Tripartite Process of Determining Hazardous Child Labour: Guide for Facilitators.* Geneva: International Labour Organization – IPEC.
ILO-IPEC (2014) *A Health Approach to Child Labour: A Synthesis Report of Four Country Studies from the Brick Industry.* Geneva: International Labour Organization – IPEC. Available at: http://www.ilo.org/ipec/Informationresources/WCMS_IPEC_PUB_25300/lang--en/index.htm (Accessed 24 April 2020).
Invernizzi, A. (2003) 'Street-working children and adolescents in Lima: work as an agent of socialization', *Childhood*, 10(3), pp 319–41.
James, A. and Prout, A. (eds) (1997) *Constructing and Reconstructing Childhood: Contemporary Issues in the Sociological Study of Childhood.* Hove: Psychology Press.
Katz, C. (1991) 'Sow what you know: the struggle for social reproduction in rural Sudan', *Annals of the Association of American Geographers*, 81(3), pp 488–514.
Katz, C. (1993) 'Growing girls/closing circles: limits on the spaces of knowing in rural Sudan and United States cities', in Katz, C. and Monk, J. (eds) *Full Circles: Geographies of Women over the Life Course.* Oxon: Routledge, pp 173–202.
Khan, A. (2007) *Representing Children: Power, Policy and the Discourse on Child Labour in the Football Manufacturing Industry of Pakistan.* Karachi: Oxford University Press.
Korbin, J. (2002) 'Culture and child maltreatment: cultural competence and beyond', *Child Abuse & Neglect*, 26, pp 637–44.
Kuimi, B.L.B. et al (2018) 'Child labour and health: a systematic review', *International Journal of Public Health*, 63(5), pp 663–72.
LeBaron, G. and Ayers, A. (2013) 'The rise of a "new slavery"? Understanding African unfree labour through neoliberalism', *Third World Quarterly*, 34(5), pp 873–92.

Liborio, R.M.C. and Ungar, M. (2010) 'Children's perspectives on their economic activity as a pathway to resilience', *Children & Society*, 24(4), pp 326–38.

Liebel, M. (2004) *A Will of Their Own: Cross-cultural Perspectives on Working Children*. New York and London: Zed Books.

Maconachie, R. and Hilson, G. (2016) 'Re-thinking the child labor "problem" in rural sub-Saharan Africa: the case of Sierra Leone's half shovels', *World Development*, 78, pp 136–47.

McKinney, K. (2015) 'Situating corporate framings of child labor: toward grounded geographies of working children in globalized agriculture', *Geoforum*, 59, pp 219–27.

Morrow, V. and Boyden, J. (2018) *Responding to Children's Work: Evidence from the Young Lives Study in Ethiopia, India, Peru and Vietnam. Summative Report*. Oxford: Young Lives. Available at: https://www.younglives.org.uk/sites/www.younglives.org.uk/files/YL-RespondingToChildrensWork-A4-Jan18_0.pdf.

Murray, U., Amorim, A. and Bland, J. (2004) *A Comparative Analysis: Girl Child Labour in Agriculture, Domestic Work and Sexual Exploitation: The Cases of Ghana, Ecuador and the Philippines (vol. 2)*. Geneva: ILO.

Myers, W. (2017) *Bizarre Bureaucratic Dysfunction in Child Labour*. (openDemocracy). Available at: https://www.opendemocracy.net/en/beyond-trafficking-and-slavery/bizarre-bureaucratic-dysfunction-in-child-labour/ (Accessed 24 April 2020).

Nieuwenhuys, O. (1996) 'The paradox of child labor and anthropology', *Annual Review of Anthropology*, 25(1), pp 237–51.

Nieuwenhuys, O. (2007) 'Embedding the global womb: global child labour and the new policy agenda', *Children's Geographies*, 5(1–2), pp 149–63.

Nieuwenhuys, S. (2020) 'Women and children in social reproduction and the global womb', *Focaal: Journal of Global and Historical Anthropology*, 82, pp 129–32.

O'Donnell, O., van Doorslaer, E. and Rosati, F.C. (2002) *Child Labour and Health: Evidence and Research Issues*. Rochester, NY: Social Science Research Network. Available at: https://papers.ssrn.com/abstract=1780320 (Accessed 24 April 2020).

Okyere, S. (2017a) 'Moral economies and child labour in artisanal gold mining in Ghana', in Brace, L. and O'Connell Davidson, J. (eds) *Revisiting Slavery and Antislavery*. London: Palgrave Macmillan, pp 29–55.

Okyere, S. (2017b) '"Shock and awe": a critique of the Ghana-centric child trafficking discourse', *Anti-Trafficking Review*, (9), pp 92–105.

Pankhurst, A., Crivello, Gina and Tiumelissan, A. (2015) 'Work in children's lives in Ethiopia: examples from Young Lives communities', in Pankhurst, A., Bourdillon, M., and Crivello, G (eds) *Children's Work and Labour in East Africa: Social Context and Implications for Policy*. Addis Ababa: Organization for Social Science Research in East Africa, pp 41–74.

Punch, S. (2000) 'Children's strategies for creating play spaces: negotiating independence in rural Bolivia', in Holloway, S.L. and Valentine, G. (eds) *Children's Geographies: Playing, Living, Learning*. Oxon and New York: Routledge, pp 48–62.

Punch, S. (2002) 'Youth transitions and interdependent adult-child relations in rural Bolivia', *Journal of Rural Studies*, 18(2), pp 123–33.

Punch, S. (2007) 'Negotiating migrant identities: young people in Bolivia and Argentina', *Children's Geographies*, 5(1–2), pp 95–112.

Razavi, S. (2007) *The Political and Social Economy of Care in a Development Context. Conceptual Issues, Research Questions and Policy Options*. Geneva: United Nations Research Institute for Social Development.

Robson, E. (2004) 'Children at work in rural northern Nigeria: patterns of age, space and gender', *Journal of Rural Studies*, 20(2), pp 193–210.

Rogoff, B. (2014) 'Learning by observing and pitching in to family and community endeavors: an orientation', *Human Development*, 57(2–3), pp 69–81.

Rogoff, B. et al (2017) 'Noticing learners' strengths through cultural research', *Perspectives on Psychological Science*, 12(5), pp 876–88.

Sabates-Wheeler, R. and Sumberg, J. (2020) *Understanding Children's Harmful Work in African Agriculture: Points of Departure. ACHA Working Paper 1*. Brighton: Action on Children's Harmful Work in African Agriculture, IDS.

Sarkar, J. and Sarkar, D. (2016) 'Why does child labor persist with declining poverty?', *Economic Inquiry*, 54(1), pp 139–58.

Sarr, F. (2016) *Afrotopia*. Paris: Philippe Rey.

Shendell, D.G. et al (2016) 'Exposures resulting in safety and health concerns for child laborers in less developed countries', *Journal of Environmental and Public Health*, 2016, p 3985498.

Sheth, A. and Buhr, E. (2012) 'Refiguring global narratives on child labour: how much safer is the school option?', *Inclusive, Journal of Kolkata Centre for Contemporary Studies*, 1(2). Available at: http://www.inclusivejournal.in/posts/2012-02-spart-02.html (Accessed 26 November 2022).

Sturrock, S. and Hodes, M. (2016) 'Child labour in low- and middle-income countries and its consequences for mental health: a systematic literature review of epidemiologic studies', *European Child & Adolescent Psychiatry*, 25(12), pp 1273–86.

Swift, A. (1997) *Children for Social Change: Education for Citizenship of Street and Working Children in Brazil*. Shrewsbury: Educational Heretics Press.

Taft, J.K. (ed) (2013) *Nothing About Us, Without Us: Critiques of the International Labor Organization's Approach to Child Labor from the Movements of Working Children*. Lima: IFEJANT.

Taft, J.K. (2021) 'Intergenerational activism as an alternative to child saving: the example of the Peruvian Movement of Working Children', in Okyere, S. and Howard, N. (eds) *International Child Protection: Towards Politics and Participation*. Basingstoke: Palgrave Macmillan, pp 57–75.

Thorsen, D. (2014) 'Jeans, bicycles and mobile phones: adolescent migrants' material consumption in Burkina Faso', in Veale, A. and Dona, G. (eds) *Child and Youth Migration: Mobility-in-Migration in an Era of Globalization*. Basingstoke: Palgrave MacMillan, pp 67–90.

UNESCO (2006) *HIV/Aids Education: Teacher Training and Teaching; a Web-Based Desk Study of 10 African Countries*. Paris: UNESCO.

Werner, E. and Smith, R. (1992) *Overcoming the Odds: High Risk Children from Birth to Adulthood*. Ithaca: Cornell University Press.

White, S.C. (2015) *Relational Wellbeing: A Theoretical and Operational Approach. Bath Papers in International Development and Wellbeing*. Bath: University of Bath.

White, S.C. and Blackmore, C. (eds) (2016) *Cultures of Wellbeing: Method, Place, Policy*. Basingstoke: Palgrave MacMillan.

Woodhead, M. (1998) *Children's Perspectives on Their Working Lives: A Participatory Study in Bangladesh, Ethiopia, The Philippines, Guatemala, El Salvador and Nicaragua*. Stockholm: Save the Children.

Woodhead, M. (2004) *Psychosocial Impacts of Child Work: A Framework for Research, Monitoring and Intervention. Working Paper 4*. Rome: Understanding Children's Work Project, University of Rome.

3

Understanding Children's Harmful Work: The Methodological Landscape

Keetie Roelen, Inka Barnett, Vicky Johnson, Tessa Lewin, Dorte Thorsen and Giel Ton

Introduction

Children' work is notoriously difficult to identify, assess and understand. Common definitions of child labour, light work, the worst forms of child labour and hazardous child labour, as put forward by the International Labour Organization (ILO), are premised on notions of hazard and risk[1] but do not include an explicit consideration of harm (Chapter 2, this volume). Harm can be broadly considered 'an identifiable negative impact on an individual or household' (see Chapter 2, this volume) and children's harmful work (CHW) can be thought of as 'any work that children undertake that actually results in harm to the child and/or their household' (Sabates-Wheeler and Sumberg, 2020, p 8). Forms of CHW are often hidden from sight and its prevalence, drivers and impacts are highly context specific (see Chapter 2, this volume). Research on CHW therefore requires careful consideration of both methodological approach and individual methods. This chapter provides a review of methods that are commonly used for studying child labour and children's engagement with work; considers their value for understanding prevalence, drivers and dynamics, and impact of CHW; discusses the role of mixed methods approaches; and proposes a set of methodological principles for studying CHW.

We review three types of methods in this chapter, namely (1) quantitative survey methods, (2) qualitative and participatory methods, and (3) certification methods. In addition, we review studies that adopt mixed methods research designs, explicitly seeking to achieve both breadth and depth by combining a variety of methods, either in parallel or sequentially. Inevitably this typology oversimplifies the variety of available methods. Furthermore, many studies adopt a combination of methods and data, often in implicit ways, without making specific reference to a mixed methods approach (such as using different qualitative and participatory tools in small-scale studies). Thus, the typology categorization serves as a framework for organizing this review as opposed to a strict delineation.

The remainder of this chapter is structured as follows. First, we provide an overview of methods as outlined earlier, exploring their use within studies of child labour and children's work. Second, we assess the merits and challenges of specific methods for assessing the prevalence of forms of children's harmful work, drivers and dynamics, and impact. Finally, we propose a set of research design principles for studying CHW.

Review of methods

Quantitative survey methods

A wide range of survey methods exist for studying children's engagement with work, ranging from large-scale surveys that collect information about work alongside many other topics, to purposive small-scale and child-centred surveys. We explore some of the most common survey methods.

Nationally representative, multi-purpose household surveys

National multi-purpose household surveys collect information across a range of issues and are designed to be representative at country level. Living Standards Measurement Surveys (LSMS), Multiple Indicator Cluster Surveys (MICS), Demographic Health Surveys (DHS) and Labour Force Surveys (LFS) have been used to gain insight into the prevalence and patterns of child labour (Bhalotra and Tzannatos, 2003; ILO/IPEC-SIMPOC, 2007; UCW, 2017). These surveys often do not produce detailed information on child labour but collect information on employment of household members, characteristics of the household and its members and household living standards, which can help to understand the context in which child labour takes place (Verma, 2008). In regard to child labour, most large-scale multi-purpose household surveys are guided by ILO Convention No. 138 (Minimum Age) (C138), ILO Convention No. 182 (Worst Forms) (C182) and United Nations Convention on the Rights of the Child (CRC) (UNICEF and ILO, 2019). In turn, the International Conference of Labour Statisticians (ICLS) translates these conventions in statistical terms and sets standards for measurement of child labour (UNICEF and ILO, 2019).

The narrow focus of these conventions and their rigid definitions and standards result in a similarly narrow remit in most multi-purpose surveys. Nevertheless, surveys differ in their potential to explore children's engagement with work. Within LSMS, for example, the ability to cross reference information about children's work with data on school attendance and educational attainment, as well as demographic and socioeconomic characteristics of the household and its members, contributed to its popularity for studying child labour (Bhalotra and Tzannatos, 2003). MICS provide insight into children's engagement with unpaid household chores, which are not captured in many other surveys (Dayıoğlu, 2013). A notable downside of MICS is that information about health and nutrition is only collected for children under five years of age and this limits the ability to link information about children's engagement in work to health and nutrition outcomes (ILO/IPEC-SIMPOC, 2007). Similarly, the use of DHS data is constrained due to the limited range of questions about employment being asked to individuals between 15 and 49 years of age. LFS are the most comprehensive in terms of capturing information about employment but age brackets vary across surveys, with lower age thresholds to be included in the survey ranging from 10 to 15 years (Desiere and Costa, 2019). Table 3.1 provides a comparative overview of national household surveys and their potential use for studying child labour.

Child labour surveys

Child labour surveys range from large scale household-based surveys to small scale surveys with street children (Verma 2008). The Statistical Information & Monitoring Programme on Child Labour (SIMPOC) and the Statistics and Monitoring Unit of ILO's International Programme on the Elimination of Child Labour (IPEC) have played key roles in developing survey-based instruments and in advising national governments on how to generate high quality data on child labour (SIMPOC, nd). Whether standalone or integrated into a larger instrument, questionnaires commonly consist of three parts: (1) household roster, (2) adult questionnaire and (3) child questionnaire (aged 5–17) (ILO, 2017). As expected, National Child Labour Surveys (NCLS) provide more detailed information about child labour than multi-purpose household surveys. For example, they usually include children aged five and upwards, thus allowing for an assessment of the age at which children start working (ILO, 2015). The questionnaires do not capture engagement in domestic chores or unpaid care work and therefore do not fully represent children's engagement with work, particularly for girls who are more likely to be engaged in housework.

Child-focused surveys include children and/or youth as respondents. A well-established survey is the School-to-Work Transition Survey (SWTS), which aimed to gain better insights into transitions from school into work and to understand youth transitions into the labour market (Elder, 2009).

Table 3.1: Overview of national household surveys and measurement of child labour

Type	Objectives	Multi-topic	Age bracket	Data availability
LSMS	(a) Foster evidence-based policy formulation on agriculture, assets ownership, health, education, income and employment; (b) Monitor the SDGs and the living condition dynamics of rural and urban households; (c) Facilitate randomized impact evaluations; and (d) Assess women and youth employment and child activities.	Yes	Varies from 7 or 10 years and above	Public
MICS	Provide internationally comparable data on children and women's lives to monitor progress towards SDGs and national development goals.	Yes	5 years and above	Public
DHS	(a) Monitor changes in population, health, and nutrition; (b) Provide an international database that can be used by researchers investigating topics related to population, health, nutrition.	Yes	15–49 years old	Public
LFS	(a) Implement policies for decent work, employment creation and poverty reduction, income support as well as other social programmes; (b) Monitor the SDGs and the living condition dynamics of rural and urban households.	No	Varies from 10 to 15 years and above	Varies by country

Sources: Desire and Costa (2019), The DHS Program (2020) and MICS website (https://mics.unicef.org/)

The survey was directed at youth aged 15–29 years of age, and its underlying sampling methodology aimed for national representation. Although it is possible to use SWTS to produce child labour estimates, its main objective was to supplement the information collected through LFS or NCLS and provide detailed data about the supply of youth labour.

Another category of child-focused surveys includes those that are developed and implemented as part of specific research studies. These vary widely in scope, sampling and types of questions asked. Examples include a six-country study that assessed whether child domestic work can be considered among the worst forms of child labour, and which administered questionnaires to over 3,000 children aged between 6 and 18 years of age (Gamlin et al, 2015). Another is a study of work and education in slum settlements in Dhaka among 2,700 children aged 6–14 years old (Quattri and Watkins, 2016).

Young Lives and the Gender and Adolescence Global Evidence (GAGE) programme are two large-scale and longitudinal child-focused studies that generate quantitative information about children's engagement with work. Young Lives is a cohort study that provides five waves of cross-sectional and panel data for two cohorts of children in Ethiopia, India, Peru and Bangladesh, including a total of approximately 12,000 children across all countries (Boyden et al, 2019). GAGE collects quantitative longitudinal data on approximately 18,000 adolescents between ages 10 and 19 in seven countries: Bangladesh, Ethiopia, Jordan, Lebanon, Nepal, Palestine and Rwanda (Jones et al, 2018).

School-based surveys collect information about how work affects school attendance or performance and attitudes to schooling (SIMPOC, nd). Schools are used as primary sampling units with questionnaires being administered to students. Interviews with teachers, administrative staff and parents may also be included, and some surveys include a control group of out-of-school children (Verma, 2008). While other surveys generally limit questions to school enrolment and attendance, school-based surveys seek to generate data about how much time children spend in school, how often they miss school because of work, and their engagement with homework and extracurricular activities (Guarcello et al, 2005). Large-scale school-based surveys were undertaken in the early 2000s with support from ILO-IPEC in Brazil, Kenya, Lebanon, Sri Lanka and Turkey, among other countries (Guarcello et al, 2005).

Establishment surveys focus on the demand-side of child labour and collect information from employers or labour intermediaries. These seek to interrogate the situation in the workplace with questions focusing on the nature of work, hours of work, remuneration and pay, injuries and illnesses and other conditions of work. Establishment surveys are rarely representative as identification of establishments employing children is inherently problematic (Verma, 2008). However, they use the place of employment as an entry point so they can be valuable for collecting information about forms of labour undertaken by children living outside of the household unit or at non-registered locations, such as children living on the streets (ILO et al, 2012).

Impact evaluation surveys

Impact evaluation represents a growing body of research within which surveys are used to collect information on the effects of interventions, which often includes information about children's engagement with work. Evaluations often employ multi-purpose surveys with varying degrees of detail on children's work, typically drawing on the survey types reviewed earlier. The quality of this information varies. Evaluations of programmes that seek to reduce child labour as a primary objective tend to include more detail about children's engagement with work than is the case when reducing child labour is a secondary objective. A case in point is social protection, which has become a key policy area for reducing child labour (ILO, 2018; Chapter 7, this volume). An increasing number of studies consider the impact of social protection programmes – including schemes such as unconditional cash transfers, conditional cash transfers and public works programmes – on children's engagement in work (de Hoop and Rosati, 2014; Dammert et al, 2018). In the majority of cases, evaluations aim to capture the programme effects on an array of outcomes, and child labour tends to be only one such outcome, resulting in relatively narrow collection of information. Also the private sector, especially certification bodies such as Rainforest Alliance and Fairtrade, increasingly commission impact evaluation that incorporate issues of child labour.

Small-scale surveys

The use of survey methods is not limited to collection of large-scale data. Qualitative researchers also use survey methods to develop their knowledge of the research setting, introduce themselves and to collect specific data that are important to their analysis of children's lifeworlds, work, education and social positions (Reynolds, 1991; Hashim, 2004; Katz, 2004; Dyson, 2014).

In her research on child labour in the Zambesi Valley, Reynolds conducted a census of 12 families (Reynolds, 1991): she had previously worked in the same community and thus already had a broad knowledge of the context. By contrast, in her study in south-eastern Sudan, Katz saw her village-wide household survey as a way to introduce herself and her research while constructing a socio-economic and cultural profile of the community. The survey illuminated the diversity of economic activities both on and off-farm, and their seasonality (Katz, 2004). In the context of a child-centred study of everyday involvement in rural household labour in a remote village in the high Himalayas in Nepal, Dyson (2014) undertook a full village census that included the age, educational background and occupation of all household members.

Qualitative and participatory methods

Qualitative studies and participatory methods span a range of scales, from small case studies focused on a limited number of people to studies working with samples of several hundreds. A wide range of methods are available, and increasingly, more traditional methods such as interviews and observations are used alongside more creative methods that have long been used in research with children and in relation to their engagement with work (Boyden and Ennew, 1997; Punch, 2001b; Leach and Mitchell, 2006).

Participant and other types of observation

Qualitative research with children about work has made use of a variety of observational methods. Many, such as participant observation, time-use studies, writing diaries and photography, are borrowed from ethnography. These have proved useful in helping to understand the role of children and their work in households and society. Examples include Pamela Reynolds' (1991) *Dance, Civet Cat*, based on her work with Tonga children in the Zambezi Valley, and Cindy Katz's (2004) *Growing up Global*, a comparative ethnography of children's lives in a Sudanese village and New York.

Participant observation is a key element of ethnographic research and has been used to discover the range of activities in which children engage (Reynolds, 1991; Johnson et al, 1995; Punch, 2001a; Katz, 2004; Dyson, 2014). At the same, questions have been raised about the extent to which adult researchers can do participant observation with children; while researchers can join children's games and work, they will always be a different type of player in the game (Punch, 2001b, p 165; Atkinson, 2019).

Other forms of observation include 24-hour reported recall, extended periods of detailed observation and diaries, allowing for children's work to be recorded in different ways such as random 'snapshots' of labour allocation, (Reynolds, 1991; Robson, 2004). In recall interviews and diaries, children are asked to recount their activities in as much detail as possible paying attention to the timing and duration of activities. However, both methods tend to under-report work because children forget tasks that they do not find important or are done alongside other work; and are unwilling to disclose work they find embarrassing (Reynolds, 1991; Johnson et al, 1995; Robson, 2004, p 199). The recording of time-use needs careful planning vis-à-vis the agricultural calendar, school holidays and even within the day (Robson, 2004; Tudge and Hogan, 2005).

Participatory and creative methods

Photography has also been used to observe children's day-to-day activities, including their work. For example, Bolton et al (2001) tasked

11- to 16-year olds with 'making photographs'[2] of their part-time jobs. However, the method goes beyond mere observation. In South Africa, the photovoice method was used to understand children's concept of 'self' (Benninger and Savahl, 2016) and perceptions of the natural spaces around them (Adams et al, 2017). Participatory photography helps in 'making the familiar strange' to both researchers and participants and thus serves as a useful mediation tool to broaden discussions with participants, complementing, augmenting, confirming and enlarging insight from other methods (Bolton et al, 2001, p 517; Mizen and Ofosu-Kusi, 2010). The method has been adapted for use with disabled children (Wickenden and Elphick, 2016).

Other creative methods, including drawing, mapping and drama have been used to encourage children's free expression and reveal 'subjugated knowledges' (Mizen and Ofosu-Kusi, 2010; Thomas De Benitez, 2011; Johnson et al, 2014) and children's understanding of place, space and their everyday lives (Mitchell, 2006; Johnson, 2011; Bolzman et al, 2017; Bowles, 2017). Methods like drawing have been successfully used in large-scale studies (Kilkelly et al, 2005; Crivello et al, 2009; Crivello et al, 2013). Katz (2004) used 'geodramatic play' to gain insight into children's social and environmental knowledge. In South Africa, theatre-based research helped to unveil emotional challenges and notions of vulnerability among undocumented migrant youth in Cape Town (Opfermann, 2020).

Interviews

Interviews can help to explore a topic or issue in detail. Life history or life cycle interviews, for example, aim 'to explore aspects of the social spaces of children and childhood' to understand the relationships that are central to children's psychosocial and material well-being (Abebe, 2008, p 57). Semi-structured interviews focusing on children's everyday activities can elicit time-use information. Katz (2004) showed how ethno-semantic interviews could be used to effectively probe children's practices and their understanding of environmental processes and interrelationships. Participatory, creative and/or ethnographic methods can be integrated into in-depth interviews to make them more child friendly (Greene and Hill, 2005; Johnson et al, 2014). Involving children in conducting interviews may also help to break down the boundaries between the researcher and the researched but also presents challenges that must be carefully negotiated (Boyden and Ennew, 1997; Hecht, 1998; Chin, 2007; Hoechner, 2015).

Focus group discussions (FDG) can create a space for children to share their understandings and experiences without having to engage in a one-on-one interview (Hashim, 2004; Gibson, 2007, p 24; Abebe, 2008; Dyson, 2014; Hoban, 2017, p 2).

Certification data

Certification systems in agricultural value chains gather a wide range of information about participating households, including background, engagement with work in priority sectors and the activities of children. These data are generated mostly by private sector organizations as part of their monitoring activities, and we therefore treat them separately from research surveys. Certification schemes and voluntary standard systems are often centred on tropical export crops, especially bananas, cocoa, coffee, sugar and palm oil. A significant part of the total production of cocoa produced in Ghana and Côte d'Ivoire is under one or more certification schemes (ISEAL, 2019b).

Certification programmes emerged in the 1980s in response to consumer demands for sustainability and fairness. The first programmes concerned organic production, especially in Organisation for Economic Cooperation and Development (OECD) countries. Later, in the 1990s, Fairtrade emerged in response to a greater focus on fairness in value chain relations involving small farmers in developing countries. At the same time, the retail sector in Europe started certification schemes around food safety and good agricultural practices, which resulted in the EurepGAP and later GLOBALG.A.P. standards (Oya et al, 2018). Dozens of new certification systems emerged in the last 20 years with varying systems and levels of credibility. In response, through International Social and Environmental Accreditation and Labelling (ISEAL), the most serious certification programmes developed minimum 'credibility standards' for monitoring and reporting impact. ISEAL is a membership organization of certification schemes and sustainability initiatives that plays a key role in data harmonization and exchange (ISEAL, 2019a).

Four data collection mechanisms used within certification systems can shed light on children's engagement with work.

Audit reports

Audit reports represent the main tool for information gathering within these schemes and systems. Audit reports present information about the compliance of individual farmers or farmer groups with the procedures and requirements, document cases where issues are observed and recommend areas for improvement. Typically, control points in the audit differ when individual producers (for example, plantations or larger producers) are certified, versus group certification (that is, where the production is scattered among many small producers). Group certification requires an accredited Internal Control System (ICS), through which data quality is managed by each group or firm. Medium or larger producers are subject to external audits. The quality of these internal and external audits is a critical concern for the credibility of a certification scheme. Often there is a layered system with an entity that controls the quality of accredited audit firms, that in turn control the compliance of certification holders (especially producers). For example, the Forest Stewardship Council (FSC) has an agency (Accreditation Services International – ASI) that provides this control-on-control.

Common core indicators

Despite the diversity of data collection across schemes, there is a tendency to harmonize the information collected using common core indicators in surveys and in-company monitoring systems. For example, ISEAL supported the development of linked, geographically referenced sets of basic data. These common core indicators can be mapped against the indicators for the UN Sustainable Development Goals (SDG).[3] Some refer directly to children's activities, including school attendance, distance to primary school, number of farms restricting the use of chemicals by pregnant women and children, food security, perceived change in quality of life and perception of change in level of control over household decisions.

ISEAL works on a range of projects to harmonize data flows within and between certification schemes (ISEAL, 2019a). This is to identify common and easily collectable data by implementers, auditors and evaluators. It is also to generate systems to store, link and analyse this information, and open it to researchers. In addition, ISEAL has developed guidance for structuring data sharing agreements for personal and sensitive data.

Outcome and impact evaluations

In addition to data generated within certification schemes, the minimum requirement of ISEAL members is for certification schemes (that is, scheme owners) to undertake at least one in-depth impact evaluation per year that addresses two questions: (1) Is the certification scheme or voluntary standard system producing the desired and intended sustainability outcomes or impacts?, and (2) What unintended effects (positive or negative) resulted from the scheme or system?

In the last 15 years, this requirement has resulted in a large body of research on the impact of certification systems, which have been the object of various systematic reviews (Blackman and Rivera, 2010; Blackmore et al, 2012; Oya, et al, 2018; Schleifer and Sun, 2020). Most of these studies focus on intended outcomes, like income and yield. Only a fraction of them discusses the impact or outcomes related to children's work as (intended or unintended) effects of certification.

Data on intended and unintended outcomes constitute a potentially useful source of information in relation to children's work, whether covering all or a sample of certification holders. The Rainforest Alliance's approach to assessing its certification system (which was developed together with the Sustainable Agriculture Network [SAN]), for example, includes three levels of data collection: programme wide monitoring, sampled monitoring and focussed research. While data for the first two types of assessments are collected within operations and as part of audits, data for focussed research is collected by an independent third party (ISEAL, 2017).

Child labour monitoring and remediation systems

Several certification schemes have explicit requirements related to children's work, such as Child Labour Monitoring and Remediation Systems (CLMRS). These schemes tend to use local facilitators to collect in-depth information on all households in a defined area. Nestlé, Mars and other brands, for example, implement CLMRS as part of their voluntary standards systems. Nestlé (2019) reports that, by the end of 2019, they had identified 18,000 cases of children working under conditions classified as child labour. This includes hazardous children's work according to the definition used in Côte d'Ivoire. In other words, these systems offer purposive quantitative information on child labour or hazardous work associated with the production and processing of specific products.

Investigating prevalence, drivers and dynamics, and impact

In this section we move on to discuss the use of these methods to investigate the (1) prevalence, (2) drivers and dynamics and (3) impact of CHW. We explore the opportunities or challenges associated with each method.

Prevalence

Prevalence refers to the scale and scope of different forms of children's harmful work, and Table 3.2 presents an overview by method.

Surveys have been widely used to gain insight into whether or not children work, and to generate quantitative information about prevalence at a wide (national or sub-national) scale. The ability to collect information across a representative sample allows for quantification of the occurrence of children's work across age, gender and other lines of disaggregation. Indeed, household surveys such as LSMS, MICS, LFS and others represent key instruments for generating estimates about child labour and monitoring progress towards SDG 8 (UNICEF and ILO, 2019). Nevertheless, there are three reasons why surveys are relatively ill-equipped to provide insights into more nuanced understandings of children's work, and particularly CHW.

Table 3.2: Prevalence of CHW: opportunities and challenges

Method	Opportunities	Challenges
Surveys	Able to provide population-wide/representative estimates of prevalence – put a 'number' to the issue	Relatively ill-equipped to uncover hazardous/harmful types of work, particularly if work or workers are hidden; lack of inclusion of marginalized groups; lack of active participation of respondents
Qualitative/ participatory methods	Vital to gaining detailed insights into what girls and boys are doing, what children and adults perceive as harm, who may experience harm; allow for mapping of the temporality, places and spaces of hazard and harm	Do not provide representative statistics; require strong link into other methods that can take insights to scale
Certification methods	Potential for using data from certification schemes to gain insight into prevalence in industries/supply chains	Prevalence estimates are not representative beyond industry/supply chain; issues with reliability of data

Source: Authors

First, the rigid nature of survey questionnaires generally limits opportunities for understanding CHW. As noted by Bhalotra and Tzannatos (2003) and supported by our review of survey methods, the work categories used tend to be crude and generally only allow for distinguishing between work for wages, work on family farms or in family enterprises, and domestic work. Surveys that underpin impact evaluations of social protection programmes also vary in the level of detail and the type of data that is collected about children's work (de Hoop and Rosati, 2014; Chapter 7, this volume). Purposive child labour surveys tend to be less bounded by stipulations within the ICLS resolution and therefore offer more flexibility. A downside of most of these purposive surveys – in terms of estimating prevalence – is that they are not nationally representative and thus only provide a partial picture.

Second, a prerequisite for identifying whether or not children engage in certain types of activities is their inclusion in data collection exercises. National household surveys are notorious for excluding the most marginalized household members, to say nothing of refugee populations, children living on the streets and in institutions (Bhalotra and Tzannatos 2003; Global Coalition to End Child Poverty 2019). This is particularly problematic when studying CHW as these children tend to be at greater risk (Bhalotra and Tzannatos, 2003).

Third, information is often provided by a proxy respondent rather than by the children themselves. This may lead to inaccurate reporting: while caregivers may be well informed about their children's engagement in work, they may not have precise information about how children allocate their time or about working conditions, and social and cultural values may lead to underreporting (Dammert et al, 2018). Equally, children may overestimate time spent on certain work or domestic activities (Dziadula and Guzman, 2020). While self-reporting is generally seen as more accurate and therefore preferable (Desiere and Costa, 2019), it has been suggested that administering questionnaires to both adults and children provides the most accurate results (Dziadula and Guzman, 2020).

Qualitative and participatory methods are vital for obtaining detailed and context-specific data about children's activities, their engagement with different forms of work and the extent to which these are considered harmful, and by whom. Participatory and observation methods can help to develop relevant categories and aid in the development of survey questionnaires (see, for example, ILO et al [2012]).

Finally, certification methods can also provide insight into children's participation in certain work activities. CLMRS systems, for example, generate data on the extent of children working in agriculture and doing specific hazardous tasks (based on CLMRS' own definitions). This offers information about prevalence within a certain industry or value-chain, but the reliability of these data needs to be ascertained.

Drivers and dynamics

As summarized in Table 3.3, the different methods can provide insights into the drivers and dynamics of child labour and children's engagement with work but also present limitations.

Surveys are widely used to study drivers and dynamics of children's work. Macro-level studies focus on correlates at country-level and are mostly premised on cross-country data. The Understanding Child Work (UCW) programme, for example, considered country-level variables such as gross domestic product (GDP) per capita, ratification of ILO Convention No. 138, exports of clothing and textiles and the Fragile States Index to understand differences in trends across countries (UCW, 2017). Micro-level studies are more common and typically explore the role of demographic and socio-economic characteristics of households and their members. In Bangladesh, for example, the Household Expenditure Survey was used to investigate the role of household poverty and wealth in child labour, with regression modelling used to estimate associations between independent variables such as household income and educational achievement of households and the dependent variable of children's work

Table 3.3: Drivers and dynamics of CHW: opportunities and challenges

Method	Opportunities	Challenges
Surveys	Ability to estimate association and sometimes causation between socio-economic and demographic factors and children's work	Analysis is limited to a relatively small set of factors; limited ability to estimate causation as the majority are cross-sectional
Qualitative/ participatory methods	Well-equipped to uncover drivers and dynamics of harmful work from multiple perspectives and respondents (girls, boys and adults); crucial for gaining detailed insight into social norms, values and power dynamics in decision making	Require careful sampling to ensure a range of perspectives across respondents; require time to build capacity in skills and on-going ethical procedures to facilitate some of these methods
Certification data	Localized longitudinal information can support analysis of changes in household conditions and harmful work	Local facilitators in CLMRS can help collect more in-depth information but are unskilled as researchers

Source: Authors

(Amin et al, 2004). Young Lives has studied the determinants of work and school attendance and their trade-off in Ethiopia (Haile and Haile, 2012). School-based surveys have also been used to understand the relationship between children's engagement with work and academic performance (Guarcello et al, 2005).

The caveats identified earlier concerning the limitations of surveys in relation to the prevalence of children's hazardous or harmful work also hold for drivers and dynamics. The sets of questions that are included are often too limited to allow for detailed understandings of factors that are associated with, or drive, CHW. It is also important to note that due to the cross-sectional nature of many surveys, they allow for investigating association but not causality. Exceptions include studies that use longitudinal data and econometric methods that allow for estimating causal effects. In Ghana, for example, three waves of the Living Standards Survey were used to investigate determinants of child labour (Blunch et al, 2002).

Qualitative and participatory methods – and their combination – should help illuminate the drivers and dynamics of CHW. However, there are no examples of longitudinal mixed methods studies specifically on the dynamics of child labour (for example, how children's workloads changed over time; how changes in a household's poverty level may affect children's labour participation). This shortcoming has also been highlighted by others (Camfield, 2014; Kuimi et al, 2018; Ibrahim et al, 2019).

Table 3.4: Impact: opportunities and challenges

Method	Opportunities	Challenges
Surveys	Ability to estimate impact of harmful children's work on children/success of interventions on reducing harmful children's work	Measuring impact requires longitudinal or comparative research design over a long period; existing impact surveys adopt simplistic definition of children's work
Qualitative/ participatory methods	Useful to understand impact of hazardous and harmful work/intended and unintended impact of interventions; can uncover impact of harmful children's work on children/success of interventions on reducing harmful children's work from multiple perspectives	Difficult to attribute impact (although can be useful to assess contribution); questions can be scaled (to be administered to large samples) but methods need to be combined with other methods to gain full insight
Certification methods	Provide insight into impact of certification systems on harmful work	Data may not be reliable

Source: Authors

Relatedly, narratives of change can provide insight into the drivers and dynamics of children's work. CLMRS may begin to provide such narrative accounts within households that are at risk. Local facilitators may be able to identify illustrative cases, for example, particularly as children are not attending school or may not be registered in the health post when injured or ill. However, the monitors are likely to have few research skills.

Impact

We explore how different methods can shape an understanding of (1) how CHW impacts children, and (2) how interventions impact CHW (Table 3.4).

Impact of child labour on children's lives

Survey methods are commonly used to assess the impact of child labour or children's work on different aspects of their lives. Many studies are particularly interested in associations between work and education. For example, NCLS data from 12 countries were used to investigate associations between child labour and educational attainment (ILO, 2015). Young Lives data underpinned a study of the impact of child labour on educational attainment in Vietnam (Mavrokonstantis, 2011). Several mixed methods studies also explored the impact of child labour on school attendance in Ethiopia (Woldehanna et al, 2008; Orkin, 2012). Qualitative and participatory studies can help uncover intended and unintended consequences of work, placing these within contextual understandings of harm.

Four observations are important. First, as noted earlier, most analyses are based on cross-sectional data and thus provide no insight into causality. Second, survey-based studies of the impact of children's work on children's outcomes tend to be limited to readily measurable aspects of children's work and lives. In other words, they focus on whether or not children work, the types and conditions of work, and outcomes such as education, nutrition or health. These studies are not well-equipped to investigate the impact of the worst forms of child labour (for example, trafficking, child slavery and bonded labour) on less tangible aspects of children's lives (for example, psychosocial wellbeing, relationships and aspirations). Qualitative and participatory methods are vital for understanding the wide range of positive and negative impacts of work on children's lives. Third, and relatedly, the impact of work on children should also be understood from the perspective of children. Their views of what is harmful or not can be understood through exploring what they do in their everyday lives, what they think of as work, and what they do or do not enjoy. This requires insights into why they are doing certain tasks and how decisions are made about their work: here, experience with 'child centred evaluation' is certainly relevant (Nurick and Johnson, 2001).

Fourth, the issue of temporality is key in understanding how work affects children, and whether or not it may be harmful (Chapter 2, this volume). Work may only cause harm if it is done over an extended period, and harm may present itself long after children have stopped engaging with this work. While the range of methods reviewed here are relatively well-equipped to pick up on intensity of exposure to particular risks through studying time-use, few methods have enough of a longitudinal perspective to pick up on medium- to long-term effects, particularly if the potential for those effects is not yet known.

Impact of interventions on child labour

Surveys are central to the research design of many impact evaluations, and constitute the primary data source for estimating programme effects, particularly in (quasi-)experimental settings. Evaluations cover programmes that have the reduction of child labour as a primary objective (for example, educational interventions) or a secondary objective (for example, social protection).

An important observation in relation to quantitative impact evaluations is that child labour (or children's work) tends to be loosely defined.

Studies – and their underlying surveys – are often designed without clear reference to either the international guidelines or the academic literature that problematizes dominant understandings of child labour or children's engagement in work (Chapter 2, this volume). This is certainly the case in relation to social protection, where evaluations of programmes and their effects on child labour rarely follow the ICLS resolution (Dammert et al, 2018). Notions such as child labour or children engaged in productive activities are used interchangeably, with some evaluations denoting any type of work as child labour. Some evaluations of programmes that focus squarely on reduction of child labour even suggest that there is no agreed definition of child labour and therefore adopt their own (for example, Andisha et al, 2014).

As described previously, there would appear to be scope for integrating participatory and creative methods into programme evaluations, while CLMRS may offer useful data and provide scope for collecting additional data about the impact of certification on children's engagement with hazardous or harmful work.

Mixed methods design

Next, we consider the use of mixed methods design in studies of child labour and children's work. We define mixed methods as the combination of quantitative and qualitative approaches in different phases of the research process (see Creswell et al, 2003). We exclude studies that only combine multiple qualitative or quantitative approaches. Also, for feasibility purposes, only studies that focused on child labour or children's engagement with work as a main point of interest were considered. A total of ten studies were identified to fit these criteria, mixing methods to triangulate findings across data sets, to use findings from one method to inform another (primarily qualitative informing quantitative methods) or to gather information using multiple rounds of data collection over a longer period of time.

Overall, mixed methods designs can be powerful as they combine strengths of various methods (Table 3.5). They often help to challenge perceptions and assumptions about children's work and thus can facilitate a more holistic understanding of CHW. The review of existing mixed methods studies shows that this potential has so far been largely under-exploited. The level of integration between the quantitative and qualitative components is generally weak: in the majority of these studies, these components were conducted separately and to a large degree independently.

With respect to the prevalence of CHW, mixed methods design offers real potential for generating more meaningful and reliable estimates. As noted in one study, national-level prevalence data were important to highlight the magnitude of child labour for advocacy work, but were of limited use

Table 3.5: Mixed methods designs: opportunities and challenges

Research focus	Opportunities	Challenges
Prevalence	Allow for providing representative estimates of prevalence and to contextualize the 'number'	Sequencing of methods often not used to full potential with survey methods often grounded in limited understandings of harmful work
Drivers and dynamics	Mix of information allows for estimating and contextualizing drivers and dynamics of harmful work	Lack of longitudinal mixed methods studies and data
Impact	Mix of information allows for assessing whether impacts do/do not exist and understanding why, combining insights about causal mechanisms primarily from the qualitative research component, and about prevalence primarily from the quantitative research component	Often there is a mismatch between understanding gleaned from quantitative and qualitative components due to different operationalizations of harmful work (although this can also be an opportunity to deepen understanding further)

Source: Authors

in guiding action and programmes, with local-level data and qualitative approaches being needed (Bhatia et al, 2020). It follows that mixed methods offer promising opportunities for estimating prevalence of CHW by first gaining more detailed insight into working conditions and then estimating prevalence using quantitative data. As noted earlier, various mixed methods studies used both qualitative and quantitative methods to gain insights into the conditions in which children worked (Al Ganideh and Good, 2015; Bhatia et al, 2020). Nevertheless, few studies have made full use of the opportunity to preface survey data collection with in-depth qualitative data generation.

In terms of the drivers and dynamics of child labour, many pure quantitative studies neglect the heterogeneity of child labour, which can significantly reduce the usefulness of findings to inform policy and practice (Krauss, 2017). Mixed method designs can facilitate the identification of meaningful sub-groups of child workers and what influences their participation in work, thereby ensuring that research is more inclusive. Orkin (2012) employed a sequential, multi-phased mixed methods design to explore the drivers of both child labour participation and school attendance in Ethiopia. Qualitative methods with parents and children were used to identify characteristics of work and school that influenced participation, which were then used to inform and improve analysis using quantitative models of intra-household bargaining with regards to children's time allocation to either school or labour. In other studies with sequential designs, the quantitative analysis proposed one or more potential drivers of child labour while the qualitative data provided details on the potential causal mechanisms behind the observed association (Shaffer, 2013). For example, based on an econometric analysis, Woldehanna et al (2008) found that children with highly educated mothers were more likely to work. Qualitative findings indicated that educated mothers were often more likely to work outside the home, thereby increasing domestic work for their children at home.

A considerable shortcoming, also observed in relation to other methods, is the lack of longitudinal data. This hampers the ability to explore what drives children's work over time, and limits the ability to understand the impact of children's work on, for example, children's health and wellbeing (Kuimi et al, 2018; Ibrahim et al, 2019). Young Lives is a notable exception to this and has undertaken various investigations into the impact of children's work. Several studies explore the impact of child labour on school attendance (Woldehanna et al, 2008; Orkin, 2012). Drawing on both qualitative and quantitative evidence, the authors found that work and school attendance may be successfully combined depending on the time each activity takes and their characteristics. A potential pitfall when it comes to mixing methods is that tools may be premised on different understandings of what constitutes child labour or harmful forms of work, thereby potentially limiting the extent to which findings can be combined and complement each other. At the same time, these alternative views can help facilitate a richer understanding.

A key observation is the overall lack of mixed methods studies on children's engagement with work. This seems to reflect the perennial and persistent divide between quantitative and qualitative researchers observed within development studies (Jones and Sumner, 2009). Findings suggest that quantitative studies still mainly focus on assessing the prevalence, drivers and impact of child labour. By contrast, qualitative and participatory research are more interested in children's experiences of work and the dynamics and complexities surrounding it. We also find that the majority of studies focus on obtaining larger scale data that can be contextualized with more qualitative methods. Relatively few studies adopt fully integrated designs or use child-centred and participatory methods in combination with quantitative methods.

Ethics of research with children

Research on children's economic activities must navigate the same basic ethical dilemmas as other research on or with children. Approaches to these dilemmas sit within wider discourses on childhood, intergenerational and institutional power dynamics, children's roles in research and the politics of evidence. A fundamental challenge is posed by the category 'children', which by many official definitions – for example, any person under the age of 18 (UNICEF, 1989) – encompasses and extraordinary range of physical, mental and emotional capabilities, and social positions.

Informed by the UN Convention on the Rights of the Child, protocols for research on children's engagement with work must certainly address ethical issues including: transparency, confidentiality, informed consent, protection for vulnerable children, differences and inequalities between children, motivations for participation and expectations, withdrawal or opt out, intergenerational and peer power dynamics and social norms, and decision-makers views of children's opinions and evidence (Johnson et al, 1998; Johnson and West, 2018). A key question that can arise, for example in household surveys, is who is allowed to speak for children – for example, is the household head's view of the extent of a child's economic activity, or experiences of work-related harm, likely to be the same as the child's?

In addition, four broad dilemmas deserve particular attention. The first arises if the research is likely to touch on children's work activities that are illegal, or if issues of criminality (such as child trafficking or abuse) arise or are disclosed during the research. In the former case, it will be difficult to obtain institutional ethical approval. In the latter case, the roles and responsibilities of the researchers (who are neither police nor civil authorities) must be articulated, and supported by clear procedural guidelines including referral to support services when appropriate (see, for example, Johnson and West, 2022).

The second dilemma arises when images of children are used in the research itself and/or the communication around it (Wells, 2018). While it goes without saying that consent by children and parents is required, there are still challenges around the use of photos, even when the imagery is positive. Children are often keen to have their pictures and quotations included; however, this may lead to unforeseen risks to them or their families. Data management of visuals also raises important ethical questions (Johnson et al, 2013, pp 49–51).

The third dilemma is linked to the question of payment or other remuneration, particularly if children's participation means some loss of wages. This can entail a complex deliberation as it touches on power dynamics and perceptions of peers, adults and employers, as well as local research norms. As always, the possibility that payment will compromise the research process must be considered. Alternatives to cash payments might be appropriate.

Finally, there is an important dilemma around how vulnerability and agency are represented in the communication of research on children's work (Mizen and Ofosu-Kusi, 2013; Johnson and West, 2018; Wells, 2018). Including children in data analysis and verification has been shown to provide perspectives on their realities that may be otherwise missed, although adults may not recognize the validity of these perspectives (Johnson, 2017). In any case, confidentiality and anonymity must be respected in the selection of quotes and images.

Conclusion

This review leads to reflections about implications for future research on CHW. In light of the existing methodological landscape, there is real potential for future research to do something new, innovative and exciting from a methodological point of view. The review identifies two research gaps. First, despite the wealth of research on child labour and children's work, few studies use a truly integrated mix of methods. This integration would enable researchers to think beyond and challenge standard notions of children's engagement with work. Second, only a relatively small body of literature (across all research looking at forms of child labour and children's engagement with work) seems to be concerned with children's hazardous and harmful work. This literature is primarily informed by smaller-scale ethnographic and participatory research due to the complexities and sensitivities surrounding these types of work. Future research that integrates methods across disciplinary divides in more holistic ways can help to understand the breadth and depth of children's engagement with work – harmful and harmless.

In other words, it is now time to envisage a new generation of research on the prevalence, dynamics and impacts of children's work and harm. We argue that this research should be designed around nine principles:

1. Use fully integrated mixed methods designs, and make full use of secondary data to inform research design.
2. Link to, but challenge, standard definitions and mainstream understandings of child labour, including that which is hazardous and/or harmful.
3. Take a child-focused approach, giving space and weight to children's voices.
4. Be inclusive of a wide range of respondents.
5. Take context into account.
6. Account for temporality.
7. Build and build on local capacity.
8. Adhere to ethical principles and protocol.
9. Take time; allow for messiness.

As previously discussed, most of these are self-explanatory. Nevertheless, the second principle requires some further explanation. The reality is that international agencies (like the ILO), national policy makers, industry partners and most other actors continue to rely on mainstream understandings and definitions of child labour, children's work and harm as articulated in the international conventions and instruments (see Chapter 2, this volume). While it is clear that these understandings and definitions leave much to be desired, research that seeks to bring more nuanced, context-sensitive perspectives into the policy process, and into the practice of for example certification schemes, must necessarily start on this well-established (and often aggressively defended) home ground.

Taken together, these design principles, should result in research that differs significantly from the bulk of research on children's engagement with work in a number of important ways. First, the mixed methods approach is more holistic and all-encompassing, fully integrating survey methods, qualitative and participatory methods and certification methods. Second, greater weight is given to qualitative and participatory methods. The complexities and sensitivities involved in research of children's harmful work merit the use of such methods, particularly in the early stages of the research and in relation to prevalence. Third, stronger linkages between methods should yield integrated mixed methods designs as opposed to purely sequential or parallel designs. The research process will be more iterative, data from qualitative and participatory methods feeding into survey design and findings from survey data feeding into ethnographic activities. Finally, methods are integrated across the research process to make full use of insights from individual methods and the expertise of respective researchers from design through to uptake of research findings. Crucially this requires ample allocation of time in order to make full use of learning opportunities created through the research.

Notes

1 Some countries also adopt their own definitions of hazardous child labour, such as Côte d'Ivoire.

2 The authors suggest that 'making' is more accurate than 'taking' here, in recognition that the visual image is framed by the young people.

3 The full list and SDG mapping can be found here: https://app.smartsheet.com/b/publish?EQBCT=e6ad0af940b44d94ac0f2f7fdc119f30

References

Abebe, T. (2008) *Ethiopian Childhoods: A Case Study of the Lives of Orphans and Working Children.* Trondheim: Norwegian University of Science and Technology.

Adams, S., Savahl, S. and Fattore, T. (2017) 'Children's representations of nature using photovoice and community mapping: perspectives from South Africa', *International Journal of Qualitative Studies on Health and Well-being*, 12(1), Article 1333900. doi: 10.1080/17482631.2017

Al Ganideh, S. and Good, L. (2015) 'Understanding abusive child labor practices in the shadow of the Arab spring', *Journal of Children's Services*, 10, pp 76–91.

Amin, S., Quayes, S. and Rives, J. (2004) 'Poverty and other determinants of child labor in Bangladesh', *Southern Economic Journal*, 70, pp 876–92.

Andisha, N. et al (2014) 'Reducing child labour in Panama: an impact evaluation', *Journal of Development Effectiveness*, 6(2), pp 128–46.

Atkinson, C. (2019) 'Ethical complexities in participatory childhood research: rethinking the "least adult role"', *Childhood*, 26(2), pp 186–201.

Benninger, E. and Savahl, S. (2016) 'The use of visual methods to explore how children construct and assign meaning to the "self" within two urban communities in the Western Cape, South Africa', *International Journal of Qualitative Studies on Health and Well-being*, 11, Article 31251. doi: 10.3402/qhw.v11.31251

Bhalotra, S.R. and Tzannatos, Z. (2003) *Child Labor: What Have We Learnt? Social Protection Discussion Paper Series No. 0317*. Washington, DC: Social Protection Unit, World Bank.

Bhatia, A. et al (2020) 'Analyzing and improving national and local child protection data in Nepal: a mixed methods study using 2014 Multiple Indicator Cluster Survey (MICS) data and interviews with 18 organizations', *Child Abuse & Neglect*, 101, Article 104292. doi: 10.1016/j.chiabu.2019.104292

Blackman, A. and Rivera, J. (2010) *The Evidence Base for Environmental and Socioeconomic Impacts of "Sustainable" Certification. Discussion paper RFF DP 10–17*. Washington, DC: Resources for the Future.

Blackmore, E. et al (2012) *Pro-poor Certification: Assessing the Benefits of Sustainability Certification for Small-Scale Farmers in Asia*. London: International Institute for Environment and Development.

Blunch, N.H., Canagarajah, S. and Goyal, S. (2002) *Short-and Long-term Impacts of Economic Policies on Child Labor and Schooling in Ghana. Social Protection Discussion Paper Series No. 0212*. Washington, DC: Social Protection Unit, The World Bank.

Bolton, A., Pole, C. and Mizen, P. (2001) 'Picture this: researching child workers', *Sociology*, 35(2), pp 501–8.

Bolzman, C., Bernardi, L. and LeGoff, J.-M. (eds) (2017) *Situating Children of Migrants across Borders and Origins: A Methodological Overview*. Dordrecht: Springer Netherlands.

Bowles, L.R. (2017) 'Doing the snap: storytelling and participatory photography with women porters in Ghana', *Visual Anthropology Review*, 33(2), pp 107–18.

Boyden, J. et al (2019) *Tracing the Consequences of Child Poverty: Evidence from the Young Lives Study in Ethiopia, India, Peru and Vietnam*. Bristol: Policy Press.

Boyden, J. and Ennew, J. (1997) *Children in Focus: A Manual for Participatory Research with Children*. Sweden: Save the Children.

Camfield, L. (2014) 'Growing up in Ethiopia and Andhra Pradesh: the impact of social protection schemes on girls' roles and responsibilities', *European Journal of Development Research*, 26, pp 107–23.

Chin, E. (2007) 'Power-puff ethnography/guerrilla research: children as native anthropologists', in Ball, A.L. (ed) *Representing Youth: Methodological Issues in Youth Studies*. New York and London: New York University Press, pp 269–83.

Creswell, J.W., Clark, V.P. and Garrett, A.L. (2003) 'Advanced mixed methods research', in *Handbook of Mixed Methods in Social and Behavioural Research*. Thousand Oaks, CA: Sage, pp 209–40.

Crivello, G., Camfield, L. and Woodhead, M. (2009) 'How can children tell us about their wellbeing? Exploring the potential of participatory research approaches within young lives', *Social Indicators Research*, 90(1), pp 51–72.

Crivello, G., Morrow, V. and Wilson, E. (2013) *Young Lives Longitudinal Qualitative Research Guide: A Guide for Researchers. Technical Note 26*. Oxford: Young Lives.

Dammert, A.C. et al (2018) 'Effects of public policy on child labor: current knowledge, gaps, and implications for program design', *World Development*, 110, pp 104–23.

Dayıoğlu, M. (2013) *Impact of Unpaid Household Services on the Measurement of Child Labour. MICS Methodological Paper No. 2*. New York: Statistics and Monitoring Section, Division of Policy and Strategy, United Nations Children's Fund.

Desiere, S. and Costa, V. (2019) *Employment Data in Household Surveys. Taking Stock, Looking Ahead*. Policy Research Working Paper 8882. Washington, DC: World Bank.

Dyson, J. (2014) *Working Childhoods: Youth, Agency and the Environment in India*. Cambridge: Cambridge University Press.

Dziadula, E. and Guzman, D. (2020) 'Sweeping it under the rug: household chores and misreporting of child labor', *Economics Bulletin*, 40(2), pp 901–5.

Elder, S. (2009) *ILO School-to-Work Transition Survey: A Methodological Guide*. Geneva: International Labour Office. Available at: https://www.ilo.org/wcmsp5/groups/public/---ed_emp/documents/instructionalmaterial/wcms_140857.pdf (Accessed 26 November 2022).

Gamlin, J. et al (2015) 'Is domestic work a worst form of child labour? The findings of a six-country study of the psychosocial effects of child domestic work', *Children's Geographies*, 13(2), pp 212–25.

Gibson, F. (2007) 'Conducting focus groups with children and young people: strategies for success', *Journal of Research in Nursing*, 12(5), pp 473–83.

Global Coalition to End Child Poverty (2019) *Child Poverty Measurement and Monitoring: The Missing Children*. New York: Global Coalition to End Child Poverty. Available at: https://static1.squarespace.com/static/56588879e4b0060cdb607883/t/5d893af76528657d97a126cf/1569274615839/Child+poverty+measurement+and+monitoring+-+The+missing+children.pdf (Accessed 26 November 2022).

Greene, S. and Hill, M. (2005) 'Researching children's experience: methods and methodological issues', in Greene, S. and Hogan, D. (eds) *Researching Children's Experiences: Methods and Approaches*. London: SAGE, pp 1–21.

Guarcello, L., Lyon, S. and Rosati, F.C. (2005) *Impact of Children's Work on School Attendance and Performance: A Review of School Survey Evidence from Five Countries*. Rome: Understanding Children's Work Project.

Haile, G. and Haile, B. (2012) 'Child labour and child schooling in rural Ethiopia: nature and trade-off', *Education Economics*, 20(4), pp 365–85.

Hashim, I.M. (2004) *Working with Working Children: Child Labour and the Barriers to Education in Rural Northeastern Ghana*. Unpublished PhD thesis. University of Sussex.

Hecht, T. (1998) *At Home in the Street: Street Children of Northeast Brazil*. Cambridge and New York: Cambridge University Press.

Hoban, E. (2017) 'Creative methodologies to stimulate children's participation during focus group discussions in rural Cambodia', *Journal of Healthcare Communications*, 2(S1:71), Article 100112. doi: 10.4172/2472-1654

Hoechner, H. (2015) 'Participatory filmmaking with Qur'anic students in Kano, Nigeria: "speak good about us or keep quiet!"', *International Journal of Social Research Methodology*, 18(6), pp 635–49.

de Hoop, J. and Rosati, F. (2014) *Cash Transfers and Child Labour*. Rome: Understanding Children's Work Project.

Ibrahim, A. et al (2019) 'Child labor and health: a systematic literature review of the impacts of child labor on child's health in low- and middle-income countries', *Journal of Public Health*, 41(1), pp 18–26..

ILO (2015) *World Report on Child Labour 2015. Paving the Way to Decent Work for Young People*. Geneva: International Labour Organization. Available at: https://www.ilo.org/ipecinfo/product/download.do?type=document&id=26977 (Accessed 26 November 2022).

ILO (2017) *Methodology of the Global Estimates of Child Labour, 2012–2016*. Geneva: International Labour Organization.

ILO (2018) *Ending Child Labour by 2025: A Review of Policies and Programmes*. Geneva: International Labour Organization.

ILO, SAP-FL and ILO-IPEC (2012) *Hard to See, Harder to Count: Survey Guidelines to Estimate Forced Labour of Adults and Children.* Geneva: ILO, Special Action Programme to Combat Forced Labour (SAP-FL) and International Programme on the Elimination of Child Labour (IPEC). Available at: https://www.ilo.org/wcmsp5/groups/public/---ed_norm/---declaration/documents/publication/wcms_182096.pdf (Accessed 26 November 2022).

ILO/IPEC-SIMPOC (2007) *Comparison of Survey Instruments for Collecting Data on Child Labour.* Geneva: International Labour Organization – IPEC. Available at: https://www.ilo.org/ipecinfo/product/download.do?type=document&id=7873 (Accessed 26 November 2022).

ISEAL (2017) *Sustainable Agriculture Network/Rainforest Alliance Impact Code.* Member Public System Reports. London: ISEAL-Alliance.

ISEAL (2019a) *Aligning and Combining: What We've Learned about Metrics and Data Sharing.* London: ISEAL-Alliance.

ISEAL (2019b) *Reaching Far and Wide: Collective Presence and Growth Trends of ISEAL Member Schemes Across Seven Commodities.* London: ISEAL-Alliance.

Johnson, G.A. (2011) 'A child's right to participation: photovoice as methodology for documenting the experiences of children living in Kenyan orphanages', *Visual Anthropology Review*, 27(2), pp 141–61.

Johnson, V. et al (1998) *Stepping Forward: Children and Young People's Participation in the Development Process.* London: Intermediate Technology Publications. Available at: http://agris.fao.org/agris-search/search.do?recordID=GB1999008907 (Accessed 19 March 2020).

Johnson, V. et al (2013) *Children and Young People's Participation Training Workshop Guide.* London: ChildHope UK. Available at: https://research.brighton.ac.uk/en/publications/children-and-young-peoples-participation-training-workshop-guide (Accessed 13 May 2020).

Johnson, V. (2017) 'Moving beyond voice in children and young people's participation', *Action Research*, 15(1), pp 104–24.

Johnson, V., Hart, R. and Colwell, J. (2014) *Steps for Engaging Young Children in Research: The Guide and Toolkit.* The Hague: The Bernard van Leer Foundation. Available at: https://research.brighton.ac.uk/en/publications/steps-for-engaging-young-children-in-research-the-toolkit (Accessed 15 April 2020).

Johnson, V., Hill, J. and Ivan-Smith, E. (1995) *Listening to Smaller Voices: Children in an Environment of Change.* Chard, Somerset: ActionAid. Available at: https://www.cabdirect.org/cabdirect/abstract/19961803480 (Accessed 15 April 2020).

Johnson, V. and West, A. (2018) *Children's Participation in Global Contexts: Beyond Voice.* Abingdon: Routledge.

Johnson, V. and West, A. et al (2022) *Youth and Positive Uncertainty: Negotiating Life in Post Conflict and Fragile Environments*. Rugby: Practical Action Publishing.

Jones, N., Baird, S. and Lunin, L. (2018) *GAGE Research Design, Sample and Methodology*. London: Gender and Adolescence: Global Evidence. Available at: https://www.gage.odi.org/publication/gage-research-design-sample-and-methodology/ (Accessed 26 November 2022).

Jones, N. and Sumner, A. (2009) 'Does mixed methods research matter to understanding childhood well-being?', *Social Indicators Research*, 90, pp 33–50.

Katz, C. (2004) *Growing Up Global: Economic Restructuring and Children's Everyday Lives*. Minneapolis: University of Minnesota Press.

Kilkelly, U. et al (2005) *Children's Rights in Northern Ireland*. Belfast: Northern Ireland Commissioner for Children and Young People.

Krauss, A. (2017) 'Understanding child labour beyond the standard economic assumption of monetary poverty', *Cambridge Journal of Economics*, 41(2), pp 545–74.

Kuimi, B.L.B. et al (2018) 'Child labour and health: a systematic review', *International Journal of Public Health*, 63(5), pp 663–72.

Leach, F.E. and Mitchell, C. (2006) *Combating Gender Violence in and Around Schools*. London: Trentham Books Limited.

Mavrokonstantis, P. (2011) *The Impact of Child Labour on Educational Attainment: Evidence from Vietnam*. Oxford: Young Lives. Available at: https://www.younglives.org.uk/sites/www.younglives.org.uk/files/YL-SP-Mavrokonstantis%20-%20MSc%20Dissertation_2011.pdf (Accessed 26 November 2022).

Mitchell, L. (2006) 'Child-centered? Thinking critically about children's drawings as a visual research method', *Visual Anthropology Review*, 22(1), pp 63–73.

Mizen, P. and Ofosu-Kusi, Y. (2010) 'Unofficial truths and everyday insights: understanding voice in visual research with the children of Accra's urban poor', *Visual Studies*, 25(3), pp 255–67.

Mizen, P. and Ofosu-Kusi, Y. (2013) 'Agency as vulnerability: accounting for children's movement to the streets of Accra', *The Sociological Review*, 61(2), pp 363–82.

Nestle (2019) *Nestle Cocoa Plan. Tackling Child Labor, 2019 Report*. Geneva: Nestlé-International Cocoa Initiative. Available at: https://www.nestle.com/sites/default/files/2019-12/nestle-tackling-child-labor-report-2019-en.pdf (Accessed 31 March 2020).

Nurick, R. and Johnson, V. (2001) 'Putting child rights and participatory monitoring and evaluation with children into practice: some examples in Indonesia, Nepal South Africa, and the UK', *PLA Notes*, 42, pp 39–44.

Opfermann, L.S. (2020) '"If you can't beat them, be them!": everyday experiences and "performative agency" among undocumented migrant youth in South Africa', *Children's Geographies*, 18(4), pp 379–92.

Orkin, K. (2012) 'Are work and schooling complementary or competitive for children in rural Ethiopia? A mixed-methods study', in Boyden, J. and Bourdillon, M. (eds) *Childhood Poverty: Multidisciplinary Approaches.* London: Palgrave Macmillan UK, pp 298–313.

Oya, C., Schaefer, F. and Skalidou, D. (2018) 'The effectiveness of agricultural certification in developing countries: A systematic review', *World Development*, 112, pp 282–312.

Punch, S. (2001a) 'Household division of labour: generation, gender, age, birth order and sibling composition', *Work, Employment & Society*, 15(4), pp 803–23.

Punch, S. (2001b) 'Multiple methods and research relations with children in rural Bolivia', in Limb, M. and Dwyer, C. (eds) *Qualitative Methodologies for Geographers.* London: Arnold, pp 165–180.

Quattri, M. and Watkins, K. (2016) *Child Labour and Education: A Survey of Slum Settlements in Dhaka.* London: ODI. Available at: https://www.odi.org/sites/odi.org.uk/files/resource-documents/11145.pdf (Accessed 26 November 2022).

Reynolds, P. (1991) *Dance, Civet Cat: Child Labour in the Zambezi Valley.* London: Zed Books.

Robson, E. (2004) 'Children at work in rural northern Nigeria: patterns of age, space and gender', *Journal of Rural Studies*, 20(2), pp 193–210.

Sabates-Wheeler, R. and Sumberg, J. (2020) *Understanding Children's Harmful Work in African Agriculture: Points of Departure. Acha Working Paper 1.* Brighton: Action on Children's Harmful Work in African Agriculture, IDS.

Schleifer, P. and Sun, Y. (2020) 'Reviewing the impact of sustainability certification on food security in developing countries', *Global Food Security*, 24, Article 100337.

Shaffer, P. (2013) 'Ten years of "q-squared": implications for understanding and explaining poverty', *World Development*, 45, pp 269–85.

SIMPOC (nd) *SIMPOC At a Glance.* Geneva: IPEC – International Labor Office.

The DHS Program (2020) *DHS Questionnaires and Manuals.* Available at: https://dhsprogram.com/publications/publ ication-DHSQ8-DHS-Questionnaires-and-Manuals.cfm (Accessed 26 November 2022).

Thomas De Benitez, S. (2011) *State of the World's Street Children: Research.* London: Consortium for Street Children. Available at: https://www.streetchildren.org/resources/state-of-the-worlds-street-children-research/ (Accessed 15 April 2020).

Tudge, J. and Hogan, Diane (2005) 'An ecological approach to observations of children's everyday lives', in Greene, S. and Hogan, D (eds) *Researching Children's Experiences: Methods and Approaches*. London: SAGE, pp 102–212.

UCW (2017) *Understanding Trends in Child Labour*. Rome: ILO, UNICEF and World Bank.

UNICEF (1989) *Convention on the Rights of the Child*. New York: UNICEF.

UNICEF and ILO (2019) *Indicator 8.7.1: Proportion and Number of Children Aged 5–17 Years Engaged in Child Labour, by Sex and Age*. New York: United Nations. Available at: https://unstats.un.org/sdgs/metadata/files/Metadata-08-07-01.pdf (Accessed 26 November 2022).

Verma, V. (2008) *Sampling for Household-Based Surveys of Child Labour*. Geneva: IPEC – International Labour Office.

Wells, K. (2018) *Childhood Studies: Short Introduction*. Cambridge: Polity Press.

Wickenden, M. and Elphick, J. (2016) 'Don't forget us, we are here too! Listening to disabled children and their families living in poverty', in Grech, S. and Soldatic, K. (eds) *Disability in the Global South: The Critical Handbook*. Cham, Switzerland: Springer International Publishing, pp 167–85.

Woldehanna, T., Jones, N. and Tefera, B. (2008) 'The invisibility of children's paid and unpaid work: implications for Ethiopia's national poverty reduction policy', *Childhood*, 15(2), pp 177–201.

4

Education and Work: Children's Lives in Rural Sub-Saharan Africa

Máiréad Dunne, Sara Humphreys and Carolina Szyp

Introduction

The need to better understand the relationship between education (formal schooling in particular) and child work is urgent because sub-Saharan Africa (SSA) has the highest number of young people 'in child labour' (ILO and UNICEF, 2021) as well as the greatest number of young people 'out of school' (UNESCO-UIS, 2019). It is estimated that around 98 million young people of school-going age – almost a third in SSA – are not enrolled in school, with participation rates having stagnated since around 2008 (UNESCO-UIS, 2019). There are also many millions who may be enrolled but not attending regularly, or attending but not learning. Estimates show that in SSA 85 per cent of boys and 95 per cent of girls of primary-school age are 'not achieving minimum proficiency standards' (ACPF, 2018). As the impact of COVID-19 exacerbates socio-economic inequalities, these figures will likely rise, as will the gendered burdens of work that many children will have to take on (United Nations, 2020).

The children least likely to be in school are female, from the poorest households and over-age for grade of entry. Other factors associated with non-participation include living in a remote, rural area or a conflict-affected region; coming from an ethno-linguistic minority or nomadic community; and living with a disability (UNESCO, 2015a). Since SSA includes many of the world's poorest countries, even children who are in formal education frequently combine schooling with unpaid and/or paid work (ILO and UNICEF, 2021). Since the main employment sector in SSA is agriculture, which accounts for more than half the total workforce, many children are inevitably engaged in subsistence or commercial farming (ILO and UNICEF, 2021).

Globally, financial constraints are often cited as the main reason many children are either not in school or attend sporadically and juggle schooling and work (UNESCO, 2015a). In Ghana, too, poverty has been identified as an important driver of non-attendance – although distance to school is also a major factor in rural areas (Ghana Ministry of Education, 2018). However, as we elaborate further, the realities are inevitably more complex and contingent, and subject to change, with wide variations across and within countries. Thus, the importance of context – in its multiple configurations and manifestations – is paramount.

Aim and scope of the chapter

The aim of this chapter is to explore children's lives as they relate to the education–work nexus in rural SSA. This we achieve, initially, through a selective and purposive summary of the education literature that highlights some of the key issues. We then elaborate an analytical framework with which to better understand the dynamics of education and work in rural children's lives.

First, we situate the issue of children's access to schooling within the broader discourse of child rights and the global development agenda, before identifying the children most likely not to be in school and the reasons why. We then explore some of the key tensions between schooling and work identified in the literature, which we relate specifically to the lives of rural children. Next, we present a relational analytical framework – an 'edu-workscape' – that aims to support more holistic understandings of the dynamics of children's lives as they relate to schooling, work and harm across household, school and work environments. In the final section, we reflect on key issues that are highly pertinent to policy interventions aimed both at increasing educational participation and addressing children's harmful work.

Concepts and definitions

The relationship between schooling and children's work is characterized by tensions. These are exacerbated by conceptual adherence to terms that have been framed in the Global North (Nieuwenhuys, 1998; Twum-Danso Imoh, 2013), and which are often used as oppositional binaries: child/adult; in school/out of school; traditional/modern; rural/urban; harmful/not harmful; female/male. Although seemingly useful for the purposes of making national and international comparisons, they oversimplify our understandings of rural realities as they are gradually solidified into universal categories and truths through the dominant discourse of development (Boyden, 1997;

Twum-Danso Imoh, 2013). We return to some of these terms and binaries later in the chapter.

For the moment, we gloss our usage of three key terms: 'education', 'child labour' and 'harm'. While we recognize 'education' to be a broad term related to all types of learning – for example, informal, non-formal and formal – the focus in this chapter is on basic schooling (meaning primary and junior secondary). There are three reasons for this: first, educational provision in SSA (as elsewhere) since colonial times has primarily been structured through formal education; second, educational research and educational interventions in SSA have, up until relatively recently, primarily been directed at this area of education; and third, debates surrounding the tensions between education and child labour are generally articulated with regard to formal schooling.

'Child labour', too, we recognize to be a contested and value-laden term. However, it is not the aim of this chapter to (re)define and/or measure child labour; rather, we align ourselves with academics who prefer the more neutral term 'children's work' (for example Boyden, Bourdillon and Woodhead). That said, we also use the term 'child labour' (sometimes distinguishing it from 'child work', as does the ILO) as it appears in the various studies reviewed, elaborating on the authors' understandings where necessary. Similarly, we employ the term 'child' to signify someone under the age of 18, as the term is predominantly understood in the literature, though we also revisit it critically.

The notion of 'harm', since it is central to ILO definitions of what counts as 'hazardous work' or the 'worst forms of child labour', is also of concern. Maconachie et al (Chapter 2, this volume), note that 'despite its voluminous writings, the ILO has itself never formally defined "harm"'. We agree that 'the concept of harm is ambiguous, relative and contextual and it may be unhelpful (or even problematic) to present harm as an "objective" concept that can be defined, measured, and assessed with discrete criteria' (p 41).

It is also worth noting that in much of the education literature (outside the area of social protection) the discussion is more about 'violence' rather than 'harm' despite the fact that they are interconnected. For example, in the UN definitions both of corporal punishment (Committee on the Rights of the Child, 2006) and school-related gender-based violence (UNESCO, 2015b) the word 'harm' does not feature. Similarly, in the UN report on school violence worldwide (United Nations, 2016), the word 'harm' occurs only five times, whereas 'violence' occurs over 400 times.

Education for all

Educational access

The right to full-time education for those under 18 years of age is enshrined in the UN Convention on the Rights of the Child (1989) and the African

Charter on the Rights and Welfare of the Child (1996, and implemented in 1999). It is also recognized as a global development priority that is reinforced through commitment to the global Education for All (EFA) initiative and Millennium and Sustainable Development Goals (MDGs and SDGs).

Since access to full-time education is considered a universal human right, any denial of that right is by definition a harm. Thus, from the outset, children's work, if it takes time away from children's educational activities (be they in class or at home doing homework), is positioned as antithetical to, or at the very least, in competition with schooling (Myers and Boyden, 1998). Indeed, in the dominant development discourse (epitomized by the United Nations Development Programme [UNDP], ILO, Overseas Development Institute [ODI][1] and World Bank, for example) child work and child labour are predominantly framed negatively as an impediment to achieving EFA (for example, Guarcello et al, 2015), even though a child's earnings may provide the means to attend school in the first place (Wambiri, 2014; Pankhurst et al, 2016).

From the end of the 20th century, school enrolments mushroomed across SSA, albeit unevenly, as demonstrated by improving enrolment rates, diminishing repetition and drop-out rates, and narrowing 'gender gaps' (UNESCO, 2015a). However, in resource-constrained contexts, including in parts of Ghana, increases in school participation have not necessarily been matched by improvements in school quality and learning opportunities (Lewin and Akyeampong, 2009). As the 2004 EFA Global Monitoring Report acknowledged, 'the focus on access often overshadows the issue of quality' even though quality stands at the heart of the EFA movement (UNESCO, 2005, p 12, see sections 5 and 6). Moreover, as we argue later in the chapter, the non-provision of 'inclusive, equitable and quality education' (as articulated in SDG 4) to children who *are* in school, is as much a denial of their rights to education as non-participation in schooling is to children who are *out of* school.

Who's not in school, and why?

Globally, as stated earlier, SSA has the largest number of school-age children out of school, with a disproportionately high number of out-of-school children (OOSCs) found in a handful of countries,[2] including Ghana and Nigeria. As the 2015 EFA Global Monitoring Report noted, many OOSCs are caught up in conflict, or have been displaced by conflict. Others are migrants, fostered children, children with disabilities, children from the nomadic communities, who account for around 20 per cent of the population in East Africa, and those who come from minority ethno-linguistic groups. Otherwise, in very broad terms, across SSA, children are more likely to be out of school if they come from rural areas, from poorer families, are girls, and are older (UNESCO, 2015a).

Importantly, however, figures for OOSCs are thought to be huge underestimations; neither one-off annual school enrolments (as recorded in education management information systems [EMIS] data), nor household survey attendance data, reflect the amount of time that children are actually at school or in the classroom engaged in meaningful learning (Fair, 2016). What is more, EMIS data in many contexts are inconsistent, unreliable and incomplete (Husein et al, 2017), making it even more challenging to gauge who is 'in' or 'out of' school.

Within the dominant statistical research on school access, as exemplified by World Bank and UNESCO Global Monitoring Reports, reasons for not being in school are generally categorized as supply- or demand-side constraints. In SSA, supply-side constraints include a lack of schools nearby, which also relates to school travel time and costs and safety concerns, especially regarding young children and girls; a shortage of classrooms, water and other necessary infrastructure; and inadequate supplies of teaching and learning materials and qualified teachers (Bashir et al, 2018). Many of these same 'inputs', however, are also commonly identified indicators of school quality, which, when inadequate, reduce demand for schooling (Hunt, 2008). Additional factors include curriculum and pedagogy, disciplinary regimes, as well as informal teacher-student and peer interactions (UNESCO and UNICEF–UIS, 2014; Bashir et al, 2018), which are addressed in more detail later.

Demand-side reasons for not being in school include economic hardship (as discussed later), which tends to be exacerbated in large households with many school-age children; child or family health issues, including hunger; early marriage and pregnancy; perceptions of the low value of education, due variously to its poor quality and lack of relevance to local socio-economic realities (Tafere and Pankhurst, 2015); and absence of employment opportunities for school graduates (UNESCO, 2015a; Bashir et al, 2018).

Across SSA, however, poverty and the high direct and indirect costs of education (including loss of children's labour) have been identified as the main reasons children in the very poorest communities are out of school (UNESCO-UIS and UNICEF, 2015; Bashir et al, 2018). To address this, most governments have abolished school fees, at least for primary education, and are increasingly committed to providing more resources for educational development (ACPF, 2018). At the same time, they struggle to keep pace with expanding school-going populations while simultaneously investing to improve quality. However, costs to households still persist in the form of parent teacher association (PTA) levies, school development funds, exam fees, uniforms, stationery, textbooks and transport. As a result, completing even a cycle of primary schooling is unachievable for children in the very poorest households (UNESCO, 2015a). Children from families living in poverty have to work both to help themselves and their family satisfy basic needs (Sabates-Wheeler and Sumberg, 2020), including paying for their schooling or that of siblings (Boyden, 1994; Okyere, 2012; Wambiri, 2014). Put another way, for many children living in extreme poverty, schooling would not be possible if they did not work (Woodhead, 1999; Jonah and Abebe, 2019).

What is being done about widening access?

Programmes designed to increase participation in basic education are premised on the assumption that the main reason that children are out of school is because families cannot afford to educate them, and/or (to a lesser extent) because parents are presumed to be unaware of the value of education, particularly with respect to girls (UNESCO, 2015a). To address the economic constraints poor households face, and reduce their reliance on children's labour, social safety net strategies aimed at widening access – such as school feeding programmes (SFPs), scholarships for girls, fee waivers and cash transfers – are spreading across Africa, undergoing particularly rapid expansion in Ghana, Kenya, Senegal and Tanzania (Beegle et al, 2018).

School feeding programmes have been particularly effective at increasing participation especially in poorer rural areas, where enrolments are usually low (Bundy et al, 2009), and in a few instances have been shown to contribute to improved test scores (within the project's limited time period) (Bashir et al, 2018). Cash transfers have also consistently been associated with improved school participation (Fisher et al, 2017). This has been the case with the Livelihood, Empowerment Against Poverty (LEAP) programme in northern Ghana, although it has also been noted that not all children within a household necessarily benefit equally (Roelen et al, 2015).

Yet, there is very little evidence on the long-term impact and sustainability of such programmes in ensuring sustained access (Snivstveit et al, 2016), especially if funded by outside donors for a limited period. Edmonds and Shrestha's (2014) paper, entitled *You Get What You Pay For*, is a cautionary tale in this respect. Sixteen months after it had ended, the researchers returned to the site of a one-year programme aimed at combatting child labour in a carpet-weaving factory in Nepal. They found that all the educational gains accrued during the project had been erased, and the children were back weaving carpets. This example may be an extreme case – we don't know – but it highlights the urgent need to carry out impact assessments well beyond the end of development projects.

What is more, as shown by an assessment of cash transfer programmes in six countries in SSA, including Ghana, the impact on children's work patterns is never straightforward (Fisher et al, 2017). Although such interventions may increase access to school, they do not necessarily reduce either absenteeism or 'child labour' (in this case, paid employment outside the home). Rather, they often signal a shift to unpaid work on the family farm as increased assets, such as livestock, generate further work (de Hoop et al, 2020). As discussed in Chapter 7 (this volume), public works programmes (in which households offer adult labour in return for cash and/or food) can have similarly ambiguous impacts on children's educational participation and their patterns of work, as they often get drawn into paid and unpaid gendered labour as a result (Devereux, 2000; Devereux et al, 2008).

The relationship between education and work

Education and work in competition

The dominant discourse sustains a hierarchical education–work binary, which positions education above work (Jonah and Abebe, 2019). This is problematic for a number of reasons. First, it reflects neither the situation within the lives of children, nor the views of the children themselves (Twum-Danso Imoh, 2013). In addition, it assumes that school is a benign space for education and learning, and therefore the proper place for children (Myers and Boyden, 1998). Further, this is the default rationale in much anti-child labour literature even when it is acknowledged that the education on offer is sub-standard, and that children both need and want to combine schooling with work (for example, Quattri and Watkins, 2016; ILO, 2017a). A recent regional ILO brief on Africa exemplifies this attitude: 'There is an on-going need for investment in what we know works in getting children out of work and into the classroom – and keeping them there' (ILO, 2017b, p 8).

In this influential literature, work is frequently understood narrowly as 'productive work' related to income generation. This excludes much domestic work – often described as 'household chores' – which is considered to 'constitute a "non-economic" form of production' (ILO, 2017a, p 17), as we elaborate later.

Within this context, a number of large-scale surveys and multi-country studies (including randomized control trials – RCTs) have compared school attendance of 'working' and 'non-working' children (itself a problematic dichotomy, given the limitations about what counts as work and the fact that children's workloads are constantly changing), and concluded that generally children who work above a particular threshold of hours and/or intensity of work are less likely to be 'in school' (ILO, 2017a; UCW, 2017). Yet the classification of children as being either 'in' or 'out-of-school' constitutes a further unhelpful binary, especially since being 'in school' may not necessarily involve much time within the school grounds, let alone in a classroom (Tafere and Pankhurst, 2015). As more longitudinal mixed methods research (for example, Young Lives, Orkin, 2012; Pankhurst et al, 2016)[3] and qualitative and ethnographic studies (for example, Berlan, 2009; Okyere, 2012) have shown, the reality of being 'in school' is inevitably nuanced. Working children from poor rural backgrounds, in particular, may move in and out of being physically at school within a single day, or over much longer periods of time, and learning-related activities may only constitute a small portion of that in-school time (Humphreys et al, 2015; Tafere and Pankhurst, 2015).

A second common assumption is that work prevents children from persisting and/or achieving well in school. While work may be a major factor, evidence from more contextually situated studies in SSA point to other challenges that children and families face (Bourdillon et al, 2015, p 6). For example, rural farming households are especially vulnerable to environmental shocks, such as drought or flooding, which may also disrupt children's schooling (Rose and Dyer, 2008). In addition, family crises (such as a death, illness or divorce) can force children out of school, as they have to cover other labour needs, such as caring for a sick relative or taking over an adult working role (Pankhurst et al, 2016). This may necessitate moving to another area (Robson, 2004; Hashim, 2005), which may well disrupt schooling. Children's own ill-health is another reason for missing or dropping out of school (Hunt, 2008), as is hunger, both of which affect the ability of children to learn even if they manage to stay at school (Jomaa et al, 2011; Morrow et al, 2017).

Crucially, the poor quality of schooling available in many rural areas is central to determining whether children attend or persist in school, and whether they learn (Odonkor, 2007; UNESCO, 2015a). So too, is the perceived benefit of schooling by children and parents or caregivers, when viewed within the context of local employment opportunities (Hashim, 2004; Jones et al, 2019). Poor households make strategic choices regarding their children's schooling based on a complex interaction of factors including available finances, the multiple and varied needs of the whole household, and the quality and the likely future benefits of education. In Ghana, the fact that the annual income for household heads who are self-employed in agriculture is the same whether they have no formal schooling or have completed basic education is likely to be a consideration (Krauss, 2017).

In addition, young people may themselves make their own choice of work over education at different times, especially if the schooling on offer is of low quality and they are failing to learn (for example, Chant and Jones, 2005; Tafere and Woldehanna, 2012). Thus, although work demands put on children may prevent them from attending school, it does not follow necessarily that if these children were not in work, they would attend or persist in school.

In contrast to the limited learning afforded by low quality schooling, adults and children may consider children's work and home environments to afford better learning opportunities (Myers and Boyden, 1998; Admassie, 2003). In a similar vein, the harm that is often attributed to many types of what the ILO terms 'hazardous work' may actually be just as evident within the school environment (Berlan, 2004), or even the home (Odonkor, 2007). Ampiah and Adu-Yeboah's (2009) study on 90 school dropouts in Ghana provides supporting evidence. Although critical incidents related to poverty and/or the need to work were the most commonly cited tipping points that finally kept the children out of school permanently, children identified a combination of out-of-school and (predominantly) in-school factors that led to dropping out, including harmful school processes such as indiscriminate corporal punishment and forced manual labour for teachers.

Schooling and fit with rural lives and livelihoods

The rigid structures of schooling demand that children's work, including within the household, should fit round the regimes of schooling (Bourdillon et al, 2015; Humphreys et al, 2015). Thus, if working children (or their families) do not adjust schedules to enable them to attend school, then work is blamed for their loss of education. Since almost all children in SSA are engaged in some form of work, whether in the home or outside, unpaid or paid, or in the formal or informal sectors (ILO and UNICEF, 2021), school's lack of flexibility concerning annual, weekly and daily timetables has profound effects on children's ability to attend school regularly and on likely learning outcomes (Orkin, 2012; Dyer, 2013).

In Ethiopia, for example, the nationally standardized main school holidays coincide with key events in the agricultural calendar in the grain-producing regions in the north but do not suit the crop calendar in the south (Abebe, 2011). The clashing annual cycles mean that children returning to school mid-year after an absence for seasonal work may be told to come back at the beginning of the next academic year, and repeat the grade (Colclough et al, 2003). This may discourage the child from re-entering school (Hashim, 2004; Wouango, 2013), sometimes due to feelings of shame or embarrassment at having to repeat and/or study with younger children (Ananga, 2011). In addition, since the child will be a year older, they are less likely to stay in school because grade repetition increases both the direct and opportunity costs of education (Lewin, 2009).

That said, some types of work may be more compatible with school timetables than others. Evidence from Ethiopia, for example, suggests that while minding cattle, boys may be able to study whereas girls doing household chores cannot (Orkin, 2012). Double-shift schooling, which is common in rural areas, offers slightly more flexibility as the half-day timetable gives children more time to contribute to their households' livelihoods (Wambiri, 2014; Pankhurst et al, 2016; also see Chapter 9, this volume).

The dissonance provoked by the spatial and temporal disconnects between rural lives and formal education is compounded by other tensions. These include the curricular irrelevance of much of modern schooling to the lives and needs of rural communities (Odachi, 2011; Dyer, 2013). Such curricula take no account of the skills that children have learned outside school (Bourdillon et al, 2010) while schools position working students as childlike, irrespective of the adult responsibilities they have outside school (Dunne and Ananga, 2013).

In conclusion, contextually situated research provides insights into the complex ways in which education and work interact and the multiple influences and demands on children's time. In the next section, we focus on three key social arenas, namely the household, school and work environments, which together we term the edu-workscape.

The edu-workscape: learning, labour and harm

As we illustrated in the previous section, whether or not rural children can realize their right to education depends upon a host of factors. The interactions between these place competing demands on children's time in three key overlapping social arenas: the household, workplaces and school. In order to better understand these dynamics, we propose a conceptual model that we term 'the edu-workscape'.

The triangular relational matrix illustrated in Figure 4.1 not only includes interactions between the workplace(s), the school and the household, but

Figure 4.1: The edu-workscape

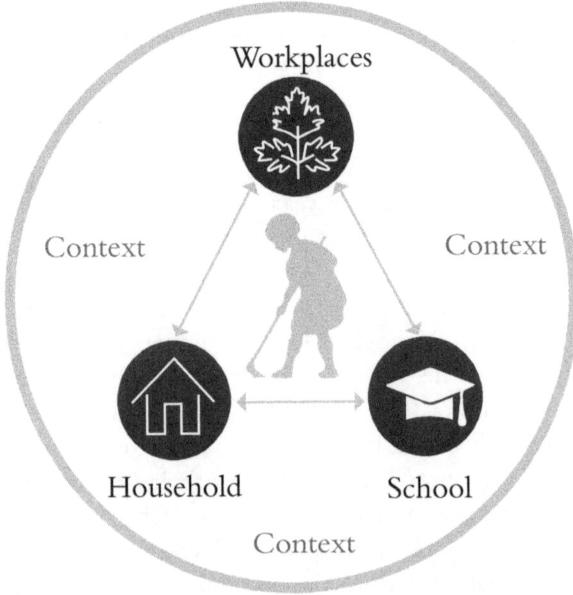

Source: Authors

it centralizes the child within these interactions. In so doing, it offers a reconceptualization and contextualization of the relationships between children's work and education. It acknowledges that both learning and work take place within each of the arenas of the edu-workscape, and that the potential for harm exists in all three arenas. Further, the matrix highlights the fact that children's experiences are shaped by social relations within and between home, school and work. The edu-workscape foregrounds the dynamic interplay within and between each arena and emphasizes how the child navigates and experiences this nexus. There are multiple tensions between the three social arenas: schools (embedded within education systems), households (with their multiple, often changing, family and community configurations) and workplaces (in multiple locations including family farms and businesses, and commercial farms). These are also subject to conditions and power relations in the wider economic, social, temporal and spatial contexts, as we elaborate later.

This conceptual framework represents the complex and overlapping relations that are the nexus of children's lives. Given the relational and contextual contingencies, childhoods are never singular or uniform but rather complex, evolving and diverse. As we discuss later, they are experienced through the symbolic and material significance of a range of social variables including gender as well as histories of migration, settlement and work in different contexts (Burman and Stacey, 2010; Jonah and Abebe, 2019; Rai et al, 2019). This means, for example, that gender practices within community and household contexts will produce operational understandings of appropriate work (domestic, unpaid, paid and/or hazardous) for both girls and boys in ways that delimit and define childhoods, future social trajectories and on-going engagements in social and economic life. Schools too often reaffirm these understandings of gender, through their formal and informal processes, such as gender-differentiated teacher–student classroom interactions or allocation of school responsibilities. This gendering will also be intersected by ethnicity, religion, age, disability and migration status, among other variables, to produce edu-workscapes within which childhoods are constructed and lived out.

In the next three sections, we explore the three social arenas of the edu-workscape, focusing in particular on the school since details on schooling are frequently absent in much of the literature on child labour. Understanding how children navigate the edu-workscape offers the potential for more nuanced and socially sensitive insights into their education and work, wherever they take place. It allows us to consider more holistically the total burden of work on children in the school, household and workplace, as well as recognizing learning across the three arenas. Further, judgements about potential harm to children should not only be focused on the workplace but should refer to the whole edu-workscape.

Harm and work in school

In contrast to the dangers that are associated with agricultural work, the school environment is presumed to be free of harm and hard physical labour. However, it is important to recognize that both are often present in rural schools and that they are important 'push' factors that are likely to encourage children to prefer work to life in school.

Violence and bullying

For a long time, international development literature on the Global South – outside feminist and post-colonial critiques – has considered formal schooling to be an unequivocal good and school as a benign institution (Vavrus and Bloch, 1998; Stromquist and Monkman, 2014). However, the United Nations' *World Report on Violence against Children* (Pinheiro, 2006) was seminal in bringing to global attention the fact that many children experience various forms of violence in and around schools worldwide.

In SSA, gender violence, corporal punishment and bullying are the three areas of obvious harm that have come to greatest prominence over the last two decades (Dunne et al, 2006; Leach et al, 2014; Parkes et al, 2016), propelled by high-profile international campaigns for their global eradication, usually framed within the discourse of child rights. These forms of violence can all be conceptually linked within an analysis of school as a gendered institution operating within broader societal gender norms and power relations (Connell, 1987; Bhana et al, 2021) and within violent historical processes, such as colonialism and apartheid (Epstein and Morrell, 2012; Adzahlie-Mensah, 2014). Yet corporal punishment and bullying, in particular, are more often studied separately and decontextualized, within gender-neutral discourses of 'victim' and 'perpetrator/bully', with gender only considered as a categorical variable (Dunne et al, 2006). Many of these forms of school-based violence are acutely felt by children from poorer households.

Central to school regulation is corporal punishment, backed up by systems of prefects and monitors, who often have the authority to physically discipline their peers (Morrell, 2001; Humphreys, 2008). Although corporal punishment is now illegal in schools in most SSA countries, there has been 'little progress' toward its elimination (ACPF, 2018, p 31). This is largely due to the fact that it is widely accepted as a legitimate disciplinary practice by teachers, parents, caregivers and children themselves – provided it is done in moderation and with the aim of correcting errant behaviour (Twum-Danso Imoh, 2013; Masko and Bosiwah, 2016). However, its application is often excessive and children are frequently punished for issues outside their control, especially children living in poverty who are late or absent from school due to heavy household or external work commitments (Pankhurst et al, 2016; Isimbi et al, 2017; Devonald et al, 2021).

In addition to violence by teachers against students, a recent global synthesis of survey data confirmed high rates of school bullying, with nearly half of all students in SSA saying that they had been bullied, while just over a third reported physical attacks or being involved in fights (UNESCO, 2019). Physical bullying was more commonly reported by boys rather than girls (25.4 per cent to 18.7 per cent), while one in ten boys *and* girls complained of sexual bullying. Peer violence is often compounded by teacher complicity in ignoring its occurrence, thereby normalizing violence in schools (Leach et al, 2003; Dunne et al, 2005).

Studies of gender violence in schools have predominantly focused on sexual violence against girls (Dunne et al, 2006; Leach et al, 2014). Only more recently have national prevalence surveys among children and youth indicated that many boys also suffer sexual violence in school, though largely from their peers (UNESCO, 2019). There is evidence of (predominantly) male teachers demanding sexual favours from girls (or, to a lesser extent boys) in exchange for preferential treatment, including better grades and/or monetary assistance (Jones and Norton, 2007; Antonowicz, 2010). A review of reports and studies on gender violence in West and Central Africa also reported boys 'procuring' girls for teachers in exchange for reduced fees (Antonowicz, 2010). In some cases, however, girls may actively seek out sexual relationships with teachers as part of the sexual economy. As with 'sugar daddies' outside school, such relationships often enable girls to pay school expenses and may be encouraged by the family (Parkes et al, 2013). In such ways, education is implicated in sexually exploitative activities.

The ill-effects of violence experienced by children in schools in SSA include increased anxiety, preventing children from participating in class (for fear of being wrong and risking further punishment) (Feinstein and Mwahombela, 2010) and depression (Cluver et al, 2010). School violence can also affect students' concentration and learning, resulting in poor attainment (Talwar et al, 2011; Stein et al, 2019), and lead to truancy, absenteeism and eventual dropout (Ananga, 2011; Pankhurst et al, 2016). Sexual violence against girls may result in unwanted pregnancy, which generally spells the end of formal schooling. Even where school policies allow these young women to continue, bullying by classmates, economic constraints and/or lack of childcare usually make it impracticable (Wekesa, 2011).

Child work in school

To date, schools have yet to be given much consideration as sites of labour. Yet, the gendered child work regimes of schools in SSA add to the burden of work that many children already experience at home and in the work place, and to the potential harm that schools can cause children. For example, Berlan's (2009) ethnographic study in a cocoa-producing area of Ghana found that work in school can be more arduous and dangerous than that carried out on family-owned cocoa farms. In school, children were clearing the ground with machetes in the hot sun, whereas on the cocoa farms there was more shade, and the work was less strenuous, and carried out under greater supervision. Such evidence highlights the need to account for the labouring that goes on in school in debates about the tensions between child work and education, and in judgements about school quality.

Studies in various national contexts in SSA, including in Ghana, have noted how children can spend anything from an hour to a whole day cleaning, working on the school farm or fetching water and sand for school construction projects (Boyle et al, 2002; Benavot and Gad, 2004; Adonteng-Kissi, 2018). Classroom and school cleaning, in particular, is often officially timetabled. Given that scheduled teaching time may be no more than 3–5 hours per day, especially in double-shift schools, the time children spend working can represent a considerable proportion of school time. This exploitative labour in school is in contrast to the valuable learning that can arise from supervised agricultural activities, where children and their families may also get to share the benefits (for example, Okiror et al, 2011, in Uganda).

Often it is schools in the poorest rural communities that require more student and community labour to build new classrooms and furniture and/or carry out school repairs (Swift-Morgan, 2006; Essuman and Akyeampong, 2011). Even school feeding programmes can result in extra labour demands on children's time (Sulemana et al, 2013).

In Ghana, there is also ample evidence that some schools insist on students undertaking paid work on farms to generate income to help run the school (Berlan, 2004; Ananga, 2011; also see Chapter 9, this volume). Teachers also use students as unpaid workers on their own farms and in their homes (Casely-Hayford et al, 2013; Maconachie and Hilson, 2016). Cleaning male teachers' accommodation puts girls (in particular) at risk (Antonowicz, 2010; Shumba and Abosi, 2011). Cases have been reported from Central and West Africa of communities and schools (or school staff) having agreements on using children's labour as a form of remuneration or incentive for teachers (Hashim, 2004; Aronowitz, 2019). Older students may absent themselves from school on days dedicated to labour or, when threatened with punishment for non-compliance, may drop out altogether (Alhassan and Adzahlie-Mensah, 2010; Ananga, 2011).

Frequently, work in school replicates the gendered patterns of labour within the household, with girls and younger children shouldering the greater burden (Antonowicz, 2010; Casely-Hayford et al, 2013). Generally, girls sweep classrooms, collect firewood and water (especially if school meals are cooked on site [Sulemana et al, 2013]) and clean toilets, whereas boys will move furniture and do heavier manual jobs (Casely-Hayford et al, 2013; Leach et al, 2014). Work tasks may also be allocated as punishments, as explained earlier, such as cleaning toilets (for girls), digging trenches or weeding (for boys) or working on the farm (Porter et al, 2011; Levison et al, 2018).

In summary, the evidence indicates that rather than a safe haven from the presumed harm of work elsewhere, schools can be sites of multiple forms of violence and harm – both sanctioned and unsanctioned – and spaces for physically demanding gendered work. Collectively, these common features of rural education in SSA can drive students out of school. What's more, the evidence shows that these multiple harms are likely to be greater for children from the poorest households as schools' inflexible timetables, poor quality teaching and harsh, inequitable disciplinary regimes compound the challenges that working children face when attempting to combine schooling with work and other commitments.

Learning (gender) work at home

The second arena in the edu-workspace is the household. Until relatively recently, research on child labour has taken scant account of the work done in households, which is integral to the child's experiences of their edu-workscape. Unpaid work within the home makes an important contribution to sustaining the household and is integral to the daily life of many children, whether working elsewhere or not (Chant and Jones, 2005; Abebe, 2011; Tafere, 2013). In Ghana, for example, more than 90 per cent of children in cocoa-growing areas do some household work (Tulane University, 2015). Children's contribution to household labour is part of an intergenerational social contract that both adults and children value (Abebe, 2011), but is renegotiated as children grow up and try to balance collective responsibilities and obligations with individual needs and desires (Tafere, 2013; Kassa, 2016). By helping parents and carers with domestic work, including sibling care and farm work, children also free up the adults to undertake paid employment (Pankhurst et al, 2016).

Despite the household being a significant site for child work, especially for girls (Chant and Jones, 2005; World Bank, 2005; Webbink et al, 2012), it is only relatively recently that household chores have been formally categorized as 'work' (ILO, 2017a). That said, the numbers are considered separately (see, for example, ILO and UNICEF, 2021); most surveys still discount domestic work (FAO, 2020); and even the term 'chore' suggests something less serious than 'work'. In underplaying the importance of domestic labour, the dominant discourse reinforces the gender hierarchies within the household.

The intensity of household work increases with age and tasks become increasingly gender-differentiated. Young boys and girls may both collect firewood and water, for example (Kassa, 2016; Levison et al, 2018), whereas as they get older, boys tend towards farming while girls' domestic load includes cleaning, cooking, care work and household management, as well as paid and unpaid farm work (Abebe, 2011; Pankhurst et al, 2016). In general, girls take the greater domestic work burden, which, along with expectations of marriage and child-bearing, frame judgments about what work and education is appropriate (Tetteh, 2011). While this may prepare children for stereotypical gendered work opportunities in both the domestic and 'productive' arenas of adulthood (Hashim, 2004; Abebe, 2011), it also has direct implications for schooling.

The household is also an important site for learning. Through participation in work, children use their mental and physical abilities beyond those required in school, and this can build children's confidence, self-esteem, social status and sense of belonging (Young Lives, 2018). In addition, the collaborative contribution of children to their household is reputed to encourage pro-social behaviour and a willingness to help (Coppens et al, 2016).

Gender relations, interacting with age, seniority and other social markers of identity, are central to the social dynamics of household and community life. Social learning through household work instantiates these social hierarchies (Heissler and Porter, 2013), and is often regulated through the use of corporal punishment. This is permitted in the African Charter on the Rights and Welfare of the Child (1990), provided it is 'with humanity and [is] consistent with the inherent dignity of the child'. Indeed, physical disciplining is regarded as a necessary process of socialization into responsible adulthood and a sign of love (Frankenberg et al, 2010; Chuta et al, 2019). If children return home late from school, or insist on going to school rather than doing chores, they may be beaten in the home (Soneson, 2005; Murphy et al, 2021), or deprived of food (Pankhurst et al, 2016; Adonteng-Kissi, 2018). As part of this socialization, as children get older they, in turn, physically discipline their younger siblings for similar misdemeanours (Twum-Danso Imoh, 2013; Isimbi et al, 2017). GAGE evidence from Ethiopia highlights how adolescent girls are frequently disciplined for contravening gender norms, which may foreshadow later domestic violence (Murphy et al, 2021).

Notwithstanding the significant learning that takes place within households, not least about gender identity and position, domestic work reinforces gendered hierarchical relations through social regulation in the form of physical, psychological and symbolic violence. These are often normalized as part of 'growing up' and rarely included in notions of harm. Contextual understandings of these conditions of daily life within households and their bearing on schooling and life outside are essential to enhancing our understanding the relationship between education and children's work (Abebe and Bessell, 2011).

Learning at work

In this section we focus on the third element of the edu-workscape – the workplace. While there are clearly contexts and conditions in which children's work may be detrimental, the overall picture is inevitably more nuanced. Importantly, in much of SSA, the notion of working hard (in both domestic and waged labour) is part of being a 'good child' (Tafere, 2013; Jonah and Abebe, 2019) and, as highlighted earlier, integral to the reciprocal intergenerational social contract that is central to children's transition to adulthood (Tafere, 2013; Kassa, 2016).

Studies have shown that, at least initially, many children manage to combine paid work – of some sort – and schooling (Okyere, 2013; Maconachie and Hilson, 2016; Mussa et al, 2019). With respect to children working in cocoa, for example, it has been reported that that 71 per cent in Côte d'Ivoire and 96 per cent in Ghana attended school in 2013/14. Only 5 per cent reported negative effects of working on their schooling (Tulane University, 2015). However, combining school and work becomes harder as children get older and opportunity costs increase, and as they progress from primary to secondary school (Lewin, 2009). What is more, to attend secondary school, rural children often have to travel further and may have to pay for boarding, which adds to the already high costs of secondary education (Ohba, 2011; Porter et al, 2011).

As in the home, however, the different kinds of waged work available have a significant bearing on the compatibility of work and schooling. In parts of Ghana, boys may have to give up the whole day to fish or farm, whereas girls may be able to engage in petty trading outside school hours (Ananga, 2011). Whether work can be broken up into small blocks of time outside school hours is also a factor, as in Ethiopia when children worked for individual farmers, or helped on the family farm, and could finish the work after school (Orkin, 2012). In contrast, piecework tasks on commercial farms, fishing or herding cattle required a whole day, and therefore competed with schooling. However, as discussed earlier, the compatibility or incompatibility of certain types of work with schooling depends as much on the flexibility in the structures and processes of schooling, as on the nature or location of the work (Orkin, 2012). As with domestic chores, the ability of children to juggle paid or unpaid work and schooling will also depend on various contextual factors.

Increasing demands on children's time can lead them on the gradual path to dropout as attendance becomes more irregular and it is hard to keep up with school work (Ananga, 2011; Pankhurst et al, 2016). It then becomes increasingly challenging for these older or 'over-age' working children to find a pathway back to education (Hunt, 2008; Dunne and Ananga, 2013).

In contexts of rural poverty, children's work often enables them to contribute to household income (Young Lives, 2018; Sabates-Wheeler and Sumberg, 2020), which can be a source of pride (Jonah and Abebe, 2019). Importantly, beyond the vital economic contribution to sustaining their household, children are learning vital work-related practical and social skills (Woodhead, 1999; Abebe and Bessell, 2011). Working alongside parents or other adults, be it farming or fishing, may be similar to an informal apprenticeship (Krauss, 2017; Moreira et al, 2017), or 'situated education' (Dyer, 2013, p 606) – preparation for becoming adult members of society (Abebe, 2011; Tafere and Pankhurst, 2015; Bourdillon, 2017; Young Lives, 2018). Learning about their inter-dependence in both their social and natural environments is important for young people's future livelihoods (Bolin, 2006).

Several studies outside Africa indicate there can be learning synergies for children engaging in both school and work, with some suggestion that work may be linked to improved attainment of low-performing students (Staff and Mortimer, 2007). Work experiences can be drawn upon to learn new vocabulary, explain abstract concepts and in understanding some aspects of the curriculum (Aufseeser, 2014; Banerjee et al, 2017). There is some limited evidence that work provides children with greater confidence, skills and connections to enable them to develop small businesses to generate funds and savings to support future studies (Marsh and Kleitman, 2005; Tafere and Pankhurst, 2015).

Yet while there are plenty of potential benefits of combining work and education, it should not be forgotten that violence, harsh discipline or abuse can be a feature of life in the workplace as it can be at home and in school. Indeed, as our earlier discussions have illustrated, harm can occur across the whole edu-workscape.

Moving forward

This chapter has focused on schooling in relation to children's work and harm. In this final section, we elaborate on some of the evident conceptual and theoretical problematics, especially as they pertain to the contingent and relational matrix of the edu-workscape. We begin with context, childhood and gender, then propose areas and methodologies for further research.

Context

The notion of context is itself multi-layered and relational, encompassing household, community, national and international levels, and including connections, disjunctions and tensions within and across these overlapping and permeable categories. Exploration of the education-work nexus 'in context' calls for research to be socio-historically and politically situated, paying attention to international and local economic and political forces, and sensitive to changing and competing cultures, traditions and identities. Geographical and climatic contexts are also critical to consider as agricultural livelihoods in rural SSA, including in northern Ghana, are considered to be the most vulnerable to the impacts of climate change (Challinor et al, 2007; UNDP, 2018). These intersecting contextual elements have substantive and methodological implications for the 'what' and 'how' of researching children's edu-workscapes.

Childhoods

Conceptions of the child, as discussed in Chapter 1 (this volume), are central to our concerns with education, child work and harm. Many critical studies point to a 'banal developmentalism' that refers both to approaches to economic and social development in the Global South as well as in the conceptual framing of childhood (Nieuwenhuys, 1998; Burman, 2010). Overbearing Western developmental models are seen in the projection of singular, linear, staged trajectories of both capitalist economies and of childhood (Agbu, 2009). These models are associated with the production of the child as a 'modern' subject through a northern cultural imaginary characterized by 'affective investment in childhood', the normalization of children at 'play', and pathologizing children at work, all saturated with moral opprobrium and occluded assumptions around household organization, gender, wealth, class, race and so on (Burman, 2010, p 14; Burman and Stacey, 2010).

A universalized linear chronology used to define age-related stages is a key reference for many of the international development goals. Age life-stage hierarchies are instrumentalized to define the extent and kind of work appropriate to particular ages in ways that effect a separation of childhood from work. This conceptual separation is then reiterated in the opposition between work and schooling. The latter is deemed to be an appropriate activity for children defined by years of age, even in contexts where birth age is not always recorded or known (Berlan, 2009) and where children carry out adult roles and may not self-identify as children (Abebe and Ofosu-Kusi, 2016). Assumptions of age-appropriate activities are also integral to a definition of what constitutes harm and for whom, irrespective of traditions, practices and levels of poverty in particular contexts (Jonah and Abebe, 2019; Yeboah and Daniel, 2019).

Against these normalizing definitions, newer research underlines the significance of the relational complexities of contexts in providing more contingent understandings of childhoods (for example, Abebe and Ofosu-Kusi, 2016, Chapter 2, this volume). The gender neutrality of 'child', 'childhood' and 'child work' have been specifically highlighted in this regard (Abebe and Bessell, 2011), as it obscures gendered processes and inequalities at work. These contextual and relational perspectives represent a shift in theoretical ground away from conceptions of the child in atomized behaviourist terms making individualistic rational choices about their lives and livelihoods (Bourdieu and Wacquant, 1992).

Gender

Normalization of gender hierarchies and the subordination of women are echoed in the gender regimes in multiple arenas of social life including households, schools and workplaces (Butler, 1997; Oyěwùmí, 2005; Lugones, 2007). Understanding the particularities of just how gender (as it interacts with other markers of identity) operates in different contexts is critical to addressing the gendered division of labour and the production of gender identity narratives that sustain these fundamental inequalities.

Turning more specifically to work, in the dominant development discourse, waged labour is used as the key definitional category and as a default against which all other kinds of work (formal versus informal, paid versus unpaid) are constructed. That said, such distinctions are, in practice, more blurred (Dar et al, 2002). More than 85 per cent of work in Africa is in the informal sector, which involves high proportions of women, young people and those with low educational outcomes (ILO, 2018; Sumberg et al, 2020). Importantly here, the dominance of these intersecting binaries has added to the invisibility of women's labour and largely obscured how the very notion of work is gendered (Rai et al, 2019; UN Women, 2019). Despite the eventual recognition of household chores as work (World Bank, 2005; ILO, 2017a), Finlay (2019) points out that the Living Standards Measurement Survey (LSMS), overseen by the World Bank, continues to position women's work as secondary to that of men. Similarly, although the UN System of National Accounts recognizes that 'production' may also include unpaid work, it nevertheless excludes unpaid care and domestic work from such calculations (UN Women, 2019, p 143). The privileging of regular, paid activity continues to make it likely that much of women's and girls' work is still not recognized as work at all.

Further, women's reproductive work, acknowledged as central to capitalist economies (Butler, 1997; Oyěwùmí, 1997), remains largely out of sight even though it overshadows the ways that girls navigate their edu-workscapes and future lives. As a result, many quantitative analyses sustain the invisibility and misrecognition of women's and children's work (ILO, 2013; Prügl, 2020).

Indeed ILO (2017c) has highlighted that almost 70 per cent of those with jobs across SSA, and especially women and young people, are in 'vulnerable' employment, which is defined as working within the household or on their 'own account'. This 'own account' work is highly gendered as girls face higher expectations than boys that they fulfil domestic chores and work on the household farm alongside their schooling (Bourdillon et al, 2015; Crossouard et al, 2022). In addition, boys generally have greater and more lucrative employment opportunities than girls (Abebe, 2011; Okyere, 2013). The reported prevalence of 'transactional sex', often to pay for education, is in part because better paid jobs are often not available to girls (Leach, 2003; Jones and Norton, 2007; Petroni et al, 2017). To add to this, anticipated futures of marriage and child-bearing intensify a gendered/sexual economy in which girls and women must struggle against systematic subordination. In these precarious conditions, the ways that girls and boys navigate their edu-workscapes are subject to the wider social and economic landscape, gendered expectations and the opportunity costs of schooling.

It is evident that decontextualized research that relies on quantifying girls' and boys' work hours, or comparing enrolment or dropout rates, or attainment outcomes, cannot begin to engage with the complex, contingent and everchanging scenarios of social and cultural life within which children go to school and/or work.

New research spaces: the edu-workscape

We have argued strongly for a dynamic conceptual framework that centres the child and takes account of the work, learning and potential harm that can take place across three key social arenas – school, household and workplaces – and which situates these interactions within broader contexts. This re-conceptualization also demands a shift away from dominant discourses of development to better explore and understand the dynamics of local contexts; provision of space for more fluid, contingent and emergent constructions of childhood; and an increase in the visibility of multiple forms of learning and work, especially those submerged in assumptions around gender.

Through the edu-workscape we suggest a conceptual framing that focuses on the social geographies of children's lives as they move within and between the social relations of school, workplace and household. This framing has multiple implications for how we explore and address children's work. For example, as elaborated earlier, the notion of childhood related to chronological serial time may be neither universal nor relevant for all contexts in SSA. The proliferation of expectations of time-staged hierarchies of progress that reverberate in development discourses are a theoretical imposition. While we may wish to retain childhood, and other similar constructs, it is important remain open to alternative theoretical structures and assumptions emergent in the field. In the discourses of rights, development and education, a shift is required from generic universalized references to children, to make visible the ways these are highly gendered and intersected by socio-economic status, ethnicity, race, age, location, migration and other markers of social identity. These all make a difference to how and when children access education, and to their experiences within the school system.

Far from being a sanctuary, the school often requires children to work and experience violence and harm. Beyond corporal punishment or sexual abuse, violence also includes more invisible harms of gender socialization or having one's culture and language excluded from the curriculum. This raises critical questions about the normalization of violence in schools and other arenas in the edu-workscape, and the point at which they can be considered as harm. The ways work and harm are stipulated for different children within different contexts and institutions appears to be an important set of issues to explore (Chapter 2, this volume). These are likely to elucidate not only the worst forms of child work but also relate to improving working conditions in general for adults and children alike.

Successful efforts to plan, regulate or intervene in child work depend on the development of contextually specific understandings of children's lives. The implications here are for a broader range of research methodologies (Chapter 3, this volume). Policy-influencing research on education and children's work in SSA, as elsewhere, has been dominated by quantitative data from randomized control trials, quasi-experimental studies, regression analyses of household and EMIS data and impact evaluations (Cornwall and Aghajanian, 2017). The World Bank's *Facing Forward: Schooling for Learning in Africa* (Bashir et al, 2018), which reports exclusively on quantitative data, is a case in point. These studies have been matched with a plethora of 'systematic' or 'rigorous' literature reviews on key policy areas. Some only include quantitative research (for example, Guerrero et al's 2012 systematic review on improving teacher attendance). Yet, as one such review reflected, many of the 'high quality' (predominantly quantitative) studies paid no attention to the effect of context (Unterhalter et al, 2014). That said, there has been a more recent move towards the inclusion of qualitative data in 'mixed methods' research, including in impact evaluations (Cornwall and Aghajanian, 2017; Chapter 3, this volume). The studies on working children's lives from the mixed methods research of Young Lives offer more contextually situated insights (Young Lives, 2018). As part of a longitudinal research programme, these studies captured the importance of changing contexts and circumstances on children's lives. At the same time, as some qualitative researchers have noted, much 'mixed methods' research 'favours the forms of analysis and truth finding associated with positivism' (Giddings and Grant, 2007).

Thus, while acknowledging the contributions of mixed methods research, this chapter highlights the need to invest in more exploratory qualitative studies (as similarly argued in Chapter 3, this volume). In particular, spatial analyses can help untangle the complex social geographies of edu-workscapes (Twum-Danso Imoh et al, 2018; Dunne et al, 2021). Such research will require more negotiated, participatory, collaborative and emergent methodologies. There is a need to understand what is going on in all its complexities and to gain insights into how and why this is the case from multiple local perspectives, including those of children. The scope of these studies may be narrowed or widened according to the research focus, its motivating questions and the processes of research. Iterations with more macro-data will also be informative. The edu-workscape that we have elaborated provides a framework for undertaking reflexive social research, which is vital for re-shaping conceptual, theoretical, methodological and empirical approaches to the study of children's education, work and harm.

Notes

1 The Gender and Adolescence Global Evidence (GAGE) programme is an exception.

2 Burkina Faso, Chad, Ghana, Mali, Niger, Nigeria and Senegal, in West and Central Africa; and Ethiopia, Kenya, Somalia, South Sudan and Tanzania, in East and Southern Africa. Smaller countries such as the Central African Republic, Chad, Djibouti and Mali have high numbers of school-age children not in school.

3 Young Lives is a longitudinal study of poverty and inequality that has been following the lives of 12,000 children in Ethiopia, India (Andhra Pradesh and Telangana), Peru and Vietnam since 2001. The programme is led by the University of Oxford.

References

Abebe, T. (2011) 'Gendered work and schooling in rural Ethiopia: exploring working children's perspectives', in Evers, S., Notermans, C. and van Ommering, E. (eds) *Not Just a Victim: The Child as Catalyst and Witness of Contemporary Africa*. Leiden and Boston: Brill, pp 147–71.

Abebe, T. and Bessell, S. (2011) 'Dominant discourses, debates and silences on child labour in Africa and Asia', *Third World Quarterly*, 32(4), pp 765–86.

Abebe, T. and Ofosu-Kusi, Y. (2016) 'Beyond pluralizing African childhoods: introduction', *Childhood*, 23(3), pp 303–16.

ACPF (2018) *The African Report on Child Wellbeing 2018*. Addis Ababa: African Child Policy Forum (ACPF).

Admassie, A. (2003) 'Child labour and schooling in the context of a subsistence rural economy: can they be compatible?', *International Journal of Educational Development*, 23(2), pp 167–85.

Adonteng-Kissi, O. (2018) 'Parental perceptions of child labour and human rights: a comparative study of rural and urban Ghana', *Child Abuse & Neglect*, 84, pp 34–44.

Adzahlie-Mensah, V. (2014) *Being 'Nobodies': School Regimes and Student Identities in Ghana*. Unpublished PhD thesis. University of Sussex.

Agbu, O. (2009) 'Introduction', in Agbu, O. (ed) *Children and Youth in the Labour Process*. Dakar: Council for the Development of Social Science Research in Africa, pp 6–9.

Alhassan, S. and Adzahlie-Mensah, V. (2010) *Teachers and Access to Schooling in Ghana. Create Pathways to Access Research Monograph No. 43*. Brighton: CREATE, Centre for International Education, University of Sussex.

Ampiah, J. and Adu-Yeboah, C. (2009) 'Mapping the incidence of school dropouts: a case study of communities in Northern Ghana', *Comparative Education*, 45(2), pp 219–32.

Ananga, E.D. (2011) 'Typology of school dropout: the dimensions and dynamics of dropout in Ghana', *International Journal of Educational Development*, 31(4), pp 374–81.

Antonowicz, L. (2010) *Too Often in Silence: A Report on School-Based Violence in West and Central Africa*. UNICEF, Plan West Africa, Save the Children Sweden West Africa and Action Aid.

Aronowitz, A.A. (2019) 'Regulating business involvement in labor exploitation and human trafficking', *Journal of Labor and Society*, 22(1), pp 145–64.

Aufseeser, D. (2014) 'Limiting spaces of informal learning among street children in Peru', in Mills, S. and Kraftl, P. (eds) *Informal Education, Childhood and Youth: Geographies, Histories, Practices*. London: Palgrave Macmillan UK, pp 112–23.

Banerjee, A.V. et al (2017) *The Untapped Math Skills of Working Children in India: Evidence, Possible Explanations, and Implications*. Working paper. Boston, MA: Abdul Latif Jameel Poverty Action Lab (J-PAL).

Bashir, S. et al (2018) *Facing Forward: Schooling for Learning in Africa. Africa Development Forum Series*. Washington, DC: The World Bank.

Beegle, K., Coudouel, A. and Monsalve, E. (eds) (2018) *Realizing the Full Potential of Social Safety Nets in Africa*. Washington, DC: World Bank.

Benavot, A. and Gad, L. (2004) 'Actual instructional time in African primary schools: factors that reduce school quality in developing countries', *Prospects*, 34(3), pp 291–310.

Berlan, A. (2004) 'Child labour, education and child rights among cocoa producers in Ghana', in van den Anker, C. (ed) *The Political Economy of New Slavery*. London: Palgrave Macmillan, pp 158–78.

Berlan, A. (2009) 'Child labour and cocoa: whose voices prevail?', *International Journal of Sociology and Social Policy*, 29(3/4), pp 141–51.

Bhana, D., Singh, S. and Msibi, T. (2021) 'Introduction: gender, sexuality and violence in education: a three-ply yarn approach', in Bhana, D., Singh, S., and Msibi, T. (eds) *Gender, Sexuality and Violence in South African Educational Spaces*. Cham, Switzerland: Palgrave Macmillan.

Bolin, I. (2006) *Growing Up in a Culture of Respect: Child Rearing in Highland Peru*. Austin, TX: University of Texas Press. Available at: https://utpress.utexas.edu/books/bolgro (Accessed 3 April 2020).

Bourdieu, P. and Wacquant, L. (1992) *An Invitation to Reflexive Sociology*. Chicago: Polity Press.

Bourdillon, M. (2017) *Ignoring the Benefits of Children's Work. Beyond Trafficking and Slavery Blog. openDemocracy*. Available at: https://www.opendemocracy.net/en/beyond-trafficking-and-slavery/ignoring-benefits-of-children-s-work/ (Accessed 3 April 2020).

Bourdillon, M. et al (2010) *Rights and Wrongs of Children's Work*. New Brunswick, New Jersey and London: Rutgers University Press.

Bourdillon, M., Crivello, G. and Pankhurst, A. (2015) 'Introduction: children's work and current debates', in Pankhurst, A., Bourdillon, M, and Crivello, G (eds) *Children's Work and Labour in East Africa*. Addis Ababa: Organization for Social Science Research in East Africa, pp 1–17.

Boyden, J. (1994) *The Relationship Between Education and Child Work. Innocenti Occasional Papers, Child Rights Series Number 9*. Florence, Italy: UNICEF International Child Development Centre.

Boyden, J. (1997) 'Childhood and the policy makers: a comparative perspective on the globalization of childhood', in James, A. and Prout, A. (eds) *Constructing and Reconstructing Childhood: Contemporary Issues in the Sociological Study of Childhood*. London: Falmer Press, pp 190–229.

Boyle, S. et al (2002) *Reaching the Poor: The 'Costs' of Sending Children to School. Synthesis Report*. London: UK Department for International Development.

Bundy, D. et al (eds) (2009) *Rethinking School Feeding: Social Safety Nets, Child Development, and the Education Sector*. Washington, DC: World Bank.

Burman, E. (2010) 'Un/thinking children in development: a contribution from northern anti-developmental psychology', in Cannella, G. and Soto, L. (eds), *Childhoods: A Handbook*. New York: Peter Lang, pp 9–26. Available at: https://www.research.manchester.ac.uk/portal/en/publications/unthinking-children-in-development-a-contribution-from-northern-antidevelopmental-psychology(4f1e7592-dad1-484e-b363-f30a788a9f5b)/export.html (Accessed 28 May 2020).

Burman, E. and Stacey, J. (2010) 'The child and childhood in feminist theory', *Feminist Theory*, 11(3), pp 227–40.

Butler, J. (1997) *Excitable Speech: A Politics of the Performative*. New York: Routledge.

Casely-Hayford, L. et al (2013) *The Quality and Inclusivity of Basic Education Across Ghana's Three Northern Regions: A Look at Change, Learning Effectiveness and Efficiency*. Accra: Associates for Change.

Challinor, A. et al (2007) 'Assessing the vulnerability of food crop systems in Africa to climate change', *Climate Change*, 83(3), pp 381–99.

Chant, S. and Jones, G.A. (2005) 'Youth, gender and livelihoods in West Africa: perspectives from Ghana and the Gambia', *Children's Geographies*, 3(2), pp 185–99.

Chuta, N. et al (2019) *Understanding Violence Affecting Children in Ethiopia: A Qualitative Study*. Oxford: Young Lives.

Cluver, L., Bowes, L. and Gardner, F. (2010) 'Risk and protective factors for bullying victimization among AIDS-affected and vulnerable children in South Africa', *Child Abuse & Neglect*, 34(10), pp 793–803.

Colclough, C. et al (2003) *Achieving Schooling for All in Africa: Costs, Commitment and Gender*. Aldershot: Ashgate.

Committee on the Rights of the Child (2006) *General Comment No. 8. The Right of the Child to Protection from Corporal Punishment and Other Cruel or Degrading Forms of Punishment (Articles 19, 28(2) and 37, inter alia), CRC/C/GC/8, para 11*. New York: United Nations.

Connell, R. (1987) *Gender and Power: Society, the Person and Sexual Politics*. Cambridge: Polity Press.

Coppens, A. et al (2016) 'Children's contributions in family work: two cultural paradigms', in Punch, S. and Vanderbeck, R.M. (eds) *Families, Intergenerationality, and Peer Group Relations: Geographies of Children and Young People*. Singapore: Springer Nature, pp 1–27.

Cornwall, A. and Aghajanian, A. (2017) 'How to find out what's really going on: understanding impact through participatory process evaluation', *World Development*, 99, pp 173–85.

Crossouard, B. et al (2022) 'Rural youth in southern Nigeria: fractured lives and ambitious futures', *Journal of Sociology*, 58(2), pp 218–35.

Dar, A. et al (2002) *Participation of Children in Schooling and Labor Activities: A Review of Empirical Studies. Social Protection Discussion Paper No. 0221*. Washington, DC: Social Protection Unit, The World Bank.

Devereux, S. (2000) *Social Safety Nets for Poverty Alleviation in Southern Africa*. Brighton: Institute of Development Studies (IDS) (ESCOR report R7107). Available at: https://www.ids.ac.uk/publications/social-safety-nets-for-poverty-alleviation-in-southern-africa/ (Accessed 28 May 2020).

Devereux, S. et al (2008) *Ethiopia's Productive Safety Net Programme 2008 Assessment*. Available at: https://www.cashdividend.net/wp-content/uploads/2013/05/Devereux-et-al.-2008.pdf (Accessed 28 May 2020).

Devonald, M., Jones, N. and Yadete, W. (2021) 'Addressing educational attainment inequities in rural Ethiopia: leave no adolescent behind', *Development Policy Review*, 39(5), pp 740–56.

Dunne, M. et al (2005) *Gendered School Experiences: The Impact on Retention and Achievement in Botswana and Ghana*. London: UK Department for International Development (DFID Educational Report, 56).

Dunne, M. and Ananga, E.D. (2013) 'Dropping out: identity conflict in and out of school in Ghana', *International Journal of Educational Development*, 33(2), pp 196–205.

Dunne, M., Humphreys, S. and Bakari, S. (2021) 'Troubled spaces: negotiating school–community boundaries in northern Nigeria', *Journal of Education Policy*, 36(6), pp 843–64.

Dunne, M., Humphreys, S. and Leach, F. (2006) 'Gender violence in schools in the developing world', *Gender and Education*, 18(1), pp 75–98.

Dyer, C. (2013) 'Does mobility have to mean being hard to reach? Mobile pastoralists and education's "terms of inclusion"', *Compare*, 43(5), pp 601–4.

Edmonds, E.V. and Shrestha, M. (2014) 'You get what you pay for: schooling incentives and child labor', *Journal of Development Economics*, 111, pp 196–211.

Epstein, D. and Morrell, R. (2012) 'Approaching Southern theory: explorations of gender in South African education', *Gender and Education*, 24(5), pp 469–82.

Essuman, A. and Akyeampong, K. (2011) 'Decentralisation policy and practice in Ghana: the promise and reality of community participation in education in rural communities', *Journal of Education Policy*, 26(4), pp 513–27.

Fair, K. (2016) *Estimation of the Numbers and Rates of Out-of-School Children and Adolescents Using Administrative and Household Survey Data*. Information Paper No. 35. Montreal, Canada: UNESCO Institute for Statistics.

FAO (2020) *FAO Framework on Ending Child Labour in Agriculture*. Rome: Food and Agriculture Organization (FAO).

Feinstein, S. and Mwahombela, L. (2010) 'Corporal punishment in Tanzania's schools', *International Review of Education / Internationale Zeitschrift für Erziehungswissenschaft / Revue Internationale de l'Education*, 56(4), pp 399–410.

Finlay, J. (2019) *Fertility and Women's Work in the Context of Women's Economic Empowerment: Inequalities Across Regions and Wealth Quintiles*. Working paper. Boston: The Chan School of Public Health, Harvard University.

Fisher, E. et al (2017) 'The livelihood impacts of cash transfers in sub-Saharan Africa: beneficiary perspectives from six countries', *World Development*, 99, pp 299–319.

Frankenberg, S.J., Holmqvist, R. and Rubenson, B. (2010) 'The care of corporal punishment: conceptions of early childhood discipline strategies among parents and grandparents in a poor and urban area in Tanzania', *Childhood*, 17(4), pp 455–69.

Ghana Ministry of Education (2018) *Education Sector Report 2018*. Accra, Ghana: Ministry of Education.

Giddings, L.S. and Grant, B.M. (2007) 'A Trojan horse for positivism?: a critique of mixed methods research.', *ANS. Advances In Nursing Science*, 30(1), pp 52–60.

Guarcello, L., Lyon, S. and Valdivia, C. (2015) *Evolution of the Relationship Between Child Labour and Education Since 2000*. Background paper for EFA Global Monitoring Report 2015. Paris: UNESCO.

Guerrero, G. et al (2012) *What Works to Improve Teacher Attendance in Developing Countries? A Systematic Review*. London: EPPI-Centre, Social Science Research Unit, Institute of Education, University of London.

Hashim, I.M. (2004) *Working with Working Children: Child Labour and the Barriers to Education in Rural Northeastern Ghana*. Unpublished PhD thesis. University of Sussex.

Hashim, I.M. (2005) *Exploring the Linkages between Children's Independent Migration and Education: Evidence from Ghana*. Falmer: Development Research Centre on Migration, Globalisation and Poverty.

Heissler, K. and Porter, C. (2013) 'Know your place: Ethiopian children's contributions to the household economy', *The European Journal of Development Research*, 25(4), pp 600–20.

de Hoop, J., Gichane, M.W. and Zuilkowski, S.S. (2020) *Cash Transfers, Public Works and Child Activities: Mixed Methods Evidence from the United Republic of Tanzania*. Innocenti Working Paper. Florence, Italy: UNICEF Office of Research – Innocenti.

Humphreys, S. (2008) 'Gendering corporal punishment: beyond the discourse of human rights', *Gender and Education*, 20(5), pp 527–40.

Humphreys, S. et al (2015) 'Counted in and being out: fluctuations in primary school and classroom attendance in northern Nigeria', *International Journal of Educational Development*, 44, pp 134–43.

Hunt, F.M. (2008) *Dropping Out from School: A Cross-Country Review of Literature*. Falmer: Consortium for Research on Educational Access, Transitions and Equity (CREATE).

Husein, A., Saraogi, N. and Mintz, S. (2017) *Lessons Learned from World Bank Education Management Information System Operations: Portfolio Review, 1998–2014*. World Bank Studies. Washington, DC: The World Bank.

ILO (2013) *Unpaid Household Services and Child Labour. Working paper. Presented at 19th International Conference of Labour Statisticians*. Geneva: International Labour Organization. Available at: https://www.ilo.org/wcmsp5/groups/public/---dgreports/---stat/documents/meetingdocument/wcms_221638.pdf (Accessed 27 May 2020).

ILO (2017a) *Global Estimates of Child Labour: Results and Trends, 2012–2016*. Geneva: International Labour Organization. Available at: https://www.ilo.org/wcmsp5/groups/public/---dgreports/---dcomm/documents/publication/wcms_575499.pdf (Accessed 19 April 2020).

ILO (2017b) *Regional Brief for Africa: Global Estimates of Modern Slavery and Child Labour*. Geneva: International Labour Organization.

ILO (2017c) *World Employment and Social Outlook: Trends 2017*. World Employment and Social Outlook. Geneva: International Labour Organization.

ILO (2018) *Women and Men in the Informal Economy. A Statistical Picture*. Geneva: International Labour Organization. Available at: https://www.ilo.org/wcmsp5/groups/public/---dgreports/---dcomm/documents/publication/wcms_626831.pdf (Accessed 28 May 2020).

ILO and UNICEF (2021) *Child Labour: Global Estimates 2020, Trends and the Road Forward*. New York: International Labour Office and United Nations Children's Fund.

Isimbi, R., Umutoni, F. and Coast, E. (2017) *Exploring Rwandan Adolescents' Gendered Experiences and Perspectives*. London: Gender and Adolescence: Global Evidence.

Jomaa, L.H., McDonnell, E. and Probart, C. (2011) 'School feeding programs in developing countries: impacts on children's health and educational outcomes', *Nutrition Reviews*, 69(2), pp 83–98.

Jonah, O.-T. and Abebe, T. (2019) 'Tensions and controversies regarding child labor in small-scale gold mining in Ghana', *African Geographical Review*, 38(4), pp 361–73.

Jones, N. et al (2019) *Adolescent Education and Learning in Ethiopia: A Report on GAGE Baseline Findings*. London: Gender and Adolescence: Global Evidence.

Jones, S. and Norton, B. (2007) 'On the limits of sexual health literacy: insights from Ugandan schoolgirls', *Diaspora, Indigenous, and Minority Education*, 1(4), pp 285–305.

Kassa, S.C. (2016) 'Negotiating intergenerational relationships and social expectations in childhood in rural and urban Ethiopia', *Childhood*, 23(3), pp 394–409.

Krauss, A. (2017) 'Understanding child labour beyond the standard economic assumption of monetary poverty', *Cambridge Journal of Economics*, 41(2), pp 545–74.

Leach, F. (2003) 'Learning to be violent: the role of the school in developing adolescent gendered behaviour', *Compare: A Journal of Comparative and International Education*, 33(3), pp 385–400.

Leach, F. et al (2003) *An Investigative Study of the Abuse of Girls in African Schools*. London: UK Department for International Development. Available at: https://ideas.repec.org/p/ags/dfider/12849.html (Accessed 8 June 2020).

Leach, F., Dunne, M. and Salvi, F. (2014) *School-Related Gender-Based Violence*. New York: UNESCO. Available at: http://www.unesco.org/new/fileadmin/MULTIMEDIA/HQ/HIV-AIDS/pdf/SRGBV_UNESCO_Global_ReviewJan2014.pdf (Accessed 8 June 2020).

Levison, D., DeGraff, D.S. and Dungumaro, E.W. (2018) 'Implications of environmental chores for schooling: children's time fetching water and firewood in Tanzania', *The European Journal of Development Research*, 30(2), pp 217–34.

Lewin, K.M. (2009) 'Access to education in sub-Saharan Africa: patterns, problems and possibilities', *Comparative Education*, 45(2), pp 151–74.

Lewin, K.M. and Akyeampong, K. (2009) 'Education in sub-Saharan Africa: researching access, transitions and equity', *Comparative Education*, 45(2), pp 143–50.

Lugones, M. (2007) 'Heterosexualism and the colonial/modern gender system', *Hypatia*, 22(1), pp 186–209.

Maconachie, R. and Hilson, G. (2016) 'Re-thinking the child labor "problem" in rural sub-Saharan Africa: the case of Sierra Leone's half shovels', *World Development*, 78, pp 136–47.

Marsh, H.W. and Kleitman, S. (2005) 'Consequences of employment during high school: character building, subversion of academic goals, or a threshold?', *American Educational Research Journal*, 42(2), pp 331–69.

Masko, A.L. and Bosiwah, L. (2016) 'Cultural congruence and unbalanced power between home and school in rural Ghana and the impact on school children', *Comparative Education*, 52(4), pp 538–55.

Moreira, C.N., Rabenevanana, M.W. and Picard, D. (2017) 'Boys go fishing, girls work at home: gender roles, poverty and unequal school access among semi-nomadic fishing communities in South Western Madagascar', *Compare: A Journal of Comparative and International Education*, 47(4), pp 499–511.

Morrell, R. (2001) 'Corporal punishment in South African schools: a neglected explanation for its existence', *South African Journal of Education*, 21(4), pp 292–99.

Morrow, V. et al (2017) '"I started working because I was hungry": the consequences of food insecurity for children's well-being in rural Ethiopia', *Social Science & Medicine*, 182, pp 1–9.

Murphy, M. et al (2021) 'Gender-norms, violence and adolescence: exploring how gender norms are associated with experiences of childhood violence among young adolescents in Ethiopia', *Global Public Health*, 16(6), pp 842–55.

Mussa, E.C. et al (2019) 'Does childhood work impede long-term human capital accumulation? Empirical evidence from rural Ethiopia', *International Journal of Educational Development*, 66, pp 234–46.

Myers, W. and Boyden, J. (1998) *Child Labour: Promoting the Best Interests of Working Children*. London: International Save the Children Alliance.

Nieuwenhuys, O. (1998) 'Global childhood and the politics of contempt', *Alternatives*, 23, pp 267–89.

Odachi, I.O. (2011) *Transforming Education and Development Policies for Pastoralist Communities in Kenya through the Implementation of Indigenous Knowledge Systems*. Addis Ababa: Organization for Social Science Research in Eastern and Southern Africa.

Odonkor, M. (2007) *Addressing Child Labour Through Education*. Accra, Ghana: Frontier Analysis Consulting Associates Ltd.

Ohba, A. (2011) 'The abolition of secondary school fees in Kenya: responses by the poor', *Access, Equity and Transitions in Education in Low Income Countries*, 31(4), pp 402–8.

Okiror, J., Matsiko, B. and Oonyu, J. (2011) 'Just how much can school pupils learn from school gardening? A study of two supervised agricultural experience approaches in Uganda', *Journal of Agricultural Education*, 52, pp 24–35.

Okyere, S. (2012) 'Re-examining the education-child labour nexus: the case of child miners at Kenyasi, Ghana', *Childhoods Today*, 6(1), pp 1–20.

Okyere, S. (2013) 'Are working children's rights and child labour abolition complementary or opposing realms?', *International Social Work*, 56(1), pp 80–91.

Orkin, K. (2012) 'Are work and schooling complementary or competitive for children in rural Ethiopia? A mixed-methods study', in Boyden, J. and Bourdillon, M. (eds) *Childhood Poverty: Multidisciplinary Approaches*. London: Palgrave Macmillan UK, pp 298–313.

Oyěwùmí, O. (1997) *Invention of Women: Making An African Sense of Western Gender Discourses*. Minneapolis: University of Minnesota Press.

Oyěwùmí, O. (2005) *African Gender Studies: A Reader*. New York: Palgrave MacMillan.

Pankhurst, A., Crivello, G. and Tiumelissan, A. (2016) *Children's Work in Family and Community Contexts: Examples from Young Lives Ethiopia. Working Paper 147*. Oxford: Young Lives.

Pankhurst, A., Negussie, N. and Mulugets, E. (2016) *Understanding Children's Experiences of Violence in Ethiopia: Evidence from Young Lives*. Florence, Italy: UNICEF Office of Research.

Parkes, J. et al (2013) 'Conceptualising gender and violence in research: Insights from studies in schools and communities in Kenya, Ghana and Mozambique', *Gender Justice, Education and International Development: Theory, Policy and Practice*, 33(6), pp 546–56.

Parkes, J. et al (2016) *A Rigorous Review of Global Research Evidence on Policy and Practice on School-Related Gender-Based Violence*. New York: UNICEF. Available at: https://eric.ed.gov/?id=ED573791 (Accessed 8 June 2020).

Petroni, S. et al (2017) 'New findings on child marriage in sub-Saharan Africa', *Annals of Global Health*, 83(5–6), pp 781–90.

Pinheiro, P.S. (2006) *World Report on Violence Against Children*. Geneva: United Nations.

Porter, G. et al (2011) 'Mobility, education and livelihood trajectories for young people in rural Ghana: a gender perspective', *Children's Geographies*, 9(3–4), pp 395–410.

Prügl, E. (2020) 'Untenable dichotomies: de-gendering political economy', *Review of International Political Economy*, 28, pp 295–306.

Quattri, M. and Watkins, K. (2016) *Child Labour and Education: A Survey of Slum Settlements in Dhaka*. London: Overseas Development Institute (ODI).

Rai, S.M., Brown, B.D. and Ruwanpura, K.N. (2019) 'SDG 8: decent work and economic growth – a gendered analysis', *World Development*, 113, pp 368–80.

Robson, E. (2004) 'Hidden child workers: young carers in Zimbabwe', *Antipode*, 36(2), pp 227–48.

Roelen, K., Karki-Chettri, H.K. and Delap, E. (2015) 'Little cash to large households: cash transfers and children's care in disadvantaged families in Ghana', *International Social Security Review*, 68(2), pp 63–83.

Rose, P. and Dyer, C. (2008) *Chronic Poverty and Education: A Review of Literature. Chronic Poverty Research Centre Working Paper 131*. London: Chronic Poverty Research Centre.

Sabates-Wheeler, R. and Sumberg, J. (2020) *Understanding Children's Harmful Work in African Agriculture: Points of Departure. ACHA Working Paper 1*. Brighton: Action on Children's Harmful Work in African Agriculture, IDS.

Shumba, A. and Abosi, O.C. (2011) 'The nature, extent and causes of abuse of children with disabilities in schools in Botswana', *International Journal of Disability, Development and Education*, 58(4), pp 373–88.

Snivstveit, B. et al (2016) *The Impact of Education Programmes on Learning and School Participation in Low and Middle-Income Countries*. London: International Initiative for Impact Evaluation.

Soneson, U. (2005) *Ending Corporal Punishment of Children in Swaziland: He Should Talk to Me, Not Beat Me*. Pretoria, South Africa: Save the Children Sweden.

Staff, J. and Mortimer, J.T. (2007) 'Educational and work strategies from adolescence to early adulthood', *Social Forces: A Scientific Medium of Social Study and Interpretation*, 85(3), pp 1169–94.

Stein, M., Steenkamp, D. and Tangi, F. (2019) 'Relations of corporal punishment to academic results and achievements in secondary schools in Tanzania', *International Journal of Education Research*, 7(8), pp 85–104.

Stromquist, N.P. and Monkman, K. (eds) (2014) *Globalization and Education: Integration and Contestation across Cultures* (2nd edn). Lanham, Maryland: Rowman & Littlefield.

Sulemana, M., Ngah, I. and Majid, M.R. (2013) 'The challenges and prospects of the school feeding programme in Northern Ghana', *Development in Practice*, 23(3), pp 422–32.

Sumberg, J. et al (2020) 'Formal-sector employment and Africa's youth employment crisis: irrelevance or policy priority?', *Development Policy Review*, 38(4), pp 428–40.

Swift-Morgan, J. (2006) 'What community participation in schooling means: insights from Southern Ethiopia', *Harvard Educational Review*, 73(3), pp 339–68.

Tafere, Y. (2013) *Intergenerational Relationships and the Life Course: Changing Relations between Children and Caregivers in Ethiopia*. Oxford: Young Lives.

Tafere, Y. and Pankhurst, A. (2015) 'Children combining work and school in Ethiopian communities', in Pankhurst, A., Bourdillon, M., and Crivello, G. (eds) *Children's Work and Labour in East Africa: Social Context and Implications for Policy*. Addis Ababa: OSSREA. Available at: https://www.younglives.org.uk/content/children-combining-work-and-school-ethiopian-communities (Accessed 3 April 2020).

Tafere, Y. and Woldehanna, T. (2012) *Beyond Food Security: Transforming the Productive Safety Net Programme in Ethiopia for the Well-being of Children*. Oxford: Young Lives.

Talwar, V., Carlson, S.M. and Lee, K. (2011) 'Effects of a punitive environment on children's executive functioning: A natural experiment', *Social Development*, 20(4), pp 805–24.

Tetteh, P. (2011) 'Child domestic labour in (Accra) Ghana: a child and gender rights issue?', *The International Journal of Children's Rights*, 19(2), pp 217–32.

Tulane University (2015) *Final Report: 2013/14 Survey Research on Child Labor in West African Cocoa-Growing Areas*. New Orleans: School of Public Health and Tropical Medicine, Tulane University.

Twum-Danso Imoh, A. (2013) 'Children's perceptions of physical punishment in Ghana and the implications for children's rights', *Childhood*, 20(4), pp 472–86.

Twum-Danso Imoh, A., Bourdillon, M. and Meichsner, S. (2018) 'Introduction: exploring children's lives beyond the binary of the global north and global south', in Twum-Danso Imoh, A., Bourdillon, M. and Meichsner, S. (eds) *Global Childhoods Beyond the North-South Divide*. Cham, Switzerland: Springer Nature, pp 1–10.

UCW (2017) *Understanding Trends in Child Labour*. Rome: ILO, UNICEF and World Bank.

UN Women (2019) *Progress on the Sustainable Development Goals*. New York: UN Department of Economic and Social Affairs (The Gender Snapshot 2019).

UNDP (2018) *2018 Northern Ghana HDR*. Accra: UNDP Ghana.

UNESCO (2005) *Education for All: The Quality Imperative; EFA Global Monitoring Report, 2005*. Paris: UNESCO.

UNESCO (2015a) *Education for all 2000–2015: Achievements and Challenges. EFA Global Monitoring Report 2015* (1st edn). Paris: UNESCO.

UNESCO (2015b) *United Nations Resolution on SRGBV at the 196th Session of the Executive Board of the United Nations Educational, Scientific and Cultural Organization (UNESCO) (196/EX/30, 2015).* Paris: UNESCO.

UNESCO (2019) *Behind the Numbers: Ending School Violence and Bullying.* Paris: UNESCO.

UNESCO and UNICEF–UIS (2014) *Regional Report: West and Central Africa. Global Initiative on Out-of-School Children.* Dakar: UNICEF and UNESCO–UIS. Available at: http://uis.unesco.org/sites/default/files/documents/out-of-school-children-west-central-africa-regional-report-education-2014-en.pdf (Accessed 27 May 2020).

UNESCO-UIS (2019) *New Methodology Shows that 258 Million Children, Adolescents and Youth Are Out of School. UIS Fact Sheet No. 56.* Paris: UNESCO Institute for Statistics. Available at: http://uis.unesco.org/sites/default/files/documents/new-methodology-shows-258-million-children-adolescents-and-youth-are-out-school.pdf (Accessed 31 March 2020).

UNESCO-UIS and UNICEF (2015) *Fixing the Broken Promise of Education for All: Findings from the Global Initiative on Out-of-School Children.* Montreal: UNESCO Institute for Statistics.

United Nations (2016) *Tackling Violence in Schools: A Global Perspective.* New York: United Nations.

United Nations (2020) *Policy Brief: Education During Covid 19 and Beyond.* New York: United Nations.

Unterhalter, E. et al (2014) *Interventions to Enhance Girls' Education and Gender Equality. Education Rigorous Literature Review.* London: UK Department for International Development.

Vavrus, F. and Bloch, M. (1998) 'Gender and educational research, policy, and practice in Sub-Saharan Africa: Theoretical and empirical problems and prospects: power, opportunities and constraints', in Bloch, M., Beoku-Betts, J. and Tabachnick, B.R. (eds) *Women and Education in Sub-Saharan Africa: Power, Opportunities and Constraints.* Boulder, CO: Lynne Rienner Publishers, pp 1–24. Available at: https://experts.umn.edu/en/publications/gender-and-educational-research-policy-and-practice-in-sub-sahara (Accessed 8 June 2020).

Wambiri, G. (2014) 'Compatibility of work and school: Informal work arrangements in central Kenya', in Bourdillon, M. and Mutambwa, G.M. (eds) *The Place of Work in African Childhoods.* Dakar: CODESRIA (Conseil pour le Developpement de la Recherche Economique et Sociale en Afrique), pp 165–84.

Webbink, E., Smits, J. and de Jong, E. (2012) 'Hidden child labor: determinants of housework and family business work of children in 16 developing countries', *World Development*, 40(3), pp 631–42.

Wekesa, A. (2011) *Bending the Private–Public Gender Norms: Negotiating Schooling for Young Mothers from Low-Income Households in Kenya. Working Paper 515*. The Hague: International Institute of Social Studies.

Woodhead, M. (1999) 'Combatting child labour: listen to what the children say', *Childhood*, 6, pp 27–49.

World Bank (2005) *Gender Issues in Child Labor*. PREMnotes Number 100. Washington, DC: The World Bank (Available at: http://www1.worldbank.org/prem/PREMNotes/premnote100.pdf (Accessed 28 May 2020).

Wouango, J. (2013) 'Travail des enfants et droit à l' éducation au Burkina Faso', *Cahiers de la recherche sur l'éducation et les savoirs*, 10, pp 127–41.

Yeboah, S.A. and Daniel, M. (2019) '"Silent exclusion": transnational approaches to education and school participation in Ghana', *Africa Today*, 66(2), pp 2–26.

Young Lives (2018) *Summary: Responding to Children's Work. Evidence from the Young Lives Study in Ethiopia, India, Peru and Vietnam*. Oxford: Young Lives. Available at: https://www.younglives.org.uk/sites/www.younglives.org.uk/files/YL-Summary-ChildWork.pdf (Accessed 3 April 2020).

5

Disabled Children and Work

Mary Wickenden

Introduction

The argument in this chapter is that children with disabilities need focused attention when children and work are being investigated. Those with disabilities make up a large minority of all children and it is not tenable to ignore them. Currently, they are largely ignored when important issues related to the wellbeing of children are interrogated. It is the exception that data are collected about them and so we cannot usually disaggregate them from the general population and reveal clear evidence about whether they are more disadvantaged than others. Yet, this is something that many agencies working on issues relating to disability and/or with children report anecdotally. In relation to work specifically, while there is very little evidence, the suspicion is that children with disabilities may be working at least as much as other children, possibly more, and potentially in more hazardous or invisible forms of work, and perhaps with less protection and support.

Child protection systems may not be sufficiently alert to the need for disability inclusive approaches in order to protect disabled children who are particularly at risk of harm. Disabled children may be working because they are more likely to be out of school. Their relationship with school attendance is complex and intertwined with attitudes (of parents, teachers, communities), family finances and other pressures. They are often devalued as citizens and seen as a drain on family resources, and not worth the investment that schooling entails. They may, therefore, be more likely to be sent to work or to seek it out themselves in order to demonstrate their worth to the family.

Being labelled as disabled usually precipitates individuals into a lifetime of disadvantage, where they continuously struggle to be valued and recognized as family and community members. Doing work at an early age may be one way in which disabled children try to counter this negativity, especially if their opportunities to exercise agency in other ways are limited. In addition, doing harmful work results in injury and possibly lasting impairment, or may exacerbate pre-existing impairments. In short, this is a topic which is neglected and needs attention.

There is an ongoing discussion in the disability community about language. The UK disability movement and academic community favour 'disabled people' in recognition that people are disabled *by* society (as per the social model of disability). In contrast, in many other international contexts 'people with disabilities' is favoured, with a rationalization that this puts the *person first*. UN bodies use the latter. In this chapter I use the two forms – 'disabled people' and 'people with disabilities' – interchangeably, with no particular significance.

The lives of adults or children with disabilities have been viewed as a minority or specialist (and often medical) interest, and these populations have not generally been included or considered either in livelihoods research or interventions. However, since the launch of the ground-breaking UN Convention on the Rights of Persons with Disabilities (CRPD) (United Nations, 2007) this has begun to change. Bolstered by the convention, there has been very active lobbying by the disability movement, made up of organizations of people with disabilities (OPD), for recognition of these rights including the right to decent work (Article 27) and the rights of disabled children (Article 7). In parallel, evidence about the numbers of people with disabilities, and their persistent marginalization is increasingly available.

Disability is not predominantly a medical or health matter. Being disabled has consequences for individuals across all aspects of their lives. There is now increased acknowledgement of the need to consider this group in all community and development initiatives and across all sectors. Disability is mentioned in the Sustainable Development Goals (SDG) (UN, 2015) in a number of key areas (for example, goals: 4 Education, 8 Growth and Employment, 10 Inequity, 11 Accessible Human Settlements, and 17 Data Collection and Monitoring). Recognition of disability, as an important characteristic and identity for people, is implied more generally throughout the SDGs, for example with the extensive use of the word inclusion, which emphasizes the participation of people with a whole range of diverse identities (genders, sexualities, ages, ethnicities, beliefs, living situations and so on). Disability clearly comes under this banner, referring to a group of people who are often particularly excluded. However, the term 'disability inclusion' is sometimes used to emphasize the specific considerations needed to ensure equal rights for members of this group as opposed to inclusion more generally.

It is now widely agreed that the most effective way to ensure that development programmes do not exclude persons with disabilities is by adopting 'disability mainstreaming' as a matter of policy and practice. This implies including a disability component and 'lens' as part of all activities being rolled out to the general population. Of course, including a disability element into policies and plans can be tokenistic and does not ensure real changes in practice. However, it is generally regarded as a first and important step, getting awareness of an inclusive approach onto the agenda of both planners and implementers. Mainstreaming contrasts with the now outdated idea that disability issues (and people) should be dealt with in separate and segregated ways. Many governments and funders recognize a need for measurement, monitoring and evaluation of disability inclusion through the use of specific targets and indicators so that the extent of any disadvantage may be seen. The idea is that this will gradually incentivize agencies of all types to embrace approaches that are truly disability inclusive.

However, this may be a utopian ambition and there is of course a danger of tick box approaches that do not change either understanding or the underlying discriminatory attitudes which lead to stigma. Deep change and recognition of people with disabilities as equals in society requires some fundamental shifts at individual, organizational and institutional levels. The tendency to discriminate against people who are different is a strong human habit (as classically demonstrated by social psychology work on 'ingroups' and 'outgroups', Brewer, 1999). Despite these difficulties it is imperative that in relation to the understanding of children, work and harm, disabled children should be considered alongside their nondisabled peers.

Many global funders now favour, or demand, a disability component or perspective as part of their programmes and projects. This is sometimes seen to echo changes that started 30 years ago in relation to gender mainstreaming. It would now be unthinkable to disregard gender in almost any development initiative, although again this can still have a tokenistic feel. In relation to disability this journey is only just starting, and many development actors are still learning about what disability inclusive development might mean and how it might be made a reality.

Structure of the chapter

This chapter starts by outlining shifts in concepts and terminology about disability over the last 20–30 years, which have had a major impact on policy and practice globally. Essentially, all the focus now is on disability-inclusive mainstreamed programmes rather than specialist or separate initiatives. An overview of issues related to disabled people and work is also provided: the promotion of inclusive employment for adults with disabilities is currently a key topic for research and intervention. Then follows a brief overview of disability research and implementation programmes in sub-Saharan Africa (SSA), following by a specific emphasis on Ghana.

The chapter then focuses on children with disabilities as a significant minority group. The particular 'double bind' of exclusion that often affects them (as children and disabled) is highlighted. Although theoretically protected by two UN conventions – CRPD (United Nations, 2007) and the Convention on the Rights of the Child (UNICEF, 1989) – disabled children are often excluded, overlooked and neglected, both as a population of interest and materially. There is a paucity of research that proactively includes them, especially in low-and-middle income countries, where disability inclusive approaches are still relatively rare.

The chapter explores how and why disabled children (and their families) experience extreme disadvantage, which arguably may force or incentivize them to work and possibly to do hazardous work. The limited evidence that is available about disabled children and work is reviewed, and possible reasons why disabled children might be disproportionately involved in hazardous work are discussed. Finally, the chapter concludes with a plausible narrative about disabled children, work and harm in rural SSA.

A disability primer

History and changing concepts

Humans have always noticed and responded to sameness and difference in others, and some sorts of difference precipitate more particular patterns of response. Disability is fundamentally about difference, and for people perceived in this way, responses have been almost universally negative and pejorative.

The way that disability is understood has shifted fundamentally over the last 30–40 years. Before the 1980s, disability was mainly seen as a matter of individual 'deviance' from a supposed norm, in the functioning of the physical body, the senses (hearing and vision) and/or the mind (cognitive function and mental state). This was essentially a 'medical model' of disability, which sought to discover the cause and preferably a cure for the individual's 'defect', so that the person could, as far as possible, be restored to what was assumed to be a 'normal' state.

Given that most types of impairment are not curable and that they are inherent unchangeable features of the person, this view was rejected by disabled people themselves (Oliver and Barnes, 2012), who argued that these differences are better understood as common variations of the human condition. Disabled activists increasingly saw the roots of their disadvantage and marginalization as being not in their individual bodily or cognitive differences, but in how society responds to those differences. Thus, the idea emerged that disability is socially constructed (Shakespeare, 2013). It has since been elaborated and combined with a human rights approach, so the terms 'social model' (Oliver and Barnes, 2012) and or more recently 'human rights model' (Degener, 2016) are both used and espoused quite widely across the world.

A reconceptualized model of disability developed by WHO in 2001 clarifies the combination of and interaction between the different elements that contribute to a person being regarded as disabled (WHO and World Bank, 2011). Claiming to be 'biospsychosocial', the International Classification of Functioning, Disability and Health (ICF), has been helpful in promoting a more relational and interactive understanding of disability, where different factors, at both individual and societal levels, combine to generate a view of a person being seen as more or less disabled. The type and severity of their impairment is thus only part of the picture. This focus on the way that impairment (the individual difference or difficulty) and disability (society's response to the person) interact is important because it shifts the onus for change from the person (no longer expecting them to be or become 'normal'), to society. It is then others who need to adapt the environment (physical, attitudinal, communication, structural) to enable people who are different to be included in all aspects of everyday life. This shift, which expects that everyone should have access to the same services and opportunities (for example, health, education, work) is the logical follow-on from the social model described previously. Strengthened by human rights and equity perspectives, it has informed a move away from segregated provision. Implementation of these ideas of course lags behind the launch of treaties and policies but has gained momentum since the CRPD in 2007.

More recently, with growing awareness of the variety of ways in which people with disabilities are excluded, and could be included, the importance of an intersectional lens is emphasized in a small body of feminist disability theory (Garland-Thomson, 2002). Evidence is building that gender and disability often combine to produce cumulative disadvantage usually for women and girls more than men and boys: the former usually having less access to education, health care and employment than the latter. There is also a clear interaction with age, so as people grow older they tend to acquire impairments (for example deafness, blindness, mobility difficulties, dementia), and so the percentage of the population who could be described as disabled increases dramatically. Additionally, within each of the major types of functional difficulty (impairment) – mobility, hearing and communication, vision and cognitive – there is a range of severities. In fact, like gender, the category 'disabled' is not a binary (Wickenden, 2019), it is both culturally constructed and variable in context – so that an individual person may feel disabled in one situation but not in another.

Until a decade ago the prevalence of disabled people globally had been a matter of conjecture. The *World Report on Disability* was the first comprehensive review and synthesis of available data (WHO and World Bank, 2011). It suggested that a best extrapolation was that 15 per cent of the global population has a disability. The report hypothesized that with uniform and systematic identification and measurement this figure would be more or less consistent across cultures and contexts. While the 15 per cent figure is now regularly cited, in many countries, national censuses and other surveys (including general instruments such as Multiple Indicator Cluster Surveys (MICS) and Demographic and Health Survey (DHS)) have generated other, usually lower estimates.

In recent years a new method for identifying people with five broad types of 'functional difficulties', which put them at risk of being disabled, has been developed (Washington Group, 2017). The use of this method is generating more consistent figures, and there is now some evidence that 15 per cent may have been an overestimate, with a more realistic figure being around 7–9 per cent. However, there will never be one definitive figure because conceptualizations of disability vary across cultures and there are disagreements about where to locate cut-off points (that is, between disabled vs nondisabled) (Mitra, 2018; Mont, 2019).

Children with disabilities

The difficulties described earlier with collecting accurate disability figures for adults are exacerbated by the fact that children's capabilities and skills change over time. Using a definition of children as under 18 years of age, disabled children probably make up about 7–10 per cent of all children globally (UNICEF, 2013), while UNICEF (2021) estimate 240 million children have disabilities globally. Earlier work suggested that 95 million girls and boys had a moderate or severe functional difficulty or disability, of whom 13 million had a severe disability (WHO and World Bank, 2011). Percentages for younger children (under 5) are especially uncertain as in many countries child development surveillance is poor or non-existent. In parallel with the evolution of more systematic methods for measuring prevalence of adult disability mentioned previously, a tool for identifying children with disabilities has been developed (Washington Group, 2016). It can be expected that statistics about disabled children, disaggregated by type and severity of difficulty, and gender, will improve markedly in the coming years (Zia et al, 2020).

Most children with impairments will have had these from birth. However, not all impairments are identified or indeed possible to spot at birth or in the early years. Additionally, in many countries, early check-ups for vision, hearing, physical, social and cognitive development are not routine or even available. Many children's difficulties may only be noticed by families as the child fails to reach expected milestones. A smaller number of children will acquire an impairment, through illness or accident (for example, head injury, poisoning or landmines). It is unclear whether and how many children become disabled (or are further disabled) through work.

Very broadly, the pattern of types of disabilities is similar globally, although some impairment types such as dyslexia may not be identified in some contexts. Some types are more common because of the lack of health care or a disadvantageous structural or environmental situation (for example weak perinatal surveillance, lack of immunization, malnutrition, poor water and sanitation or where there is a natural disaster or ongoing conflict). These latter factors will increase the proportion of disabled children in the population. Mortality rates for disabled children may also be higher as survival is more precarious, and the needs of other family members may be prioritized (Kuper et al, 2014).

The population of children with impairments is skewed towards the mild end of the range, so there are many more children with a single, mild impairment, than there are with severe and multiple difficulties (UNICEF, 2021). Children with mild difficulties are often not labelled as 'disabled', either by the family or the child.

Disabled children come under the purview of two UN Conventions, the Convention on the Rights of the Child (CRC) (UNICEF, 1989) and the more recent Convention on the Rights of Persons with Disabilities (CRPD) (2006). However, it has been argued that children are poorly served by both (Lansdown, 2012): the UNCRC only mentions disability very briefly and in what now seems an outdated way, while the CRPD concentrates mostly on adults (United Nations, 2006).

Thus, the needs and rights of disabled children are arguably easily overlooked because they are often not seen in the community, and these children remain substantially unprotected. They are easily forgotten and exploited, and evidence suggests that they are often excluded from education, health care, social support and so on (UNICEF, 2013). Their parents and families are often among the poorest in their communities (Groce and Kett, 2013), and the additional costs incurred in having a disabled child can impact the whole family (Mitra, 2018). Disabled children and their families are sometimes referred to as experiencing a 'double disadvantage' (that is poverty and disability) (Lansdown, 2012). They are recognized now to be an overlooked group who are often to be found at the bottom of a number of population metrics relating to wealth, school enrolment and completion, and health status. Although analysis of the seemingly intractable impoverishment of families with a disabled member is an important aspect of disability research, and has made use of capability theory (Mitra, 2018), this perspective is not the predominant theoretical perspective among disability scholars (Grech, 2009). Multi-dimensional poverty is a useful lens, but human rights and equality arguments are used more universally. Perhaps not surprisingly, there has been very little work on measuring wellbeing of disabled children specifically: as Sabatello (2013) correctly observes, they are 'invisible citizens'.

In childhood research, there is often only a cursory or tokenistic mention of disability as being one of the intersecting identities that might confer disadvantage (WHO and World Bank, 2011). Often the causes and mechanism for this cumulative exclusion are not explored or dissected. There is also an assumption that disability means physical difficulties, so that the other categories of impairment (deaf, blind, cognitive, psychosocial) are not discussed or explored and these individuals' marginalization is not recognized (Wickenden and Kembhavi, 2014). In fact, the same 'hierarchy of exclusion' experienced by adults also plays out with children, leading those with physical or visual impairments to be proportionately less excluded than those with hearing, communication or behavioural difficulties.

Children's own perspectives are instructive. Sometimes children are only vaguely aware that they are labelled as disabled by others. It is not until older childhood (possibly 8–10 years+) that they start to realize that they are categorized in this way (Wickenden, 2019) or that this has a (usually negative) social meaning. Disabled children want to be treated like their siblings and have the same opportunities as them. Within their families, they are to a large extent treated like everyone else, although there is some evidence of differential treatment by parents (for example, in relation to access to food, paying for healthcare, school fees). It is quite common to hear of a disabled child being taken out of the parental home to be looked after by a grandparent, or other relative, or for one parent to refuse to support the child. In a context of poverty, this is evidence of the parents making what for them is a pragmatic choice about who is 'worthy' of investment. Assessment by children of their experiences within and outside families vary greatly, from very supportive to rejecting and cruel (Wickenden and Elphick, 2016). When they are asked about their lives, disabled children often focus on poverty rather than on their impairment or disability status per se (Wickenden and Elphick, 2016). However, not many studies have explored this in depth, so we do not know if they are talking about poverty more broadly or whether this is specific to being disabled (Feldman et al, 2013).

Although data are limited, rates of neglect and abuse of disabled children are found to be higher than for other children, sometimes by as much as four times (Handicap International and Save the Children, 2011; Jones et al, 2012; Coe, 2013). This maltreatment can occur inside the family home, in school and/or in the community. Girls with disabilities are at particular risk of abuse, including sexual abuse as they reach puberty. They may be regarded as an 'easy target' as their ability to report may (often wrongly) be assumed to be limited. Perpetrators can continue this behaviour with impunity, sometimes with families colluding in it or feeling unable to intervene (Handicap International and Save the Children, 2011). Because of the increased risks for disabled children, some parents may be very (overly) protective of them, and this can be a reason why they do not go to school, thus exacerbating their isolation and potential for social exclusion.

Disabled children themselves are aware of some of these risks to their full citizenship. If asked, they express the desire to feel safe, to go to school, to have friends, to join in with community activities and so on, in short to be 'normal' children. They see other people's attitudes to their differences as a hindrance to this, in fact they usually emphasize that they are 'normal' in more ways than they are different, and would like to be treated as such (Wickenden and Elphick, 2016).

Disability in Africa and a focus on Ghana

Awareness, research and intervention around disability are widespread and increasing throughout Africa. Some countries, such as Uganda, have been particularly active in promoting the rights enshrined in the CRPD and incorporating them into their domestic laws (Ministry of Gender, Labour and Social Development, 2006). There are centres of excellent research on various aspects of the lives of people with disabilities, including in South Africa, Uganda, Kenya and Ghana. Studies investigate a wide range of issues, from health related and clinical topics through to economic and social concerns, realization of rights, inclusive education and livelihoods and the multi-sectorial training of community-based rehabilitation workers (CBR). However, none have to date focussed particularly on the lives of children with disabilities, or specifically on their involvement in work. A search of the *African Journal of Disability* generated more than 60 papers broadly focusing on children with disabilities, but none of these dealt with working children. The majority focus on parents' experiences and concerns (for example, their difficulty with getting work as parents with caring responsibilities), on inclusive education or on aspects on disabled children's participation in community activities (Huus et al, 2021). There is some literature about young adults with disabilities and their transition into work from education and training, which suggests unsurprisingly that rates of employment are higher for those with less severe impairments (Goodall et al, 2018).

Focusing on Ghana

Demographic data and research evidence about disabled people in Ghana are both limited.[1] There have been few empirical studies to date and a search found none specifically about disabled children who work. Studies exploring traditional beliefs are discussed later; Ghana having been highlighted in the local and international press as a particularly harsh and unaccepting environment for disabled children and adults, although whether it is really more so than other West African or low/middle income countries is unclear.[2] Table 5.1 presents the available statistics on some key disability-related indicators taken from a data bank collated in preparation for a World Summit on Disability in 2018. Data for Ghana are not extensive and there is little elaboration or qualitative data to support or explain the observed patterns.

Ghana has several constitutional and legal provisions which aim to protect socially disadvantaged people including those with disabilities. There are anti-discrimination clauses covering disability in the constitution (WHO and World Bank, 2011), and the government enacted a Disability Act in 2006 (Act 715) (Asante and Sasu, 2015), signed the CRPD in 2007 and ratified it in 2012. Ratification of the CRPD is viewed as an indication of a country's commitment to protecting the rights of disabled people but does not always lead to change in practice on the ground.

Table 5.1: Some disability statistics about Ghana

	With disabilities		**Without disabilities**	
Indicator	**Male**	**Female**	**Male**	**Female**
Prevalence*	12.8%			
Primary school completion**	51%	57%	63%	65%
Secondary school completion**	23%		34%	
Participation rate of youth in formal & non-formal education & training in previous 12 months**	42%	33%	52%	41%
% Employed in informal sectors **	69%		64%	
% Living below the national poverty line**	67%		60%	

Sources: *World Health Survey (WHS) 2002–2004, see: https://dss.princeton.edu/catalog/resource1757; **2010 Population and Housing Census, see: https://www.disabilitydataportal.com/explore-by-country/country/Ghana/

Like most other countries there are a number of OPDs in Ghana for which the Ghana Federation of Disability Organisations (GFD) acts as a national umbrella. GFD seeks to influence policy on human rights, access to services, discrimination and so on. OPDs are generally viewed as being made up of people with disabilities (so 'of them') rather than organizations who might be working 'for them' such as non-governmental organizations (NGOs). This is an important distinction: the OPDs are seen to be representing people with disabilities and aim to influence policy and practice directly, espousing a global mantra used in the disability movement 'nothing about us without us'.[3]

Disability, poverty and work

It is generally accepted that for adults, being in work is good for both health and wellbeing (Waddell and Burton, 2006). For any given individual this will, of course, depend on the type of work and the working conditions. Depending on their role, how well the job is matched to their skills and whether they feel valued and supported in the workplace, an individual will feel more or less committed and comfortable with their work. Feelings of contributing to family and community are important elements which can increase an individual's sense that they are a valued member of the community and can participate alongside others. Not surprisingly, the reverse is also true – a lack of work can negatively affect health and wellbeing (WHO and World Bank, 2011).

For many years there has been anecdotal evidence that families with a disabled member tend to be poorer than their neighbours (Trani and Loeb, 2012), and empirical evidence around this important point is now mounting (Groce and Kett, 2013). So, households with a disabled member are likely to be disproportionately located in the lowest wealth quintiles. There appears to be a vicious cycle, where being poor increases chances of being disabled, and conversely being disabled increases chances of being poor. This seems to hold true across contexts and cultures, in both high- and low-income settings (Groce and Kett, 2013). There is some evidence that in the very poorest communities, households containing people with disabilities are not much poorer than others (because everyone is poor). However, when countries or communities move out of poverty, disabled people and their families are often left behind. This has been called the 'disability development gap' (Groce and Kett, 2013).

The mechanisms for and nuances of the interrelationship between disability and poverty are not entirely clear and vary culturally, but a key element is that disabled people have much lower rates of employment. When they do get work, it is predominantly informal, low paid, insecure and low status, such as in small family businesses, agriculture and small-scale craft work (Mizunoya and Mitra, 2013). One explanation often given for this is disabled children and young people's low school enrolment and completion rates, resulting in them becoming adults with low literacy and other skills. However, even for those who do attain qualifications, including up to degree level, levels of employment are disproportionately low, and they tend to have particular difficulty entering the formal labour market and accessing higher status jobs (Mitra et al, 2013). Other factors associated with poverty are likely to include: the extra health costs of having an impairment; opportunity costs in relation to lost earnings for the disabled person themselves not working and for others (often women) not being able to work outside the home because of caring responsibilities; smaller social networks and reduced social capital (because of stigma and discrimination driven by negative beliefs and attitudes about disability).

Both families and employers often have very low expectations about the ability of disabled people to work (Wickenden et al, 2020). Additionally, disabled person themselves may have low self-esteem sometimes called 'internalised oppression' (Reeve, 2014) and reduced aspirations because of negative attitudes from others and a lack of encouragement to find work. As a result, many disabled people who could work do not or are employed in occupations that are well below their potential or are not of their choosing.[4] Once labelled disabled (either as a child or when acquiring impairment later), they very often start on a journey of stigma, discrimination and marginalization. There are reportedly high rates of neglect and abuse of disabled people in the workplace (particularly of women and girls) (Mizunoya and Mitra, 2013): they can be forced to do work that is difficult for them, or be bullied and otherwise maltreated.

Disabled people face various types of barriers in the labour market and the workplace, and these are usually classed as: environmental, attitudinal, communication related and institutional (or structural) (Van Ek and Schot, 2017). In formal workplaces, 'accessibility' is often assumed to be about mobility impairment and physical infrastructure (for example, lack of ramps, rails, lifts, toilets). These are relatively obvious and there are easy adaptations to understand and provide. However, required changes in communication modes and formats (for example, sign language, easy read, pictures, slower pace) or attitudinal changes may be less visible and more difficult to achieve satisfactorily.

The relative disadvantage experienced by people with different impairments can result in a 'hierarchy of impairments' (Deal, 2007). In many spheres of life, people with physical and visual impairments are relatively less disadvantaged than other disabled people. Impairment group identities also intersect with gender so that often men with physical or visual impairments are to be found as leaders of OPDs while disabled women are less likely to be seen in prominent positions. People with cognitive, psychosocial-emotional and communication difficulties, and those with multiple impairments (for example, deafblind), are consistently the most excluded from society, including from the labour market (Mitra, 2018).

These barriers help account for the fact that most disabled people who work, do so close to home, for example, in a small family business or in agriculture (WHO and World Bank, 2011). Here, a form of 'natural inclusion' can sometimes be seen, where the person is well known, understood and supported in a role that suits their strengths. Someone with no mobility impairments (but who has a sensory impairment such as deafness or blindness, or a cognitive impairment such as learning difficulty) may be included in a physical job with little apparent difficulty. However, there may be no additional safety, protection or appropriate support in place in these informal work arrangements. Evidence about work conditions for people with disabilities is increasingly becoming available, but most studies are still from the Global North.

There is paucity of information from SSA about disabled people's involvement in agricultural work specifically, although we know anecdotally that many people do work or 'help out' on family farms.

From segregation to inclusion

Until relatively recently, programmes to facilitate disabled people's entry into the workplace focused on placement in separate and protected work settings (WHO and World Bank, 2011). Such 'sheltered workshops' provided a limited range of work – for example, arts and crafts, carpentry, basket weaving and so on (although in recent years some have moved to more contemporarily work such as computing and desk top publishing) – and some people, such as those who entered as teenagers after dropping out of school, might remain for many years. There was generally little choice as to the trade or specialism the person learnt, and virtually no career progression or personal development beyond perhaps some initial on-the-job training. Segregated workplaces like these are now regarded as counter to the CRPD and are gradually being closed. Some people are being supported or mentored to enter the labour market and take on 'real' jobs (Van Ek and Schot, 2017). This transition can be tricky, as many will have worked in protected environments for decades and will naturally be anxious about moving to a new less protected workplace.

The notion of 'inclusive employment' captures the idea that disabled people should and can find work within the open labour market and be supported to do so. In some settings this is gaining support among both the disability and business communities. Working with the ILO, a global movement of large, formal-sector employers has emerged – the Global Business Disability Network (GBDN) – that recognizes the positive business case for employing disabled people.[5] In its most progressive form, this is not driven by charity, corporate social responsibility (CSR) or virtue signalling, but by seeing that disabled people have the skills to work, that diversity within the workforce is a positive influence, and that disabled people make-up a substantial proportion of consumers, so being inclusive is good for business. Being 'disability-friendly' should be advantageous for firms in a number of ways. This approach is increasing in many countries, as are research and interventions at different levels to improve disabled people's employment opportunities and outcomes (Wickenden et al, 2020).

Inclusive employment as part of the mainstream job market is favoured by many disabled people, who in some situations are becoming more vocal in advocating for their right to decent work (as laid out by the CRPD in article 27 on Work and Employment). It is also supported by global treaties (United Nations, 2006; Hashemi et al, 2017) and national disability policies in many countries.

In theory, most or arguably all jobs could and should be accessible to disabled people if the individual's skills are matched to the job and the appropriate adaptations are made. Clearly the kind of work that someone could do, if exclusion and discrimination were removed, is still to some extent dictated by their impairment type and severity, and the particular adaptations and 'reasonable accommodations' (the technical term for supportive changes to the environment) that might be needed. The CRPD (2006) dictates that disabled people should not be prevented from working because of lack of adaptations (for example, a lift for a wheelchair user, sign language interpreter for a deaf person, braille or an adapted IT software for blind person and so on). Hopefully, their work will also be of interest to them.

Research about and with disabled children

There are some clear parallels between the discourses over the last 20–30 years in the two multidisciplinary arenas of Childhood Studies and in Disabilities Studies (Wickenden, 2019). The new 'sociology of childhood' kick-started the idea that children are a socially constructed group whose agency is often overlooked and about whom assumptions of incompetence and vulnerability are often (wrongly) made (James et al, 1998; Skelton, 2008; Tisdall and Punch, 2012). These ideas have been applied, but not without controversy, in various settings in the Global South, where concepts of children and childhood may be very different (White and Choudhury, 2007). However in these settings, as elsewhere, there has also been increasing recognition of the importance of engaging with children about matters that concern them (Hart, 2008). This recognizes children as being competent and having agency (Hunleth, 2011). Nevertheless, it is still often the case that children have a lower status than others in their families and communities (and in policy), and have little say or choice about what happens. Their voices are muted or drowned out by others; sometimes their views are gathered but in ways which are tokenistic (James, 2007). Participatory and inclusive approaches to research with children have gathered pace in the last decade or so (Ansell et al, 2012; also see Chapter 3, this volume). But to date, there are very few studies with or about disabled children in the Global South that really engage them directly and ask for their views about their lives and what could improve their wellbeing (Wickenden and Kembhavi, 2014; Zuurmond et al, 2016).

Methodologically, the same kinds of debates take place about how to do research with disabled children as with children more broadly (see Chapter 3, this volume). However, there is the added need to consider how to make studies sufficiently inclusive to enable disabled children to participate in meaningful and equal ways to their non-disabled peers (Thompson et al, 2020). Arguments about participation of children centre around seeing them as agentive, having optimistic expectations of what they can do, providing choice and using methods that will appeal to them in their cultural context. With appropriate support there is also potential to include them as 'peer researchers' in some or all aspects of studies (including design, data collection, analysis, dissemination) (Kellett, 2010). Discussions have also centred on whether the same methods can be used with children as with adults, and when and why these methods might need to be adapted (Punch, 2002). All these aspects are applicable and perhaps amplified for disabled children (Hansen et al, 2014). Judgements about competence are similarly relevant, although rigid age-based stipulations are even more likely to be problematic for disabled children.

The specific adaptations to create accessibility (called reasonable adjustments) that might be needed to make research inclusive of all children are many and varied. This will depend on the type of functional difficulty that the children have. Access needs should be anticipated, inquired about and provided for as a basic right and as part of the planning and budgeting of activities (Wickenden and Lopez Franco, 2021). If this is not done then accidental, unwitting exclusion can occur, which risks exacerbating the marginalization already experienced by disabled children. They are regularly not included in consultations with the 'mainstream' population of children, who are increasingly asked for their views on a variety of topics including work, school, home life, their hopes for the future and so on (National Children's Bureau, 2012; Wickenden and Elphick, 2016).

Finally, it is important not to patronize children by underestimating their skills or put them off by expecting too much of them without providing appropriate levels of support and so inadvertently excluding them. Disabled children are highly sensitive to both of these possibilities and given the chance will say what they can and can't do, what they are interested in and what help they need from others in order to join in (Thompson et al, 2020).

Disabled children and work

There is a large body of literature on child labour that discusses the various types of work that children do, and whether children's work should be regarded as unacceptable under any circumstances or whether a more nuanced and conditional view should be taken (Boyden and Ling, 1998; ILO, 2017; Bourdillon and Carothers, 2019). The age at which work is permitted varies across countries and there are also varying definitions for 'hazardous' work and 'light' work. It is noticeable that consideration of disabled children and work is almost completely missing. However, this does not mean that these children are not working. It is likely that many of them do work, but that data are not collected on disability status.

So, what can we say about disabled children and work? Search engine queries produce little on the topic. There is a related body of work on the employment concerns of parents of disabled children (who find it hard to get work because of their extra caring responsibilities), but practically nothing on the children themselves working. Training schemes and apprenticeships for adolescents with disabilities do feature and there is currently heated debate about whether these should be inclusive, that is part of programmes for all young people, or whether there is a place for specialist, segregated programmes to prepare young people with disabilities for work. The current trend, guided by the principles in the CRPD, is to move away from the latter and towards 'mainstreaming' of training and employment.

There is some literature on children and injuries in the workplace, but this does not make explicit links with potentially permanent disabling consequences of such injuries (for example, Salminen, 2004; Rhaman, 2018). Thus, the marginalization and exclusion of disabled children in many societies is echoed in the research arena, where they are largely invisible.

Groce (2004) in her overview of various aspects of the lives of disabled young people (aged 10–24 years) points out that although official data about employment is largely lacking, we know anecdotally that they work informally:

> Most young people with disabilities world-wide do work, although they usually are officially listed as unemployed. Millions work outside the home, doing menial tasks or working as street beggars. Millions more work long hours within the family home or on the family farm. (Groce, 2004, p 21)

Probably the most visible form of work that disabled children do in contexts of poverty is begging, but again this has not been explored in detail except in one study about disabled adults in Ethiopia (Groce et al, 2013).

Two studies, from Mexico and India respectively, specifically address the issue of disabled children working. Villalobos et al (2017) in Mexico carried out a large quantitative study that shows that children with functional difficulties (often used as a proxy for disability) are disproportionately more likely to be working than other children. They find that of all disabled children, those with have psychosocial or emotional difficulties are the most likely to be working. This is not surprising as members of this group are likely to be physically unimpaired (and so arguably more able to do physical work), may have been excluded from school because of their behaviour or may have been considered difficult to teach or include in the classroom. In their analysis, the authors express uncertainty about the direction of causation of their findings but reflect on the links between poverty, school enrolment and child labour. They suggest: 'Worrisome indications of a vicious cycle of limited education and poverty for those who do child labor, perhaps especially for children who have a functioning difficulty or disability' (p 381). They conclude by suggesting that: 'Guaranteeing educational opportunities and respect for the rights of children with severe functioning difficulties and disability is essential to achieve development of their full potential' (p 387).

Rakshit et al (2019) report on an econometric analysis of educational attainment and child labour status among disabled children in Tamil Nadu, India. The findings suggest that whether or not a child works depends on their type of impairment. They show that physically and mentally disabled children are more likely to attend school than those with other impairments (deafness and blindness) and, surprisingly, to participate less in child labour than children with multiple disabilities. This finding is quite difficult to interpret. It might possibly be because adaptations in school for these two groups might be perceived as easier to provide by the schools, whereas adaptations for deaf and blind children may be too difficult. Disabled children living in urban areas are more likely to go to school and are less likely to drop out compared to their rural counterparts, and this may be because schools are physically nearer, whereas a long walk or other journey to a rural school might be impossible. No gender difference in workforce participation was found but more boys go to school, disabled girls more often being regarded as not worthy of the investment required for school attendance. It is likely then that disabled girls are working within the home, but this is not evidenced. They also found an interaction with child marriage, revealing that those who were married were more likely to be working, thus they also suggest a vulnerability of disabled children to child marriage as well as working rather than attending school. One might interpret this as parents making a short-term decision to gain some financial advantage by arranging marriages for their disabled children, rather than a long-term and uncertain investment in their education. It is suggested that the Tamil Nadu Disabled Persons Act (2007) has not made a marked difference to the educational achievements of learning-disabled children, perhaps because children with this type of disability are among the most excluded.

Rakshit et al (2019) point to some evidence from ILO that disabled children who are not in school are not involved with income-generating activities or household tasks, but the authors argue that in contexts of poverty (in India), disabled children *are* working rather than going to school. It is not clear whether their lack of school attendance is linked to the other reasons often cited for disabled children's non-attendance (as well as economic ones) such as stigma and discrimination, and lack of a welcoming and inclusive approach by the schools.

Groce (2004) makes an important point about the visibility and recognition of nondisabled children's work activities, as a route towards later more formal employment and independence as adults, compared with the view of disabled children for whom:

> Identical work is frequently viewed as an end in itself for those with disabilities, or as a way of helping to justify the costs of their food and housing. Such work, even when it is of great financial significance to the household, may go unnoticed by economists, local communities and even by their own families. Moreover, many young people with disabilities working on the family farm or assembling piece-work in the kitchen, may have their work brought to the marketplace by others who receive the credit and collect the wages for that work. (p 21)

Conclusion

Most countries have signed human rights conventions and put laws and policies in place to promote the rights and protection of disabled people, but often these are not enacted or implemented sufficiently strongly. Thus, there is a tension between the treaties, laws and policies, and what actually happens on the ground. Long-standing attitudes and beliefs, which have tended to define people with disabilities as abnormal, deficient, and sometimes as not human, still prevail. Disability activists and practitioners often cite this as a major frustration, where people's lived experience is very different and much more inequitable than indicated by the global and national rhetoric of human rights and inclusion. Often these bold statements are not backed up with sufficient local training, awareness raising and resources. Traditional and local practices which exclude or exploit those with disabilities can still be found, perhaps more so in rural areas and informal workplaces.

In rural SSA, families with a disabled member are likely to be disproportionately poorer and disabled children often do not attend or complete school. There is also a potential paradox, where disabled adults have difficulty getting into employment, but disabled children may be working. Much of their work is likely to be informal, perhaps alongside their siblings and peers, but possibly with worse conditions, or less attention paid to their welfare and protection. They may be working instead of going to school, rather than in parallel with school attendance as is common among their peers. However, the facts are extremely sparse.

The global promise of the CRPD and the CRC is that disabled children should be regarded like other children, as citizens with rights and as people who should be considered in the mainstream development agenda (UNICEF, 2011). Empirical data about the lives of disabled children, including their engagement with work, the nature of their work, and their experience of harm are urgently needed. Such information could inform policymaking, planning and resourcing of initiatives designed to benefit all children, but which currently regularly exclude disabled children. In this context, the edu-workspace framework discussed in Chapter 4 (this volume) is valuable.

Based on the very limited data from SSA, and what is available from other regions, it is possible to construct a plausible narrative about disabled children, work and harm in rural SSA as follows:

> Disabled children in rural SSA likely represent 7–15 per cent of population of children and tend to live in poorer households. They live with a range of types and severity of disability, and access to specialised services is extremely limited. These children are more likely to be working *instead of* going to school, in contrast to non-disabled children who often work *alongside* attending school. Disabled children, particularly girls, will do more hours of domestic work than their school attending siblings. Disabled boys and girls will accompany parents or older siblings to the family farm or business, and may choose, be encouraged or forced to work. Families who are poor are more likely to be involved in more hazardous forms work, and there is an increased probability that their disabled children will do hazardous work and suffer harm which may lead to further permanent impairment.
>
> Families understand their children's capacities and will identify work that is appropriate to them. Tasks, equipment and processes are likely to be adapted to enable a disabled child to join in; nevertheless, a disabled child is likely to need more supervision and protection than other children. At the same time, negative attitudes and assumptions of incompetence are likely to encourage disabled children to want to 'prove their worth', by getting involved in work wherever and however they can, even if the work is hazardous.

This narrative identifies multiple opportunities for further research on the lived experience of disability, work and harm. Any such research must certainly be built around the voices and perspectives of disabled children, their families and their communities.

But if we assume for the moment that the narrative is broadly correct, the question is, what are the implications for policy and programmes that seek to address harmful children's work in rural SSA. In other chapters of this volume (for example, Chapter 4) the trade-offs between school and work are highlighted. The argument is that parents' and children's perspectives on these trade-offs will likely reflect the often-poor quality of education available in rural areas. This will only be exaggerated when it comes to disabled children, as they are unlikely to have access to appropriately adapted and inclusive education. Further, attending school may well involve exposure to additional harm (bullying, physical abuse and so on) by teachers and/or students.

Two things are clear. First, the particular challenges faced by disabled children working in agriculture in rural SSA are unlikely to be addressed by the kinds of value chain interventions (Chapter 6, this volume), or living wage/living income initiatives (Szyp, 2020), that are now widely promoted to address child labour. Second, disabled children and the families are being buried under multiple layers of failing social policy which has not embraced a disability inclusive approach across sectors, a situation that only the state is in a position to address.

Notes

1 There is very limited literature on disabled children in Ghana. Kassah et al (2012) in a small qualitative study identified four types of abuse experienced by disabled children: social, capital (killing), physical and emotional. They link abuse to traditional belief systems. Ghana has been cited as one of the countries practicing killing of disabled children.

2 See BBC television documentary *The World's Worst Place to be Disabled, 2015,* https://www.bbc.co.uk/programmes/b064449w

3 See for example: International Disability Alliance (IDS) – https://www.internationaldisabilityalliance.org

4 See Global Business and Disability Network (GBDN) – http://www.businessanddisability.org

5 http://www.businessanddisability.org/

References

Ansell, N. et al (2012) 'Learning from young people about their lives: using participatory methods to research the impacts of AIDS in southern Africa', *Children's Geographies*, 10(2), pp 169–86.

Asante, L.A. and Sasu, A. (2015) 'The Persons with Disability Act, 2006 (Act 715) of the Republic of Ghana: the law, omissions and recommendations', *Journal of Law, Policy and Globalization*, 36, pp 62–8.

Bourdillon, M. and Carothers, R. (2019) 'Policy on children's work and labour', *Children & Society*, 33(4), pp 387–95.

Boyden, J. and Ling, B. (1998) *What Works for Working Children?* Florence: Innocenti Publications International Child Development Centre and Rädda Barnen.

Brewer, M.B. (1999) 'The psychology of prejudice: ingroup love and outgroup hate?', *Journal of Social Issues,* 55(3), pp 429–44.

Coe, S. (2013) *Outside the Circle: A Research Initiative by Plan International into the Rights of Children with Disabilities to Education and Protection in West Africa.* Dakar: Plan West Africa.

Deal, M. (2007) 'Aversive disablism: subtle prejudice toward disabled people', *Disability & Society*, 22(1), pp 93–107.

Degener, T. (2016) 'A human rights model of disability', in Blanck, P. and Flynn, E. (eds) *Routledge Handbook of Disability Law and Human Rights.* London: Routledge, pp 47–66.

Feldman, M.A. et al (2013) 'Inclusion of children with disabilities in mainstream child development research', *Disability & Society*, 28(7), pp 997–1011.

Garland-Thomson, R. (2002) 'Integrating disability, transforming feminist theory', *Feminist Foundations*, 14(3), pp 1–32.

Goodall, J. et al (2018) 'Stigma and functional disability in relation to marriage and employment in young people with epilepsy in rural Tanzania', *Seizure*, 54, pp 27–32.

Grech, S. (2009) 'Disability, poverty and development: critical reflections on the majority world debate', *Disability & Society*, 24(6), pp 771–84.

Groce, N. (2004) 'Adolescents and youth with disability: issues and challenges', *Asia Pacific Disability Rehabilitation Journal*, 15(2), pp 13–32.

Groce, N. et al (2013) *Disabled Beggards in Addis Ababa. Employment Working Paper No. 141.* Geneva: International Labour Organization (ILO).

Groce, N. and Kett, M. (2013) *The Disability and Development Gap. Working Paper 21.* London: Leonard Cheshire Disability and Inclusive Development Centre, University College London.

Handicap International and Save the Children (2011) *Out from the Shadows: Sexual Violence Against Children with Disabilities.* London: Save the Children UK.

Hansen, A.M.H., Siame, M. and van der Veen, J. (2014) 'A qualitative study: barriers and support for participation for children with disabilities', *African Journal of Disability*, 3(1), Article 112, pp 1–9.

Hart, J. (2008) 'Children's participation and international development: attending to the political', *The International Journal of Children's Rights*, 16(3), pp 407–18.

Hashemi, G., Kuper, H. and Wickenden, M. (2017) 'SDGs, inclusive health and the path to universal health coverage', *Disability and the Global South,* 4(1), pp 1088–111.

Hunleth, J. (2011) 'Beyond on or with: questioning power dynamics and knowledge production in "child-oriented" research methodology:', *Childhood*, 18(1), pp 81–93.

Huus, K. et al (2021) 'Barriers and facilitators to participation for children and adolescents with disabilities in low- and middle-income countries: a scoping review', *African Journal of Disability*, 10, p 771.

ILO (2017) *Global Estimates of Child Labour: Results and Trends, 2012–2016*. Geneva: International Labour Organization.

James, A. (2007) 'Giving voice to children's voices: practices and problems, pitfalls and potentials', *American Anthropologist*, 109(2), pp 261–72.

James, A., Jenks, C. and Prout, A. (1998) *Theorizing Childhood*. Cambridge: Polity Press.

Jones, L. et al (2012) 'Prevalence and risk of violence against children with disabilities: a systematic review and meta-analysis of observational studies', *Lancet*, 380(9845), pp 899–907.

Kassah, A.K., Kassah, B.L.L. and Agbota, T.K. (2012) 'Abuse of disabled children in Ghana', *Disability & Society*, 27(5), pp 689–701.

Kellett, M. (2010) 'Small shoes, big steps! Empowering children as active researchers', *American Journal of Community Psychology*, 46(1–2), pp 195–203.

Kuper, H. et al (2014) 'The impact of disability on the lives of children; cross-sectional data including 8,900 children with disabilities and 898,834 children without disabilities across 30 countries', *PLOS One*, 9(9), e107300.

Lansdown, G. (2012) *Using the Human Rights Framework to Promote the Rights of Children with Disabilities: Working Paper. An Analysis of the Synergies Between CRC, CRPD and CEDAW*. New York: UNICEF.

Ministry of Gender, Labour and Social Development (2006) *National Policy on Disability in Uganda*. Kampala: Ministry of Gender, Labour and Social Development, Government of Uganda.

Mitra, S. (2018) *Disability, Health and Human Development*. New York: Palgrave MacMillan.

Mitra, S., Posarac, A. and Vick, B. (2013) 'Disability and poverty in developing countries: a multidimensional study', *World Development*, 41, pp 1–18.

Mizunoya, S. and Mitra, S. (2013) 'Is there a disability gap in employment rates in developing countries?', *World Development*, 42, pp 28–43.

Mont, D. (2019) 'Differences in reported disability prevalence rates: is something wrong if I don't get 15%?', *Washington Group on Disability Statistics Blog*, 22 August. Available at: https://www.washingtongroup-disability.com/wg-blog/differences-in-reported-disability-prevalence-rates-is-something-wrong-if-i-dont-get-15-120/ (Accessed 26 November 2022).

National Children's Bureau (2012) *The Viper Project: What We Found*. London: National Children's Bureau Research Centre.

Oliver, M. and Barnes, C. (2012) *The New Politics of Disablement*. Basingstoke: Palgrave Macmillan.

Punch, S. (2002) 'Research with children: the same or different from research with adults?', *Childhood*, 9(3), pp 321–41.

Rakshit, I. et al (2019) 'Educational attainment and child labor status among disabled children in Tamil Nadu, India', *Journal of Developing Areas*, 53(3), pp 183–98.

Reeve, D. (2014) 'Psycho-emotional disablism and internalised oppression', in Swain, J. et al (eds) *Disabling Barriers: Enabling Environments* (3rd edn). London: SAGE Publications, pp 92–8.

Rhaman, S. (2018) 'Occupational injuries among children in Bangladesh', *International Research Journal of Social Sciences*, 7(10), pp 17–20.

Sabatello, M. (2013) 'Children with disabilities: a critical appraisal', *The International Journal of Children's Rights*, 21(3), pp 464–87.

Salminen, S. (2004) 'Have young workers more injuries than older ones? An international literature review', *Journal of Safety Research*, 35(5), pp 513–21.

Shakespeare, T. (2013) *Disability Rights and Wrongs Revisited*. London and New York: Routledge.

Skelton, T. (2008) 'Research with children and young people: exploring the tensions between ethics, competence and participation', *Children's Geographies*, 6(1), pp 21–36.

Szyp, C. (2020) *Living Wage, Living Income, and Child Labour-Free Zones: Arguments and Implications for Children's Work. ACHA Rapid Review No. 1*. Brighton: Action on Children's Harmful Work in African Agriculture, IDS.

Thompson, M., Cannon, M. and Wickenden, M. (2020) *Exploring Critical Issues in the Ethical Involvement of Children with Disabilities in Evidence Generation and Use. Office of Research – Innocenti Working Paper WP 2020–04*. Florence: UNICEF Office of Research – Innocenti.

Tisdall, E.K.M. and Punch, S. (2012) 'Not so "new"? Looking critically at childhood studies', *Children's Geographies*, 10(3), pp 249–64.

Trani, J.-F. and Loeb, M. (2012) 'Poverty and disability: a vicious circle? Evidence from Afghanistan and Zambia', *Journal of International Development*, 24(S1), pp S19–52.

UN (2015) *Sustainable Development Goals*. New York: United Nations.

UNICEF (1989) *Convention on the Rights of the Child*. New York: UNICEF.

UNICEF (2011) *UNICEF Calls for Children with Disabilities to Be Included in All Development*. New York: UNICEF.

UNICEF (2013) *The State of the World's Children 2013: Children with Disabilities*. New York: UNICEF.

UNICEF (2021) *Seen, Counted, Included: Using Data to Shed Light on the Well-Being of Children with Disabilities*. New York: UNICEF.

United Nations (2006) *Convention on the Rights of Persons with Disabilities and Optional Protocol*. New York: United Nations.

United Nations (2007) *Convention on the Rights of Persons with Disabilities*. New York: United Nations.

Van Ek, V. and Schot, S. (eds) (2017) *Towards Inclusion: A Guide for Organisations and Practitioners*. Netherlands: Light for the World, Mission East and ICCO Cooperation.

Villalobos, A. et al (2017) 'Child labor and severe functioning difficulties and disability in Mexican children and adolescents 5–17 years of age', *Salud Publica De Mexico*, 59(4), pp 380–8.

Waddell, G. and Burton, A.K. (2006) *Is Work Good for Your Health and Well-Being?* Norwich: The Stationary Office.

Washington Group (2016) *Child Disability Question Set: Child Functioning Module*. Hyattsville, Maryland: Washington Group on Disability Statistics.

Washington Group (2017) *Short Set of Disability Questions*. Hyattsville, Maryland: Washington Group on Disability Statistics.

White, S. and Choudhury, S. (2007) 'The politics of child participation in international development: the dilemma of agency', *The European Journal of Development Research*, 19(4), pp 529–50.

WHO and World Bank (2011) *World Report on Disability*. Geneva: World Health Organization.

Wickenden, M. (2019) 'Disabled versus nondisabled: another redundant binary', in Twum-Danso Imoh, A., Bourdillon, M., and Meichsner, S. (eds) *Global Childhoods Beyond the North-South Divide*. Cham, Switzerland: Palgrave, pp 123–44.

Wickenden, M. et al (2020) *Accelerating Disability Inclusive Formal Employment in Bangladesh, Kenya, Nigeria, and Uganda: What are the Vital Ingredients?* Brighton: Institute of Development Studies (IDS).

Wickenden, M. and Elphick, J. (2016) 'Don't forget us, we are here too! Listening to disabled children and their families living in poverty', in Grech, S. and Soldatic, K. (eds) *Disability in the Global South: The Critical Handbook*. Cham, Switzerland: Springer International Publishing, pp 167–85.

Wickenden, M. and Kembhavi, G. (2014) 'Ask us too! Doing participatory research with disabled children in the Global South', *Childhood*, 21, pp 400–17.

Wickenden, M. and Lopez Franco, E. (2021) 'Chapter 24: Don't leave us out: disability inclusive participatory research – why and how?', in Burns, D., Howard, J. and Ospina, S. (eds) *The SAGE Handbook of Participatory Research and Inquiry*. London: SAGE Reference.

Zia, N. et al (2020) 'Adaptation and validation of UNICEF/Washington group child functioning module at the Iganga-Mayuge health and demographic surveillance site in Uganda', *BMC Public Health*, 20(1), p 1334.

Zuurmond, M. et al (2016) 'Childhood disability in Turkana, Kenya: understanding how carers cope in a complex humanitarian setting', Article a277, *African Journal of Disability*, 5(1).

6

Value Chain Governance and Children's Work in Agriculture

Giel Ton, Jodie Thorpe, Irene Egyir and Carolina Szyp

Introduction

The vast majority of children's work in rural Africa is in agriculture (Dachille et al, 2015) and, with the exception of what is used for home consumption, all agricultural produce – whether sold and consumed locally, or exported – moves through a value chain. All such chains link processes of production, trade, processing and distribution, and determine how costs, benefits and risks are distributed. It follows therefore that children's work should never be seen as simply a farm- or household-level phenomenon, isolated from the broader web of economic and social relations, institutions and politics. For some crops and livestock products, these relations, institutions and politics will be predominately local, national or regional; but in the case of commodities such as coffee, cocoa, tea and sugar, they reach around the globe, linking working children to some of the world's largest markets and most powerful corporations.

Because much of the work performed by rural children is embedded in agricultural value chains, and all such chains are governed in one way or another, the core argument developed in this chapter is that an understanding of value chain governance can help identify entry points for research on children's work and for interventions to address harmful work. Although it is widely accepted that private sector actors, from local traders to international agri-business firms, can (and must) contribute positively to development, the reality of market competition and stakeholder interests still presents huge challenges (Scheyvens et al, 2016). We start with the assumption that agricultural value chain actors have some room for manoeuvre that allows them to influence the extent and nature of children's harmful work (CHW). However, the question is which actors, in what kinds of value chains and in what settings, are likely to have the motivation to exercise such influence?

In this chapter we introduce the concepts of agricultural value chain and value chain governance in order to highlight the embedded nature of children's work. Value chains are governed through combinations of coordination modalities between producers, traders, processors, retailers, consumers, and other stakeholders. A typology of such governance modalities is proposed and used to identify entry points for research on children's work and for value chain-based interventions to address CHW. For the purpose of this chapter, interventions are understood to be all activities undertaken with the objective of addressing CHW: as such, they are social processes that aim to affect the lives of individuals and groups, and to enable and constrain their social strategies (Long and van der Ploeg, 1989). The examples that we use in the chapter are predominately from the West African cocoa sector. However, the eight value chain governance modalities can be observed in agricultural value chains more generally.

Value chains

The term value chains is used in both the professional and development literatures to refer in a generic way to linked processes of production, trade, processing and distribution (Kaplinsky and Morris, 2001; Roduner and Gerrits, 2006; M4P, 2008; Donovan et al, 2015). In the academic literature, the term global value chains (GVC) is more common, with this literature focusing particularly on chain governance – that is, who exercises power to influence the distribution of risks and rewards (Gereffi et al, 2005; Lee et al, 2012)? GVC analyses are common in the manufacturing sector (including garments and automobiles), but less so in agriculture that in much of the Global South is dominated by smallholders and intermediate traders. Other academics prefer the term global production and distribution networks (Yeung and Coe, 2015), which extends the analysis beyond vertical value chain linkages, and highlights the heterogeneity of company strategies and differences in territorial outcomes of these strategies. Recently, the term food chain analysis has become popular (FAO, 2014; Lentink, 2016), which covers production, distribution and consumption within the 'food system', often with more emphasis on nutrition and health. In this chapter, we follow the development literature and use the term value chain to refer to the actors linked in the production, trade, processing and distribution of specific agricultural commodities, among whom there is coordination in relation to quantity, quality and transaction terms. We analyse these value chains with a focus on power relations between these actors and the resulting dynamics that influence the inclusion, and terms of inclusion, of rural households as suppliers of agricultural products and labour, with a special focus on implications for CHW.

Value chain maps depict the flow of a product from upstream to downstream through a chain of intermediating actors (Hellin and Meijer, 2006; KIT and IIRR, 2010; Frederick, 2019). At each link in the chain there is horizontal coordination between similar actors (for example, farmers, traders, processors and so on) and vertical coordination with the other links, both upstream and downstream. Around these transacting parties, there is a network of other stakeholders that indirectly influences their transactions. Figure 6.1 provides a simple schematic of stakeholders involved in a generic value chain and differentiates between 'chain actors' involved in transactions and 'chain supporters' who influence their room for manoeuvre. Both types of stakeholders are, in turn, constrained by the agronomic, economic and legal realities of the 'chain context'. There are multiple ties, interdependencies and power relations between these different actors, which create emergence, synergies, resilience, uncertainties, surprises and other system dynamics.

We focus our attention on those links in the value chain where, under conditions of interdependency, smallholders, local agents, farmer groups and traders exchange agricultural products or related services, and in so doing interact around quality attributes, risks and rewards. We are particularly interested in the roles that agri-business – both large multinational agribusinesses and small and medium-sized enterprises – plays in and around these links. Understanding the roles and motivations of agribusiness in value chain governance will be critical in addressing CHW.

Power relations between value chain actors can manifest themselves in multiple forms. Power is expressed not only directly (for example, the buying company imposing specific terms of trade) but also indirectly through relations with chain supporters and institutions in the chain context. For example, large companies have more political influence than smaller firms in how export or import procedures, quality control parameters or labour legislation are codified and regulated; they have more power to influence, shape and/or defend their interests. Other elements of power that are important for CHW are entrenched in norms that structure gender, race and other social relations in and around a value chain (ICI, 2011; ILO, 2018; Constant et al, 2020).

In this chapter, we are primarily interested in farming areas in sub-Saharan Africa (SSA), where children's work is most prevalent, and second in the local, national and international contexts in which consumers make their decisions around food, such as in urban areas in Africa. The role of importing countries in the Global North is especially significant for value chains involving cocoa, coffee and cotton, where certification schemes are important and discussions around CHW are particularly active (ICI, 2011; ILO, 2018).

Figure 6.1: Schematic of actors involved in a value chain

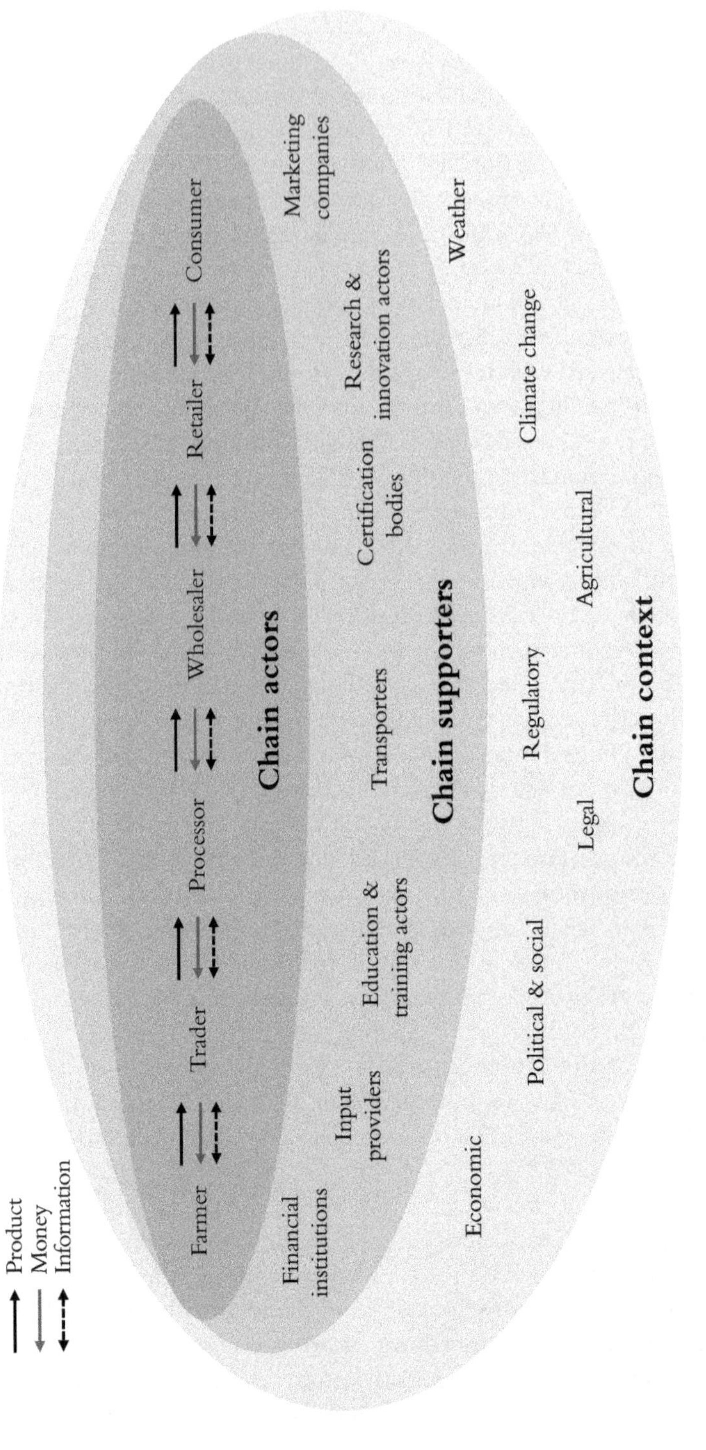

Product
Money
Information

Farmer
Trader
Processor
Wholesaler
Retailer
Consumer

Chain actors

Financial institutions
Input providers
Education & training actors
Transporters
Certification bodies
Research & innovation actors
Marketing companies

Chain supporters

Economic
Political & social
Legal
Regulatory
Agricultural
Climate change
Weather

Chain context

Source: KIT and IIRR (2010)

Value chain governance

In linking agricultural value chains to children's work and CHW we focus on value chain governance and coordination dynamics. Coordination is embedded in specific institutional arrangements, such as spot markets, contract farming and certification programmes (Williamson, 2002). We call these coordination mechanisms 'governance modalities'. Governance modalities are structuring properties (Giddens, 1979): they structure the flow of knowledge and information in the chain, and the distribution of risks and rewards (Handayati et al, 2015). In so doing, they both enable and constrain the agency of actors regarding the characteristics of a product transacted in the value chain. These modalities often make use of a combination of (sometimes conflicting) formal and informal rules and regulations that shape how actors discuss or negotiate issues, including those related to CHW. In the case of smallholder agriculture, informal, unwritten norms and rules are generally more common than formal ones.

Value chain interventions

Many national governments, international organizations and procuring companies undertake activities – 'value chain interventions' – that directly or indirectly address CHW. Some such interventions are directed to improve the implementation of national and international laws and regulations, others promote voluntary codes of conducts and some are localized direct actions to prevent brand damage. Ultimately, most of these interventions try to change the behaviour of households (for example, to keep their children away from activities that are considered hazardous) or companies (for example, to change hiring practices or reduce children's exposure to hazards and their experience of harm).

To analyse the way that interventions try to change behaviour at micro-level, following Michie et al (2011), we focus on the relative capabilities, opportunities, and motivations of the actors involved. However, we want to emphasize that these micro-level behaviours are conditioned by macro- and meso-level structures in the value chain context, depicted as rules and resources in Figure 6.2, that enable and constrain the capacity of actors to effectively change their behaviour. These structures mean, for example, that many households or children do not have the opportunity or capability to act in a particular way, even when they are motivated to do so.

A typology of value chain governance modalities

In this section, we present a typology of governance modalities present in agricultural value chains. We argue that this typology provides insights into

Figure 6.2: Actor behaviour conditioned by access to rules and resources

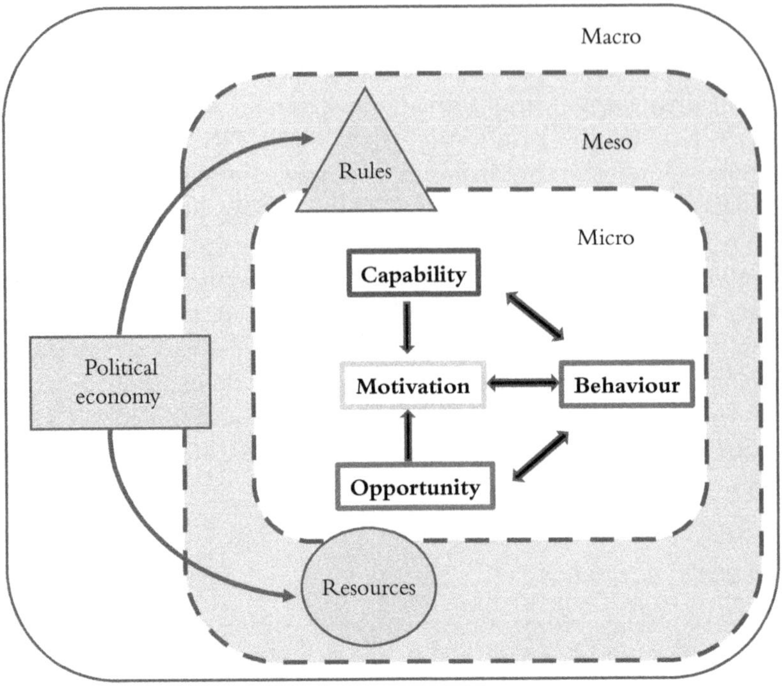

Source: Modified from Ton et al (2021), based on Michie et al (2011)

useful entry points for research on children's work in African agriculture and can help identify interventions that could be used to address CHW. Any particular value chain is likely to involve several of these modalities.

The typology consists of eight modalities, which vary based on the complexity of the arrangements they employ to coordinate value chain actors, and the web of actors and supporters involved. These differences in turn reflect the nature of the coordination challenge being addressed, which depends in part on the degree of interdependency between chain actors. Where product specifications are simple, where little input is needed from buyers, and where scarcity or uncertainty is limited, such as with many staple commodities, there will be little or no coordination (Gereffi et al, 2005). On the other hand, value chains that involve highly specific (and highly valuable) product characteristics, or require investment in specific assets and complex information exchange, imply a higher degree of interdependency between chain actors. As a result, businesses will engage in more complex modalities to coordinate the value chain and secure supply (Ménard, 2004; Gereffi et al, 2005; Chamberlain and Anseeuw, 2019). Although they come with high transaction costs associated with implementation, monitoring and enforcement, such arrangements are intended to better align the incentives of value chain participants and minimize the risk of opportunistic behaviour (Ménard, 2004; Chamberlain and Anseeuw, 2019).

However, agricultural value chains do not only involve economic relationships. They are also embedded in a web of social and political relations and institutions that encompass value chain actors, supporters and other stakeholders (Henderson et al, 2002; Bolwig et al, 2010). The interactions between these multiple and heterogenous actors often generate non-linear outcomes, which cannot be attributed to a single mechanism, but which emerge from interactions between actors (Hammond, 2009; Gardeazabal et al, 2021). The implication is that where such outcomes are undesirable or problematic, such as in the case of CHW, no single actor can drive change independently of other stakeholders (Bitzer et al, 2013). However, the more complex the configuration of stakeholders, the more likely they will have differing interests, values and priorities which will need to be reconciled if undesirable non-linear outcomes are to be addressed (Dentoni et al, 2018; Thorpe et al, 2021).

In Figure 6.3 we present eight value chain governance modalities, which are differentiated by (1) the number of different stakeholders involved, reflecting the differing interests, values and priorities that the arrangements seek to reconcile, and (2) the institutional and administrative complexity of the rules and agreements, reflecting the balance between the need for coordination and the transaction costs involved. These modalities are evident to varying degrees across African agriculture and are present in both 'traditional' and 'modern' value chains.

Modality 0: self-consumption

This modality comes into play when households produce their own food and do not source inputs like seeds or fertilizers externally. It is seen primarily in remote areas where markets are absent or where households also have non-farm cash-generating activities and only produce part of their food themselves. With this modality, the product is not traded in a market so there are no other chain actors involved. Decisions about children's work are made by the household and/or the child, and interventions to reduce CHW will need to provide the household with resources that modify their capabilities, opportunities and/or motivation. For example, new information about the toxicity of plant protection measures or long-term health risks due to carrying heavy loads could motivate households to change the types of work done by children.

Modality 1: direct exchange

When a farmer sells the product directly to a consumer, such as their neighbours, without any intermediation, they are engaged in direct

Figure 6.3: Value chain governance modalities according to the number of stakeholders involved and degree of institutional and administrative complexity

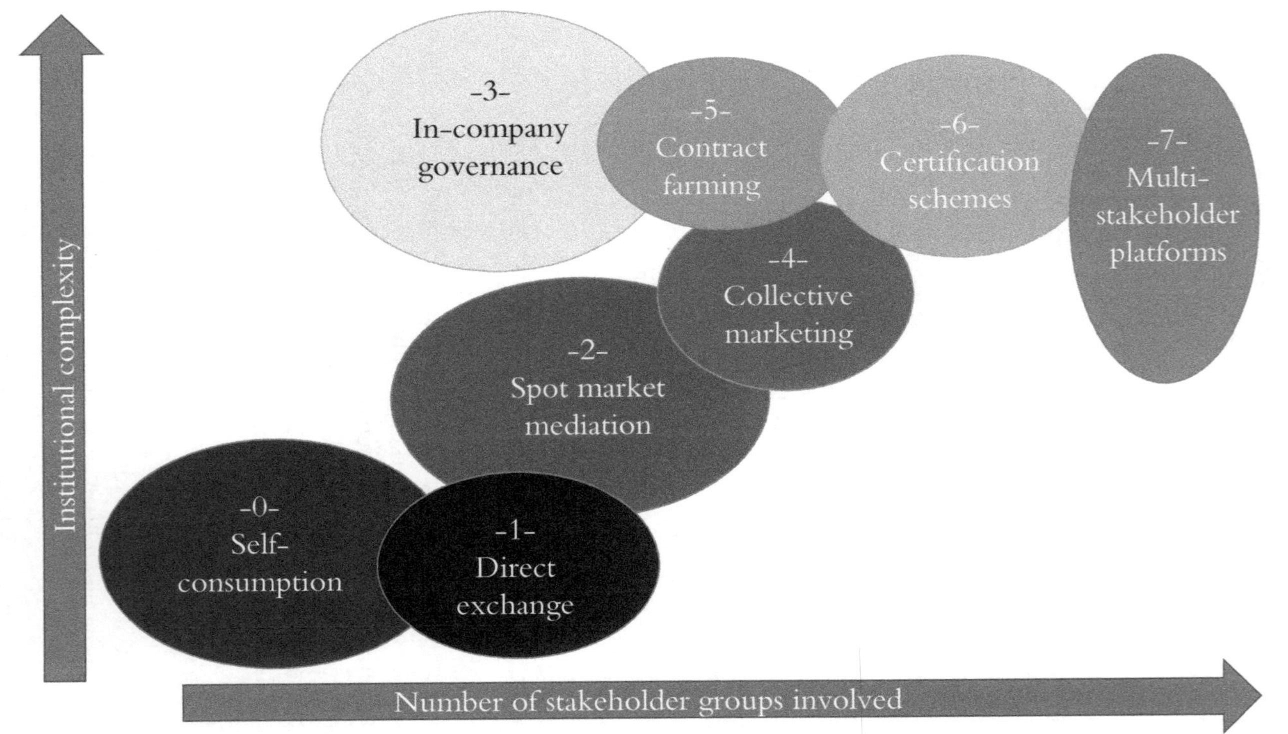

Source: Author

marketing. With this modality the coordination between the two value chain actors is direct and all aspects of the transaction, including any involvement by children, are potentially open for discussion. Generally, this modality will follow or reflect local norms and traditions.

Interventions to address CHW could target the capabilities, opportunities and motivation of producers and/or buyers. New information could change not only the motivation of the producing household to modify its practices but also the motivation of the buyer to undertake or repeat the transaction. Ultimately, the buyer could look for alternative ways to procure the product.

Modality 2: spot market mediation

If buyers and sellers of a product transact through an intermediary, then price is the main coordination mechanism. This is a classic spot market transaction. The intermediary is generally a trader but can also be an electronic trading platform or auction. With relatively straightforward institutional arrangements and multiple buyers and sellers, this modality differs significantly from direct marketing. Spot market mediation is not confined to rural market centres. It is also the dominant modality in situations where farmers sell without prior obligations to passing traders at the farm gate. In this case the farmer can switch to another buyer, as he or she will not have incurred expenses specific to a particular transaction or buyer (Gereffi et al, 2005). The dynamics of spot market mediation changes when repeated transactions over time generate a level of trust that shifts toward the direct marketing modality.

In what follows we identify two broad sub-types, each providing a somewhat different context for value chain interventions to address CHW. However, a major assumption about spot markets and CHW, for which the evidence remains inconclusive (Ravetti, 2020), is that there is a relationship between market price and the prevalence of CHW.

Anonymous spot market transactions

Anonymous spot market arrangements are of interest because small-scale producers are very commonly involved in them. Such producers are not formally organized or trading with large companies; rather they operate in informal and trader-driven contexts, which are primarily influenced by the price that other buyers offer. The nature of the interaction between farmer and trader varies in relation to the type of product, frequency of interactions (for example yearly, weekly, daily) and the place where the interaction takes place (for example, in open food markets, auctions and commodity exchanges). The information that the buyer has about the quality of the product is limited to what is visible: attributes such as the social conditions of production are impossible to determine. Thus, anonymous spot-market transactions do not provide an entry point for discussions about whether or how children are involved in production. Because CHW is not a visible product attribute, farmers are unlikely to face (or fear) a price penalty.

If it is assumed that poverty is the primary driver of children's work and CHW (Basu and Van, 1998; ILO, 2022), the focus should be on addressing structural factors that depress prices or otherwise reduce household income. Interventions might include, for example, measures that increase the bargaining power of farmers, such as increasing access to market information, or a greater diversity of markets and/or to financial services (which could enable storage in anticipation of higher prices). Another entry point could be strengthening the ability of households to withstand shocks by improving land rights, irrigation and/or other services. More resilient households are likely to be better able to negotiate with traders.

A different approach would be to change the chain context, through for example, stricter competition policy or legally enforced floor prices which might reduce the bargaining power of buyers. For example, Ghana has a system of regulated minimum prices for cocoa and licensed buying companies (Vellema et al, 2016). In 2020, in an effort to combat poverty among cocoa farmers and to increase the farmer's share in the value added of the global chocolate market, the governments of Ghana and Côte d'Ivoire jointly introduced the living income differential (LID). The LID consists of a levy of US$400 to be used to stabilize and sustain farm gate prices in case the international price drops (Boysen et al, 2021). Systems that raise or stabilize farm prices are present in many countries, and can be politically sensitive. For example, in India, farmers mobilized in 2020–21 to keep the decades-old system of floor prices to stabilize the market for essential commodities (Meijerink and Joshi, 2021). They feared that commercial traders would be able to distort spot markets, resulting in short-term price increases but a long-term price decline with negative impacts on farm income (Jodhka, 2021).

Spot market with repeated personal interactions

The second type of spot market also involves mediated exchanges in which price is the primary coordination mechanism but where repeated transaction over time result in the development of relationships between buyers and sellers (Webster, 1992). Although not requiring explicit and formalized governance modalities such as contracts or other types of pre-harvest arrangements, these conditions allow for some degree of negotiation, cooperation and traceability.

In addition to the interventions identified previously, with repeated transactions there is at least some potential for additional measures that reward producers – for example, through a price premium – for addressing CHW.

However, better on-farm labour conditions do not change the resulting product in any observable way, which makes it easy for transacting partners to 'cheat'. Interpersonal relations can support a learning and trust-building process between buyer and seller, and lower both the risk of opportunistic behaviour and transactions costs to some extent (Williamson, 1975; Goldbach et al, 2003; Cadilhon et al, 2007). To really reduce this risk of opportunistic behaviour, a certification-like governance modality linked to a credible verification system, would be needed (see Modality 6).

Modality 3: in-company governance

Not all companies rely on market transactions to procure or sell their products – for some, these transactions occur 'in-house'. Compared with the modalities already discussed, this means that most links in the value chain where market transactions would take place are eliminated (so-called vertical integration), and objective market prices are replaced by normative internal pricing considerations. Generally, the goal of such an arrangement is to ensure resources are used most efficiently (Shinde, 2018). In-company coordination requires transactions and coordination between different units of the same firm or holding. This modality can involve relatively complex institutional arrangements, but generally include few stakeholder groups.

The ability to address CHW in the context of in-company governance depends to a large extent on the degree of separation between management and ownership. While management exists in theory to achieve the owners' goals, in practice, managers have their own incentives which mean their decisions and behaviour may not always align with the interests of owners. Thus, the incentives and interests of both management and owners, and how they might be influenced, must be considered. This is as true for efforts to address CHW as for any other social or environmental issue.

In-company governance in public firms

The shares of stock-listed firms are owned by individuals and/or institutions who are legally separated from the firm itself. Depending on their objectives, shareholders groups, such as pension funds, mutual funds and hedge funds, can pressure companies to focus on short-term strategies to maximize shareholder profits or longer-term concerns such as social or environmental sustainability.

Although direct involvement of these firms in agricultural production is relatively rare, some operate large farms or estates producing tea, sugar or biofuel-crops. In SSA, due to the land tenure regimes, direct foreign investment in large-scale agricultural production is less common than in Latin America, but may be on the rise (Havnevik et al, 2011; Batterbury and Ndi, 2018). These firms may combine some in-house production with an outgrower scheme (see Modality 5). Reputational risk is probably the most important motivation for public firms to consider and act on children's work and CHW in their supply chains. For example, in Organisation for Economic Cooperation and Development (OECD) countries, the advocacy strategy of non-governmental organizations (NGOs) to address CHW in agricultural value chains often includes public naming and shaming.

In public firms, shareholders influence management by asking for transparency, mainly in financial reporting, but, increasingly relating to the broader environmental, socio-economic and/or governance dimensions of business performance. Such reporting requirements provide incentives for companies to develop corporate social responsibility (CSR) programmes that may pilot approaches that showcase their social commitment, including initiatives to address CHW. CSR initiatives reflect the voluntary behaviour of companies to go beyond the legal requirements of the country in which they operate (Jamali and Mirshak, 2007). In some cases, what started as philanthropy-motivated CSR policies have subsequently become in-company requirements to monitor social conditions of production.

In-company governance in family-owned firms

Family-owned firms are less subject to the short-term demands of equity markets. Especially in small and medium enterprises, the owners of the firm are often also the managers. This closer relationship of owners and workers, and a direct relationship with farmers, may motivate them to support social causes that transcend profit-seeking. Equity and management responsibility are often transferred to the next generation within the same family, which may enable the firm to pursue a long-term vision.

While there is little evidence or literature, our expectation is that family-owned firms, with less pressure to respond to short-term interests of shareholders, may be in a better position to address CHW in their agricultural supply chains. However, because of limited transparency and public scrutiny, these firms can also be particularly secretive and ruthless, and many large family-owned firms that are active in African agriculture are also politically connected. In relation to policy aimed at addressing CHW this can play out in one of two ways. On the one hand, these firms may be more pro-active in implementing policy; and on the other hand, they may also in a better position to hinder the implementation or effectiveness of interventions.

In-company governance in parastatal firms

The picture changes again when the ownership of the company is partly or entirely public. When parastatal firms function in domestic markets, the close link between the business and the state provides opportunities for these firms to influence public policy but also to be very directly influenced by policy and politics. Trade unions often have an important presence in parastatal firms and play a role in fostering discussions of the social relations of production, including children's work and CHW. Therefore, it might be expected that implementation of international conventions and national labour regulations, including those relating to children's work, would be faster and easier in parastatal firms. It is important to note, however, that this is not so straightforward. For example, in Ghana the Ghana Cocoa Board (COCOBOD) often publicly denies the existence of child labour in the cocoa sector in spite of the formal Ghanaian government policies (see Chapter 10, this volume) and significant coverage of the problem in the local media (Okali et al, 2022).

Modality 4: collective marketing

Collective marketing is used by small-scale farmers to compete more effectively, and might include additional storage, processing or packaging of the crop, with the costs shared by the collective. These marketing groups often start small and develop activities to improve the conditions of production and marketing of specific crops. In relation to the typology, this modality can be characterized as involving more complex institutional arrangements and having interactions with a more diverse group of stakeholders. This is particularly the case when such initiative become larger and start to have subgroups of members with slightly different interests because they live in different geographical areas or use different farming systems.

When collective marketing groups are small, the village is the logical entry points for interventions to address CHW. Village authorities often have an important role in conflict mediation and may be informed about intra-household conflicts related to children's work or abuse. However, village-based groups tend to have an automatic membership based on geographical residence; they tend to include everyone as member. As a village will likely include households engaged in multiple activities, the leaders are not necessarily the most knowledgeable about the work and working conditions within any particular value chain (for example, fisheries, high-value horticultural crops), and not be best placed to facilitate discussion of issues related to CHW.

The major feature of collective marketing, relevant for CHW, is the existence of an institutionalized coordination and communication mechanism: a leader or leadership group that can speak for a group of farmers. In many rural areas, economic farmer organizations develop into important forms of social capital (Ton, 2015). Collective marketing groups provide a platform to discuss issues in addition to marketing, and can play a bridging role between rural communities and development NGOs (Bebbington,

1997; World Bank, 2007). Interventions to address CHW can use this coordination and deliberation mechanism to start a discussion or collect data about the incidence of CHW. In the following, we distinguish between two (somewhat overlapping) types of collective marketing that differ in the way that membership is defined and the intensity of social interaction. Collective marketing groups are sometimes linked to other governance modalities, such as contract farming (Modality 5), certification schemes (Modality 6), and spot market mediation (Modality 2).

Village-based marketing groups

Farmers within a particular village may work together around a specific commodity or value chain. They often start with activities to make themselves more attractive to urban traders, such as arranging storage or transport, or agreeing a place and time to sell, and if successful, move to collective marketing or facilitating procurement of agricultural inputs or other products. Other groups are organized around processing or post-harvest value-addition (for example milling, coffee or cocoa washing and fermentation) and then decide to sell these products collectively.

Village-based groups are often informal due to the limited number of members and the relatively simple processes of coordination and decision making. Awareness of the founding history of these groups is key to understanding how they create trust and organizational capability through collective action (Lyon, 2000). They often emerge from pre-existing networks of individuals who trust each other, or as a result of development interventions of NGOs. For example, Ton et al (2010) report the varying origins of village-based farmer organizations active in sunflower production in Uganda, including groups that started as fellow believers, choir groups and extension groups (formed, for example, as Farmer Field Schools).

Economic farmers organizations

When village-based groups grow, for example through merging with others, and become more institutionally complex, they can be considered as economic farmer organizations. These include cooperative-like farmer organizations as well as not-for-profit associations and farmer-led commercial enterprises (formally registered companies with farmers as co-owners). Economic farmer organizations develop specialized functions and begin to require an explicit commitment from members. In so doing, they cease to be all-inclusive. Due to the multiplicity of tasks, these organizations involve members in interactions and transactions during most of the year, which makes them an important form of social capital. They may be constituted formally as cooperatives, as quasi-cooperatives or informal groups.

Cooperative procurement of inputs such as seed and agrochemicals, hiring of vehicles and determining output price is well known among cassava, fish and meat processors in southern Ghana. Often, they aim to bypass local markets and send their products directly to traders, processors or retailers in urban areas. Managing collective marketing at scale is not easy, and many groups face challenges due to opportunistic behaviour of members. However, with good management they can avoid the dangers of side-selling so that group functions are maintained. Collective marketing implies coordination and communication about the quantity and quality of the product being sold by members or purchased from members, and often implies a division of tasks and responsibilities in negotiations about these attributes (Ton, 2015).

Most collective marketing groups ask for only a small contribution from members and do not compensate board members for their time. Therefore, often the better-off farmers are elected to leadership positions, as they can more easily cover the related expenses. Some cooperatives (for example, Kuapa Kokoin Ghana) play an important role in the efforts of multinational chocolate companies to address child labour in the cocoa sector (Nestle Cocoa Plan and ICI, 2017). Training and capacity building efforts aim to increase the effectiveness of these organizations in, for example, identifying, monitoring and addressing child labour and issues that threaten to deprive children of education, health care and development (Tulane University, 2015). The stronger and larger the groups, and with increasing ability to communicate with members, the more attractive they are to buyers or stakeholders, or as potential participants in other value chain governance modalities such as contract farming (Modality 5) and multisector partnerships (Modality 7).

Modality 5: contract farming

Contract farming is a commercial relationship between a firm and a group of farmers through which farm production is purchased in advance in exchange for specific services and other benefits (Ton et al, 2018). Although principally a commercial initiative, contract farming is also a way to overcome the challenges that smallholder farmers face when linking to markets or accessing inputs and services. As a governance modality it operates at an intermediate level of institutional complexity and involves a group of stakeholders that is more heterogenous than in the modalities discussed so far. Contract farming concerns an amalgam of different value chain actors – a firm and farmers, often with a financial institution and/or service provider (for example, providing ploughing, irrigation and/or extension).

Contract arrangements and provisions can range from strict to lax. This wide variety reflects different contexts, crops, quality attributes, type of services provided and power relations. Generally, when a new contract farming modality is initiated, the relations between the value chain actors are quite loose. But over time, due to repeated cycles of contracting and re-contracting, the modality leads to the self-selection of farmers, farmer organizations and contracting firms (Ton et al, 2018). Each faces specific constraints related to opportunities, capabilities and motivation (Michie et al, 2011), which are partly the result of the particularities of the contract attributes proposed (Sartorius and Kirsten, 2007; Abebe et al, 2013; Bellemare and Lim, 2018).

Similar to the collective marketing modality, contract farming provides a coordination mechanism that can be used to reach farming households in relation to CHW. When contractual relations are formal, this modality allows for the specification of requirements relating to children's work, with only products that comply with these requirements being acceptable to the procuring firm. Depending on the scale of the arrangements, compliance with these CHW-related attributes can be controlled by the farmer group, the contracting firm, or through a relevant certification scheme (Modality 6). In contrast, when contractual arrangements are informal, as they often are, this modality will have similar entrance points for work on CHW as discussed for Modality 1 (direct exchange). We therefore distinguish two sub-types to represent the ends of a continuum.

Informal resource-providing agreements

As is common with some cash crops, buyers may prefer certain varieties and provide seeds in advance, sometimes on subsidized terms or on credit. Buyers may also provide packaging material, or cash in advance of the harvest to pay seasonal workers. When the price is not the only coordination mechanism, but additional services and expectations play a role, the arrangement between producers and buyers moves towards a pre-harvest agreement – a common informal contract farming modality especially in vegetable production (Fafchamps, 2004). The services provided vary considerably: for example, in African savannah areas, tractor services and seeds are commonly part of a package of services provided to oil seed producers. Sometimes, this informal contracting is known as sharecropping, with the owner contributing seeds, inputs and market relations and the farmer contributing land and labour, while the harvest is split between them.

The interpersonal relations on which these arrangements are built can be heavily power-laden, as reflected in the fact that this modality can sometimes be forced on farmers due to previous indebtedness. Often, the individual with whom the farmer has a contract plays a pivotal role in the social networks that help households withstand shocks. These dense interpersonal relations and mutual dependencies have implications for whether and how CHW can be addressed when this modality is part of a value chain. Informal agreements make it possible to trace the product and, in principle, allows communication about the (un)desirability of certain kinds of labour relations, with the threat to withhold resources from the producer when he or she does not comply with the quality attributes. However, informal contracting might very well be inequitable and involuntary, and force households to do things that may negatively affect the wellbeing of their children. For example, children might be required to help during harvest time not only on the land worked by their parents, but also on farm of the buyer.

Formal resource-providing contracts

Although covering only a relatively small volume of Africa production, the use of formal pre-harvest contracts is increasing, reflecting the growth of urban populations and changes in the food systems that serve them. The urban food market is replacing self-consumption, principally because urban areas have higher incomes than rural areas (Tschirley et al, 2015; Reardon et al, 2019). Also, processed foods have penetrated both rural and urban markets in SSA: Tschirley et al (2015) reported that 56 per cent of urban, and 29 per cent of rural household food expenditures (in value terms) went to processed foods. Processing firms generally prefer to purchase agricultural products of a uniform quality and look for stable prices to be able to better plan their transformation activities and assure the volume they can deliver to supermarkets. This creates an incentive to find preferred suppliers and shorten the chain of intermediation. Both processors and supermarkets tend to work with medium or large producers, even if they start initially with smallholders (Dolan and Humphrey, 2000). When they work with smallholders at scale, they almost always combine two governance modalities: contract farming and collective marketing by farmer groups (Ton et al, 2018).

Processing firms face more public scrutiny than informal village-based agents, which provides additional entry points to address CHW. Formal, written agreements codify the rights and obligations of the different parties and increase transparency to third parties. For example, to prevent negative publicity, and to comply with the demands of international buyers, the Horticultural Crops Development Authority (HCDA) in Kenya developed a 'model contract' that clearly specifies risks, rewards and conflict resolution mechanisms. A company is required by the 1995 export order to use formal contracts and to adhere to certain practices that are specified in the HCDA Code of Conduct (Waarts and Meijerink, 2010). The same processing firms will often manage a national brand and because of this may be susceptible to negative publicity in the local media if it becomes known that children are involved in their operations.

Modality 6: certification schemes

Certification is the formal attestation or confirmation of certain characteristics of a product, person or organization, often based on some form of external review, assessment, or audit. Certification programmes emerged in the 1980s in response to consumer demands for sustainability and fairness: they represent a governance modality with a high level of institutional complexity and involvement of many different stakeholder groups.

The first certification programmes concerned organic production, especially in OECD countries. Later in the 1990s, Fairtrade emerged in response to the low prices received by producers of tropical commodities and the need to support collective action of smallholders. At the same time, the Forest Stewardship Council (FSC) was launched to protect forests and regulate the timber trade, and Rainforest Alliance developed a certification scheme aimed to reduce biodiversity loss. The retail sector in Europe also started certification schemes around food safety and good agricultural practices, which resulted in the EurepGAP and later GLOBALG.A.P. schemes (GLOBALG.A.P., 2022). Despite this diversity, certification schemes have some common characteristics, in large part as a result of the work of the International Social and Environmental Accreditation and Labelling organization (ISEAL), a global platform representing those voluntary standards or schemes that comply with specified credibility requirements (ISEAL Alliance, 2022).

In agriculture, certification schemes are mainly focused on tropical export crops, especially banana, cocoa, coffee, tea, sugar and palm oil. For some crops, the share of certified production has increased rapidly: for example, in 2016 it was estimated that 35 and 44 per cent of cocoa produced in Ghana and Côte d'Ivoire respectively was covered under one or more certification schemes (ISEAL, 2019). The European General Food Law Regulation of 2002 gave an immense boost to certification because it mandated a traceability system and made distributing companies and retailers legally responsible for the products they sell (European Parliament and Council of the European Union, 2002).

Field-level certification

Most certification schemes make a distinction between indirect, group-based certification through an internal control system (ICS), and direct certification of production on an estate or plot. Almost invariably, smallholder production is certified through group membership. The required ICS can be managed by a private firm (for example, a trader or processor) or by the farmer group. Certification schemes have different auditing modalities and critical control points that take this distinction into account. The audit function will primarily look at the credibility of the ICS through the way that internal control is organized and registered. Auditors have a list of control points, some of which relate to children's work. Generally, these will be based on the ILO definitions of child labour. But increasingly, they introduced requirements that ask for processes to address child labour and refrain from considering the detection of child labour as a reason to reject a product or decertify a producer.

Certification of medium and large producers is directly monitored by a third-party verification body. Here rural workers are the central focus, and among others, auditors consider social issues related to workers and families that live on-site, as well as certain environmental issues (Rainforest Alliance, 2018). Because medium and large producers generally have a high level of control over land and production processes, the power of the firm to comply with the requirements of the certification body is greater than in smallholder group certification. Correspondingly, the threat of decertification based on child labour related criteria is greater for medium and larger producers. This implies a more direct influence of the abolitionist approach on larger producers, with all its associated intended and unintended effects.

Certification schemes collect large amounts of data that offer a potentially useful entry point for both awareness raising and evaluation of interventions related to CHW (Chapter 3, this volume). One of the most CHW-relevant interventions that emerged in the certification community is the Child Labour Monitoring and Remediation System (CLMRS). At the end of 2019, Nestlé implemented CLMRS in 87 cooperatives covering 45,000 households with an estimated 18,000 children considered to be in child labour (Nestle, 2019). Remediation activities are at the heart of CLMRS, including access to education, health services, awareness of laws and so on, and also encompass supporting children, their families and communities to remove children from risky situations (Nestle, 2019). In 2022, Nestlé announced the Income Accelerator programme that introduces a cash incentive paid directly to cocoa-farming households for certain activities such as enrolment of children in school and implementation of good agricultural practices.[1]

Landscape-level certification

The discussion of certification and sustainable development has gradually evolved from a focus on field and household level effects, to the higher-level systemic effects (Ruben, 2019; Termeer et al, 2019). Value chain actors operate in large social systems and field-level certification is often patchy. Therefore, especially when ecological outcomes are key, certification schemes need to work on a larger scale, with additional stakeholders. Some certification schemes are experimenting with landscape-level effects and jurisdictional approaches, which involve not only the producers of a commodity of interest, but also the wider village or region. International climate funds may trigger the emergence of these more 'systemic' impacts of certification, for example, by requiring forest management plans that imply the involvement of users on a geographical scale larger than the plots that are being certified, or irrigation and water management plans that require consent from upstream and downstream users.

The fact that these landscape-level approaches consider the wider social system around a production site or process make them particularly conducive to multistakeholder processes (Modality 7). Thus, in addition to direct value chain actors, other interest groups and government agencies working on health and education, biodiversity conversation and water management will influence the governance of the social attributes of a crop, product or production process. This system-wide focus may help to create the incentives for individual firms or households to change their practices in order to benefit children's wellbeing. CLRM-type monitoring systems increasingly work at landscape-level, and are considered one of the most promising interventions to address hazardous child labour (ICI, 2011; ILO, 2018).

Modality 7: multistakeholder partnerships

Multistakeholder partnerships or platforms (both terms are used, abbreviated as MSP) are institutionalized, but voluntary collaborations between private, public and/or civil society stakeholders that seek sustainable solutions to complex, systemic challenges. First popularized at the World Summit on Sustainable Development in Johannesburg in 2002, MSPs exist in sectors from water, energy and health to food and agriculture. In the agri-food sector, MSPs have been defined as 'a process of interactive learning, empowerment and participatory governance that enables stakeholders with interconnected problems and ambitions, but often differing interests, to be collectively innovative and resilient when faced with the emerging risks, crises and opportunities of a complex and changing environment' (Brouwer et al, 2016, p 14).

As such, MSP can be characterized as a value chain governance modality with a medium to high level of institutional complexity and involving a very large number of different stakeholder groups. MSPs are intended to achieve transformational change through convening stakeholders and facilitating exchange between them. They aim to foster an enabling environment for collaboration that stimulates new investments, innovations, policies and activities in response to collective challenges. They use networked governance (Rhodes, 1997; Jessop, 2000; Thorpe et al, 2021) to respond to collective action problems which arise from conflicting short-term interests between groups or individuals and which discourage mutually beneficial cooperation (Olson, 1965). The theory is that through dialogue, collaboration and the experience of working together, stakeholders build trust and mutual respect that promotes problem-solving, rather than bargaining based on individual interests as the key decision-making style (Bache, 2008). Existing studies have classified MSPs based on either structure and arrangements, or the domain or purpose (Treichel et al, 2017; HLPE, 2018). By focusing on the primary purpose, we discuss three analytical sub-types that enable identification of entry points for addressing CHW. For all sub-types, the first entry point is the direct involvement of civil society groups and/or representatives of working children.

Norm and standard-setting multistakeholder partnerships

Norm and standard-setting MSPs are primarily designed to develop, strengthen and enforce global or national norms and standards in a particular industry, sector or crop (Buckup, 2012; Beisheim and Simon, 2016). They are generally industry-led efforts, developed in response to perceived public-sector failures to promote appropriate social and/or environmental practices. Typically, they are dominated by industry leaders and/or civil society.

There are several such MSPs within the food and agriculture sector, including: the International Cocoa Initiative (ICI), the World Cocoa Foundation, Roundtable for Sustainable Palm Oil, Bonsucro, World Banana Forum, Global Roundtable for Sustainable Beef, the Better Cotton Initiative, the Ethical Trading Initiative, the Global Coffee Platform and 4C. Some of these use product certifications as a value chain governance modality, but they also tend to have a broader portfolio of activities addressing sustainability challenges. Large multinational companies are key participants, and through their market power and influence, they seek to enforce agreed standards among chain intermediaries and farmers. Entry points to address CHW include the introduction of specific principles, commitments and/or reporting requirements, the provision of training on CHW for members and auditors, and general industry awareness raising.

Action and service-oriented multistakeholder partnerships

Action and service-oriented MSPs are primarily designed to deliver goods and services or implement policies, programmes and projects (HLPE, 2018). They are common in the food and agriculture sector, with examples including Grow Africa, the Global Food Security Cluster, Global Agenda for Sustainable Livestock, Kudumbashree, German Initiative on Sustainable Cocoa, New Alliance for Food Security and Nutrition, Malawi Tea 2020 and the Farm to Market Alliance.

While these MSPs may be involved to some degree in standard-setting, knowledge co-generation and capacity building, they are more directly outcome- and impact-focused (Buckup, 2012), with goals that focus on social or environmental issues (potentially including CHW), or particular geographies or value chains. Unlike industry norm and standard-setting MSPs, which are more prevalent in high-value export crops, these MSPs cover both export crops and domestic staples. Membership is typically based on actors' ability to contribute resources (financial or other) (Witte et al, 2005), and may include governments, private sector operators, donors, UN agencies and farmers groups, among others.

Action and service-oriented MSPs work through facilitating joint action, innovation and pooling of resources (Buckup, 2012) to deliver 'positive externalities' that are undersupplied through the market (Witte et al, 2005). These positive externalities may include policy change, better natural resource management, value chain upgrading, innovation and resource mobilization (Witte et al, 2005; Pattberg and Widerberg, 2014; Muoio and Rimland Flower, 2016; HLPE, 2018). They also seek to improve the allocation of scarce resources by avoiding duplication of effort.

Operationally, action and service-oriented MSPs are often set up in specific national and sub-national geographies, even if they are under a global umbrella organization. For example, while the Farm to Market Alliance is a global initiative, implementation takes place in specific value chains and countries. Entry points for addressing CHW include providing technical know-how and support, for example on measures to identify, address and mitigate harmful work, or to improve value chain competitiveness, and enable higher wages (for example, Malawi Tea 2020; Malawi, 2020; Platform, 2015)). These MSPs may also facilitate access to finance for investment and innovation, as well as knowledge exchange, and support for pilot projects to address CHW.

Multistakeholder partnerships for knowledge sharing and learning

MSPs for knowledge sharing and learning tend to start from the perspective that solutions already exist but are not being used (Loveridge and Wilson, 2017). The focus, therefore, is on awareness-raising via reports, conferences and digital media. They may also involve an element of building trust and respect between different stakeholder groups. In some cases, these MSPs also focus on knowledge co-generation and capacity building (HLPE, 2018), by bringing together stakeholders with relevant information and experiences. This is seen to be especially important in complex contexts, where transdisciplinary and participatory approaches may be particularly important (HLPE, 2018).

In the food and agriculture sector, examples include the Pan-Africa Bean Research Alliance (PABRA), the African Orphan Crops Consortium (AOCC), the Southern Africa Food Lab (SAFL), and the Voice for Change

Partnership (V4CP) Programme. Awareness raising and knowledge sharing are the most obvious entry points for intervention around CHW, through facilitating discussions of CHW-related issues, including challenging assumptions and drawing attention to potentially negative effects of existing interventions.

Next steps

This chapter started with the argument that an awareness of agricultural value chain governance is essential to understand and address CHW in African agriculture. Interventions need to provide relevant stakeholders with the right incentives to change practices that harm children but without negatively impacting the livelihoods of farm households. To design these kinds of interventions, there is a need for greater insight into the ability of various actors to change, by understanding their capabilities, opportunities and motivations. Value chain governance modalities influence these incentives (price, risk and so on) and, even more importantly, point to the communication processes that may be used to initiate discussion and coordination around CHW.

Table 6.1 provides an overview of the typology of eight governance modalities and associated entry points for interventions to address CHW. The modalities differ in institutional complexity and the number and type of stakeholder groups involved. This means that the potential for discussion and decision-making with respect to CHW-related practices varies considerably. Many value chains include several of these modalities, and within a sector there are different configurations of modalities that coexist and compete with each other, such as Fairtrade-certified cocoa production versus bulk trade or plantation production versus smallholder production. Also, farmers might well take part in a certain modality for a specific cash crop, while they are part of another modality for the food crops that they produce.

The increasing incidence of collective marketing, contract farming and certification schemes in sectors such as cocoa provides a way to trace products to their source and thus to discuss CHW as part of the quality parameters of a transaction. The price premiums that tend to be part of these governance mechanism provide a motivation for farm households to comply with more stringent quality requirements, such as the reduction of CHW. There is increasing interest among buyers in the Global North (especially those linked to retailers and consumer brands) in incorporating issues related to household wellbeing and children's work in their procurement practices. However, it is important that these intentions do not translate into obstacles for smallholder farmers, but rather help them change their practices in ways that reduce CHW.

Table 6.1: Potential entry points to change behaviours of value chain actors regarding CHW

Governance modality	Capabilities	Opportunities	Motivations
Modality 0. Self-consumption	Provide information about long-term effects of CHW related with specific agricultural tasks	Facilitate alternative livelihood strategies that involve less CHW	Increase the attention to children's wellbeing in household decision-making
Modality 1. Direct exchange			
Modality 2. Spot market mediation	Increase households' livelihood options (for example land rights, irrigation)	Address structural factors that help household to negotiate better prices (for example storage facilities, competition policy)	Increase price levels in markets (for example, living income differential)
Modality 3. In-company governance	Design a reward system for CHW reducing business practices	Transparency and traceability of social conditions of production	Shareholder and consumer pressure (for example, brand shaming) CSR-reporting requirements
Modality 4. Collective marketing	Training and capacity-building to identify, monitor and address CHW Improve collective action capacities	Create an enabling environment for culturally appropriate internal regulations of CHW practices	Improve prices for products that involve collective action. Use group leaders as a channel to convoke and discuss CHW issues
Modality 5. Contract farming	Generate credible information about the social conditions of production	Offer social services, such as proper education facilities, as part of the transaction	Fair prices that incorporate costs of CHW monitoring Discuss CHW issues as part of the contract

Table 6.1: Potential entry points to change behaviours of value chain actors regarding CHW (continued)

Governance modality	Capabilities	Opportunities	Motivations
Modality 6. Certification schemes	Training on Internal Control System and CLMRS Improve collective action capacities	Mobilize consumer preferences for fair and sustainable products Culturally appropriate requirements and indicators of CHW (for example, refine ISEAL common indicators)	Use certification-related monitoring to identify cases CHW for social remediation (CLMRS) Conditional cash transfers to increase children's education and wellbeing
Modality 7. Multistakeholder partnerships	Challenge the narrative about child labour, with a more attention to unintended negative effects of interventions	Address CHW as an additional issue in existing standard-setting MSPs. Fine-tune ongoing interventions in action-oriented MSPs related to (drivers of) CHW	Facilitate multi-stakeholder processes to discuss CHW-related issues

Source: Authors

We argue that with the more sophisticated governance mechanisms depicted in Figure 6.1 there is real potential to address CHW. Provided interventions are locally appropriate, they offer ways to address the capability, opportunity and motivation of farmers to change practices in ways that benefit children's wellbeing, and capitalize on the consumers' willingness to pay for extrinsic qualities. On the other hand, where the less sophisticated governance mechanisms predominate, it is likely to be more effective to address CHW through broader social and economic policy (see Chapter 7, this volume).

The typology has considerable potential to inform future analytical research on the drivers of CHW in different contexts. Here the focus should be on economic factors and the nature and distribution of power in transactions, and how these dynamics limit or enhance effective discussions and coordination to address CHW. Moreover, the typology could be useful in the design of more effective interventions to tackle the drivers of CHW. An in-depth understanding of specific value chain governance modalities will be essential if such interventions are to be effective in addressing children's harmful work in African agriculture.

Note

1 https://www.nestle.com/media/pressreleases/allpressreleases/tackle-child-labor-risks-farmer-income-cocoa-traceability

References

Abebe, G. et al (2013) 'Contract farming configuration: smallholders' preferences for contract design attributes', *Food Policy*, 40, pp 14–24.

Bache, I. (2008) *Researching Multi-Level Governance*. Paper presented at the CINEFOGO/University of Trento conference on The Governance of the European Union: Theory, Practices and Myths, Brussels, 25–6 January 2008.

Basu, K. and Van, P.H. (1998) 'The economics of child labor', *The American Economic Review*, 88(3), pp 412–27.

Batterbury, S. and Ndi, F. (2018) 'Land-grabbing in Africa', in Binns J.A., Lynch, K. and Nel, E. (eds) *The Routledge Handbook of African Development*. London: Routledge, pp 572–82.

Bebbington, A. (1997) 'Reinventing NGOs and rethinking alternatives in the Andes', *The Annals of the American Academy of Political and Social Science*, 554(1), pp 117–35.

Beisheim, M. and Simon, N. (2016) 'Multi-stakeholder partnerships for implementing the 2030 agenda: improving accountability and transparency. Analytical paper for the 2016 ECOSOC Partnership Forum', *SSRN Electronic Journal*. doi: 10.2139/ssrn.2767464.

Bellemare, M.F. and Lim, S. (2018) 'In all shapes and colors: varieties of contract farming', *Applied Economic Perspectives and Policy*, 40(3), pp 379–401.

Bitzer, V., Glasbergen, P. and Arts, B. (2013) 'Exploring the potential of intersectoral partnerships to improve the position of farmers in global agrifood chains: findings from the coffee sector in Peru', *Agric Hum Values*, 30, pp 5–20.

Bolwig, S. et al (2010) 'Integrating poverty and environmental concerns into value-chain analysis: a conceptual framework', *Development Policy Review*, 28(2), pp 173–94.

Boysen, O. et al (2021) *Impacts of the Cocoa Living Income Differential Policy in Ghana and Côte D'ivoire*. Luxembourg: Publications Office of the European Union. Available at: https://data.europa.eu/doi/10.2760/984346 (Accessed 13 January 2022).

Brouwer, H. et al (2016) *The MSP Guide: How to Design and Facilitate Multi-Stakeholder Partnerships*. Wageningen: Centre for Development Innovation, Wageningen University.

Buckup, S. (2012) *Building Successful Partnerships: A Production Theory of Global Multi-Stakeholder Collaboration*. Wiesbaden: Gabler Verlag.

Cadilhon, J. et al (2007) 'Business-to-business relationships in parallel vegetable supply chains of Ho Chi Minh City (Viet Nam): reaching for better performance', in Batt, P. and Cadilhon, J. (eds) *Proceedings of the International Symposium on Fresh Produce Supply Chain Management*. Rome: FAO. Available at: http://www.fao.org/3/ah996e/ah996e00.pdf (Accessed 29 April 2020).

Chamberlain, W. and Anseeuw, W. (2019) 'Inclusive businesses in agriculture: defining the concept and its complex and evolving partnership structures in the field', *Land Use Policy*, 83, pp 308–22.

Constant, S. et al (2020) *Social Norms and Supply Chains: A Focus on Child Labour and Waste Recycling in Hlaing Tharyar, Yangon, Myanmar. CLARISSA Evidence Report 2*. Brighton: Institute of Development Studies (IDS).

Dachille, G., Guarcello, L. and Lyon, S. (2015) *Child and Youth Agricultural Work in Sub-Saharan Africa: Perspectives from the World Bank Integrated Surveys on Agriculture Initiative. Working Paper*. Rome: Understanding Children's Work Programme, ILO and Centre for Economic and International Studies (CEIS).

Dentoni, D., Bitzer, V. and Schouten, G. (2018) 'Harnessing wicked problems in multi-stakeholder partnerships', *Journal of Business Ethics*, 150(2), pp 333–56.

Dolan, C. and Humphrey, J. (2000) 'Governance and trade in fresh vegetables: the impact of UK supermarkets on the African horticulture industry', *The Journal of Development Studies*, 37(2), pp 147–76.

Donovan, J. et al (2015) 'Guides for value chain development: a comparative review', *Journal of Agribusiness in Developing and Emerging Economies*, 5(1), pp 2–23.

European Parliament and Council of the European Union (2002) *General Food Law Regulation. EC Regulation No. 178/2002*. Brussels: European Union.

Fafchamps, M. (2004) *Market Institutions in Sub-Saharan Africa: Theory and Evidence*. Cambridge, MA: The MIT Press.

FAO (2014) *Developing Sustainable Food Value Chains. Guiding Principles, Policy Support and Governance*. Rome: Food and Agriculture Organization (FAO). Available at: http://www.fao.org/policy-support/resources/resources-details/en/c/422953/ (Accessed 22 April 2020).

Frederick, S. (2019) 'Global value chain mapping', in Ponte, S., Gereffi, G., and Raj-Reichert, G. (eds) *Handbook on Global Value Chains*. Cheltenham: Edward Elgar Publishing, pp 29–53.

Gardeazabal, A. et al (2021) 'Knowledge management for innovation in agri-food systems: a conceptual framework', *Knowledge Management Research & Practice*, pp 1–13.

Gereffi, G., Humphrey, J. and Sturgeon, T. (2005) 'The governance of global value chains', *Review of International Political Economy*, 12(1), pp 78–104.

Giddens, A. (1979) *Central Problems in Social Theory: Action, Structure, and Contradiction in Social Analysis*. Oakland, CA: University of California Press.

GLOBALG.A.P. (2022) *GLOBALG.A.P. About Us*. Available at: https://www.globalgap.org/uk_en/who-we-are/about-us/ (Accessed 13 January 2022).

Goldbach, M., Seuring, S. and Back, S. (2003) 'Co-ordinating sustainable cotton chains for the mass market', *Greener Management International*, 43, pp 65–78.

Hammond, R.A. (2009) 'Complex systems modeling for obesity research', *Preventing Chronic Disease*, 6(3), Article 97. Available at: https://stacks.cdc.gov/view/cdc/20387.

Handayati, Y., Simatupang, T.M. and Perdana, T. (2015) 'Agri-food supply chain coordination: the state-of-the-art and recent developments', *Logistics Research*, 8(5), Article 5. doi: 10.1007/s12159-015-0125-4

Havnevik, K., Matondi, P.B. and Beyene, A. (2011) *Biofuels, Land Grabbing and Food Security in Africa*. London and Uppsala: Zed Books and Nordiska Afrikainstitutet. Available at: http://urn.kb.se/resolve?urn=urn:nbn:se:nai:diva-1331 (Accessed 13 January 2022).

Hellin, J. and Meijer, M. (2006) *Guidelines for Value Chain Analysis*. Rome: Food and Agriculture Organization (FAO).

Henderson, J. et al (2002) 'Global production networks and the analysis of economic development', *Review of International Political Economy*, 9(3), pp 436–64.

HLPE (2018) *Multi-Stakeholder Partnerships to Finance and Improve Food Security and Nutrition in the Framework of the 2030 Agenda. HLPE Report 13*. Rome: HPLE, Food and Agriculture Organization (FAO).

ICI (2011) *Emerging Good Practice in Combating the Worst Forms of Child Labour in West African Cocoa Growing Communities*. Geneva: International Cocoa Initiative (ICI).

ILO (2018) *Ending Child Labour by 2025: A Review of Policies and Programmes*. Geneva: International Labour Organization.

ILO (2022) *Child Labour: Causes*. Available at: http://www.ilo.org/moscow/areas-of-work/child-labour/WCMS_248984/lang--en/index.htm (Accessed 13 January 2022).

ISEAL (2019) *Reaching Far and Wide: Collective Presence and Growth Trends of ISEAL Member Schemes Across Seven Commodities*. London: ISEAL-Alliance.

ISEAL Alliance (2022) *About ISEAL, ISEAL Alliance*. Available at: https://www.isealalliance.org/about-iseal (Accessed 13 January 2022).

Jamali, D. and Mirshak, R. (2007) 'Corporate social responsibility (CSR): theory and practice in a developing country context', *Journal of Business Ethics*, 72(3), pp 243–62.

Jessop, B. (2000) 'The dynamics of partnership and governance failure', in Stoker, G. (ed) *The New Politics of Local Governance in Britain*. Basingstoke: Macmillan, pp 11–32.

Jodhka, S.S. (2021) 'Why are the farmers of Punjab protesting?', *The Journal of Peasant Studies*, 48(7), pp 1356–70.

Kaplinsky, R. and Morris, M. (2001) *A Handbook for Value Chain Research*. Ottawa: IDRC. Available at: http://www.ids.ac.uk/ids/global/pdfs/VchNov01.pdf (Accessed 22 April 2020).

KIT and IIRR (2010) *Value Chain Finance beyond Microfinance for Rural Entrepreneurs*. Amsterdam & Nairobi: Royal Tropical Institute & International Institute of Rural Reconstruction.

Lee, J., Gereffi, G. and Beauvais, J. (2012) 'Global value chains and agrifood standards: challenges and possibilities for smallholders in developing countries', *Proceedings of the National Academy of Sciences of the United States of America*, 109(31), pp 12326–31.

Lentink, A. (2016) 'FAO's approach to gender-sensitive and sustainable food value chains', in Meybeck, A. and Redfern, S. (eds) *Sustainable Value Chains for Sustainable Food Systems*. Rome: Food and Agriculture Organization (FAO), pp 117–28.

Long, N. and van der Ploeg, J.D. (1989) 'Demythologizing planned intervention: an actor perspective', *Sociologia Ruralis*, 29(3–4), pp 226–49.

Loveridge, D. and Wilson, N. (2017) *Engaging with the Private Sector Through Multi-Stakeholder Platforms*. London: Donor Committee for Enterprise Development.

Lyon, F. (2000) 'Trust, networks and norms: the creation of social capital in agricultural economies in Ghana', *World Development*, 28(4), pp 663–81.

M4P (2008) *Making Value Chains Work Better for the Poor: A Toolbook for Practitioners of Value Chain Analysis. Version 3*. Phnom Penh, Cambodia: Agricultural Development International. Available at: http://www.fao.org/sustainable-food-value-chains/library/details/en/c/265290/ (Accessed 22 April 2020).

Malawi 2020 Platform (2015) 'Malawi 2020 Tea Revitalisation Programme: working towards a competitive tea industry with living wages & living income', UN Forum on Business & Human Rights, Session 'Multi-stakeholder engagement across all three pillars (case studies)' 16 November, Geneva.

Meijerink, G. and Joshi, P. K. (2016) 'India's price support policies and global food prices', in Brouwer, F. and Joshi, P. K. (eds) *International Trade and Food Security: The Future of Indian Agriculture*. Wallingford: CABI, pp 134–49.

Ménard, C. (2004) 'The economics of hybrid organizations', *Journal of Institutional and Theoretical Economics (JITE) / Zeitschrift für die gesamte Staatswissenschaft*, 160(3), pp 345–76.

Michie, S., van Stralen, M.M. and West, R. (2011) 'The behaviour change wheel: a new method for characterising and designing behaviour change interventions', *Implementation Science*, 6(1), Article 42, pp 1–11.

Muoio, A. and Rimland Flower, N. (2016) *Participate: The Power of Involving Business in Social Impact Networks*. Stamford, CT: Deloitte Development. Available at: https://www.slideshare.net/RockefellerFound/participate-the-power-of-involving-business-in-social-impact-networks (Accessed 29 April 2020).

Nestle (2019) *Nestle Cocoa Plan. Tackling Child Labor, 2019 Report*. Geneva: Nestlé-International Cocoa Initiative. Available at: https://www.nestle.com/sites/default/files/2019-12/nestle-tackling-child-labor-report-2019-en.pdf (Accessed 31 March 2020).

Nestle Cocoa Plan and ICI (2017) *Tackling Child Labour: 2017 Report*. Vevey, Switzerland: Nestlé and ICI. Available at: https://www.nestlecocoaplanreport.com/sites/default/files/2017-10/NestleCocoaPlanReport2017_EN_0.pdf.

Okali, K., Frimpong Boamah, E. and Sumberg, J. (2022) 'The quantification of child labour by Ghana's mass media: a missed opportunity?', *Africa Spectrum*, 57(2), pp 155–77.

Olson, M. (1965) *The Logic of Collective Action: Public Goods and the Theory of Groups*. Cambridge: Harvard University Press.

Pattberg, P. and Widerberg, O. (2014) *Transnational Multi-Stakeholder Partnerships for Sustainable Development: Building Blocks for Success*. Report R-14/31. Amsterdam: IMV Institute for Environmental Studies.

Rainforest Alliance (2018) *Rainforest Alliance Sustainable Agriculture Standard Applicable for Smallholder Farms: Draft 1.0 – for Public Consultation*. Available at: https://cgspace.cgiar.org/bitstream/handle/10568/100180/SMALLHOLDERS_RAINFOREST%20ALLIANCE%20SUSTAINABLE%20AGRICULTURE%20STANDARD.V1.1.pdf?sequence=1&isAllowed=y (Accessed 26 November 2022).

Ravetti, C. (2020) *The Effects of Income Changes on Child Labour: A Review of Evidence from Smallholder Agriculture*. Geneva: International Cocoa Initiative (ICI). Available at: https://cocoainitiative.org/knowledge-centre-post/the-effects-of-income-changes-on-child-labour-a-review-of-evidence-from-smallholder-agriculture/ (Accessed 24 April 2020).

Reardon, T. et al (2019) 'Rapid transformation of food systems in developing regions: Highlighting the role of agricultural research & innovations', *Agricultural Systems*, 172, pp 47–59.

Rhodes, R. (1997) *Understanding Governance: Policy Networks, Governance, Reflexivity and Accountability*. Buckingham and Philadelphia: Open University Press.

Roduner, D. and Gerrits, A. (2006) 'The role of donors in value chain interventions', *Rural Development News*, pp 10–15.

Ruben, R. (2019) 'Impact assessment of commodity standards: pathways for sustainability and inclusiveness', in Schmidt, M. et al (eds) *Sustainable Global Value Chains*. Cham, Switzerland: Springer, pp 327–45.

Sartorius, K. and Kirsten, J. (2007) 'A framework to facilitate institutional arrangements for smallholder supply in developing countries: an agribusiness perspective', *Food Policy*, 32, pp 640–55.

Scheyvens, R., Banks, G. and Hughes, E. (2016) 'The private sector and the SDGS: the need to move beyond "business as usual"', *Sustainable Development*, 24(6), pp 371–82.

Shinde, S. (2018) *Functions of Management*. Raleigh, NC: Lulu Publications.

Termeer, C.J.A.M. et al (2019) 'The dynamics of new governance arrangements for sustainable value chains', in Koppenjan, J., Karré, P.M., and Termeer, C.J.A.M. (eds) *Smart Hybridity: Potentials and Challenges of New Governance Arrangements*. The Hague: Eleven International Publishing, pp 85–98. Available at: https://research.wur.nl/en/publications/the-dynamics-of-new-governance-arrangements-for-sustainable-value (Accessed 22 April 2020).

Thorpe, J. et al (2021) 'Are multi-stakeholder platforms effective approaches to agri-food sustainability? Towards better assessment', *International Journal of Agricultural Sustainability*, 20(2), pp 168–83.

Ton, G. (2015) *Measuring Tensions and Intentions: Mixing Methods in the Impact Evaluation of Development Support to Farmer Organisations*. PhD thesis. Wageningen: Wageningen University. Available at: https://library.wur.nl/WebQuery/wurpubs/493804 (Accessed 13 January 2022).

Ton, G. et al (2018) 'Contract farming for improving smallholder incomes: what can we learn from effectiveness studies?', *World Development*, 104, pp 46–64.

Ton, G., Opeero, D.M. and Vellema, S. (2010) '"How do we get it to the mill?" A study on bulking arrangements that enable sourcing from smallholders in the Ugandan vegetable oil chain', *SSRN Electronic Journal*. doi: 10.2139/ssrn.1636204

Ton, G., Thorpe, J., Egyir, I. and Szyp, C. (2021) *Value Chain Governance: Entrance Points for Interventions to Address Children's Harmful Work in Agriculture*, ACHA Working Paper 6. Brighton: Action on Children's Harmful Work in African Agriculture, IDS.

Treichel, K. et al (2017) *Multi-Stakeholder Partnerships in the Context of Agenda 2030. A Practice Based Analysis of Potential Benefits, Challenges and Success Factors*. Bonn and Eschborn: Partnerships 2030, c/o Deutsche Gesellschaft für Internationale Zusammenarbeit (GIZ). Available at: https://www.partnerschaften2030.de/wp-content/uploads/2018/10/Multi-stakeholder-partnerships-in-the-context-of-Agenda-2030.pdf (Accessed 22 April 2020).

Tschirley, D. et al (2015) 'The rise of a middle class in east and southern Africa: implications for food system transformation', *Journal of International Development*, 27(5), pp 628–46.

Tulane University (2015) *Final Report: 2013/14 Survey Research on Child Labor in West African Cocoa-Growing Areas*. New Orleans: School of Public Health and Tropical Medicine, Tulane University.

Vellema, S. et al (2016) 'Policy reform and supply chain governance: insights from Ghana, Côte d'Ivoire and Ecuador', in Squicciarini, M.P. and Swinnen, J. (eds) *The Economics of Cocoa*. Oxford: Oxford University Press, pp 228–46.

Waarts, Y. and Meijerink, G. (2010) *The HCDA Code of Conduct in Kenya: Impact on Transaction Costs and Risks. VC4PD Research Papers*. Wageningen: Wageningen University.

Webster, F.E. (1992) 'The changing role of marketing in the corporation', *Journal of Marketing*, 56(4), pp 1–17.

Williamson, O.E. (1975) *Markets and Hierarchies: Analysis and Antitrust Implications: A Study in the Economics of Internal Organization*. Rochester, NY: Social Science Research Network. Available at: https://papers.ssrn.com/abstract=1496220 (Accessed 29 April 2020).

Williamson, O.E. (2002) 'The lens of contract: private ordering', *The American Economic Review*, 92(2), pp 438–43.

Witte, J.M., Benner, T. and Streck, C. (2005) 'Partnerships and networks in global environmental governance', in Petschow, U., Rosenau, J. and von Weizsacker, E. (eds) *Governance and Sustainability: New Challenges for States, Companies and Civil Society*. London: Routledge, pp 141–52.

World Bank (2007) *World Development Report 2008: Agriculture for Development.* Washington, DC: World Bank.

Yeung, H.W. and Coe, N.M. (2015) 'Toward a dynamic theory of global production networks', *Economic Geography*, 91(1), pp 29–58.

7

Blurred Definitions and Imprecise Indicators: Rethinking Social Assistance for Children's Work

Rachel Sabates-Wheeler, Keetie Roelen, Rebecca Mitchell and Amy Warmington

Introduction

Children's work, and more specifically child labour, has received increasing attention over the last two decades. This has been due in large part to the rise in global commitments to children's rights, but also to the heightened concerns of consumers from the Global North informed by western imaginaries of childhood (Sabates-Wheeler and Sumberg, 2022). In this view, childhood should be all about home (family) and school (learning). Children working long hours for little reward is not part of this version of childhood.

Historically, most policy responses and actions to stop children working have been punitive in nature. But given the many structural constraints that families face, and the fact that the majority of children's work takes place away from the public eye, these responses have had limited effect (Hanson et al, 2015; Bourdillon and Carothers, 2019; Chapters 2 and 8, this volume). This has given rise to alternative and more supportive policy initiatives, including social protection[1]: instead of punishing children or families, these schemes provide incentives to make the 'right' choices. They are often linked to education and include reduction or elimination of school fees and scholarship programmes: the assumption being that cheaper or more accessible education will shift preferences. Social assistance initiatives – a sub-set of social protection – such as school feeding and cash or asset transfers have also become increasingly popular, based on the idea that they will reduce household poverty and thus reduce the need for children to contribute to family income through work.

There is increasing evidence to suggest that social assistance has the potential to reduce children's engagement with work (de Hoop and Rosati, 2014; Dammert et al, 2018). However, we know very little about its impact on children's engagement with harmful work. The potential for social assistance to reduce harmful and exploitative forms of children's work may be limited given the importance of social norms, labour relations and other structural and socio-political factors that attach value to children's work, and in contexts where income opportunities are limited (Thompson, 2012). In addition, evaluations generally do not pick up on the nuances beyond whether a child engages with paid or unpaid work, missing information on the why, how and when of the work. A prime reason for this is because in many evaluations children's engagement with work is often only a secondary interest (Chapter 3, this volume).

We believe that children everywhere are entitled to a childhood where they are able to learn and do not need to engage in harmful work. However, the trade-off between the benefits and harms from the work that children do is seldom clear cut. Is all hazardous (potentially harmful) work to be avoided under all circumstances? The nexus between school, work and home is fluid and complex (Chapter 4, this volume). The spheres of activity are not exclusive and do not trade-off in equal measure against each other, nor are they either inherently good or bad in nature. In fact, the spheres of activity frequently complement rather than substitute for each other, especially in poor households and where decisions are constrained by limited income and other opportunities.

This chapter argues that the design and delivery of social assistance does not take adequate account of the nuanced role of work in children's lives, and that current interventions are therefore ill-equipped to tackle children's harmful work. Based on a comprehensive review of evaluations of social assistance schemes across low and middle-income countries (LMICs), we find a lack of engagement with the complex role of children's work in the lives of children and families, with the theories of change underpinning such interventions often rendering *any* and *all* work as undesirable. Few studies look beyond prevalence or intensity of work, resulting in a substantial knowledge gap about the extent to which, and how, social assistance may reduce harm through work, if at all. We propose an alternative way of understanding benefits and harms of children's work.

The chapter is structured as follows. First, we outline the debate on harms and benefits of children's work. Second, we provide an overview of the behavioural model that underpins the majority of social assistance provisioning. Next, we review evaluations of interventions in LMICs over the last decade in reference to their impact on children's engagement with work and the definitions and indicators used to track such impacts. We conclude by framing children's work in relation to hazardscapes that cut across children's spheres of activity and propose social assistance as one of several policy levers to address children's harmful work.

The harms and benefits of children's work

There is broad social and political consensus around the need to eliminate children's harmful work, not least because it can have life-long negative and irreversible impacts (ILO, 2011; Burgard and Lin, 2013). This consensus is made explicit in the UN Sustainable Development Goals (SDGs), which seek to eliminate all forms of child labour by 2030, with its worst forms[2] targeted for eradication by 2025 (Target 8.7).

The International Labour Organization (ILO) has an international mandate to establish definitions and guidelines for what constitutes acceptable and unacceptable work. In relation to children, the two key conventions are 138 and 182, the *Minimum Age* and *Worst Forms of Child Labour* conventions respectively (ILO, 1973, 1999). These are supplemented by Recommendation 190 (ILO, 1999). As reported in Chapter 2 (this volume) these three texts, plus the ILO's many clarifying publications, break children's economic activity down into four categories: (1) children's work; (2) child labour; (3) the worst forms of child labour; and (4) hazardous child labour, with the distinction between the first two categories representing the line between what is considered acceptable versus harmful.

According to ILO, *children's work* is a 'a non-technical term for economic activities of children', where these activities are acceptable because they fall outside any of the following detrimental categories (for example, ILO-IPEC, 2012, p 31). *Child labour* is 'work which may affect their [children's] health, safety, morals, or which might interfere with their schooling' (p 31). The distinction between children's work and labour is classified by age, with legitimate activities for younger children including 'helping their parents around the home, assisting in a family business or earning pocket money outside school hours and during school holidays' (ILO, n.d.). *The worst forms* and *hazardous child labour* comprise work which, by its nature or the circumstances in which it is carried out, is likely to harm the health, safety or morals of children (ILO-IPEC, 2012, p 32).

It is clear from the definitions previously discussed, and the supporting documentation, that what differentiates work and labour are the notions of hazard and harm. Conventions, policies and programmes that aim to address the range of issues associated with work and labour are embedded in assumptions about what is and is not harmful. However, as argued in Chapter 2 (this volume), to date no coherent theory or definition of harm exists among the institutions working on child labour. The vagueness in the definition of children's work has meant that the focus on eliminating harm has increased pressure to more precisely define child labour, allowing the scope of child labour to expand and become almost synonymous with children's work. This fuzziness in boundaries frequently translates into an objective of eliminating all work done by children, not just harmful work.

A case in point has been the appropriation of the term child labour by the ILO's Statistical Information and Monitoring Programme on Child Labour (SIMPOC) following the Minimum Age Convention (138 of 1973). SIMPOC extends the concept to include: (1) all economic activity by children under the age of 12 (including unpaid contributions to family enterprises), (2) more than 14 hours per week in economic work by children aged 12–14 and (3) more than 27 hours per week of household chores by children aged 7–15 (ILO and UNICEF, 2021).

These standards and monitoring criteria are used to guide both global and national policy on children's work as well as private sector standards and interventions on child labour. The key assumption is that work for children is a 'bad' that is frequently trading off against 'goods' such as schooling, play and home-time. However, as convincingly established through extensive empirical work by Bourdillon et al (2010), these standards do not correlate well with whether work is harmful or beneficial to children. What is absent is an acknowledgement that not all forms of work are undesirable and that a combination of engaging in school and work may be preferred by, and beneficial for, children (and their families).

There are many reasonable explanations for why children continue to work, even when the work is hazardous or harmful. Economic reasons include the need for income or in-kind contributions from children's work to support subsistence needs or to help overcome financial barriers to education and health (for example transport, books or a uniform, see Admassie, 2003). So, in this sense, work and school are complementary. In cases where work and school cannot be combined, the temporal trade-off means that families and children have to balance short-term gains of work against potential long-term benefits of schooling (Orkin, 2012), with poverty tipping the balance in favour of short term gains. There may also be educational reasons for children's work such as building skills and gaining experience, which can be superior to benefits accrued from formal schooling if quality of provision is low. Work experience can also complement and augment schooling, for example with business, technical and life skills. Social and cultural reasons for children's work include psycho-social factors, with research showing that children acquire status, autonomy and a sense of achievement by contributing to the family economy. Cultural and social norms may support an expectation that children work (Abebe and Bessell, 2011), which may push children toward work even when family income increases.

This does not mean that the work is necessarily 'good', in fact it can be hazardous, exhausting and interfere with school. Nevertheless, the loss of household income from insisting the child does not work will leave the child and family worse off. Bourdillon and colleagues have shown that on the limited occasions when holistic outcomes in children's lives are investigated in relation to a specific child labour intervention, 'many children are shown to be worse off, often ending up in more exploitative or hazardous work, particularly when their livelihood and education depend on their work' (Bourdillon et al, 2010, pp 1–6; 181–92). In other words, there are real life-changing trade-offs to consider when designing policy that modifies the work–school-life balance of poor households. Insistence on the elimination of child labour might leave children in a worse position. However, interventions that provide income support, such as cash transfers or microfinance, can positively affect these trade-offs such that children may be able to reduce their hours of work and increase hours in school (de Hoop and Rosati, 2014).

An increasing body of literature has questioned the idea of a simple trade-off between school and work, and the notion that school is always good and work always bad. Dominant narratives that focus on the negative aspects of work not only overlook its potential educational and social benefits, they also feed a rigid form of policymaking that can put children at risk of even greater harm (Aufseeser et al, 2018; Bourdillon and Carothers, 2019). Pitting school against work offers limited theoretical or practical traction. A better framing is to consider the total burden of work and potential for harm across the multiple spheres of a child's life – in school, at home and in the workplace. As argued in Chapter 4 (this volume), children's work takes place within a negotiated space of three interdependent arenas; schools (embedded within education systems), households (with their multiple family and community configurations) and workplaces (in multiple locations including family and commercial farms and enterprises). This school-home-work nexus further sits within, and is influenced by, the wider economic, social, temporal and spatial contexts. The tensions and choices that occur as children and their families navigate this nexus illustrate the paucity of the standard behavioural model and of the classically posed binary trade-off between children's work and school.

Is it any wonder, then, that so many interventions have failed in their efforts to tackle harmful forms of work? The lack of attention to the harm-benefit trade-offs facing children and their families has not only created a policy environment that does not adequately represent or serve the interests of children and their families, but has meant that most interventions and evaluations that have been rolled out employ (1) ineffective criteria for defining and identifying children's work, and (2) inadequate indicators for monitoring and evaluating whether the intervention is fit for purpose. Social assistance is a case in point.

The behavioural model underpinning social assistance provision

Social protection, particularly in the various forms of publicly financed social assistance such as cash transfers, school subsidies, school feeding and pensions, is a classic way in which policy relies on programmes to leverage behaviour change. Cash transfers, for instance, work through two mechanisms to incentivize change. First, the provision of extra income is supposed to create an 'income effect' whereby the household is able to purchase more of a good or service (food, education, health).[3] Second, if social assistance is made conditional on uptake of a service like education or health, or if it is provided in-kind as a food or education subsidy, this will change the relative price of goods and services leading to a substitution effect. In addition, soft conditions, such as nutrition or education messaging and sensitization campaigns, are sometimes used to influence the balance of choice between 'goods' and 'bads'.

Singh and McLeish (2013) describe these effects in relation to the ways that social assistance can reduce or avoid children's work. First, by improving a household's economic position, thereby increasing resilience to shocks, the need for children to work to contribute to family income (either over the long-term or as a short-term coping mechanism) is reduced. Second, by creating positive incentives to get and keep children in school and away from work, such as through the provision of school meals and making the receipt of cash transfers conditional upon school attendance.

The first represents the income effect. For a household that, before the social assistance, had been underinvesting in children's education due to lack of income, the cash transfer is expected to enable them to increase investment in children's education, with the assumption that it would reduce the need for the child to work. A similar outcome can be achieved through the provision of an education subsidy. For those households who were not previously sending the child to school due to lack of income, the subsidy will now change the cost-benefit ratio of schooling – the substitution effect. The family will weigh up the pros and cons of sending the child to school, and if schooling is a normal good (that is as income increases more of the good is consumed) then the policy change should lead to an increase in schooling. The assumption is that social assistance would change the price of education relative to other activities, such as work on or off-farm, or in the home. For a household without an income constraint that is already investing in their child's education, a cash transfer or education subsidy would be the equivalent of a pure income effect to the household. It would not affect education choices but would be extra money for other goods and services, or investment.

However, unlike what is portrayed in the virtuous hypotheses previously discussed, the net effect is far from straightforward as it will depend on whether the income or the substitution effect dominates. This depends, first, on the magnitude of the price change: if the transfer or subsidy is not large enough then the poorest household may not be able or 'persuaded' to change their preference for education over work. Second, it depends on the nature of the good. The assumption is that, for children, education is a normal good and work is an inferior good, meaning that an increase in income will lead to an increase in education and a reduction in work. However, as will be discussed later, in some cultures work is seen as positive, even for children, and can attribute status. Third, it depends on the relation of one good to another – for example, children's work (due to the income received) can actually complement rather than substitute their education, in the sense of allowing them to go to school.

Furthermore, in the case of a household, as opposed to an individual decision-making model, there will be other substitution effects. If the opportunity cost of an adult staying at home increases (for instance, if a public works programme is introduced), then the adult might choose to go to work. However, any care responsibilities the adult had might be transferred to an older child, causing her/him to leave school. Indeed, research in Rwanda found that women struggled to balance their participation in a public works programme with other household work and care responsibilities, sometimes relying on children to take on these tasks (Roelen et al, 2017). Research on the public works programme in India also suggests that the added work burden has negative effects on children (Zaidi et al, 2017).

Moreover, if gender quotas or conditions are attached to cash transfers, such that only one child in the household is able to benefit from the assistance, there may be a substitution *between* children in the same household (that is between those attending school and those remaining at home or going out to work). In relation to the conditional cash transfer (CCT) programme PROGRESA in Mexico, for example, the condition that younger children must go to school was found to push older children into paid work or increase the intensity of their work to compensate for the loss of income (Bastagli et al, 2016). Conditionalities, quotas and different social protection instruments can have both intended and unintended impacts.

More generally, gender matters, with positive impacts from social assistance often being larger for boys than they are for girls. This is explained by boys being more likely, on average, to be engaged in paid work, and the income effect of cash transfers therefore playing out more strongly for boys. In turn, the fact that girls are more commonly involved in household and unpaid work means that public works programmes are more likely to negatively affect them (de Hoop and Rosati 2014). Evaluation findings from the public works component of the Productive Safety Net Programme (PSNP) in Ethiopia indicate that while the programme reduced engagement in work for all children, it increased engagement in household work among young girls (Hoddinott et al, 2010; Zibagwe et al, 2013).

The behavioural model underlying the expected change in work decisions through social assistance is predicated on a simple division between work, school and leisure, thereby overlooking the conditions of work. As elaborated previously, whether work is harmful depends on the amount of time spent on work activities but crucially, on the nature and intensity of work. Covarrubias et al (2012) show that the Malawi Social Cash Transfer Scheme (MSCTS) led to higher investment in productive assets and livestock, but adult participation in on-farm work or self-employment in household enterprises did not change. However, while children's involvement in work outside the home declined, their participation in within-household tasks increased (no increase in leisure, more chores and more participation in family farm/non-farm business activities). Efforts that aim to reduce children's engagement with harmful work should, therefore, move beyond a consideration of whether children engage in work and for how long, towards a fuller understanding of the type of work, the spheres in which the work takes place and the working conditions.

Fundamentally, the results of the provision of social assistance – in the form of cash or food transfers, public works and so on – are highly contingent. Common assumptions about the effects of assistance on children's work, based on standard theory, are overly simplistic. For this reason, the basic behavioural model, that underpins the theory of change for many social assistance interventions, is not able to deal with the complexities of choices and constraints faced by poor children and their families. Crucially, it makes no distinction between acceptable or harmful forms of work, nor does it take account of children or families' own preferences in weighing up potential benefits and harms. While the principle of 'do no harm' is an important element of social assistance, there has generally been insufficient understanding of the impacts of interventions on children's engagement with work to guarantee against additional or greater harm.

What is known about social assistance and children's harmful work

To gain a better understanding of the role of social assistance in addressing children's harmful work, this section reviews studies that include the reduction of child labour or children's work as a programme objective and/or where child labour or work are included as an outcome indicator. The review focuses on social assistance only and is restricted to articles and reports from 2010 onwards when social assistance started expanding rapidly across LMICs. As we are interested in both the effect of social assistance on children's engagement with work as well as how this effect was conceptualized in intervention design, the review is limited to studies that make mention of children's work or child labour as one of the outcome variables of interest.

Based on these criteria, 22 studies are included (Appendix, Table 7.2). Most studies that evaluate the effect on children's work refer to unconditional cash transfers (UCTs) and CCTs. Very few studies of other types of interventions, such as public work programmes (PWs), consider the effect on children's work. Most studies focus primarily on prevalence and intensity of children's work, considering any reduction in these indicators to be desirable. Only 5 of the 22 studies address whether or not the work was harmful.

The majority of studies unpack children's engagement in work by distinguishing between types of work. Categories commonly include domestic work and household chores; working in family business; and working outside of the home. Edmonds and Schady (2012), for example, analyse the effect of the *Bono de Desarrollo Humano* (BDH) programme in Ecuador on time allocation of children, distinguishing between paid economic activity, economic activity on the family farm or business and unpaid household services. Exceptions include Gee's (2010) study of *Red de Protección Social* (RPS) in Nicaragua that employs a blanket category of 'work' without further specification. Similarly, the study of the Mahatma Gandhi National Rural Employment Guarantee Scheme (MGNREGS) in India by Das and Mukherjee (2019) does not specify the type of work in which children engaged, although it does distinguish between low and high intensity of child labour based on numbers of working hours per day. Within the remit of these categorizations, studies focus on whether children participate in work or not and often also include information on intensity of work.

In the majority of studies, children's engagement with work is approached from the perspective that it is undesirable and should be reduced. This objective is often phrased in conjunction with desired improvements in education, based on the rationale that improved school enrolment or attendance is in conflict with children's engagement with work, and that engagement with education constitutes an investment in human capital, while engagement in work does not. For example, Miller and Tsoka's (2012) study on the Social Cash Transfer Programme (SCTP) in Malawi ask whether the receipt of a monthly cash transfer would lead households to 'invest in their children's human-capacity development by prioritizing child education and reducing child labour outside the home' (p 500). In their study of the Child Grants Programme (CGP) in Lesotho, Sebastian et al (2019) consider time spent on household chores and farm activities vis-à-vis time spent on educational activities. Similarly, for an evaluation of the Ghana

School Feeding Programme, Aurino et al (2018) consider children's time use spent on housework, farm work and other types of labour vis-à-vis time spent in school, studying or on leisure, as a mechanism for understanding programme effects on educational outcomes. Brauw et al (2012) hypothesize that *Bolsa Familia*'s positive effects on girls' grade progression in Brazil may be explained by reductions in time spent on domestic work. However, they indicate that this was speculative only as they had no information about time spent studying.

Work outside of the household is frequently deemed less desirable and more disruptive to children's education than domestic chores or work in a family business. Edmonds and Schady (2012) note that 'paid employment is difficult to combine with schooling because of constraints in the minimum number of hours required to work' (p 118), while schooling and engagement in unpaid work or household chores is often combined. Various studies specifically sought to test negative behaviours associated with paid work outside of the household. In a mixed methods evaluation of the South African Child Support Grant (CSG) (DSD et al, 2012), for example, participation in work outside the home is correlated with risky adolescent behaviours such as substance abuse and criminal activities. However, no such analysis is undertaken in relation to potential positive outcomes of paid work such as social capital investment or relational wellbeing.

Most studies do not differentiate between types of work in terms of desired effect. Engagement in domestic chores and care work is commonly referred to as child labour with predominantly negative connotations. In reference to the impact of UCTs in Malawi, Covarrubias et al (2012) state 'concern arose that households were relying on child labour to intensify their agricultural activities. This appears to be true … children increased participation in household tasks such as chores and caring for household members' (p 72). In their assessment of a UCT in Lesotho, Sebastian et al (2019) consider children's increased time allocation to domestic chores or farm activities to undermine 'child investment behaviour'. In a study of the Cash Transfer for Orphans and Vulnerable Children (OVC-CT) programme in Kenya, both engagement with wage labour and own farm labour is labelled as child labour and considered equally undesirable (Asfaw et al 2014). Similarly, a reduction in children's work as a result of the *Jefas* programme in Argentina is considered a beneficial impact (Juras, 2014).

Only a minority of studies take a more nuanced view of children's work. A study of UCTs in Malawi and Zambia, acknowledge that '[a]t low levels of intensity, child engagement in common economic activities and household chores may be innocuous or beneficial to children' (de Hoop et al, 2019, p 20), while Del Carpio et al (2016) consider differential effects on undesirable and more desirable types of work in their evaluation of Nicaragua's CCT programme. Specifically, they distinguish between physical labour such as farm work, and skill-forming labour including work in commerce and manufacturing. While acknowledging that skills can be gained from both, they argue that physical labour would not support social mobility in the same way as skill-forming labour. De Hoop et al (2019) find that the Pantawid programme in the Philippines incentivized both school enrolment and participation in paid work but note that without having any information about the nature of children's work, it is not possible to comment on overall welfare effects.

Finally, a few studies consider hazardous forms of work. In relation to UCTs in Malawi and Zambia, de Hoop et al (2019) consider impacts on excessive working hours (based on ILO recommendations) and whether children carry heavy loads, work with dangerous tools or are exposed to hazards such as fumes or extreme cold (in Malawi only). Similarly, in their evaluation of Tanzania's Productive Social Safety Net (PSSN), de Hoop et al (2020) adopt definitions of hazardous work and excessive hours in line with the Tanzania Mainland National Child Labour Survey 2014 (based on Tanzania legislation and ILO recommendations), collecting information about prevalence and intensity of different types of work as well as hazardous working conditions. This study also presents a rare example of unpacking differences in programme impacts on child labour versus children's work.

In their review of the effect of cash transfers on child labour, de Hoop and Rosati (2014) note that child labour affects children in different ways depending on type of work, working conditions and length of exposure to hazardous conditions, among others. They acknowledge that these complexities cannot be captured in a single indicator and that detailed information is required to gain full insight into the ramifications of children's engagement with work, and therefore into the impact of programmes such as cash transfers. Nevertheless, data constraints mean that – in practice – most evaluations are limited to considering participation in different types of work. This is echoed by individual studies, such as Sebastian et al (2019).

Impact of social assistance on children's engagement with work

A small number of studies provide sufficient detail to assess the impact of social assistance on children's harmful work. None of the studies on public works, feeding programmes or social pensions record impacts relating to children's exposure to hazards or experience of harm, or on their wellbeing. Two studies of UCT interventions investigate impact, but because neither of these explicitly examine the nature of these impacts they provide limited insights. The first analyses the productive impacts of the SCTP in Malawi (Covarrubias et al, 2012). From the limited analysis of exposure to hazards and harm, one impact that could be seen was that child labour changed from taking place outside the household to work in family enterprises or household chores.[4] De Hoop et al (2019) explicitly identify impacts on children's wellbeing and their exposure to harm and hazards in their comparison of Malawi's SCTP and the Multiple Category Targeted Programme (MCTP) in Zambia. In Malawi, for those children in households that were beneficiaries of the programme there was a four percentage point increase in the likelihood of risk of exposure to hazards such as 'carrying heavy loads, working with dangerous tools, exposure to dust, fumes or gas, and exposure to extreme cold, heat or humidity' (p 23).[5] In the case of Zambia, a five to six percentage point increase in 'excessive' engagement in economic activities and household chores was observed for children across all age-groups in beneficiary households, which the authors argue could be detrimental to children's wellbeing.

There were three studies of CCTs that noted impacts on children's exposure to hazards and harm, or on their wellbeing (two related to the CSG in South Africa and one to Pantawid in the Philippines). De Hoop et al (2020) note three impacts of the CSG: (1) fewer children working in roles outside the household, (2) more children working within their own household, and (3) a reduction in the percentage of children involved in casual or seasonal labour. The authors consider the reduction in casual labour to lower children's exposure to hazards such as exploitation by an employer. They also suggest that less casual labour would give children more opportunity for rest. However, the same study also finds a significant increase in the probability that beneficiary children would work at night and in bars, hotels and places of entertainment. An earlier study of the CSG found a potential indirect impact on adolescents' exposure to harm and hazards: in households that had started receiving the CSG when children were of a younger age, adolescents' participation in work outside the home was reduced, in particular for girls (DSD et al, 2012). Conversely, de Hoop et al (2019) find that in the Philippines, children in households that received the grant were five percentage points more likely to be working for pay outside the household than children in households that did not receive the grant.

Our review shows that evaluations that consider the impact of social assistance schemes on children's engagement with work provide ambiguous evidence and lack any critical reflection regarding the harms or benefits of engagement with work. Complex realities of work are bypassed by deeming any and all work to be undesirable, and judging the effectiveness of social assistance by its ability to reduce the time spent working and increase the time spent in formal education. Lack of critical engagement is evidenced by many studies using the terms 'child labour' and 'children's work' interchangeably, often without reference to ILO or national definitions of child labour. To our knowledge, no studies proposed alternative understandings of what constitutes harmful or potentially beneficial types or conditions of work.

In the next section, we develop the idea of hazardscapes to support a more nuanced understanding of children's engagement with work and situate social assistance as one of the policy levers to improve wellbeing for children.

Hazardscapes, incentives and policy levers

As noted previously, the notion of, and assumptions related to, harm drives the way in which social and political actors address children's work. We have seen that the ILO formally defines child labour as work that is mentally, physically, socially or morally harmful to children. It also includes in this category work that interferes with children's schooling because this is understood as harmful to future economic prospects. The problem with this definition is that harm is a contested and contingent concept, which makes it extremely difficult to develop a 'global' definition that is precise enough to be used in field research and that will be meaningful to different stakeholders in different contexts (Chapter 2, this volume). Embedded within narratives of harm are concepts of hazards and risks. Hazard might be physical, chemical, biological, environmental, ergonomic, social and so on: according to the ILO, hazard is anything with the potential to cause harm. It follows that harm is the realization of a hazard (also see Sabates-Wheeler and Sumberg, 2022).

We use the term 'hazardscape' to describe the main hazards facing children in any given situation, and their relative importance. The likelihood or probability that hazards will result in harm varies enormously. For example, a child, who through her work is regularly exposed to toxic chemicals, is more likely to experience serious harm than one who must carry loads that are only marginally too heavy. Using the notion of a home–school–workplace nexus (Chapter 4, this volume) (Figure 7.1), with all three spheres characterized to varying degrees by both work and hazards (and thus potential harm), it becomes clear that children navigate a complex, multi-layered hazardscape that extends well beyond what is generally considered child labour and children's work.

The potential for harm arises from a complex combination of factors, including: (1) the situational context, (2) the specific nature of the work and (3) the conditions that surround the work. The actual experience of harm will be influenced by the presence of any hazard management initiatives or structures, such as labour regulations, training, safeguarding measures, social norms and so on. For example, the use of protective equipment for

Figure 7.1: The nexus where children's work takes place

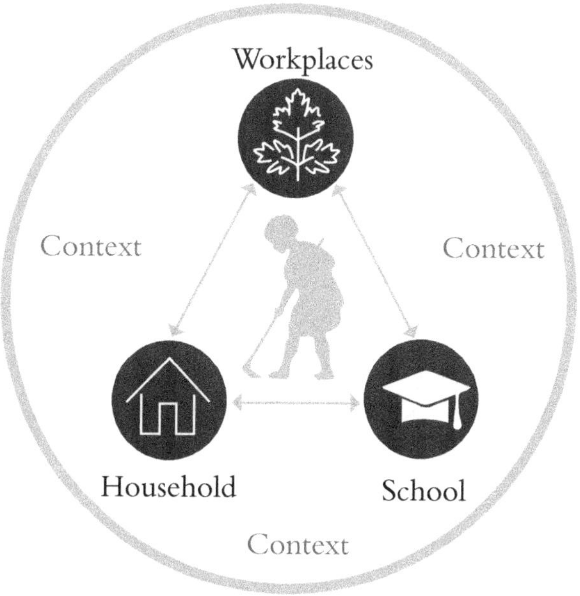

Source: Dunne, Humphreys and Szyp (Chapter 4, this volume)

the application of an agricultural chemical may change both the perception of the hazard and the likelihood that it will result in harm.

At home, children's work often includes cooking, collecting water and/or firewood, caring for other family members or working on the family farm. Some work might be supervised, some done independently (Admassie 2003; Dinku et al 2019; Robson 2004). The home environment *may be* more benign, but children will still be exposed to hazards and potential harm. Participation in household chores has been found to be associated with less time spent in school and corresponding lower academic achievements (Dinku et al, 2019; Kassouf et al, 2020), and an analysis of Young Lives data from Ethiopia found that 4+ hours per day of household chores had a large negative effect on children's body mass index (BMI) (Dinku et al, 2019).

Many children living in poor communities also work at school, including cleaning, weeding the school garden, tending small animals and assisting with school feeding programmes (Chapter 4, this volume). Some teachers use students as unpaid workers on their own farms or in their homes (Berlan, 2004; Hashim, 2004; Odonkor, 2007; Alhassan and Adzahlie-Mensah, 2010; Ananga, 2011; Casely-Hayford et al, 2013; Maconachie and Hilson, 2016). Hazards may be similar to the ones faced in other workplaces but may also include violence or/and abuse (Antonowicz, 2010; Shumba and Abosi, 2011; Humphreys et al, 2015). Work at school is predominantly carried out by girls and younger children, and girls are more likely to be targeted for abuse (Jones and Norton, 2007; Antonowicz, 2010).

By combining the notions of hazardscape and the work–school–home nexus it becomes clear that just because hazard and harm might be reduced in one sphere of the nexus, these reductions do not necessarily trade-off against higher benefits in another sphere. Reduced involvement in work at home or in a workplace might simply expose a child to new hazards and potential harms at school. Similarly, an increase in exposure to hazard and potential harm while working away from the home might lead to benefits in another sphere, such as more food or increased ability to pay school expenses. In other words, the way that harm and benefits are realized in different parts of the nexus will mean that the overall *a priori* net effect of work across the nexus will most often be ambiguous.

Gaining an understanding of the interaction between hazard, harm and benefit across these spheres is vital as children's and their family's decisions about work will be influenced by weighing up hazard and harm against benefits. As outlined in Table 7.1, within each sphere of the home–workplace–school nexus there are potential policy levers with which the hazardscape might be managed. All interventions are about changing the structure and nature of the hazardscape, which will in turn modify the potential for harm (that is, the harmscape). Many forms of work will likely remain unchanged, but the likelihood of them translating to harm will be mediated by changes in the hazardscape.

A focus on the hazardscape is particularly useful in the workplace sphere as it moves the duty of care to an institutional level – government, employers and labour unions – making it their responsibility to ensure that hazards are managed to reduce the likelihood of harm. Legislation around workplace safety, health insurance provision and provision of protective gear among others, should reduce the likelihood of hazards resulting in harm. The limitation is that such provisions are unlikely to touch the informal workplaces within which most paid work by children in Africa is situated.

In addition to legislation and accountability structures, the table shows that across the three spheres behaviour modifiers can take the form of social protection. Interventions can include conditional or unconditional social transfers (cash, food or assets), child grants, social pensions, school feeding and any poverty-targeted intervention, such as public works, that increases income and nudges households to reallocate labour across the portfolio of activities it is engaged with. Other 'soft' interventions that augment income or food transfers include training and awareness raising initiatives. Policy levers at the household level often take the form of poverty-targeted income transfers (either direct or indirect through a conditional cash transfer). These interventions aim to change the choices that households make in relation to hours spent in school and work, and will likely shift the balance of activity across the three spheres. At the school level, policy levers that

Table 7.1: Policy levers by sphere across the school–work–home nexus

Sphere	Primary policy levers	Purpose
Workplace	• Hazardscape management	
	• Legislation • Guidance and codes of conduct • Workspace regulations (health and safety) • Accountability structures • Monitoring • Information and sensitization; training • Health insurance provision	Actions to modify risk profile of work environment; reduce likelihoods of hazard presenting as harm
Household	• Incentive based 'nudging' • Social transfers: cash, food or assets • Social pensions • Child grants • Any 'income' transfer to the household • Information and training about harms and benefits of work–school–home • School feeding	Initiatives to change households and children's choices about engagement across the work–school–home nexus
School	• School based and incentive based	
	• Subsidies for school attendance • Universal Primary Education (UPE) • School grants targeted to specific groups • School feeding or take-home rations • Improve quality of school and teaching	School-conditional initiatives to 'pull' children into education

Source: Authors

influence the allocation of children's time and nature of engagement across the three spheres include education grants and subsidies, school feeding and other education-specific interventions.

Importantly, mapping out the hazardscapes and possible interventions across the three spheres highlights the way in which an intervention resulting in behavioural change in one sphere may impact another sphere, thus changing the balance and the trade-offs of harm and benefits from work (or school). Policy interventions therefore need to provide (1) modifiers to the hazardscape, (2) incentives to influence household and children's choices across the work–school–home nexus, and (3) information and training to allow people to make informed choices about hazards and potential harms.

Conclusion

In this chapter we have used a social assistance lens to open up and question the assumptions underpinning the common suite of policy actions used to incentivize 'good' behaviour in relation to children's work. We develop two lines of argument. First, we argue that most social assistance interventions aimed at shifting the balance between children's work and education are premised on a simple binary that work is always bad and education is always good, and that reduced engagement in any kind of work therefore constitutes programme success. This is despite an established and growing body of work that shows this to be a false binary, and that a combination of certain types of work and school might be most beneficial for children. Second, the definitions applied and indicators used to measure and locate children's work vary by organization, country and programme, resulting in huge challenges in being able to say anything useful about how policy interacts with children's work. As a result, making clear-cut recommendations about design and implementation of interventions is virtually impossible. What is needed is a contextualized understanding of the conditions within which children's work takes place, how it is experienced by children and families, and how policy interventions can serve to reduce harm experienced through work.

A more nuanced understanding of children's work, and which types of work may lead to harm and why, is vital for social assistance to tackle harmful children's work. By moving away from a simple binary of reducing work and increasing schooling towards the objective of reducing harmful work, various forms of complementary support could help parents and their children to consider alternative options. If social assistance is combined with forms of behaviour change communication (BCC) or sensitization about immediate and long-term harms associated with certain types of work or work situations, parents and children may choose for children to forego this work or adjust in order to reduce the potential for harm. This is even more important given the role of social norms, labour relations and other more structural issues in determining harmful and exploitative forms of children's work, suggesting that social assistance that is primarily predicated on achieving an income effect will have limited success in reducing harmful children's work (Thompson, 2012).

There is need for much greater precision and clarity when using the terms 'child labour' or 'children's work'. Evaluation studies often use these terms in a loose manner, sometimes interchangeably, with limited reference to ILO guidelines or formal definitions. Studies may refer to the impact of programmes on child labour when in fact they only consider intensity or prevalence of paid or unpaid work. This creates confused messaging about the actual programme impacts. A more precise use of language and indicators in reference to children's work is not an issue of semantics or ideology but can fundamentally shift design and implementation social protection programmes with real effects on children's lives.

Appendix

Table 7.2: Reviews included within our analysis

Programme and country	Review	Definition (or description) of child labour/work	Indicators used	Impacts (harm, hazards and wellbeing)
Unconditional cash transfers (UCTs)				
Malawi Social Cash Transfer Scheme (MSCT)	Miller and Tsoka (2012)	No explicit definition	Prevalence (engagement in household chores, other family work, and income-generating activities outside the household for money)	None
	Covarrubias et al (2012)*	No explicit definition	Prevalence (engagement in paid and unpaid domestic work outside the house, within-household tasks, and family farm/non-farm business activities)	Child labour activities changed from work outside the household to family-based work in family enterprises or in household chores
	de Hoop, Groppo and Handa (2019)*	Careful discussion of child work versus child labour and hazardous forms of work	Prevalence (engagement in farm work for the household, caring for livestock owned by the household, work in the nonfarm household business, paid work outside the household, and household chores) Intensity (engagement in farm work for the household, caring for livestock owned by the household, work in the nonfarm household business, paid work outside the household, and household chores)	Increase in the risk of exposure to hazards such as 'carrying heavy loads, working with dangerous tools, exposure to dust, fumes or gas, and exposure to extreme cold, heat or humidity'.

(continued)

Table 7.2: Reviews included within our analysis (continued)

Programme and country	**Review**	**Definition (or description) of child labour/work**	**Indicators used**	**Impacts (harm, hazards and wellbeing)**
			Working conditions (exposure to hazards including carrying heavy loads, working with dangerous tools, exposure to dust fumes or gas or to heat, cold or humidity; ill or injured in the 2 weeks or 12 months before interview)	
Multiple Category Targeted Programme, Zambia	de Hoop, Groppo and Handa (2019)*	Careful discussion of children's work versus child labour and hazardous forms of work	Prevalence (engagement in any economic activities classified as farm work for the household, caring for livestock owned household, caring for livestock owned by the household, work in the nonfarm household business, and paid work outside the household; and household chores encompassing collecting water or firewood; taking care of children, cooking, or cleaning; and taking care of elderly or sick household member)	None
Child Grants Programme, Lesotho	Oxford Policy Management (2014)	No explicit definition	Prevalence (engagement in any labour activity, own non-farm business activities, own crop/livestock production activities, paid work outside the household)	None

Table 7.2: Reviews included within our analysis (continued)

Programme and country	**Review**	**Definition (or description) of child labour/work**	**Indicators used**	**Impacts (harm, hazards and wellbeing)**
			Intensity (hours spent on a typical school day helping at home with household tasks, completing tasks on family farm, herding or other family business, activities for pay (cash or kind) outside the household)	
	Sebastian et al (2019)	No explicit definition	Prevalence (engagement in own crop or livestock production)	None
			Intensity (days worked in last week on own crop or livestock production)	
Orphans and Vulnerable Children Cash Transfer (CT-OVC), Kenya	Asfaw et al (2014)	Acknowledgement that data is insufficient to provide detailed picture of child labour according to international definitions	Prevalence (engagement in agricultural and non-agricultural wage labour or own-farm labour)	None

(continued)

Table 7.2: Reviews included within our analysis (continued)

Programme and country	**Review**	**Definition (or description) of child labour/work**	**Indicators used**	**Impacts (harm, hazards and wellbeing)**
Bono de Desarrollo Humano, Ecuador	Edmonds and Schady (2012)	No explicit definition	Prevalence (engagement in paid employment and unpaid economic activity in the family farm or business and unpaid household-based work) Intensity (hours spent on paid employment and unpaid economic activity in the family farm or business and unpaid household-based work)	None
Child Support Grant (CSG), South Africa	DSD et al (2012)*	No explicit definition; types of work differentiated by age group	Prevalence (engagement in household chores, helping with family business, working for pay outside the household for 10-year olds or engagement in paid or unpaid work inside or outside the home for 15–17-year olds) Intensity (hours spent on work inside the home and in work outside the home for 15–17-year olds)	15–17-year olds: receipt of the CSG at a younger age reduces participation in work outside the home, particularly in girls.

Table 7.2: Reviews included within our analysis (continued)

Programme and country	Review	Definition (or description) of child labour/work	Indicators used	Impacts (harm, hazards and wellbeing)
Conditional cash transfers (CCTs)				
Productive Social Safety Net (PSSN), Tanzania	Rosas and Ngowi (2019)	Programme theory of change includes reduction of number of hours spent on work; differentiation by age group	Prevalence (engagement in paid or unpaid work either outside or inside the household for 5–14-year olds and 14–19-year olds) Intensity (hours spent on work in paid or unpaid work either outside or inside the household for 5–14-year olds and 14–19-year olds)	None
	de Hoop et al (2020)*	Careful discussion of child work versus child labour and hazardous forms of work	Prevalence (engagement in paid work outside the home, in hazardous activities or in excessive hours in economic activity for 3–15-year olds at baseline and 5–17-year olds at endline) Intensity (engagement in farm work for the household, caring for livestock owned by the household, work in the nonfarm household business, paid work outside the household) Working conditions (exposure to hazards including carrying heavy loads, working with dangerous tools, exposure to dust fumes or gas; to heat, cold or humidity; loud noise or vibration)	Fewer children working in roles outside the household, and instead working within their own household Reduction in percentage of children involved in casual or seasonal labour, and therefore lower exposure to hazards associated with casual labour Significant increase in the probability that children worked at night and worked in bars, hotels and places of entertainment

(continued)

Table 7.2: Reviews included within our analysis (continued)

Programme and country	**Review**	**Definition (or description) of child labour/work**	**Indicators used**	**Impacts (harm, hazards and wellbeing)**
Bolsa Familia, Brazil	Brauw et al (2012)	No explicit definition	Prevalence (engagement in 'any work') Intensity (hours spent in typical week on domestic work)	None
Red de Protección Social, Nicaragua	Gee (2010)	No explicit definition	Prevalence (engagement in 'work') Intensity (hours spent on 'work')	None
Atención a Crisis, Nicaragua	Del Carpio et al (2016)	No explicit definition; distinction between physical and skill-forming child labour	Prevalence (engagement in economic agriculture and commerce activities and in non-economic household chores) Intensity (days and hours per week spent on economic agriculture and commerce activities and in non-economic household chores)	None
PROGRESA / Oportunidades, Mexico	Behrman et al (2011)	No explicit definition	Prevalence (engagement in agricultural and non-agricultural work)	None

Table 7.2: Reviews included within our analysis (continued)

Programme and country	Review	Definition (or description) of child labour/work	Indicators used	Impacts (harm, hazards and wellbeing)
Pantawid, the Philippines	De Hoop et al (2019)*	No explicit definition; acknowledgement that desired programme effect depends on type of work	Prevalence (engagement in paid work outside the home, unpaid work inside or outside the household, paid work inside the household)	Compared to control group, there was a 5 percentage point increase in children working for pay outside the household
			Intensity (days year and hours per week spent paid work outside the home, unpaid work inside or outside the household, paid work inside the household)	
Feeding programmes				
Take Home Rations, Burkina Faso	Kazianga et al (2012)	No explicit definition	Prevalence (engagement in farm work, non-farm work and livestock herding, and domestic work including fetching water, fetching firewood, tending for younger siblings and household chores)	None
School Meals, Burkina Faso				None
School meals, Ghana	Aurino et al (2018)	No explicit definition	Intensity (average time spent on a typical day at school, doing housework, doing farm work or other types of labour)	None
Public works				
Productive Safety Net Programme (PSNP), Ethiopia	Hoddinott et al (2010)	No explicit definition	Intensity (hours spent in last week on farm work or domestic tasks)	None

(continued)

Table 7.2: Reviews included within our analysis (continued)

Programme and country	**Review**	**Definition (or description) of child labour/work**	**Indicators used**	**Impacts (harm, hazards and wellbeing)**
PSSN, Tanzania (see previously in CCT)				
MGNREGS, India	Das and Mukherjee (2019)	No explicit definition	Intensity (hours spent per day on work; 1–4 hours is low intensity and 4–8 hours is high intensity)	None
	Shah and Steinberg (2019)	No explicit definition; differentiation by age group	Intensity (hours spent on work at home, work outside home, domestic work)	None
Programa Jefes y Jefas de Hogar Desocupados, Argentina	Juras (2014)	No explicit definition; text refers to child work only	Prevalence (engagement in work for pay)	None
Social pensions				
Social Pension, Brazil	de Carvalho Filho (2012)	No explicit definition	Prevalence (engagement in work for pay) Children 10–14 participation in wage economy School enrolment boys/girls	None

Notes: 'None' means that no description or analysis of impact on harm hazards or wellbeing is provided in the article. * Indicates inclusion of 'harm' within impacts.

Notes

1. Social protection is commonly described as comprising three elements: *social assistance*; *social insurance*; and *labour market programmes*. *Social services* are increasingly accepted as a further element. Social assistance includes social transfers (cash, food or assets), public works programmes, fee waivers and subsidies.
2. The worst forms of child labour as defined by Article 3 of ILO Convention No. 182: all forms of slavery or practices similar to slavery, such as the sale and trafficking of children, debt bondage and serfdom and forced or compulsory labour, including forced or compulsory recruitment of children for use in armed conflict; the use, procuring or offering of a child for prostitution, for the production of pornography or for pornographic performances; the use, procuring or offering of a child for illicit activities, in particular for the production and trafficking of drugs as defined in the relevant international treaties; work which, by its nature or the circumstances in which it is carried out, is likely to harm the health, safety or morals of children.
3. The *income effect* is the change in demand for a good or service caused by a change in a consumer's purchasing power resulting from a change in real *income* (in this case through the provision of cash).
4. This could be a positive impact under the assumption that work outside of the household is frequently deemed less desirable and more disruptive to children's education.
5. This finding appears to contradict the findings described previously, but this is likely due to the inconsistency in indicators used. Corravubias [et al] look only at children's time allocation: there were no indicators in [the] Covarrubias [et al] study to see whether or not the increase in children's involvement in within household tasks corresponded to increased exposure to harm, which is why [we] [considered] it as a potentially indirect impact.

References

Abebe, T. and Bessell, S. (2011) 'Dominant discourses, debates and silences on child labour in Africa and Asia', *Third World Quarterly*, 32(4), pp 765–86.

Admassie, A. (2003) 'Child labour and schooling in the context of a subsistence rural economy: can they be compatible?', *International Journal of Educational Development*, 23(2), pp 167–85.

Alhassan, S. and Adzahlie-Mensah, V. (2010) *Teachers and Access to Schooling in Ghana. Create Pathways to Access Research Monograph No. 43*. Brighton: CREATE, Centre for International Education, University of Sussex.

Ananga, E.D. (2011) 'Typology of school dropout: the dimensions and dynamics of dropout in Ghana', *International Journal of Educational Development*, 31(4), pp 374–81.

Antonowicz, L. (2010) *Too Often in Silence: A Report on School-Based Violence in West and Central Africa*. UNICEF, Plan West Africa, Save the Children Sweden West Africa and Action Aid.

Asfaw, S. et al (2014) 'Cash transfer programme, productive activities and labour supply: evidence from a randomised experiment in Kenya', *Journal of Development Studies*, 50(8), pp 1172–96.

Aufseeser, D. et al (2018) 'Children's work and children's well-being: implications for policy', *Development Policy Review*, 36(2), pp 241–61.

Aurino, E. et al (2018) *Food for Thought? Experimental Evidence on the Learning Impacts of a Large-Scale School Feeding Program in Ghana*. IFPRI Discussion Paper 1782. Washington, DC: International Food Policy Research Institute (IFPRI).

Bastagli, F. et al (2016) *Cash Transfers: What Does the Evidence Say? A Rigorous Review of Programme Impact and of the Role of Design and Implementation Features*. London: Overseas Development Institute (ODI).

Behrman, J.R., Parker, S.W. and Todd, P.E. (2011) 'Do conditional cash transfers for schooling generate lasting benefits? A five-year followup of Progresa/Oportunidades', *The Journal of Human Resources*, 46(1), pp 93–122.

Berlan, A. (2004) 'Child labour, education and child rights among cocoa producers in Ghana', in van den Anker, C. (ed) *The Political Economy of New Slavery*. London: Palgrave Macmillan, pp 158–78.

Bourdillon, M. et al (2010) *Rights and Wrongs of Children's Work*. New Brunswick, New Jersey and London: Rutgers University Press.

Bourdillon, M. and Carothers, R. (2019) 'Policy on children's work and labour', *Children & Society*, 33(4), pp 387–95.

Brauw, A. et al (2012) *The Impact of Bolsa Familia on Child, Maternal and Household Welfare*. Unpublished paper. Washington, DC: International Food Policy Research Institute (IFPRI).

Burgard, S.A. and Lin, K.Y. (2013) 'Bad jobs, bad health? How work and working conditions contribute to health disparities', *The American Behavioral Scientist*, 57(8), pp 1105–27.

de Carvalho Filho, I.E. (2012) 'Household income as a determinant of child labor and school enrollment in Brazil: evidence from a social security reform', *Economic Development and Cultural Change*, 60(2), pp 399–435.

Casely-Hayford, L. et al (2013) *The Quality and Inclusivity of Basic Education Across Ghana's Three Northern Regions: A Look at Change, Learning Effectiveness and Efficiency*. Accra: Associates for Change.

Covarrubias, K., Davis, B. and Winters, P. (2012) 'From protection to production: productive impacts of the Malawi Social Cash Transfer scheme', *Journal of Development Effectiveness*, 4(1), pp 50–77.

Dammert, A.C. et al (2018) 'Effects of public policy on child labor: current knowledge, gaps, and implications for program design', *World Development*, 110, pp 104–23.

Das, S. and Mukherjee, D. (2019) 'The impact of MGNREGS on child labour and child education: an empirical analysis', *Development in Practice*, 29(3), pp 384–94.

Del Carpio, X.V., Loayza, N.V. and Wada, T. (2016) 'The impact of conditional cash transfers on the amount and type of child labor', *World Development*, 80, pp 33–47.

Dinku, Y., Fielding, D. and Genc, M. (2019) 'Counting the uncounted: the consequences of children's domestic chores for health and education in Ethiopia', *Review of Development Economics*, 23(3), pp 1260–81.

DSD, SASSA and UNICEF (2012) *The South African Child Support Grant Impact Assessment: Evidence from a Survey of Children, Adolescents and Their Households*. Pretoria: UNICEF South Africa.

Edmonds, E.V. and Schady, N. (2012) 'Poverty alleviation and child labor', *American Economic Journal: Economic Policy*, 4(4), pp 100–24.

Gee, K.A. (2010) 'Reducing child labour through conditional cash transfers: evidence from Nicaragua's Red de Proteccion Social', *Development Policy Review*, 28(6), pp 711–32.

Hanson, K., Volonakis, D. and Al-Rozzi, M. (2015) 'Child labour, working children and children's rights', in Vandenhole, W. et al (eds) *International Handbook of Children's Rights Studies*. London: Routledge, pp 332–46.

Hashim, I.M. (2004) *Working with Working Children: Child Labour and the Barriers to Education in Rural Northeastern Ghana*. Unpublished PhD thesis. University of Sussex.

Hoddinott, J., Gilligan, D.O. and Taffesse, A.S. (2010) *The Impact of Ethiopia's Productive Safety Net Program on Schooling and Child Labor*. Unpublished paper.

de Hoop, J. et al (2019) 'Child schooling and child work in the presence of a partial education subsidy', *Journal of Human Resources*, 54(2), pp 503–31.

de Hoop, J., Gichane, M.W. and Zuilkowski, S.S. (2020) *Cash Transfers, Public Works and Child Activities: Mixed Methods Evidence from the United Republic of Tanzania*. Office of Research – Innocenti Working Paper. Florence, Italy: UNICEF Office of Research – Innocenti.

de Hoop, J., Groppo, V. and Handa, S. (2019) 'Cash transfers, microentrepreneurial activity, and child work: evidence from Malawi and Zambia', *The World Bank Economic Review*, 34(3), pp 670–97.

de Hoop, J. and Rosati, F. (2014) *Cash Transfers and Child Labour*. Rome: Understanding Children's Work Project.

Humphreys, S. et al (2015) 'Counted in and being out: fluctuations in primary school and classroom attendance in northern Nigeria', *International Journal of Educational Development*, 44, pp 134–43.

ILO (1973) *Convention C138 – Minimum Age Convention, 1973 (No. 138)*. Available at: https://www.ilo.org/dyn/normlex/en/f?p=NORMLEXPUB:12100:0::NO::P12100_ILO_CODE:C138 (Accessed 29 April 2020).

ILO (1999) *Convention C182 – Worst Forms of Child Labour Convention, 1999 (No. 182)*. Available at: https://www.ilo.org/dyn/normlex/en/f?p=NORMLEXPUB:12100:0::NO::P12100_ILO_CODE:C182 (Accessed 28 April 2020).

ILO (2011) *Children in Hazardous Work: What We Know, What We Need to Do*. Geneva: International Labour Organization.

ILO and UNICEF (2021) *Child Labour: Global Estimates 2020, Trends and the Road Forward*. New York: International Labour Organization and United Nations Children's Fund.

ILO-IPEC (2012) *The Tripartite Process of Determining Hazardous Child Labour – Guide for Facilitators*. Geneva: International Labour Organization – IPEC.

Jones, S. and Norton, B. (2007) 'On the limits of sexual health literacy: insights from Ugandan schoolgirls', *Diaspora, Indigenous, and Minority Education*, 1(4), pp 285–305.

Juras, R. (2014) 'The effect of public employment on children's work and school attendance: evidence from a social protection program in Argentina', *IZA Journal of Labor and Development*, 3(14), Article 14, pp 1–20.

Kassouf, A.L., Tiberti, L. and Garcias, M. (2020) 'Evidence of the impact of children's household chores and market labour on learning from school census data in Brazil', *Journal of Development Studies*, 56(11), pp 2097–112.

Kazianga, H., de Walque, D. and Alderman, H. (2012) 'Educational and child labour impacts of two food-for-education schemes: evidence from a randomised trial in rural Burkina Baso', *Journal of African Economies*, 21(5), pp 723–60.

Maconachie, R. and Hilson, G. (2016) 'Re-thinking the child labor "problem" in rural sub-Saharan Africa: the case of Sierra Leone's half shovels', *World Development*, 78, pp 136–47.

Miller, C. and Tsoka, M. (2012) 'Cash transfers and children's education and labour among Malawi's poor', *Development Policy Review*, 30(4), pp 499–522.

Odonkor, M. (2007) *Addressing Child Labour Through Education*. Accra, Ghana: Frontier Analysis Consulting Associates Ltd.

Orkin, K. (2012) 'Are work and schooling complementary or competitive for children in rural Ethiopia? A mixed-methods study', in Boyden, J. and Bourdillon, M. (eds) *Childhood Poverty: Multidisciplinary Approaches*. London: Palgrave Macmillan UK, pp 298–313.

Oxford Policy Management (2014) *Child Grants Programme Impact Evaluation. Follow-up Report*. Oxford: Oxford Policy Management.

Robson, E. (2004) 'Hidden child workers: young carers in Zimbabwe', *Antipode*, 36(2), pp 227–6.

Roelen, K. et al (2017) *How to Make "Cash Plus" Work: Linking Cash Transfers to Services and Sectors*. Office of Research – Innocenti Working Paper WP-2017-10. Florence: UNICEF Office of Research.

Rosas, N. and Ngowi, E. (2019) *Evaluating Tanzania's Productive Social Safety Net Findings from the Midline Survey*. Washington, DC: World Bank Group.

Sabates-Wheeler, R. and Sumberg, J. (2022) 'Breaking out of the policy enclave approach to child labour in sub-Saharan African agriculture', *Global Social Policy*, 22(1), pp 46–66.

Sebastian, A. et al (2019) 'Cash transfers and gender differentials in child schooling and labor: evidence from the Lesotho Child Grants Programme', *Population and Development Review*, 45(S1), pp 181–208.

Shah, M. and Steinberg, B.M. (2019) 'Workfare and human capital investment: evidence from India', *Journal of Human Resources*, 117–9201R2.

Shumba, A. and Abosi, O.C. (2011) 'The nature, extent and causes of abuse of children with disabilities in schools in Botswana', *International Journal of Disability, Development and Education*, 58(4), pp 373–88.

Singh, S. and McLeish, S. (2013) 'Social protection and its effectiveness in tackling child labour: the case of internal child migrants in Indonesia', in *SMERU Conference on Child Poverty and Social Protection*, Jakarta, Indonesia: SMERU Research Institute.

Thompson, H. (2012) *Cash and Child Protection. How Cash Transfer Programming Can Protect Children from Abuse, Neglect, Exploitation and Violence*. London: Save the Children.

Zaidi, M. et al (2017) *'My Work Never Ends': Women's Experiences of Balancing Unpaid Care Work and Paid Work through WEE Programming in India*. IDS Working Paper 494. Brighton: Institute of Development Studies (IDS).

Zibagwe, S., Nduna, T. and Dafuleya, G. (2013) 'Are social protection programmes child-sensitive?', *Development Southern Africa*, 30(1), pp 111–20.

8

Children's Work in Ghana: Policies and Politics

Samuel Okyere, Emmanuel Frimpong Boamah, Felix Ankomah Asante and Thomas Yeboah

Introduction

This chapter explores policy and legislation aimed at preventing, regulating and abolishing harmful children's work in Ghana, and the political debates and controversies surrounding these mechanisms. Children's work in sectors such as agriculture, trading, fishing and a host of others has emerged as an area of public concern over the last three decades. As outlined in phases 1 (2009–2015) and 2 (2017–2021) of the National Plan of Action for the Elimination of the Worst Forms of Child Labour (hereafter NPA1 and NPA2), the Government of Ghana (GoG) views harmful children's work in these and other sectors as a breach of the dignity, personhood, wellbeing, development and fundamental human rights of the child. This view is supported by UN agencies, domestic and international non-governmental organizations (NGO and INGO) and other development partners which have long called upon and supported the GoG to put in place preventative and abolitionist measures against such work. The ensuing campaigns, laws, policies, direct interventions and the human, financial and material resources targeted at these prohibited forms of work over the last three decades have seen success in areas such as school enrolment. They have also successfully ushered debates on 'child labour' into the centre of Ghanaian policymaking, civil society or NGO advocacy, academic research and wider public discourse (Okali et al, 2022).

Yet, awareness-raising and increased school enrolment have neither achieved the primary goal of disengaging children from prohibited forms of work, nor necessarily provided working children with good quality education (Hamenoo et al, 2018; Carter et al, 2020; Ghanney et al, 2020).

The number of children involved in prohibited work and those combining such work with schooling has risen rather than decreased (Baah et al, 2009; Darko, 2014; UCW, 2016b; Aboa and Ross, 2020). This ineffectiveness raises questions about the compatibility of the policies and programmes with the country's historical, socio-cultural, economic and political realities (Okyere, 2012; Thum-Danso Imoh, 2012). Actors within fishing, farming, mining and other sectors that have been the target of interventions to abolish child labour have expressed misgivings about the fact that notions like 'tutelage' and 'civilizing' are inherent to some of these measures (Nti, 2017). They challenge efforts to impose particular forms of childhood and children's socialization through campaigns and narratives which delegitimize autochthonous cultures and child socialization mechanisms and also overlook the socio-economic drivers of children's work (Okyere, 2013; Jonah and Abebe, 2019).

This chapter elaborates on the foregoing and other contestations surrounding children's work in Ghana. The next section provides a brief overview of children's economic activity. The discussion then outlines the major national legislation, policies and initiatives targeted at eliminating work deemed hazardous, harmful or inimical to children's welfare and development. The third section is an evaluative analysis of the successes and failures of these preventative interventions, highlighting obstacles or limitations where their impact has been limited. Here, the chapter highlights the fact that approaches to children's work in Ghana are located within two rights discourses and practices, that are sometimes complementary and sometimes in opposition. There is, on the one hand, a formal legislative rights discourse, with its related practices and norms on childhood, children's rights and children's work, influenced strongly by international rights conventions, NGO and INGO advocacy and demands by (mainly) Western development partners including agencies from the US and EU. On the other hand, there is an informal, traditional rights discourse with its related practices underpinned by autochthonous socio-cultural norms on childhood, children's rights and children's work. These two discourses, the chapter argues, sit at distinct levels of Ghanaian society and polity: the former dominant within government, NGOs, civil society and in urban, middle-class spheres; and the latter dominant in working-class, socio-economically marginalized communities and rural areas.

The chapter concludes that legislation and interventions aimed at preventing children's hazardous or harmful work should draw on both perspectives if they are to help advance children's development, rights and best interests. Such compromise is urgently needed because while the formal position is backed by law, its implementation continues to be stymied by the asymmetries between it and structures and norms that shape children's socialization and lived experiences in rural areas. Adopting a purely punitive approach, instead of consensus-building, unduly penalizes already marginalized and disenfranchised communities. The outcome may be further antagonism towards NGOs and government workers in these communities and rejection of child rights interventions.

Children's work in Ghana: a brief introduction

Successive studies have shown that work of various forms is integral to the lives of Ghanaian children. The ILO (2008) showed that over 88 per cent of Ghanaian children aged 5–14 years take on household chores and responsibilities. Depending on where the children live, their everyday work can range from domestic activities such as cooking, cleaning, taking care of siblings, washing dishes and running errands, to work outside the home such as herding livestock, farming, petty trading, and other economic and non-economic activities. Work constitutes a central aspect of what many Ghanaians regard as part of a normal and desirable upbringing (Yeboah, 2020). As discussed in more detail later in the chapter, this idea is reflected in some areas of the public education system where pupils are required to arrive well ahead of lessons to clean classrooms, toilets and other school facilities (Twum-Danso Imoh, 2009; also see Chapter 4, this volume). From the foregoing, while reflections on children's labour in Ghana tend to focus on poverty, probably the most important factor is that work in its diverse forms is integral to childhood socialization. With this recognition in mind, the GoG has sought to avoid blanket bans on children's work and instead to identify for elimination or regulation sectors and job types that are deemed inimical to children's wellbeing, schooling, development, and morals (Table 8.1).

Several concerns have been raised about such classifications. The line between acceptable work and unacceptable work is not easy to distinguish (as discussed more generally in Chapter 2, this volume). For example, scholars such as Berlan (2004), Okyere (2013, 2018) and Howard (2017) have questioned whether children's participation in cocoa farming, domestic work, fishing and other activities can be deemed exploitative or harmful without consideration of the specificities surrounding their involvement. Hence, while the GoG, ILO and other stakeholders identify fishing and related activities such as preparing bait, nets and fishing gear as 'categorical worst forms of child labour', following a study by the Food and Agriculture Organization (FAO) aimed at reducing child exploitation in Ghanaian agriculture (Zdunnek et al, 2008), FAO staff member Bernd Seiffert observed that 'working on the farm or on the fishing boat or herding cattle can, if it doesn't get in the way of school and occurs under safe circumstances, be very valuable. It's a means of acquiring skills, giving kids a sense of belonging and cultural identity'.[1]

Others posit that forced ritual servitude and trafficking that appear in such lists are not really 'work' *per se* (Nimbona and Lieten, 2007). A related area

Table 8.1: Children's work targeted for regulation or elimination in Ghana

Sector/ industry	Activity
Agriculture	Producing cocoa*, including land clearing, using machetes and cutlasses for weeding, collecting cocoa pods with a harvesting hook, breaking cocoa pods, working in the vicinity of pesticide spraying, and carrying heavy loads* of water.
	Production of palm oil* and cotton, including weeding, harvesting, and acting as scarecrows.
	Herding livestock, including cattle, hunting*, and work in slaughterhouses.
	Fishing*, including for tilapia; preparing bait, nets, and fishing gear; launching, paddling, and draining canoes; diving for fish; casting and pulling fishing nets and untangling them underwater; sorting, picking, cleaning, smoking, transporting, and selling fish; cleaning and repairing nets; and building and repairing boats.
Industry	Quarrying* and small-scale mining*, sometimes for gold, including using mercury, digging in deep pits, crushing rocks by hand, carrying heavy loads*, and operating machinery*.
	Manufacturing and working in sawmills*.
	Construction and bricklaying or carrying brick.
Service	Domestic work*.
	Transporting heavy loads as *kayayei**.
	Work in transportation*, activities unknown.
	Electronic waste and garbage scavenging*, including sorting scavenged items* and transporting items for sale*.
	Street work*, including begging*, small-scale vending, and working at restaurants or bars*.
Categorical worst forms of child labour**	Commercial sexual exploitation, sometimes as a result of human trafficking.
	Forced labour in begging; agriculture, including herding; fishing, including for tilapia; artisanal gold mining; domestic work; and street work, including vending and carrying heavy loads, each sometimes as a result of human trafficking.
	Forced ritual servitude for girls known as trokosi, including domestic work for priests.

*Determined by national law or regulation as hazardous and, as such, relevant to Article 3(d) of ILO C. 182 (1999).

**Child labour understood as the worst forms of child labour per se under Article 3(a)–(c) of ILO C. 182 (1999).

Sources: Bureau of International Labor Affairs (2018), Shahinian (2014), ILO-IPEC (2013) and Tulane University (2015)

of contention is the attempt to quantify the number of children involved in the activities listed in Table 8.1. The production of estimates for phenomena such as child labour and its worst forms is inherently political. Numbers (like other research data) are not neutral as they do not exist independently of the people who produce them (Best, 2008). Researchers define the problem, choose the questions to ask, what to count, how to go about the counting, and which aspects of the data to emphasize or de-emphasize. These choices are shaped by particular values, preferences, agendas, interests and resource availability, which suggest that the resultant figures should be treated with caution.

This disclaimer notwithstanding, all assessments carried out over the last two decades have shown a high prevalence of children's involvement in prohibited forms of work. In 2003, a survey by the Ghana Statistical Service (GSS) showed that over one million children under 13 years were working despite being officially prohibited from economic activities (Ghana Statistical Service, 2003). An estimated 242,074 children aged 13 to 17 years were engaged in exempted activities such as mining, fishing, stone quarrying, and others. Hence, approximately 1.3 million children or 19 per cent of the then estimated 6.4 million children in Ghana were engaged in activities prohibited by national and international policies. About a decade later, in 2012, data from the Ghana Living Standards Survey (GLSS) estimated that the number of children aged 14 years or younger who were involved in prohibited children's work was almost 1.5 million (Ghana Statistical Service, 2012). Methodological differences and other factors such as lack of information on the percentage increase or decrease in the population of children do not permit direct comparisons to be made between the 2003 and 2012 data. However, analysis by UNICEF's Understanding Children's Work (UCW) project compared an earlier (2005) version of the GLSS data with that of 2012 to provide a comprehensive and nationally-representative picture of the child labour and youth employment situations. It found that the involvement of children aged 7–14 years in prohibited activities more than doubled between 2005 (13 per cent) and 2012 (29 per cent) (UCW, 2016a).

The UCW analysis also showed that while the number of children aged 7–14 who were in prohibited work and not in school declined over the same period, there was a concomitant rise in the number of children combining schooling with work. This calls into question the commonly made argument that schooling will disengage children from work (Guarcello et al, 2006; Annan, 2012). Working children in Ghana are instead increasingly combining schooling with work, as several studies after the UCW analysis have also established (Ravallion and Wodon, 2000; Okyere, 2013; Maconachie and Hilson, 2016; also see Chapter 4, this volume). This may be seen as an improvement over the situation where working children do not attend school at all. However, over the last two decades, successive studies have shown that this situation can also result in poor quality education for working children, among other adverse consequences (Ray, 2002; Heady, 2003; Imoro, 2009; Feigben, 2010; Hamenoo et al, 2018; Carter et al, 2020). As Okyere (2013) notes, the schooling–child labour nexus in Ghana requires further scrutiny as access to schooling alone or of itself cannot address the myriad of reasons underpinning children's involvement in prohibited labour.

In terms of the distribution of children's work across economic sectors, the GSS (2012) data further shows that 80 per cent of the estimated 1,500,000 children in prohibited employment work in agriculture. Also, children working in the agricultural sector mainly do so within the family (82 per cent) (2016a, p 27). Data limitations did not permit a similar analysis of the involvement of those aged 15–17 in prohibited work. However, the GSS (2012) and the UCW (2016a) analysis concerning this group shows that 24 per cent (or 412,000 children) are engaged in activities such as head porterage, mining, quarrying, agriculture and other work forms that are considered to pose a danger to their health, safety or morals (see ILO, 1999 C182; and Section 91.2 of the Government of Ghana, 1998 Children's Act).

Altogether, an estimated 21.8 per cent (1,892,553) of children in Ghana are presently considered to be involved in child labour, and 14.2 per cent (1,231,286) in hazardous work (Government of the Republic of Ghana, 2017b). With regards to cocoa farming, which has been the focus of the most intense legislative, prevention and abolition efforts, the data suggest that during the period 2005–2012, the rise in the number of children working in cocoa-growing communities was greater than in non-cocoa communities (UCW, 2016a, p 31). Indeed, a recent major study by the University of Chicago, suggests that there has been an increase of at least 12 percentage points in the total number of children working in the Ghanaian and Ivorian cocoa sectors in 2018/19 compared to 2008/09; from 31 to 45 per cent (Sadhu et al, 2020). The number of children aged 5–17 working in Ivorian cocoa farming rose from 23 to 38 per cent and those working on Ghanaian cocoa farms from 44 to 55 per cent. This marked increase happened even as governments of the two countries, together with international cocoa companies under the Framework of Action to Support Implementation of the Harkin–Engel Protocol (US Department of Labor, 2017), pledged to reduce the worst forms of child labour in their West African supply chains by 70 per cent by 2020.

Regulatory and legislative frameworks

Over the past three decades, the GoG enacted a plethora of laws and signed international agreements aimed to regulate, prevent or eliminate prohibited forms of children's work. Key among these is Article 28 of the Constitution of Ghana (1992), which prohibits children's involvement in activities considered injurious to their health, education, or development, and provides a framework for legislation and policy to promote this ambition. Likewise, the Children's Act (Act 560) (1998) was enacted to reform and consolidate the law relating to children, to provide for the rights of the child, child maintenance and adoption, and regulate child labour and apprenticeships. Section 1 of Act 560 defines a child as a person below the age of 18 years. Section 87 makes children's involvement in exploitative labour (defined as work that deprives the child of health, education, and development) and hazardous work (defined in Section 91 as labour which poses a danger to the health, safety or morals of a person) illegal. Furthermore, Section 88 prohibits children working at night (between the hours of 8 pm and 6 am), while Sections 89 and 90 respectively set 15 years as the minimum age for employment and 13 years as the minimum age for entry into 'light work'. In addition to Act 560, other legislation addressing prohibited forms of children's work include the Child Rights Regulations instrument (LI 1705) (2002), Juvenile Justice Act (2003a) the Human Trafficking Act (Act 694) (2005), the Labour Act (Act 651) (2003b), Labour Regulations instrument (LI. 1833) (2007) and the Education Act (Act 778) (2008).

Ghana cannot be described as powerless or as playing a subservient role in the development of its national policies and programmes. Nonetheless, as several scholars have observed, few if any of Ghana's current legislative instruments on children's rights or children's labour, including the Constitution itself, have been shaped solely by domestic socio-political agendas (Gyimah-Boadi, 1994; Oquaye, 1995; Frimpong Boamah, 2018). New laws and debates on children's work and other child rights modalities have been heavily influenced by UN agencies, foreign donor governments and INGOs who demand or expect that Ghana adheres to international standards represented by various UN Conventions (Lawrance, 2010). As discussed later, there is a long-standing critique in the childhood studies and rights literature that these should not be considered as 'international standards', but as Western-derived norms.

The Child Rights Act, for instance, is a near carbon copy of the United Nations Convention on the Rights of the Child (CRC). ILO Convention Nos 138 and 182 also feature very prominently in sections touching on child labour. Likewise, the Human Trafficking Act (Act 694) (Government of the Republic of Ghana, 2005) is derived from the United Nations Protocol to Prevent, Suppress and Punish Trafficking in Persons, especially Women and Children (hereafter referred to as the Palermo Protocol). Such is the influence of foreign actors in Ghana's national legislative efforts that the country included these provisions in its flagship children's rights legislation even before it had formally ratified ILO Convention No. 138,[2] and before the adoption of ILO Convention No. 182 by the UN General Assembly in 2000. Additionally, the government's flagship programmes NPA1 (2009–2015) and NPA2 (2017–21) were both developed with technical and financial support from the ILO, UNICEF and International Cocoa Initiative (ICI) (Government of the Republic of Ghana, 2009, 2017b).

Most of the previous and current direct interventions aimed at eliminating children's work in sectors with high international visibility (such as cocoa farming, fishing, mining and rice farming) have also been carried out with funding from actors such as the US Department of Labour (USDoL) and US State Department, the World Cocoa Foundation, International Cocoa Initiative (ICI), and with technical assistance from ILO-IPEC (ILO-IPEC, 2013). The next sections highlight the key programmes and other initiatives partly or wholly targeted at the elimination or regulation of prohibited children's work over the last decade and the scale to which these activities are influenced by and dependent on funding from external development partners.

Key policies and social interventions aimed at preventing and eliminating child labour

The National Plan of Action for the Elimination of the Worst Forms of Child Labour, Phase 1 (NPA1, 2009–2015)

This was Ghana's first systematic attempt to prevent and eliminate child labour (Government of the Republic of Ghana, 2009). Among others, some key objectives were to review, update and enforce the laws; ensure social mobilization for the respect and protection of children's rights; ensure full implementation of the Free Compulsory Universal Basic Education (FCUBE) Policy with priority attention to deprived communities; put in place institutional arrangements to identify, withdraw, rehabilitate and reintegrate children unconditionally from the worst forms of child labour; and put in place measures to prevent and eliminate hazardous child labour.

NPA1 did not originate from within the GoG itself, but from ILO-IPEC through its Ghana National Programme Manager (Government of the Republic of Ghana, 2009, p 6). This is a potential explanation for the programme's lack of success (Government of the Republic of Ghana, 2017b). Although NPA1 is said to have helped make the need to address child labour a priority in many sectors and saw some actions undertaken, its overall impact was graded 'below expectation' and poor performance was identified at all stages. The Ministry of Employment and Social Welfare (MESW), through its Child Labour Unit (CLU), had responsibility for the overall coordination and supervision of NPA1. However, the assessment report states that 'apart from donor-led interventions, which were monitored by the respective donors, little was done', due to failure by implementing agencies to provide reports and share information, staff capacity issues and generally low collaborative efforts between the relevant parties (Government of the Republic of Ghana, 2017b, p 22).

The National Plan of Action for the Elimination of the Worst Forms of Child Labour, Phase 2 (NPA2, 2017–21)

This is a continuation of NPA1 and, in reality, it seeks to achieve what NPA1 could not. NPA2 has the overarching objective to: 'reduce child labour to the barest minimum (at least 10%) by 2021 while laying strong social, policy and institutional foundations for the elimination and prevention of all forms of child labour in the longer term' (Government of the Republic of Ghana, 2017b, p 27). The main difference with NPA1 is that a figure of 'at least 10%' has been cited to represent the idea of 'barest minimum' within the mission statement. Four accompanying strategic objectives are to: reinforce public awareness and strengthen advocacy for improved policy programming and implementation of child development interventions; improve capacity, collaboration, coordination and resource mobilization for effective implementation of child labour interventions; ensure effective provision and monitoring of social services and economic empowerment programmes by local government administrations; and promote community empowerment and sustainable action against child labour. NPA2 is being carried out with 'technical direction and financial support' from ICI, the United Nation Children's Fund (UNICEF), ILO and the Government of Canada (Government of the Republic of Ghana, 2017b, p 8).

The Declaration of Joint Action to Support the Implementation of the Harkin–Engel Protocol

This declaration, made in 2010, aims at a significant reduction in the worst forms of child labour in cocoa producing areas of Ghana and Côte d'Ivoire. As with the Harkin–Engel Protocol itself, the origins of the declaration's Framework of Action were not from either of the two West African countries, but the US. Additionally, it is funded in almost its entirety by the USDoL (US$10 million in 2010 and further amounts thereafter) and ICI (approximately US$10 million in the inception phase and further amounts thereafter). This protocol for public–private partnership involves activities such as continuing the child labour surveys and establishing the Ghana Child Labour Monitoring System (GCLMS) in 2010, that was subsequently constrained by inadequate funding (Owusu-Amankwah, 2015).

The National Plan of Action for the Elimination of Human Trafficking in Ghana (NPAHT, 2017–21)

This seeks to reduce the scale of child and other forms of trafficking and address the social factors that make children especially vulnerable to being trafficked (Government of the Republic of Ghana, 2017a, p iv). NPAHT is also led and funded by external actors, and as noted in the acknowledgements section of the policy document, the 'whole process' was guided and facilitated by UNICEF. The Canadian government also provided 'support', 'contributions' and 'commitments' to combat the issues of abuse, violence and exploitation of children in Ghana (Government of the Republic of Ghana, 2017a). The scheme is ongoing, and no reviews are available.

National Social Protection Programmes

The NPA2 states that child labour can be addressed when concerns for the widening inequality in the population are addressed (Government of the Republic of Ghana, 2017b, p 12). To this end, it calls for strong advocacy and public policy to enhance education outcomes and improve access to social protection services, especially in areas where child labour is endemic. Several such social protection and social welfare programmes have been instituted over the last two decades (see Chapter 7, this volume, for more detail on evaluations of social protection programmes). The most recent, which has also been linked to child labour prevention efforts, is the Livelihood Empowerment Against Poverty Programme (LEAP). Under this scheme, direct cash transfers are provided to poor families on the condition that their children continue to attend school and that the family makes use of preventive health care and nutrition services. In reality, child labour elimination was peripheral to the core objectives of the LEAP programme at its inception phase, though it has since been adapted for this purpose. Though initiated by GoG, LEAP is reliant on support from development partners. As Handa et al (2014) noted, LEAP's annual budget of US$20 million comprised GoG funds (50 per cent), donations from the UK government, and a loan from the World Bank. Over the last decade, financial assistance has also been provided by the EU, United Nations Population Fund (UNFPA), UNICEF, USAID and the World Food Programme (WFP) (World Bank, 2016). Other national social protection programmes with some potential to address child labour include the Ghana School Feeding Programme, which was initiated under the Comprehensive Africa Agricultural Development Programme (CAADP) Pillar 3, and the Capitation Grant, which is aimed at removing financial obstacles to children's school enrolment, a key objective of the FCUBE policy.

Role of external actors

While the GoG and its civil servants have participated in the development of these policies and programmes, or have provided the required human resources, leadership and skills to operationalize them, it is clear that external actors have played key roles. Significant financial, human and material resources have been provided, including by the US government and its

Table 8.2: Examples of funded child labour and social protection initiatives in Ghana

Project title	Funder	Amount (millions)
Combating Forced Labour and Labour Trafficking of Adults and Children in Ghana (2017–2021)	USDoL	US$2
Assessing Progress in Reducing Child Labour in Cocoa-Growing Areas of Côte d'Ivoire and Ghana (2015–2019)	USDoL	US$3
Mobilizing Community Action and Promoting Opportunities for Youth in Ghana's Cocoa-Growing Communities (MOCA) (2015–2019)	USDoL	US$4.5
CARING Gold Mining Project	USDoL	US$5
Child Protection Compact Partnership (CPC) (2015–2020)	US government	US$5
Accelerating Care Reform (2016–2020)	USAID	US$8
LEAP 1000 (2014–2019)	USAID	US$12
Sustainable Fisheries Management Project (2014–2019)	USAID	US$24
Complementary Basic Education Program	USAID & DFID	US$40
Learning Support program	USAID & UNICEF	US$37
Ghana Education Quality Improvement Project (EQUIP)	DFID	UK£25
Leave No-one Behind Programme in Ghana	DFID	UK£27

Notes: Some of these initiatives are specific to addressing child labour while others (for example, LEAP) are mainly social protection programmes tangentially related to child labour concerns. DFID stands for UK Department for International Development, now part of the Foreign, Commonwealth and Development Office (FCDO).

Source: US Department of Labour (2018)

agencies, especially towards the elimination or prevention of children's work in sectors such as cocoa farming, fishing, mining and other prohibited sectors. The US and UK governments alone have provided at least US$200 million for child labour and child rights related initiatives in Ghana since 2014 (Table 8.2). This reliance on foreign resources and technical guidance has important implications for the nature, scope and success of these initiatives.

As discussed previously, while some of the programmes have successfully increased the entry of children into formal education, results are mixed in terms of their core objective of decreasing the involvement of children in prohibited work. This may reflect the critique that countries that are largely reliant on foreign assistance for their development strategies risk perpetuating weakness in their institutions and a lack of clear policy direction (Whitfield, 2008; Movik, 2011). Another related issue is whether child rights and regulation of children's work would look the same if the country had greater policy space. There is, for example, a palpable absence of reference to indigenous customary constructions of and views on childhood, child rights, and children's work in Act 560.

Between a rock and a hard place: child rights and regulation of children's work

Social attitudes towards children and children's work are closely aligned with dominant socio-cultural understandings of childhood and children's place in society. Cultures and traditions are not static but change with a society's evolving political, economic, and other realities. Ghana has already undergone significant changes in attitudes, norms and standards since the re-introduction of parliamentary democracy in 1992, which ushered in child rights and children's work legislation. Nevertheless, particularly in rural areas, important elements of 'traditional' perspectives on childhood and work still hold sway. Thus, this section is rooted in the assertion by Bourdieu (1998, p 2) that the most profound logic of any social world can only be truly understood by situating oneself in the historical, cultural, and empirical reality of its inhabitants (also see Achebe, 1993; Appiah, 1993; Mbembe, 2001). The next section traces aspects of traditional ideals on children's work and explores why they have proven challenging to dismantle despite the significant financial and material resources poured into this agenda over the last three decades.

Traditional socio-cultural constructions of childhood and children's work

Defining childhood in context

In keeping with the ILO child labour conventions and the CRC definition of childhood, legislative approaches to regulating children's work in Ghana rely on calendar age and minimum age standards. However, chronological age has traditionally been peripheral to the understanding of childhood and child development in Ghanaian communities, and its validity as the sole basis for determining a person's maturity or capacity is severely critiqued in the childhood studies literature (Laz, 1998; Clark-Kazak, 2016; Akinola, 2019).

For example, in the 1950s the Talensi of Northern Ghana were described as having two distinct stages of child development: babyhood and childhood (Boakye-Boaten, 2010, p 108; citing Fortes, 1957). Babyhood, the period from birth till weaning (about 3–4 years), was a period of complete dependency during which there were no social demands on the child. Childhood then had three distinct stages: age 4–8 years, when the child was mostly free from work and mostly at play; age 8–12 years, when the child was progressively introduced to community activities, values, work and adult responsibilities; and from age 12 years onwards when they were expected to start taking on basic economic and household tasks. This represented a gradual entry into adulthood, and children were given roles to signify their developing social status. Despite decades of social change, such ideas still hold in many in rural and urban areas.

Meanwhile, in Southern Ghana, the Akans marked the transition from childhood to adulthood (or adolescence) through *bragoro*, which is translated as 'life dance' to convey the idea that adult life begins at this stage (Sarpong, 1977; Crentsil, 2014). *Bragoro* was performed (and still is in some communities) for girls following their first menstruation and was thus also described with euphemistic expressions such as *ƆayƐ bra* (she is of age) or *Ɔakum sono* (she's killed an elephant) to communicate that she had now attained womanhood (Sarpong, 1977; Agyekum, 2002). For boys, courage and bravery were seen as signs of masculinity and thus counted as part of the transition and entry to manhood. Hence, expressions such as *ne bo ayɛ duru* or *ne koko ayɛ duru* or *w'ayɛ / ɔreyɛ barima* (he's brave or he's become brave or he's become/is becoming a man) were used to refer to those who begin to show the markers of adolescence or puberty, such as the growth of pubic hair and beard or breaking of the voice, or those who commit acts of bravery or competence associated with adulthood (Adinkrah, 2012; Fiaveh et al, 2015).

These traditional conceptualizations of childhood represent one of the primary areas of contention between indigenous perspectives on childhood and the formal child-centric legislation enacted by the national Parliament over the last three decades. They set up an ongoing challenge to child rights discourses which are premised on the assumption that all communities are aware of the formal laws and support the age-based definition of childhood. This dilemma is not unique to Ghana: many scholars have identified similar problems with the operationalization of local laws based on the normative definition of childhood used by the CRC (Liebel, 2012; Abebe and Tefera, 2014; Ansell, 2014; Thum-Danso Imoh, 2019; Vandenhole, 2020). The critique is that the normative approach reduces human maturation to a Gregorian calendar age when the reality is that the extent to which, and the range of issues about which, children are able to make effective choices is related to their experience and maturity and not their calendar age (Huijsmans, 2012, p 1311). It also 'infantilises adolescents' (Abramson, 1996) and 'obscures children's differentiated levels of competence, needs, and maturity in various life stages of childhood' (Abebe, 2019, p 3).

These views and this chapter's overarching point about the tensions between indigenous perspectives on childhood and the formal child-centric legislation are exemplified by a study on children's work in Ghanaian mining communities by the NGO called Free the Slaves (FTS, 2014). Responses to this baseline study of understandings of childhood in Obuasi, a mining town in the Ashanti region, showed an overwhelming rejection of the legal definition of childhood: only 18 per cent of the survey respondents agreed with the view that the age of 18 represents the boundary between childhood and adulthood. It was evident that the community did not regard the category of young people who were involved in artisanal mining work as 'children'. Instead of exploring or seeking to understand the residents' perspective, the researchers simply concluded that parents of Obuasi were naïve or 'lacking knowledge about their roles as parents, and the rights and welfare of their children' (FTS, 2014, p 5). This example reflects what Van Dijk (2001) describes as positive self-representation and negative other-representation.

'Childhood' influenced by social mores

Respect for elders and the importance of contributing to one's community are among the core values instilled into Ghanaian children from a young age. A sense of communal obligation is associated with norms and expectations including reciprocity, altruism, and mutual contributions, all of which underpinned traditional welfare systems (Ansah-Koi, 2006). Children's upbringing was, and continues to be regarded as, the duty of the entire extended family, kinship group or community, and not only the biological parents (Goody, 1966, 1973; Oppong, 1973; Allman, 1997; Badasu, 2004). This is founded on the belief that children represent the continuity of the names, heritage and identities of the wider community. Furthermore, as Badasu (2004) notes, the child's socialization is seen as a duty that could not be performed by one person alone. This social or communal approach to child upbringing also ensures that all children are provided with guardianship and care (Alber, 2003, 2010; Frimpong-Manso, 2014, p 411). While these practices have waned due to the loosening of social bonds catalysed by urbanization, migration and adoption of alternative child-upbringing cultures, they are still prevalent in some areas and are the foundation of the traditional child fostering system (Pennington and Harpending, 1993).

Regardless of the family, household or community in which they live, children are introduced to work at an early age and expected to contribute, through their work, to their family and the wider community (Sarpong, 1974; Sackey and Johannesen, 2015; Yeboah, 2020). As Takyi (2014, p 38) notes, this is integral to children's socialization because traditionally parents and extended families were regarded as failures if their children grew up lazy or without the skills or abilities to cater for their own families in turn. The value of work is thus instilled in children at the earliest opportunity, with 'economic activities' being among the main skills and competencies which parents teach their children. Children's work ranges from domestic chores (taking care of siblings, helping to cook family meals, washing of clothes) through to subsistence and income-earning activities (including farming and tending livestock). Adult caregivers express concern that a lazy child will fail in life, and some send their children to live with relatives or others with the hope that they will encourage the child to be more diligent.

Lived experiences of work

This attitude towards work in children's lives has been maintained even in the face of urbanization and rural-urban migration (Yeboah, 2020) and is reflected in the duties and expectations of children within the public education system (Twum-Danso Imoh, 2009; Mohammed Gunu, 2018). For example, the Ghana Education Service's (GES) guidance for Water, Sanitation and Hygiene (WASH) Facilities Planning and Management lists the maintenance of school WASH facilities as the pupils' responsibility (Moojiman et al, 2013; GES, 2014). Similar policies exist elsewhere. For instance, under the 'o-soji' (cleaning) tradition in Japanese schools, pupils clean some school facilities (Tsuneyoshi et al, 2016). Likewise, in 2016, Singapore's Ministry of Education announced a decision to make daily cleaning of school canteens, corridors and classrooms (though not toilets) a mandatory task for primary and secondary school children (The Independent, 2016).

Berlan (2009) demonstrates the ubiquitous nature of work in children's lives across both informal (domestic) and formal (schooling) arenas owing to the positive associations that have been and are still made between childhood and work (also see Chapter 4, this volume). Besides their unpaid school and domestic chores, many children are called upon to assist their families with income-earning activities (Yeboah et al, 2015; Agyei et al, 2016; Ungruhe, 2019). Some of these children may be coerced or compelled, but there is ample evidence that many are entrepreneurial and take on economic activities of their own volition to earn incomes for themselves (Okyere, 2013; Yeboah, 2020). Other children work because they find it more rewarding than other options.

Bruscino (2001) originally set out to explore ways of ending children's work in Yindure, a village in Northern Ghana. She worked with children who were literate or had attended school at some point in their lives. Most expressed a desire to migrate to the south of the country to work, as they had heard they could make more money there, reflecting the long-established circuit of independent seasonal North–South labour migration (Whitehead and Hashim, 2005; Kwankye et al, 2007, 2009; Whitehead et al, 2007). Boys explained that they saw migration and work as a more rational response to their circumstances than schooling:

> The boys said they enjoyed their work and saw it as useful for their futures, which for all seemed to include becoming farmers. Their jobs

> were skill-building and seemed to be the crucial first steps toward their occupations. They said they enjoyed school too but thought that work was more useful. The gains from work are immediate – if they work today, they bring home food or money today. Although they gave most of the money to their families, the boys seemed to be working for themselves, self-initiating small service endeavours. One boy said he even farms his own plot of land. (Bruscino, 2001, p 22)

Girls were generally less enthusiastic about work – they had fewer opportunities for paid work and preferred schooling, which they hoped would help them with a future career or lead to greater independence.

Two important points emerge from Brucino's work and similar studies (Yeboah et al, 2015; Agyei et al, 2016; Ungruhe, 2019). First, it is important to listen to children carefully to gain an understanding of their worldviews, individual preferences and lived experiences. Second, there is the need to engage with the diversity of voices: those of girls which appear to align with the interests of actors seeking to prohibit certain forms of children's work, and those of boys who may be keen to pursue the prohibited work. The importance of working with individuals whose views of children and work are outside international norms, and who therefore tend not to be consulted, has been widely acknowledged (Boyden and Ling, 1998; Myers, 1999; Crivello et al, 2009; Bourdillon, 2014; Morrow and Boyden, 2018; Bourdillon and Carothers, 2019).

Complementarities, divergences, and tensions around children's work

An important part of the rationale for engaging with marginalized voices is that there can be many commonalities between the underlying visions of those seeking to prohibit children's work and those with greater tolerance for it. The traditional acceptance of diverse forms of children's work does not imply laxity toward or acceptance of work that is inimical to children's wellbeing or development. Most families and children themselves are also acutely aware of the fact that work that is not age-appropriate can cause physical harm, and is wrong (for example, Adonteng-Kissi, 2018). This view is captured in many songs, folklore and icons such as the popular Akan proverb 'the child breaks the shell of a snail and not that of a tortoise'; to wit, a child does or should do things that are appropriate for children.

The foregoing suggests that the divergence between the traditional and legal positions on children's work emanate as much from moral and political views as from objective judgements about work and harm. For example, children and families in cocoa growing and fishing communities have long held that there are activities that can be safely performed by children, while for the most part the law and mainstream child labour discourses present children's involvement in cocoa farming in wholly pathological terms. The second reason for the divergence is because in Western Europe and North America, the mention of 'child labour' conjures images of children in horrific factory conditions, sweatshops, or large plantations. In these situations, the logic of abolition by declaring such work as unconditionally bad for children is understandable.

However, children's work in rural Ghana typically occurs in small-scale agriculture in the family context, or petty trading, fishing or mining, not in industrial spaces. In all these, attention is paid to the capacities, maturities or abilities of the child to whom jobs are allocated. Traditionally in Ghana, no jobs were unconditionally denied to children or automatically barred as being unquestionably unsafe for them as the dominant view was that most jobs had light, non-hazardous or child-friendly aspects. Introducing children to these suitable elements was seen as a practical means of facilitating their development. Thus, in farming communities, for example, children could initially help gather the harvest, and then be allocated further responsibilities as they gained more farming experience and matured in age and physical stature. Families and communities considered it imperative to impart to children and youth the skills with which they could eventually build a livelihood – be this in fishing, farming, petty trading or other jobs (Nukunya, 2003; Sackey and Johannesen, 2015). Work was also an educational experience, for a lot of historical, social, cultural and political information was and still is, encoded and passed down through oral accounts and folklore, or taught through weaving, trade skills, farming practices, craft making and other modes that required hands-on involvement.

Hence, while classroom-based education was deemed important, right from Ghana's colonial-era, warnings were issued that the focus on formal education and devaluation of traditional work-based educational and knowledge systems risked undermining the scope for imparting vital practical knowledge, history and skills (Kwamena-Poh, 1975; Lord, 2011). There is also the problem that despite advances in the provision of school infrastructure and school access, formal classroom-based education in many areas is inaccessible or of such poor quality that children would rather not attend (Yeboah et al, 2015). Many children who attend poor-quality schools remain innumerate and illiterate even after completing Junior Secondary School. This challenge was recognized by NPA1 and reaffirmed in NPA2, with the identified response being an investment in alternative forms of education, including transitional programmes for out-of-school children. However, given how non-classroom based schooling or educational provision is generally stigmatized within mainstream child labour and child rights discourses, reaffirmation of this goal in the NPA2 is likely to yield only minimal action. Indeed, NPA2 formally ended in December 2021 without any tangible programme or action to implement non-formal and traditional work-based education systems.

Ultimately, though there are areas of complementarity between traditional constructions of childhood and children's work on the one hand, and the legislative and policy approach on the other, there are also clear divergences and tensions. These have mainly been brought about by the fact that laws have been formulated without due regard for the indigenous systems which predated them. The tensions largely operate at the communal or societal level but also occur at a more personal level for working children and their families. Many young people see the ability to cater for themselves and help others in the family as an important milestone on their path to maturity, and proof that they can meet societal and personal responsibilities and are thus worthy of respect and recognition. It is often overlooked that historically work was, as it is still today, tied to a young person's sense of self-sufficiency, independence, honour and respect (Hilson, 2009; Okyere, 2013). In Okyere's (2012) study, young people working in artisanal gold mining spoke with pride about being able to work to pay for education and apprenticeships. The research participants saw the policy position that they should be denied such work as potentially depriving them of the ability to access education, apprenticeships, developmental and welfare opportunities, with further adverse knock-on effects on their self-esteem.

Conclusions

This chapter started with a recognition that Ghana's legislative approach to child rights and work is a radical departure from the ideas which prevailed up until the early 1990s when democratic rule was restored. At that point, the country began adopting international children's rights instruments such as the CRC. In contrast to the understandings of childhood prevalent in rural communities, the Ghana Child Rights Act (1998) introduced a notion of childhood determined exclusively by chronological age. This was always going to be difficult to implement in contexts where not all births are registered, and many do not know their actual dates of birth.

Additionally, the presentation of education only in terms of classroom-based schooling and of schooling itself as a time that is completely incongruous with work (see, for example, UNICEF 2007) is highly problematic. Adherence to this has been very challenging because much education has historically taken place outside the classroom, through work and other activities. Furthermore, despite the introduction of measures such as FCUBE, LEAP, and others, many children do not attend school because it is too far away, whereas others consider the quality of schools and the instruction received so poor as to be a waste of their time (UCW, 2016a, p 43). Many children have to work to fund their education and pay for necessities, as shown by Okyere's (2012) research with children seeking income opportunities in artisanal mining.

While cultural acceptance of children's work is pervasive, it is also widely recognized that there are forms of work that can be too onerous or hazardous for children. The occurrence and persistence of hazardous and harmful work usually reflect socio-economic constraints. This challenge was squarely recognized by the Ghana National Commission on Children (GNCC) in drafting Act 560. Despite acceding to the various ILO Conventions, the GNCC nonetheless stated the following in its background report:

> Government documents recognise the inevitability of child labour as a direct result of poverty. As stated in the background report to the Children's Act: 'The committee takes the view that the present economic circumstances do not permit a wholesale ban on child employment and that a law which seeks to eradicate it completely would be unimplementable and unrealistic. What Ghana needs as a developing country is a piece of legislation which would allow children to work but under certain conditions'. (Cited in Bruscino, 2001, p 22)

These concerns are as true now as they were at the time, and various aspects of the Act's provisions on child labour remain unfulfilled while successive national efforts to prevent child labour have floundered. The socio-economic challenge needs to be resolved as a matter of urgency, for it is also a truism that many families whose children are engaged in harmful work aspire to the vision of childhood presented to them in media campaigns, and through NGO and governmental advocacy. These messages do not fall entirely on closed ears, but they fail to galvanize a response among some audiences because of the harsh socio-economic reality of their lives.

The chapter argues that the country's high dependency on foreign aid, technical guidance and assistance for social programmes and other interventions addressing children's work remains problematic. It lends legitimacy to critics' concerns that these are foreign impositions or designs, even if they are in step with the country's national development agenda. The inability to initiate and implement child rights and social welfare programmes without external support also exemplifies economic and political underdevelopment. As Kim puts it: 'such intervention by donors in the process of Ghanaian policymaking has further challenged state capacity, legitimacy and effectiveness' (Kim, 2015, p 1341). Against this backdrop, fairer trade practices, addressing global political and economic inequalities, and measures to right the lingering wrongs of historical events such as colonization should be seen as underpinning the future ability of Ghana and other African countries to protect their children (ActionAid, 2011; Herbert, 2011).

What this chapter argues is the importance of bridging the gap between the two dominant discourses on children's rights and childhood. Policies and programmes aimed at preventing hazardous or harmful work must now seek the middle ground and draw on both perspectives. Failure to do so will only further penalize those who are already marginalized and lead to the rejection of what may be worthwhile interventions.

We conclude with what should be an obvious point: child rights, and initiatives to address them, are intrinsically political. They occur at the intersection of different ideologies, interests, identities and other deeply embedded factors. They also raise sensitive questions about class, gender, ethnicity, nationality, power, colonialism and hegemony. We argue that it is of utmost importance that all endeavours carefully consider and understand the multiplicity of opinions and views on children's rights and children's work. This includes a willingness to consider ideas and propositions that may appear antithetical to deeply held beliefs. This is especially so with regards to the voices of the working children, their families and communities, in whose interests the laws, research studies and advocacy campaigns are so often justified.

Notes

1 http://www.fao.org/gender/insight/insight/ru/c/42487/

2 C138 was ratified by Ghana in 2011.

References

Abebe, T. (2019) 'Reconceptualising children's agency as continuum and interdependence', *Social Sciences*, 8(3), Article 81. doi: 10.3390/socsci8030081

Abebe, T. and Tefera, M. (2014) 'Earning rights: discourses on children's rights and proper childhood in Ethiopia', in Twum-Danso Imoh, A. and Ansell, N. (eds) *Children's Lives in an Era of Children's Rights: The Progress of the Convention on the Rights of the Child in Africa*. London: Routledge, pp 53–71.

Aboa, A. and Ross, A. (2020) *Child Labour Still Prevalent in West Africa Cocoa Sector Despite Industry Efforts: Report*. Abidjan: Reuters. Available at: https://www.reuters.com/article/us-cocoa-childlabour-ivory-coast-ghana-idUSKCN21R356 (Accessed 28 April 2020).

Abramson, B. (1996) 'The invisibility of children and adolescents: the need to monitor our rhetoric and our attitudes', in Verhellen, E. (ed) *Monitoring Children's Rights*. The Hague: Martinus Nijhoff Publishers, pp 393–402.

Achebe, C. (1993) *The Education of a British-Protected Child*. London: Allen Lane.

ActionAid (2011) *Real Aid: Ending Aid Dependency*. London: ActionAid.

Adinkrah, M. (2012) 'Better dead than dishonored: masculinity and male suicidal behavior in contemporary Ghana', *Social Science & Medicine (1982)*, 74(4), pp 474–81.

Adonteng-Kissi, O. (2018) 'Parental perceptions of child labour and human rights: a comparative study of rural and urban Ghana', *Child Abuse & Neglect*, 84, pp 34–44.

Agyei, Y.A., Kumi, E. and Yeboah, T. (2016) 'Is better to be a kayayei than to be unemployed: reflecting on the role of head portering in Ghana's informal economy', *GeoJournal*, 81(2), pp 293–318.

Agyekum, K. (2002) 'Menstruation as a verbal taboo among the Akan of Ghana', *Journal of Anthropological Research*, 58(3), pp 367–87.

Akinola, O. (2019) 'Who is a child? The politics of human rights, the convention on the right of the child (CRC), and child marriage in Nigeria', in Blouin-Genest, G., Doran, M.-C. and Paquerot, S. (eds) *Human Rights as Battlefields: Changing Practices and Contestations*. Cham, Switzerland: Springer International Publishing, pp 129–48.

Alber, E. (2003) 'Denying biological parenthood: fosterage in Northern Benin', *Ethnos*, 68(4), pp 487–506.

Alber, E. (2010) 'No school without foster families in Northern Benin: a social historical approach', in Haldis, H. and Tatjana, T. (eds) *Parenting After the Century of the Child – Travelling Ideals, Institutional Negotiations and Individual Responses*. London. Available at: https://www.researchgate.net/publication/283253923_No_school_without_foster_families_in_Northern_Benin_A_social_historical_approach (Accessed 18 May 2020).

Allman, J. (1997) 'Fathering, mothering and making sense of "ntamoba": reflections on the economy of child-rearing in colonial Asante', *Africa: Journal of the International African Institute*, 67(2), pp 296–321.

Annan, J. (2012) *Education is Key to Address Menace of Child Labour*. Accra: Challenging Heights.

Ansah-Koi, A.A. (2006) 'Care of orphans: fostering interventions for children whose parents die of AIDS in Ghana', *Families in Society*, 87(4), pp 555–64.

Ansell, N. (2014) 'The convention on the rights of the child: advancing social justice for African children?', in Twum-Danso Imoh, A. and Ansell, N. (eds) *Children's Lives in an Era of Children's Rights: The Progress of the Convention on the Rights of the Child in Africa*. London: Routledge, pp 228–46.

Appiah, K.A. (1993) *In My Father's House: Africa in the Philosophy of Culture*. New York: Oxford University Press.

Baah, F., Anchirinah, V. and Badu-Yeboah, A. (2009) 'Perceptions of extension agents on information exchange with cocoa farmers in the Eastern region of Ghana', *Scientific Research and Essays*, 4(7), pp 694–99.

Badasu, D.M. (2004) 'Child care among Ewe migrants in the city of Accra: cases of crisis', *Research Review of the Institute of African Studies*, 18(7), pp 17–37.

Berlan, A. (2004) 'Child labour, education and child rights among cocoa producers in Ghana', in van den Anker, C. (ed) *The Political Economy of New Slavery*. London: Palgrave MacMillan, pp 158–78.

Berlan, A. (2009) 'Child labour and cocoa: whose voices prevail?', *International Journal of Sociology and Social Policy*, 29(3/4), pp 141–51.

Best, J. (2008) 'Beyond calculation: quantitative literacy and critical thinking about public issues', in Madison, B.L. and Steen, L.A. (eds) *Calculation vs. Context: Quantitative Literacy and its Implications for Teacher Education.* Washington, DC: Mathematical Association of America, pp 125–35.

Boakye-Boaten, A. (2010) 'Changes in the concept of childhood: implications on children in Ghana', *The Journal of International Social Research*, 3(10), pp 104–15. Available at: http://www.sosyalarastirmalar.com/cilt3/sayi10pdf/boakyeboaten.pdf (Accessed 18 May 2020).

Bourdieu, P. (1998) *Practical Reason: On the Theory of Action.* Cambridge: Polity Press.

Bourdillon, M. (2014) 'Introduction: children's work in Africa', in Bourdillon, M. and Mutambwa, G.M. (eds) *The Place of Work in African Childhoods / La Place Du Travail Chez Les Enfants Africains*. Dakar: CODESRIA, pp 1–20.

Bourdillon, M. and Carothers, R. (2019) 'Policy on children's work and labour', *Children & Society*, 33(4), pp 387–95.

Boyden, J. and Ling, B. (1998) *What Works for Working Children?* Florence: Innocenti Publications International Child Development Centre and Rädda Barnen.

Bruscino, A. (2001) *Child Labor in Ghana: An Analysis of Perceptions and Practices.* African Diaspora ISPS. Paper 77. Brattleboro, VT: School for International Training.

Bureau of International Labor Affairs (2018) *2018 Findings on the Worst Forms of Child Labor: Ghana.* Washington, DC: US Department of Labour.

Carter, E. et al (2020) 'Trapped in low performance? Tracking the learning trajectory of disadvantaged girls and boys in the Complementary Basic Education programme in Ghana', *International Journal of Educational Research*, 100, Article 101541, pp 103–24.

Clark-Kazak, C.R. (2016) 'Mainstreaming social age in the sustainable development goals: progress, pitfalls, and prospects', in Huijsmans, R. (ed) *Generationing Development: A Relational Approach to Children, Youth and Development.* London: Palgrave Macmillan.

Crentsil, P. (2014) 'Bragoro: a disappearing puberty rite of the Akan of Ghana', in Roscoe, C. (ed) *Ghana: Social, Economic, Political Issues.* New York: Nova Science, pp 83–102. Available at: https://researchportal.helsinki.fi/en/publications/bragoro-a-disappearing-puberty-rite-of-the-akan-of-ghana (Accessed 18 May 2020).

Crivello, G., Camfield, L. and Woodhead, M. (2009) 'How can children tell us about their wellbeing? Exploring the potential of participatory research approaches within young lives', *Social Indicators Research*, 90(1), pp 51–72.

Darko, P.O. (2014) '"Our daily bread comes from rocks": the livelihood struggles of children at a quarry in Pokuase, Ghana', *Contemporary Journal of African Studies*, 2(1), pp 97–120.

Feigben, J. (2010) *Child Labour and Children's Education in Northern Region of Ghana. Case Study of Bunkpurugu-Yunyoo and East Mamprusi Districts.* Unpublished MA thesis. Kumasi: KNUST.

Fiaveh, D.Y. et al (2015) 'Constructions of masculinity and femininity and sexual risk negotiation practices among women in urban Ghana', *Culture, Health & Sexuality*, 17(5), pp 650–62.

Fortes, M. (1957) *The Web of Kinship Among the Tallensi: The Second Part of an Analysis of the Social Structure of a Trans-Volta Tribe.* London: Routledge.

Frimpong Boamah, E. (2018) 'Constitutional economics of Ghana's decentralization', *World Development*, 110, pp 256–67.

Frimpong-Manso, K. (2014) 'Child welfare in Ghana: the past, present and future', *Journal of Educational and Social Research*, 4(6), p 411–19.

FTS (2014) *Child Rights in Mining: Pilot Project Results & Lessons Learned Obuasi, Ghana.* Washington, DC: Free the Slaves. Available at: https://www.freetheslaves.net/wp-content/uploads/2015/03/ChildRightsinMiningPilotProjectOverview.pdf (Accessed 18 May 2020).

GES (2014) *Wash in Schools: National Implementation Model.* Accra: Ghana Education Service.

Ghana Statistical Service (2003) *Ghana Child Labour Survey*. Geneva and Accra: ILO and Ghana Statistical Service. Available at: https://www.ilo.org/ipec/Informationresources/WCMS_IPEC_PUB_690/lang--en/index.htm.

Ghana Statistical Service (2012) *Ghana – Ghana Living Standards Survey 6 (With a Labour Force Module) 2012–2013, Round Six – Data Collection.* Accra: Ghana Statistical Service (GSS). Available at: http://www2.statsghana.gov.gh/nada/index.php/catalog/72/datacollection (Accessed 18 May 2020).

Ghanney, R., Dughan, J. and Bentil, J. (2020) 'Academic performance in mining areas: the case of selected junior high schools in the Atwima Kwanwoma district, Ghana', in *Proceedings of The International Virtual Conference on Education, Policies and Politics Around Children's Work in Ghana.*

Goody, E. (1966) 'The fostering of children in Ghana: a preliminary report', *Ghana Journal of Sociology*, 2(1), pp 23–33.

Goody, E.N. (1973) *Contexts of Kinship: An Essay in the Family Sociology of the Gonja of Northern Ghana.* Cambridge: Cambridge University Press.

Government of the Republic of Ghana (1998) *The Children's Act.* Accra: Government of Ghana.

Government of the Republic of Ghana (1992) *Constitution of the Republic of Ghana.* Available at: https://www.ghanaweb.com/GhanaHomePage/republic/constitution.php (Accessed 28 April 2020).

Government of the Republic of Ghana (2002) *Child Right Regulation 2002 (LI 1705).*

Government of the Republic of Ghana (2003a) *Juvenile Justice Act (Act 653)*. Available at: https://www.ilo.org/dyn/natlex/natlex4.detail?p_lang=en&p_isn=88528 (Accessed 28 April 2020).

Government of the Republic of Ghana (2003b) *Labour Act of 2003 (Act 651)*. Available at: https://www.ilo.org/dyn/travail/docs/1199/Labour%20Act.pdf (Accessed 28 April 2020).

Government of the Republic of Ghana (2005) *Human Trafficking Act (Act 694)*. Available at: https://www.mint.gov.gh/wp-content/uploads/2017/06/Human_Trafficking_Act_2015-1.pdf (Accessed 28 April 2020).

Government of the Republic of Ghana (2007) *Labour Regulations (LI 1833)*. Available at: https://www.ilo.org/dyn/natlex/natlex4.detail?p_isn=77273&p_lang=en (Accessed 28 April 2020).

Government of the Republic of Ghana (2008) *The Education Act, Act 778*. Available at: https://www.ilo.org/dyn/natlex/docs/MONOGRAPH/83622/92463/%20F2061259086/GHA83622.pdf (Accessed 28 April 2020).

Government of the Republic of Ghana (2009) *National Plan of Action for the Elimination of the Worst Forms of Child Labour 2009 – 2015*. Accra: Ministry of Employment and Social Welfare (MESW). Available at: https://cocoainitiative.org/knowledge-centre-post/ghana-national-plan-of-action-for-the-elimination-of-child-labour-2009-2015-2/ (Accessed 16 April 2020).

Government of the Republic of Ghana (2017a) *National Plan of Action for the Elimination of Human Trafficking in Ghana*. Accra: Ministry of Employment and Social Welfare (MESW). Available at: https://www.unicef.org/ghana/media/1851/file/National%20Plan%20of%20Action%20for%20the%20Elimination%20of%20Human%20Trafficking%20in%20Ghana.pdf (Accessed 18 May 2020).

Government of the Republic of Ghana (2017b) *National Plan of Action to Eliminate the Worst Forms of Child Labour 2017–2021*. Accra: Ministry of Employment and Social Welfare (MESW).

Guarcello, L., Lyon, S. and Rosati, F.C. (2006) *Child Labour and Education for All: An Issue Paper. Working Paper 33*. Rome: Understanding Children's Work Project.

Gyimah-Boadi, E. (1994) 'Ghana's uncertain political opening', *Journal of Democracy*, 5(2), pp 75–86.

Hamenoo, E.S., Dwomoh, E.A. and Dako-Gyeke, M. (2018) 'Child labour in Ghana: implications for children's education and health', *Children and Youth Services Review*, 93, pp 248–54.

Handa, S. et al (2014) *Livelihood Empowerment Against Poverty Program Impact Evaluation*. Chapel Hill, NC: Carolina Population Center, University of North Carolina at Chapel Hill.

Heady, C. (2003) 'The effect of child labor on learning achievement', *World Development*, 31(2), pp 385–98.

Herbert, R. (2011) *Dependency, Instability and Shifting Global Power: Influences and Interests in African Foreign Policy in the 21st Century*. Occasional Paper 96. Braamfontein, South Africa: South African Institute of International Affairs (SAIIA).

Hilson, G. (2009) *Challenges with Eradicating Child Labour in the Artisanal Mining Sector: A Case Study of the Talensi-Nabdam district, Upper East Region of Ghana*. Paper delivered to the Rethinking Extractive Industries Conference, York University, Toronto, 5–7 March 2009.

Howard, N. (2017) *Child Trafficking, Youth Labour Mobility, and the Politics of Protection*. Basingstoke: Palgrave Macmillan.

Huijsmans, R. (2012) *Background Paper on Young Migrants in Urban Ghana, Focusing Particularly on Young Female Head Porters (Kayayei)*. The Hague: Institute of Social Sciences (ISS).

ILO (1999) *Convention C182: Worst Forms of Child Labour Convention, 1999 (No. 182)*. Available at: https://www.ilo.org/dyn/normlex/en/f?p=NORMLEXPUB:12100:0::NO::P12100_ILO_CODE:C182 (Accessed 28 April 2020).

ILO (2008) *Ghana: Child Labour Data Country Brief*. Accra, Ghana: International Labour Organization. Available at: http://www.ilo.org/ipec/Informationresources/WCMS_IPEC_PUB_7798/lang--en/index.htm (Accessed 18 May 2020).

ILO-IPEC (2013) *Analytical Study on Child Labour in Volta Lake Fishing in Ghana*. Geneva: International Labour Organization – IPEC.

Imoro, B. (2009) 'Dimensions of basic school dropouts in rural Ghana: the case of Asutifi District', *Journal of Science and Technology (Ghana)*, 29(3), pp 72–85.

Jonah, O.-T. and Abebe, T. (2019) 'Tensions and controversies regarding child labor in small-scale gold mining in Ghana', *African Geographical Review*, 38(4), pp 361–73.

Kim, J. (2015) 'Aid and state transition in Ghana and South Korea', *Third World Quarterly*, 36(7), pp 1333–48.

Kwamena-Poh, M.A. (1975) 'The traditional informal system of education in pre-colonial Ghana', *Présence africaine*, 95, pp 269–83.

Kwankye, S.O. et al (2007) *Coping Strategies of Independent Child Migrants from Northern Ghana to Southern Cities*. Working Paper T-23. Brighton: Development Research Centre on Migration, Globalisation and Poverty.

Kwankye, S.O. et al (2009) *Independent North-South Child Migration in Ghana: The Decision Making Process*. Working Paper T-29. Brighton: Development Research Centre on Migration, Globalisation and Poverty.

Lawrance, B.N. (2010) 'From child labor "problem" to human trafficking "crisis": child advocacy and anti-trafficking legislation in Ghana', *International Labor and Working-Class History*, (78), pp 63–88.

Laz, C. (1998) 'Act your age', *Sociological Forum*, 13(1), pp 85–113.

Liebel, M. (2012) 'Framing the issue: Rethinking children's rights', in Liebel, M. et al (eds) *Children's Rights from Below: Cross-Cultural Perspectives*. London: Palgrave Macmillan, pp 63–79.

Lord, J. (2011) 'Child labor in the Gold Coast: the economics of work, education, and the family in late-colonial African childhoods, C. 1940–57', *The Journal of the History of Childhood and Youth*, 4(1), pp 88–115.

Maconachie, R. and Hilson, G. (2016) 'Re-thinking the child labor "problem" in rural sub-Saharan Africa: the case of Sierra Leone's half shovels', *World Development*, 78, pp 136–47.

Mbembe, A. (2001) *On the Postcolony*. Oakland, CA: University of California Press. Available at: https://www.ucpress.edu/book/9780520204355/on-the-postcolony (Accessed 18 May 2020).

Mohammed Gunu, I. (2018) 'Alternatives to school exclusion in Ghana: changing the rhythm of dealing with truancy in Ghanaian high schools', *Sage Open*, 8(4). doi: 10.1177/2158244018805361

Moojiman, A., Esseku, H. and Tay, V. (2013) *Wash in Schools: Facilities Planning and Management*. Accra: Ghana Education Service.

Morrow, V. and Boyden, J. (2018) *Responding to Children's Work: Evidence from the Young Lives Study in Ethiopia, India, Peru and Vietnam. Summative Report*. Oxford: Young Lives. Available at: https://www.younglives.org.uk/sites/www.younglives.org.uk/files/YL-RespondingToChildrensWork-A4-Jan18_0.pdf.

Movik, S. (2011) 'The politics of aid: African strategies for dealing with donors', *Forum for Development Studies*, 38(2), pp 213–22.

Myers, W.E. (1999) 'Considering child labour: changing terms, issues and actors at the international level', *Childhood – A Global Journal of Child Research*, 6(1), pp 13–26.

Nimbona, G. and Lieten, G.K. (2007) *Child Labour Unions: AEJT Senegal*. Amsterdam: IREWOC.

Nti, K. (2017) *Return Our Children, You Abducted – MP Tells NGO*. Available at: https://ghananewspage.com/return-our-children-you-abducted-mp-tells-ngo/ (Accessed 18 May 2020).

Nukunya, G.K. (2003) *Tradition and Change in Ghana: An Introduction to Sociology*. Accra, Ghana: Ghana Universities Press.

Okali, K., Frimpong Boamah, E. and Sumberg, J. (2022) 'The quantification of child labour by Ghana's mass media: a missed opportunity?', *Africa Spectrum*, 57(2), pp 155–77.

Okyere, S. (2012) 'Re-examining the education-child labour Nexus: the case of child miners at Kenyasi, Ghana', *Childhoods Today*, 6(1), pp 1–20.

Okyere, S. (2013) 'Are working children's rights and child labour abolition complementary or opposing realms?', *International Social Work*, 56(1), pp 80–91.

Okyere, S. (2018) '"Like the stranger at a funeral who cries more than the bereaved": ethical dilemmas in ethnographic research with children', *Qualitative Research*, 18(6), pp 623–37.

Oppong, C. (1973) *Growing Up in Dagbon*. Accra: Ghana Publishing Co.

Oquaye, M. (1995) 'Human rights and the transition to democracy under the PNDC in Ghana', *Human Rights Quarterly*, 17(3), pp 556–73.

Owusu-Amankwah, R. (2015) *Certifications, Child Labour and Livelihood Strategies: An Analysis of Cocoa Production in Ghana*. PhD thesis. Wageningen: Wageningen University.

Pennington, R. and Harpending, H. (1993) *The Structure of an African Pastoralist Community: Demography, History, and Ecology of the Ngamiland Herero*. London: Clarendon Press.

Ravallion, M. and Wodon, Q. (2000) 'Does child labour displace schooling? Evidence on behavioural responses to an enrolment subsidy', *Economic Journal*, 110(462), pp C158–75.

Ray, R. (2002) 'The determinants of child labour and child schooling in Ghana', *Journal of African Economies*, 11(4), pp 561–90.

Sackey, E.T. and Johannesen, B.O. (2015) 'Earning identity and respect through work: A study of children involved in fishing and farming practices in Cape Coast, Ghana', *Childhood – a Global Journal of Child Research*, 22(4), pp 447–59.

Sadhu, S. et al (2020) *Assessing Progress in Reducing Child Labor in Cocoa Production in Cocoa Growing Areas of Côte d'Ivoire and Ghana*. Chicago: NORC, University of Chicago.

Sarpong, P. (1974) *Ghana in Retrospect: Some Aspects of Ghanaian Culture*. Tema, Ghana: Ghana Publishing Corporation.

Sarpong, P. (1977) *Girls' Nubility Rites in Ashanti*. Tema, Ghana: Ghana Publishing Corporation. Available at: https://trove.nla.gov.au/version/11858981 (Accessed 18 May 2020).

Shahinian, G. (2014) *Report of the Special Rapporteur on Contemporary Forms of Slavery, Including Its Causes and Consequences. a/Hrc/27/53/Add.3*. Geneva: UN Human Rights Council. Available at: http://www.ohchr.org/EN/HRBodies/HRC/RegularSessions/Session27/Documents/A-HRC-27-53-Add3_en.doc.

Takyi, E. (2014) 'Child labour in Ghana: ecological perspective', *Developing Country Studies*, 4(19), pp 35–42.

The Independent (2016) 'Cleaning common areas to be daily routine for all school students'. Available at: https://theindependent.sg/cleaning-common-areas-to-be-daily-routine-for-all-school-students/ (Accessed 23 November 2020).

Thum-Danso Imoh, A. (2012) '"This is how we do it here": the persistence of the physical punishment of children in Ghana in the face of globalizing ideals', in Thum-Danso Imoh, A. and Ame, R. (eds) *Childhoods at the Intersection of the Local and the Global*. London: Palgrave Macmillan UK, pp 121–42.

Thum-Danso Imoh, A. (2019) 'Terminating childhood: dissonance and synergy between global children's rights norms and local discourses about the transition from childhood to adulthood in Ghana', *Human Rights Quarterly*, 4(1), pp 160–82.

Tsuneyoshi, R., Kusanagi, K. and Takahashi, F. (2016) *Cleaning as Part of TOKKATSU: School Cleaning Japanese Style. Working Paper*. Tokyo: Center for Excellence in School Education, The University of Tokyo.

Tulane University (2015) *Final Report: 2013/14 Survey Research on Child Labor in West African Cocoa-Growing Areas*. New Orleans: School of Public Health and Tropical Medicine, Tulane University.

Twum-Danso Imoh, A. (2009) 'Situating participatory methodologies in context: the impact of culture on adult–child interactions in research and other projects', *Children's Geographies*, 7(4), pp 379–89.

UCW (2016a) *Child Labour and the Youth Decent Work Deficit in Ghana*. Rome: Understanding Children's Work Project.

UCW (2016b) *The Twin Challenges of Child Labour and Educational Marginalisation in the ECOWAS Region*. Rome: Understanding Children's Work (UCW) Project. Available at: https://cocoainitiative.org/knowledge-centre-post/the-twin-challenges-of-child-labour-and-educational-marginalisation-in-the-ecowas-region/ (Accessed 16 April 2020).

Ungruhe, C. (2019) 'Beyond agency's limits: "street children's" mobilities in southern Ghana', *Cadernos de Estudos Africanos*, 37, pp 41–61.

UNICEF (2007) *Child Labour, Education and Policy Options*. New York: United Nations Children's Fund (UNICEF). Available at: https://www.unicef.org/Child_Labor_Education_and_Policy_Options.pdf (Accessed 18 May 2020).

US Department of Labor (2017) *Framework of Action to Support Implementation of the Harkin–Engel Protocol*. Washington, DC: US Department of Labour.

US Department of Labor (2018) *2017 Findings on the Worst Forms of Child Labor: Ghana*. Washington, DC: US Department of Labour.

Van Dijk, T. (2001) 'Critical discourse analysis' in Schriffin, D., Tannen, D. and Hamilton, H. E. (eds) *The Handbook of Discourse Analysis*. Maldon, MA and Oxford: Blackwell Publishers.

Vandenhole, W. (2020) 'Decolonising children's rights: of vernacularisation and interdisciplinarity', in Buddle, R. and Markowska-Manista, U. (eds) *Childhood and Children's Rights between Research and Activism*. Wiesbaden: Springer, pp 187–206.

Whitehead, A. and Hashim, I.M. (2005) *Background Paper for DFID Migration Team March 2005*. Unpublished paper.

Whitehead, A., Hashim, I.M. and Iversen, V. (2007) *Child Migration, Child Agency and Inter-generational Relations in Africa and South Asia*. Working Paper T-24. Brighton: Development Research Centre on Migration, Globalisation and Poverty.

Whitfield, L. (ed) (2008) *The Politics of Aid: African Strategies for Dealing with Donors*. Oxford, New York: Oxford University Press.

World Bank (2016) *Ghana Social Protection Assessment and Public Expenditure Review*. New York: The World Bank.

Yeboah, T. (2020) 'Future aspirations of rural–urban young migrants in Accra, Ghana', *Children's Geographies*, 19(1), pp 45–58.

Yeboah, T., Owusu, L. and Arhin, A.A. (2015) 'Fighting poverty from the street: perspectives of some female informal sector workers on gendered poverty and livelihood portfolios in southern Ghana', *Journal of Economic & Social Studies (JECOSS)*, 5(1), pp 239–67.

Zdunnek, G. et al (2008) *Child Labour and Children's Economic Activities in Agriculture in Ghana. SLE Publication Series – S233*. Berlin: Centre for Advanced Training in Rural Development (SLE), Humbolt University, on behalf the Food and Agriculture Organization of the United Nations (FAO).

9

Children's Work in Shallot Production on the Keta Peninsula, South-Eastern Ghana

Thomas Yeboah and Irene Egyir

Introduction

Over the last two decades, agriculture in Africa has moved towards the top of the development agenda. The Comprehensive African Agricultural Development Programme (CAADP) was agreed in 2003, with a focus on improving food and nutrition security, and increasing incomes in Africa's largely farming-based economies. It aims to achieve this by raising agricultural productivity and increasing public investment in agriculture (NEPAD, 2003). With new public commitments by African governments, and unprecedented investment by private actors and development partners, competing visions and models of African agricultural and rural transformation have emerged. In Ghana, the Food and Agricultural Sector Development Policy has been supported by various governments through four-year medium-term investment programmes (Ministry of Food and Agriculture, 2007). The strategy has been to use flagship projects to provide subsidies and technical information, and thereby facilitate productivity enhancement (World Bank, 2017). The current programme, 'Planting for Food and Jobs', singles out vegetables and major grain crops for greater support (Ministry of Food and Agriculture, 2018; Nantui Mabe et al, 2018). As vegetable production in Ghana has historically relied on children's labour contribution, the new emphasis on vegetables will likely impact on children's work.

Children's involvement in agriculture in Ghana can be traced to the colonial period (and was presumably present long before that). The establishment of a typical export oriented colonial economy in the former Gold Coast included the development of infrastructure including railways, roads, deep water harbours and some plantations. However, it is remarkable that the cocoa sector developed without state involvement (Hill, 1963). The significant expansion in cocoa production from 536 tons in 1900 to 176,000 tons in 1920 (see Chapter 10, this volume), led to heavy demands for porters, particularly for head loading beans, and children played an important role in meeting this demand (Van Hear, 1982). The number of children undertaking head carriage increased in line with the booming cocoa industry, and by 1914, according to a report quoted by Van Hear (1982), 'a large number of the children in this colony are engaged daily in heavy weight carrying. It is in fact their daily occupation'. However, warnings about the harmful effects of head carriage and cultivation on the health of children prompted no action on the part of the colonial authorities (Van Hear, 1982).

Round 6 of the Ghana Living Standards Survey (GLSS6) estimated that in 2012–13, 39 per cent of the 1.78 million rural children aged 5–17 had engaged in economic activity during the 7 days previous to the survey, and 42.4 per cent during the previous 12 months (Ghana Statistical Service, 2014b). Eighty-seven per cent of these children worked in agriculture and fisheries (Ghana Statistical Service 2014b); and around 59 per cent of this work was classified as 'hazardous' (ILO, 2016). There is a growing body of research and policy literature from Ghana that draws attention to the negative consequences of children's involvement in farming, small-scale fisheries and livestock husbandry (Abenyega and Gockowski, 2003; Casely-Hayford, 2004; Amuzu et al, 2010; Tulane University, 2015; Sadhu et al, 2020).

Given the global significance of cocoa it is not surprising that much attention has been given to reducing child labour within the sector; however, in many ways this detracts from other sectors and crops where children's work is equally prevalent (Sabates-Wheeler and Sumberg, 2022). For example, shallot (*Allium ascalonicum*) is another crop grown by small-scale producers that has been closely linked to children's work. Shallot is a perennial plant managed as an annual for its cluster of small bulbs or cloves. It has a delicate onion-like flavour and is consumed both as dry bulbs and as green onions. Shallots are valuable, not only for flavouring dishes but also for their medicinal properties (Sinnadurai 1973; Swamy and Gowda 2006). As a vegetable, shallots have been increasing recognized as important for food and nutrition security; they can be an important source of the vitamins and minerals needed for good health.

Shallots are produced in Ghana primarily on the Keta Peninsula, which is located along the seafront near to the border with Togo. Like many vegetables, the production, processing and marketing of shallots are labour intensive, with the work of children and young people being considered essential (Patten and Nukunya, 1982). While the prevalence and drivers of children's work in Ghana's cocoa (see Chapter 10, this volume) and fisheries (Chapter 11, this volume) sectors have been studied – and contested – there is relatively little academic, political or policy interest in the involvement of children in shallot production. Indeed, over the last three decades there has been little new published literature addressing this topic.

The aim of this chapter is to provide a synthesis of the research and policy literature on the involvement of children in shallot production on the Keta Peninsula, with particular emphasis on the forms, prevalence and drivers of children's work. Overall, what emerges is that children's work remains central to shallot production, and their engagement is structured by both age and gender. Despite increased awareness of child labour in public and policy discourse in Ghana, we find little evidence that speaks directly to the issue of harm or anything close to the so-called 'worst forms of child labour' associated with children's engagement in shallot production.

The remainder of the chapter is organized as follows. The next section provides background information on the geography and local economy of the Keta Peninsula including an outline of its biophysical and socio-economic characteristics. We then provide an historical overview of the development of shallot production including a discussion of the history, economics of production, labour requirements, and the organization and governance of the shallot value chain. This is followed by a discussion of children's work including the forms, prevalence, drivers and harm associated with children's work in shallot production. The last section concludes with some questions to help orient future research.

The geography and local economy of the Keta Peninsula

The unique biophysical and socio-economic characteristics of the Keta Peninsula have been amply described (Folitse et al, 2017; Addo et al, 2018). Keta Municipality, where the peninsula is located, is one of the 25 administrative districts in the old Volta Region,[1] and lies within longitudes 0.30°E and 1.05°E and latitudes 5.45°N and 6.005°N. The peninsula shares borders with Ketu North and South Districts to the east, Akatsi South District to the north, South Tongu District to the west and the Gulf of Guinea to the south. It is essentially a very narrow stretch of sand bar, about 2.5 kilometres in width, which separates the Keta lagoon (to the north) from the sea (to the south). Its total surface area is 1,086 km^2, of which 30 per cent is covered by water bodies and swamp, interspersed with savannah woodland and short grassland mangrove (Ghana Statistical Service, 2014a).

The climatic conditions of the entire area are influenced by the twice-yearly South West monsoon winds, which give rise to a double maximum rainfall pattern; the major rainy season occurs between March and July and the minor season between August and November. The total annual rainfall varies significantly between 146 mm and 750 mm (Addo et al, 2018). The combination of limited rainfall and high evapotranspiration means that without supplemental irrigation the opportunities for vegetable production are severely limited. The water available from the lagoon is too saline for agricultural purposes, so horticulture depends on groundwater irrigation from the shallow fresh aquifer underneath the bar. Most of the peninsula is covered by sandy soils, but closer to the lagoon edge there are heavy saline clays. The preparation of sand beds for shallot production on the lagoon side of the bar is done by bringing sand from the sea side (Porter et al, 1997).

Keta Municipality has a population of around 150,000 inhabitants, with females (53.6 per cent) outnumbering the males (46.4 per cent) (Ghana Statistical Service, 2014a). The average household size is 3.8 persons, and children (aged between 0 and 17) constitute the largest share (33.3 per cent) of the household population. About 64 per cent of the population aged 15 years and older is economically active.

During the pre-colonial era, the economy of the Peninsula was dominated by fishing and salt extraction, supplemented to a lesser extent by hunting, livestock and crop production, and manufacturing. At the time, salt making, fishing and farming were highly organized (Ocloo 1996). The major crop was coconut on the seaside and near the marshes on the lagoon side, but Cape St Paul Wilt disease (a lethal yellowing disease of coconut) led to a massive decline in production (Sinnadurai, 1973; Addo et al, 2018). This, combined with the perennial difficulties caused by low water levels in Keta Lagoon and the associated decline in fish stocks stimulated interest in commercial shallot farming in and around the peninsula (Porter et al, 1997).

Today the economy of the peninsula depends essentially on agriculture, with horticultural crops, with shallot, pepper and okra being particularly important (Addo et al, 2018). However, increased temperatures combined with variable rainfall and prolonged periods of drought negatively affect agriculture (Addo et al, 2018). There are also small-scale agro-based activities including coconut-oil extraction, cassava processing, sugar cane juice distilling and fish processing, supplemented by salt mining and sand winning, kente weaving, carpentry, production of standing brooms, pottery, straw mat weaving, mechanics, masonry, tailoring and dressmaking. Thirty-five per cent of the employed population is engaged in agriculture, forestry or fishing (Ghana Statistical Service, 2014a). The agricultural sector accounts for a larger share of employment for females than males (Addo et al, 2018; Ghana Statistical Service, 2014a).

The peninsula and surrounding areas are well served by economic and social infrastructure including transport and telecommunication, hospitals, piped water, electric power, schools, community centres and financial institutions (Ghana Statistical Service, 2014a). Within the region, Keta Municipal District, which includes the peninsula, is among the relatively prosperous districts: the depth of poverty is estimated to be between 5.0

and 9.9 per cent (Ghana Statistical Service, 2015) while a ranking of all 216 districts across Ghana by poverty incidence placed Keta Municipal as 54th, with a poverty incidence of 14.6 per cent (compared to 94.2 per cent for the poorest district and 1.3 per cent for the least poor).

Overview of shallot production

History

The Keta Peninsula has been a centre of intensive irrigated shallot and other vegetables production since at least the 18th century. The crop is not considered indigenous to the area, and there is controversy around when and how it was introduced. One theory is that shallots were introduced into neighbouring Togo by early European settlers and subsequently moved into Ghana (Sinnadurai, 1973). However, Ocloo (1996) notes that there are no aspects of shallot farming in Togo, from cultivation to marketing, that suggest a common origin with Anlo. He is of the view that since the settlements in Saltpond (in the Central Region, 240 km west of Keta) had a longer European presence than any in Togo, they could have easily been the source of diffusion of the shallot crop. In 1957, the Department of Agriculture enumerated 214 shallot beds in a cluster of villages around Saltpond's lower towns including Kuntu, Ankaful, Abandzi and Kromantsi.

In any case, it is well documented that by the mid-1930s shallot production dominated the peninsula's economy (Patten and Nukunya, 1982; Ocloo, 1996), with its growth linked to extensive re-filling and reclamation of the marshy land on both the sea and lagoon sides. These lands were converted into beds, specifically for the production of shallots. Individual farmers extended their activities from Anloga to neighbouring Tegbi, Woe and Vui in the east and to Anyanui, Wuti, Dzita and Atorkor in the west. All available depressions on the peninsula, totalling around 4,500 hectares of land, were reclaimed and utilized for the purpose of shallot production. Ocloo (1996) notes that a process of intensification aimed at increasing the yield of shallots began in the 1960s, while in 1963, Hill (1986) described shallot farming on the peninsula as an 'astonishing industry' and 'among the most intensive in the world', being based on a renting system that was 'unique in the West African context'. Hill (1986) also noted that the system itself was developed without any support from the Gold Coast Department of Agriculture, and by the end of the 1960s, the peninsula had developed a truly 'practical monopoly of shallot production in Ghana'. The cultivation of shallots was initially restricted to the lagoon-side owing to the fact that the water table is relatively high and shallow wells of 1.5 to 2.0 metres depth are adequate to access the aquifer. Over time, due to the shortage of land, farmers extended cultivation to the seaward side of the bar (Porter et al, 1997).

The speed with which the shallot industry developed between 1930 and 1955 led Ocloo (1996) to describe it as a 'revolution'. He identified two immediate causes of intensification. The first was urbanization, particularly of Accra, which became and remains the main market for Anlo shallots, but also of nearby Lomé, the capital city of Togo. The second was the trade slump associated with the world economic crisis of the 1930s, and government's response, which was to promote agricultural diversification including vegetable production. A precondition of the shallot revolution was the increased commodification of land, including privatization and a system for leasing shallot beds.

High market prices and consistent demand for vegetables in urban areas allow many people on the peninsula to continue to rely on commercial production of shallot, okra, pepper and other vegetables for their livelihoods (Porter et al, 1997; Adzraku, 2017).

Production

Shallot production involves bed preparation, planting, irrigation (watering), weeding, pest and disease control, harvesting and post-harvest handling (sorting, grading and packing). Shallots are often intercropped with other crops that may be planted about 45 days after the shallots have sprouted. Bulbs are planted on beds measuring about 1.5 by 12 metres. Production requires only simple implements such as cutlasses and small-handled hoes. Traditional seed varieties grown on mainly sandy soils (with low organic matter content and poor cation exchange capacity) must be irrigated regularly. Producers commonly work up to 0.4 hectare of owned or rented beds.

The calendar of activities is well structured. Generally, the first planting of shallot is in December/January (possibly with maize intercropped), the second in April/May (generally with tomatoes) and the third in August/September (with tomatoes or peppers). Irrigation is essential for the first and third plantings. This pattern of shallot planting was established to prevent the spread of pests and diseases, particularly the insect pest 'thrips', and at least in the 1970s was reported to have been strictly adhered to on the lagoon side (Sinnadurai, 1973).

The yield in the dry season is higher than in the wet season. Yields of 10 to 20 tons per hectare per annum of dried shallots have been reported (Wills, 1962). The Ministry of Agriculture, Food and Fisheries (1994) suggested yields of 15–25 tons per hectare are possible under good management but observed that yields of 8–10 tons per hectare are more common.

Over the last two decades there has been a gradual diffusion of overhead sprinkler irrigation, with electric pumps being used to extract water from deeper wells. This shift was facilitated in part by a World Bank-sponsored programme in the 1990s, which provided funds for well-sinking and electric pumps. Investment in pumps and overhead irrigation has enabled expansion of shallot and vegetable production from the low-lying coastal areas to the 'upland' fields (Porter et al, 1997). It is now common to see shallots produced in household compounds located in the central (that is, slightly higher) part of the peninsula.

Land

In addition to owning land, men and women access land for shallot production by renting, leasing, pledging and share cropping, but the prevailing patrilineal system of inheritance makes access to land for farming skewed in favour of men (it is estimated by Folitse et al (2017) that 67 per cent of shallot farmers are male). Under the Anlo patrilineal system of inheritance, both sons and daughters may inherit land from their fathers, although sons take precedence. Ayivor (2001) found that 7 per cent of 209 beds surveyed in Torgome depression and 24 per cent of 142 beds surveyed in Tsinyui depression, both in Anloga, were acquired by women by inheritance. He suggests that women's ownership of land comes about in four ways: it is purchased outright; a landowner has daughters but no sons, and the girls inherit; a land owner decides to reward a good and 'serviceable' daughter with a plot of land; and the sons of a deceased land owner decide to share the father's land with their sisters (in such cases, however, the proportion going to sons is always larger).

Labour

Within the peninsula's intensive commercial horticulture system, labour is a critically important resource. The topography and sandy soil of the peninsula, combined with the action of the sea on one side, and flooding of the lagoon on the other, means that much of the land on which shallots are produced was created, and is maintained, through the concerted actions of local people (Nukunya, 1975; Porter et al, 1997). In addition to bed creation and maintenance, shallot production requires substantial labour inputs for manuring (Hill, 1986), bulb propagation, weeding, irrigation and post-harvest handling (Sinnadurai, 1973).

Historically, shallot farmers relied on household labour, and they continue to do so. Household members who assist male producers include the wife or wives as well as children over about eight years of age (Patten, 1990). Patten and Nukunya (1982) noted that the need to use all available family labour resulted in increasing flexibility with regards to the sexual division of labour within the family. As shallots came to dominate the local economy, farmers increasingly supplemented family labour with hired labour. But despite flexibility of gender roles within the household, the divisions between adult male and female hired labour remains strict. Men are hired to perform tasks including hoeing, planting, cultivating, harvesting and bundling for market, while women are hired for sorting of the harvest and headloading manure or sand into the fields.

The women shallot producers (about 33 per cent of all producers) mostly rely on hired labour for tasks such as weeding, watering and manuring. Tasks such as harvesting, transportation and marketing are performed by the women themselves. Depending on their gender, age and abilities, children may perform various task such as land preparation, planting and watering of shallot beds, weed control, harvesting, drying, transportation, bagging and marketing of shallots at the local market (Ocloo, 1996; Yeboah and Sumberg, 2020).

The value chain

The specific governance mechanism for the shallot value chain on the Keta Peninsula could be described as a spot market transaction (see Chapter 6, this volume). This involves the use of mediators to connect buyers and sellers. This system of value chain governance allows a relatively large group of buyers and sellers to connect given that it has relatively straightforward institutional arrangements (see Chapter 6, this volume).

Figure 9.1 illustrates the shallot value chain, with the primary actors being input suppliers, producers, traders and consumers. Unlike cocoa, there is little or no involvement by state or international actors in production or anywhere else along the shallot value chain. This is not surprising given that the crop is produced and consumed locally with no export or international market (with the exception of long-established links with Togo).

Private business actors supply seeds, fertilizers, herbicides, pesticides, manure and irrigation equipment (Adzraku, 2017). Both wholesale and retail traders work within the value chain. Between the 1970s and the 1990s shallot trading became so lucrative that women from Accra, Kumasi, Koforidua, Ho and Hohoe visited Anloga and the Keta markets to purchase (Porter et al, 1997). Today, wholesalers mainly from Accra and Tema, and to a lesser extent nearby Lomé (Togo), buy shallots directly from farmers for onward supply to retailers or consumers in the urban market. Anecdotes suggest that Ashaiman (in Tema city, 159 km west of Keta) is becoming an important town for shallot trading owing to the growth of the Anlo population. Retailers buy shallots in smaller quantities at the farm gate, in Anloga market or from wholesalers. Prices of shallots are determined through negotiation between producers and traders. Adzraku (2017) found that there is no contractual agreement between producers and traders. The

Figure 9.1: The shallot value/marketing chain on the Keta Peninsula

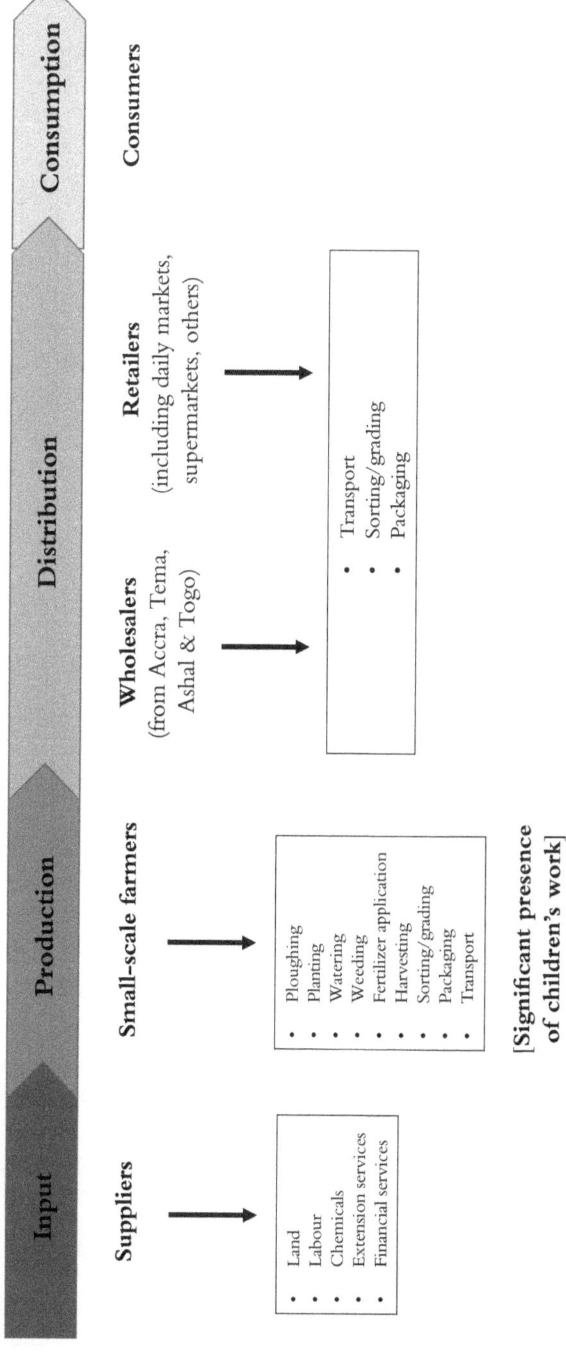

Source: Adapted and modified from Adzraku (2017)

implication is that shallot producers have the liberty to sell their produce without prior obligation to passing traders at the farm gate and can further decide to switch to different buyers and traders without any compulsion. Prices are generally low in the rainy season when supply exceeds demand and high in the dry season when the reverse is true (Adzraku, 2017).

Children's work

Children have always played a key role in shallot production on the Keta Peninsula. They start to contribute to household agriculture at an early age and begin to enter the labour market around age 12, whether they attend school or not (Patten, 1990). This still holds today. According to recent research by Yeboah and Sumberg (2020) children of school-going age (primary and junior high school) are centrally engaged shallot and other vegetable production. According to Patten and Nukunya (1982), the increasing use of hired labour during the shallot revolution provided a channel through which children could enter the labour market. The reliance on children to assist, particularly with watering, is linked to the sandy soils on which shallots are grown, which require regular watering. During the first cropping period which coincides with the rainy season, shallot farmers are concerned about too much water and potential flooding of the shallot beds. During this period, there is little if any need to hire labour to assist with watering. However, during the second and third seasons, which coincide largely with the dry season, there is continual pressure to supply water to the crop. It is during these periods that school children's involvement becomes critical.

As part of intensive PhD research in the 1970s, Patten (1990) conducted a household survey and a short questionnaire was administered in one primary and one middle school (450 respondents aged 12 to 20 and comprising 199 females and 251 males). She also interviewed 20 male and 20 female students from one of the primary schools that participated in the survey; and conducted interviews with 45 female and 85 male students in one of the middle schools. A summary of the children's participation by age and gender in the household's farming as well as household and contract work is shown in Table 9.1.

It is evident that male and female school children contributed to both household agricultural production and paid (contract) work, but across most school groups, boys were more likely than girls to contribute. Notably, the involvement of girls in shallot production began to slacken as they moved beyond Form 1, by which time they were assisting their mothers and other female relatives with petty trading. The involvement of children who worked for other farmers for a wage was structured by gender; while males were hired for watering, fertilizing, hoeing, ditching, sowing and harvesting, females

Table 9.1: Distribution of school children's involvement in shallot production

				Assist father, mother, other relative (no cash remuneration)		Assist with household agricultural work & contract work	
School group	**Age range**	**Female (no.)**	**Male (no.)**	**Female (%)**	**Male (%)**	**Female (%)**	**Male (%)**
Class 4	12–16	39	53	64	53	33	42
Class 5	13–16	38	46	61	74	50	65
Form 1	14–16	38	44	92	100	76	82
Form 2	15–17	38	37	92	86	61	65
Form 3	16–20	20	44	40	87	40	68
Form 4	16–20	26	27	58	85	38	85

Source: Patten (1990, p 183)

who hired out their labour were involved in watering and headloading. The money that the children earned was their own and they had the option to collect their wages either daily, weekly or at the end of the farming season.

Based on these findings, Patten (1990) concluded that 'without the paid labour of school children, the agricultural system would be unworkable'. She further noted that during her field research, four of six primary schools and all four middle schools operated split days, with a student attending either in the morning or the afternoon, and that this 'greatly enhanced' the feasibility of school children making such an important contribution to shallot production. Ocloo also recognizes children's labour as 'essential' (1996, p 147), particularly for watering, a task 'dominated by children'.

In 2019, Yeboah and Sumberg (2020) re-examined Patten's central conclusion – that a well-established, intensive agricultural system was reliant on the paid labour of school children – in the light of three significant changes in context. These changes relate to investment in irrigation technology (change from using buckets to draw water from shallow wells to using overhead sprinklers); re-organization of the school day so that all students attend for the whole day; and the increased attention to child labour in both policy and public discourse in Ghana. They administered a short survey covering 440 students (aged 11–24 years, 255 males and 185 females, across five schools in Anloga); interviewed 20 male and 10 female students from the schools that participated in the survey; and interviewed 10 adult shallot producers. For students in Basic School, 87 per cent of boys and 58 per cent of girls reported that they were 'sometimes' or 'often' involved in shallot or vegetable production. For students in senior high school, 64 per cent of boys and 60 per cent of girls reported that they were 'sometimes' or 'often' involved in shallot or vegetable production. These results suggest that many school children are still frequently working in shallot and vegetable production.

The literature on children's involvement in shallot production on the peninsula suggest that the most common task performed by many children is watering (Patten and Nukunya, 1982; Patten, 1990; Ocloo, 1996; Yeboah and Sumberg, 2020). This is also confirmed by observation. Watering is normally done in the mornings and the evenings, and children report waking as early as 4 am to go to the farm and water, and returning around 6 am to prepare for school. They then return to the farm again after school, normally between 4 pm and 6 pm, although some stay longer. Other common tasks performed by children include weeding, harvesting and sowing. The involvement of children in shallot production is highly gendered with boys engaged in weeding, sowing, watering and digging and girls grading bulbs after harvest and preparing them for the market. Children's engagement in activities such as spraying chemicals, ploughing, digging and fertilizer application is less widespread (Yeboah and Sumberg, 2020).

Drivers of children's work

While reliable data on the actual numbers of children engaged in both agriculture and domestic work in Ghana is not available, there is some literature on the factors that drive children's work, particularly in cocoa and fisheries (Casely-Hayford, 2004; Agbenya, 2009; Kapoor, 2017; Adonteng-Kissi, 2018; Chapters 10 and 11, this volume). Income poverty, inadequate agricultural technology, limited access to quality education, insufficient adult labour, minimal regulations and enforcement, socialization of the child, ingrained attitudes about the roles of children, lack of mechanization and family needs have all been noted to contribute to and shape children's participation in work. In comparison with cocoa or fishing, the literature on what drives children's participation in shallot production is very limited.

Patten's (1990) research demonstrated that children's sense of a need to contribute to household welfare was a significant driver for their participation in shallot production, and many parents understood this as 'culturally appropriate'. In addition to their farm work being valuable to the household, the children saw their participation as appropriate because 'my father feeds me' (1990, p 184). Similarly, Yeboah and Sumberg (2020) found that children who work on the shallot plots of family relations recognized their work as an opportunity to help parents or contribute to the welfare of the household. Many regarded their involvement in shallot production as part of their responsibility and there appeared to be no sense of compulsion or coercion to get involved. For example, a 13-year-old female explained that 'working on the farm is an opportunity to help my father, and my father provides for all my needs through the farming business'.

The involvement of children in shallot production is also driven by children's own desire to earn income that can be used to meet their socio-economic needs. Patten and Nukunya (1982) noted that children, and particularly young men, contracted their labour to earn a wage, which they could invest in land to start their own farm. With pressure on land this avenue is now likely to be closed to most young people. Patten (1990) noted that many children were also motivated by a desire to earn income, and what they earned was not all given to the household. In most cases, earnings are (and were) spent on school items (for example, textbooks, pens, pencils and exercise books) and personal items including food and clothing (Patten and Nukunya, 1982). This also appears to be the case today (Yeboah and Sumberg, 2020).

Some literature suggests that children's involvement in shallot production is driven by kinship fosterage, a system whereby rural children are recruited to carry out age-specific work for family members who may not have children of their own (Goody, 1966; Ocloo, 1996). Ocloo (1996) argues that the tradition of extensive migration during the pre-colonial era gave rise to the institutionalization of fostering, and this system was used in different ways to access children's labour during the shallot revolution. In addition to the farmers' own children, in the early 1990s, many of the family workers on shallot farms were children of relatives who were recruited to assist with farm work. Records of 40 farming households in Setsinu-Anloga indicate that in 1992, out of the total of 277 household members who assisted with shallot production (other than the head of the household), 46.6 per cent were the heads' grandchildren, 41.5 per cent were the heads' own children, and 11.9 per cent were other relatives (Ocloo, 1996).

The recruitment of children of distant relatives to assist with shallot production appears to have one particular benefit for farmers. The practice of *fiabui*[2] gives the first male son the liberty to shift residence from the family house to start his own independent life. When this is done, he is entitled to receive a parcel of land from his family to compensate for work already undertaken. According to Ocloo (1996) this practice not only makes the senior Anlo male child an unreliable source of labour for household production but also a potential competitor for family resources. In the early phases of development of the shallot industry, there was little or no difficulty for parents to fulfil their *fiabui* obligation, owing to the availability and under-utilization of marshy lands. Today, this is no longer possible because of the scarcity of land. As a result, farmers prefer to recruit distant child relatives to assist with farm work because there will be no obligation to give a share of the family land when the foster child decides to shift residence after a period of work.

Harmful work and the 'the worst forms of child labour'

There is little research, and few policy or media reports that provide direct or indirect evidence of harm associated with children's work in shallot production. We were able to identify only two studies that specifically mention any potential negative consequences. What is interesting is that these studies were not designed specifically to investigate harm or exploitation of children working on shallot plots.

Patten (1990) noted that 'women chiefs and family elders who routinely hear domestic trouble cases indicated that the school attenders increasingly complain about the heavy demands they feel on three fronts: school, home and the wage labour market' (1990, p 186). While little information was provided to substantiate this finding, we can infer that children's engagement in the shallot labour market had implications for their education, and perhaps put them under undue stress. However, having access to cash from work made it more feasible for children to express their displeasures and in some cases shift their residence to live with other relatives (Patten, 1990). Yeboah and Sumberg (2020) report that some children working on shallot beds experienced fatigue and body pain, which had implications for the time available for their studies, lateness to school and attendance. Some children reported they would perform better at school if they were not involved in shallot work. For example, an older male student interviewed said:

> 'The time I am supposed to wake up and learn, that is the time I will be going to farm and watering the plants and the crops. It is affecting my performance because I'm not getting enough time to learn what they teach us in class. Farming takes much of my time so I can't get enough time to learn.' (21-year old male, SHS 2, Yeboah and Sumberg, 2020)

These findings provide insights into the argument that at least for some children there is a potentially significant trade-off between working on the shallot beds and education. This deserves further careful analysis recognizing that such trade-offs greatly complicate any simple conclusions about harm associated with children's work. For many children, their engagement in shallot production may help defray the cost of their schooling, meet their own personal expenses and contribute to household production, all of which greatly enhances their sense of self-worth and identity as a 'good child'.

We are not suggesting that children working on shallot plots may not encounter harm. However, the lack of specific evidence that points to harm suggests the need for researchers and policy makers to reflect and begin to formulate an alternative framing of benefits associated with children's work in shallot production.

Research directions

We have established that children's labour historically played, and continues to play, a crucial role in shallot production on the Keta Peninsula. However, when one compares the volume of research relating to children's engagement in cocoa for example, the evidence on the forms, drivers and prevalence of children's work in shallot production is minimal. More research is needed to better understand the dynamics of children's work in this setting. While there is some limited evidence of harm, particularly in relation to education and physical wellbeing, we find very little research directly investigating the trade-off between the benefits and negative effects of children's involvement in this agricultural work. To be clear: we are not suggesting that some children working on shallots may not be exposed to hazards, or may not experience harm, but at this time, substantiating evidence is non-existent.

The evidence presented here also begs some specific questions for future research. What we know currently about children's work in shallot production is that much of it takes place on household plots. However, the shallot value chain goes well beyond on-farm activities (as illustrated more generally in Chapter 6). In this regard future research could examine the governance of the value chain and the gendered nature of children's involvement in all steps along the chain, including production, processing and trade. Additionally, future research could also explore how indigenous social practices such as fostering and *fiabui* reinforce or mitigate against the involvement of children in shallot production and levels of harm arising.

Finally, given that there has been no reporting of anything akin to the worst forms of child labour, yet children's work in shallot production is pervasive, perhaps the key question to interrogate is, why? Is it because shallots are produced mainly for the domestic market and in this regard have abusive practices (where these exist) escaped the attention of the media, policy makers and researchers? Or are there aspects of the technical, social or political context that mitigate against child abuse and harm? For example, Van Hear (1982) reported how during the colonial era collective actions, such as, boycotting work, violence for non-payment of agreed wages, spreading of messages about bad treatment to other workers, and solidarity among northern rural casual labourers including children, were used to help prevent exploitation and harm to child workers. Are similar actions also at play on the Keta Peninsula, and if so, what conditions have allowed them to emerge? Perhaps the limited attention to children's work on the Keta peninsula is indicative of the cultural acceptability of children working to support the household and local community. Does 'harm' need to be the framing for researchers and policy makers whenever they see or hear of children working alongside family and community? In conclusion we are of the view that it might be better for policy makers, researchers and development professionals to start with a framing of 'benefit' associated with children' rather than the simplistic assumption of 'harm'.

Notes

1 Following a referendum in 2018 the Volta Region was divided into the Volta and Oti regions.

2 A socio-traditional practice where the first male son would be entitled a share of his family resources (mainly farmland). This is done as compensation for work already undertaken in household agriculture for several years. The practice allows the first male son to shift residence from the family house.

References

Abenyega, O. and Gockowski, J. (2003) *Labor Practices in the Cocoa Sector of Ghana with a Special Focus on the Role of Children*. Kumasi: KNUST and IITA.

Addo, K.A. et al (2018) 'A biophysical and socioeconomic review of the Volta Delta, Ghana', *Journal of Coastal Research*, 345(5), pp 1216–26.

Adonteng-Kissi, O. (2018) 'Causes of child labour: perceptions of rural and urban parents in Ghana', *Children and Youth Services Review*, 91, pp 55–65.

Adzraku, M.E. (2017) *Shallot Value Chain in the Keta Municipality of Ghana: Assessing the Role of Small Scale Irrigation Vegetable Farming*. Unpublished BA dissertation. Tamale: University for Development Studies.

Agbenya, L. (2009) *Child Labour Trafficking in the Lake Volta Fishery of Ghana: A Case Study of Ogetse in the Krachi West District of the Volta Region*. Unpublished Master's thesis in International Fisheries Management. Tromso, Norway: University of Tromso.

Amuzu, C., Jones, N. and Pereznieto, P. (2010) *Gendered Risks, Poverty and Vulnerability in Ghana: To What Extent Is the LEAP Cash Transfer Programme Making a Difference?* London: Overseas Development Institute (ODI).

Ayivor, S. (2001) *Patterns of Land Tenure in Anloga, Ghana*. London: RICS Foundation.

Casely-Hayford, L. (2004) *Situational Analysis of Child Labour in the Cocoa Sector of Ghana*. (Final Report). Submitted to: The International Cocoa Initiative (ICI). Accra: Associates for Change.

Folitse, B.Y. et al (2017) 'The present status of shallot (*Allium ascalonicum* L.) farming enterprise in Ghana: the case of Keta Municipality', *Agricultural Communications*, 5, pp 8–16.

Ghana Statistical Service (2014a) *2010 Population and Housing Census. District Analytical Report. Keta Municipality*. Accra: Ghana Statistical Service.

Ghana Statistical Service (2014b) *Ghana Living Standards Survey Round 6 (GLSS 6): Child Labour Report*. Accra: Ghana Statistical Service (GSS).

Ghana Statistical Service (2015) *Ghana Poverty Mapping Report*. Accra: Ghana Statistical Service.

Goody, E. (1966) 'The fostering of children in Ghana: a preliminary report', *Ghana Journal of Sociology*, 2(1), pp 23–33.

Hill, P. (1963) *Migrant Cocoa Farmers of Southern Ghana: A Study in Rural Capitalism*. Cambridge: Cambridge University Press.

Hill, P. (1986) *Talking with Ewe Seine Fishermen and Shallot Farmers. Cambridge African Monographs 6*. Cambridge: African Studies Centre.

Kapoor, A. (2017) *Children at the Heart: Assessment of Child Labour and Child Slavery in Ghana's Cocoa Sector and Recommendations to Mondelēz International*. Hong Kong: Embode Ltd.

Ministry of Agriculture, Food and Fisheries (1994) *Agricultural Sector Investment Programme*. Accra: Ministry of Agriculture, Food and Fisheries.

Ministry of Food and Agriculture (2018) *Investing for Food and Jobs (IFJ): An Agenda For Transforming Ghana's Agriculture (2018–2021)*. Accra: Ministry of Food and Agriculture.

Ministry of Food and Agriculture, Republic of Ghana (2007) *Food and Agriculture Sector Development Policy (FASDEP II)*. Accra: Ministry of Food and Agriculture.

Nantui Mabe, F., Danso-Abbeam, G. and Ehiakpor, D. (2018) *Assessment of Implementation of Planting for Food and Jobs (PJF) Programme: Lessons and Ways Forward*. Tamali: Faculty of Agribusiness and Communication Sciences, University for Development Studies.

NEPAD (2003) *Comprehensive Africa Agriculture Development Programme*. Nidrand, South Africa: New Partnership for Africa's Development. Available at: http://www.fao.org/nr/water/aquastat/sirte2008/NEPAD-CAADP%202003.pdf.

Nukunya, G.K. (1975) 'The effects of cash crops on an Ewe Community', in Goody, J. (ed) *Changing Social Structure in Ghana*. London: International African Institute, pp 59–71.

Ocloo, C.Y. (1996) *The Anlo Shallot Revolution, 1930s–1992: A Study of the Local Agricultural History of Anloga in the Volta Region of Ghana*. Trondheim: Department of History, Norwegian University of Science and Technology.

Patten, S.E. (1990) *The Avuncular Family, Gender Asymmetry, and Patriline: The Anlo Ewe of Southeastern Ghana*. PhD thesis. Minneapolis/St Paul: University of Minnesota.

Patten, S.E. and Nukunya, G. K. (1982) 'Organizational responses to agricultural intensification in Anloga, Ghana', *African Studies Review*, 25(2–3), pp 67–77.

Porter, G., Young, E. and Dzietror, A. (1997) 'Pressures on an intensive irrigated cash-crop system in coastal Ghana', *Geoforum*, 28(3), pp 329–40.

Sabates-Wheeler, R. and Sumberg, J. (2022) 'Breaking out of the policy enclave approach to child labour in sub-Saharan African agriculture', *Global Social Policy*, 22(1), pp 46–66.

Sadhu, S. et al (2020) *Assessing Progress in Reducing Child Labor in Cocoa Production in Cocoa Growing Areas of Côte d'Ivoire and Ghana*. Chicago: NORC, University of Chicago.

Sinnadurai, S. (1973) 'Shallot farming in Ghana', *Economic Botany*, 27(4), pp 438–41.

Swamy, K.R.M., Gowda, R.V. and Peter, K.V. (2006) 'Leek and shallot', in *Handbook of Herbs and Spices. Volume 3*. Cambridge: Woodhead Publishing Limited, pp 365–89.

Tulane University (2015) *Final Report: 2013/14 Survey Research on Child Labor in West African Cocoa-Growing Areas*. New Orleans: School of Public Health and Tropical Medicine, Tulane University.

UCW (2016) *Child Labour and the Youth Decent Work Deficit in Ghana*. Rome: Understanding Children's Work Project.

Van Hear, N. (1982) 'Child labour and the development of capitalist agriculture in Ghana', *Development and Change*, 13(4), pp 499–514.

Wills, J.B. (1962) *Agriculture and Land Use in Ghana*. Oxford: Oxford University Press.

World Bank (2017) *Ghana: Agriculture Sector Policy Note: Transforming Agriculture for Economic Growth, Job Creation and Food Security*. Washington, DC: The World Bank.

Yeboah, T. and Sumberg, J. (2020) *Is Shallot Production in Anloga Still 'Unworkable' without the Paid Labour of School Children?* Unpublished paper.

10

Children's Work in West African Cocoa Production: Drivers, Contestations and Critical Reflections

Dorte Thorsen and Roy Maconachie

Introduction

In 2000–2001, widespread public concerns about children's work in cocoa production emerged in Europe and North America, following a series of high-profile media reports that referred to children in harmful work[1] in the supply chains of some of the world's largest and most well-known chocolate manufacturers (Blowfield, 2003; Ould et al, 2004). This reignited public debate about the prevalence of harm to children working in global commodity chains and spawned a wide range of initiatives to tackle exploitative labour practices in the West African cocoa sector. Influenced by the global push for children's rights, Ghana – the world's second largest cocoa producer – had already set out comprehensive regulations concerning the employment of children in the national Children's Act of 1998, part V, § 87–96 (Government of Ghana, 1998) before ratifying the International Labour Organization (ILO) Convention 182 on the worst forms of child labour[2] in June 2000 (Chapter 8, this volume). The ratification happened in tandem with the negotiation of the US-led Harkin–Engel Protocol, which brought together the cocoa industry, the ILO, trade unions and activists concerned about harmful work, with the governments of Ghana and Côte d'Ivoire in a voluntary agreement to end the worst forms of child labour in cocoa production. Subsequent to the signing of the protocol in September 2001, a series of national action plans directed specifically at the cocoa sector were developed. Although new legislation was passed in both countries, the conflict in Côte d'Ivoire hampered implementation in the first decade. Hence, the Ghanaian policy and implementation process offers compelling insights into the monitoring of potentially harmful aspects of children's work (Bertrand and de Buhr, 2015; ILO-IPEC, 2007c).

Over the past two decades, considerable debate has continued over the role that children play in the cocoa sector. Critics are largely divided between those who view all children's work as 'harmful' and unacceptable (the 'abolitionists'), and those who locate children's work on a wider canvas, and favour a more nuanced, regulatory approach based on a contextual understanding of and response to work in children's lives (see Chapter 2, this volume; Thorsen, 2012). With respect to the latter position, Berlan (2013) and Buono and Babo (2013) note that it is problematic to make judgements about the role that children play in African agriculture independent of the children's social, cultural and economic contexts. Cocoa production is embedded within local social institutions and family relations, and historical reports have documented how family labour, including that of children, played a significant role in the early development of the cocoa sector (Van Hear, 1982). A report commissioned by the Ghanaian government's National Programme for the Elimination of the Worst Forms of Child Labour in Cocoa noted:

> Traditionally, working on family farms and with family enterprises is seen as part of the process by which children are trained towards adulthood … Children's involvement in the production of cocoa is an age-old tradition which, besides the immediate labour value, constitutes a … way of imparting cocoa farming skills to them and equipping them to take over from aging parents and relatives. (NPECLC, 2007, pp 6–7)

Children's work in the cocoa sector is therefore not as easily constructed as morally bad or undesirable, as some critics would like to argue. The abstraction of labour practices from their wider historical context is common in debates on cocoa production (Berlan, 2013). Amanor (2019) further reminds us that it remains vital to examine the relationship between land tenure systems, labour markets and family relations in production, to gain a better understanding of the contemporary cocoa industry.

In this chapter we seek to provide a more dynamic assessment of children's work in the West African cocoa sector, a prerequisite for more tangible, empirically grounded, pro-poor child protection policies and interventions. Drawing predominantly upon scholarship on the Ghanaian cocoa sector, the chapter provides a synthesis of recent academic and policy debates in relation to children's work in cocoa production. In doing so, it flags up some key areas for inquiry relating to the drivers and dynamics of harmful children's work, with the intention of orienting future research.

The chapter proceeds as follows. Following this introduction, a brief historical overview of cocoa production in Ghana is presented, tracing the prevalence and importance of children's labour inputs from colonial times to the present. The next section then outlines in further detail the role that children traditionally played in cocoa farming, demonstrating how children's work is embedded in the fabric of Ghanaian society and economy, and supports the household economy at peak times in the agricultural calendar. Drawing predominantly on data from a recent study by the National Opinion Research Center at the University of Chicago (NORC), the chapter then discusses the various tasks that boys and girls of different ages perform on cocoa farms, making it apparent that the distinction between benign work and work that carries risk of harm is often blurred. The contentious relationship between schooling and children's work in cocoa communities is briefly discussed, followed by some reflection on how debates that concern children's work in the cocoa sector are shaped by policy and discourse. The chapter concludes with some reflections on future directions for research and advocates for a more holistic approach to harm, which places children at the centre of the analysis and seeks to incorporate both 'subjective' and 'objective' dimensions.

Ghanaian cocoa production and global incorporation

Trade and barter have long been part of West African economies and social relations. But, since the colonial era, farmers were incorporated into the production of commodities for export. In many respects, Europeans viewed Africa as a giant farm that could produce a host of crops including cotton, cocoa, rubber, sisal, groundnuts, tea, coffee, sugar and tobacco. In colonial Ghana (then known as the Gold Coast), this process started with the export of vast quantities of palm oil to Europe in the 19th century. However, by the latter part of the 19th century, the insatiable demand for palm oil led to the establishment of new industrial plantations in Southeast Asia, saturating the market and out-competing West African producers. Eventually, a fall in the international price of palm oil in 1885 compelled farmers in the Gold Coast to seek alternatives, with cocoa becoming the preferred crop for income generation (Kolavalli and Vigneri, 2011).[3] Commercial cocoa farming first began in the Gold Coast in the 1890s,[4] and by the 1920s, the Gold Coast was the dominant global cocoa producer, with over 50 per cent of all production (Green and Hymer, 1966).

Polly Hill's (1963) classic study of rural capitalism in Ghana provides important insights into the dynamics of labour that sustained cocoa production. Hill's detailed ethnographic work challenged orthodox thinking that cocoa was produced only by sedentary, small-scale, peasant farmers. Rather, it revealed that cocoa production in southern Ghana was dominated by entrepreneurial capitalist farmers who had initially accumulated wealth by investing in palm oil and rubber, before reinvesting in land and labour for cocoa production. Although labour for cocoa cultivation was in high demand in the early 1900s, this capitalist class of farmers was able to draw upon both migrant labour from northern Ghana and the surrounding Sahelian colonies, as well as family labour (Abdul-Korah, 2007).[5] Migrant labourers were either employed under an annual arrangement when establishing a new farm, in which case they were paid at the end of their contract, or, a sharecropping agreement when working on a mature farm. In both cases, plots for food production were usually provided to migrants so they could feed themselves throughout their stay.[6] Extended family relations increasingly became involved in production and were an important resource in the expansion of cocoa farms to new forest frontier areas. The significant expansion of cocoa production from 536 tons in 1900 to 176,000 tons in 1920 led to heavy demand for carriers, particularly for head loading cocoa, and the labour of children became central to meeting this requirement (Van Hear, 1982).

By the mid-1930s, cocoa production had reached 300,000 tons, resulting in a 'frontier economy' in which cocoa cultivation continued to expand into the forest regions under the enterprise of migrant farmers with capital (Amanor, 2019). Although labour migration was initially the domain of young, single, male adults seeking to accumulate savings, by 1935, increasing numbers of women and children began to accompany them (Van Hear, 1982). Migrants were often drawn towards frontier areas where farmers had more capital to spend on labour and where weeding was less demanding than on mature farms (Amanor, 2019). As explained by Van Hear:

> Children worked on cocoa farms as members of sharecroppers' families and were thus not directly employed by farm-owners, who nevertheless benefitted from their labour. Children also cultivated sharecroppers' food farms, thus freeing them for cocoa work, and helped to headload harvested cocoa to the marketing points. (1982, p 501)

By the 1940s, the demand for labour on cocoa farms increased dramatically once again, as the economy emerged from the impact of the Great Depression of the 1930s. This often resulted in the direct recruitment of both children and youth to work on cocoa farms. In 1947, the Cocoa Marketing Board (today widely referred to as COCOBOD) was established, which gave the colonial government a monopoly over the purchase of cocoa beans. After independence, cocoa exports continued to climb, and overall production reached an annual level of 430,000 tons, even in the face of a significant decline in global prices between 1960 and 1962 and an outright collapse in 1964 following a record high harvest in West Africa (Kolavalli and Vigneri,

2011, p 203). The effect of global prices on cocoa farmers was exacerbated by the cedi being overvalued and the fixing of low farmgate prices by COCOBOD. However, due to a time lag of three to five years from planting new trees until they bore beans and a duration of production of over 30 years, farmers could not respond quickly to changing prices (Bulíř, 2002).

During the 1970s and early 1980s, dismal farm gate prices for cocoa compared to global prices and to local prices for maize and rice, as well as the exhaustion of new frontier lands in Ghana, triggered a significant decline in cocoa production. From having supplied over 35 per cent of global cocoa production in the early 1960s, Ghana supplied less than 10 per cent by the early 1980s (Bulíř, 2002, p 414). World Bank Structural Adjustment Programmes were adopted to revive the sector and Ghana's adjustment package included a partial reform of the internal cocoa market, but it had dramatic impacts on the lives of poor farmers, through increases in the cost of living and farming inputs. The liberalization process included granting private companies licenses to trade cocoa.

During the 1990s, COCOBOD was restructured, there was a sharp and sustained increase in farm gate cocoa prices, and production continued to increase. Production peaked in the early 2000s, with output almost doubling between 2002 and 2004 (Lowe, 2017). Initially, this expansion was driven through access to new land, predominantly in forest areas, but now relies increasingly on the adoption of inputs such as insecticides and fungicides (Kolavalli and Vigneri, 2011). Although not as central to the economy as it once was, Ghana still has a vibrant cocoa sector. Recent estimates suggest that cocoa constitutes about three per cent of Ghana's GDP and 20–25 per cent of total export receipts (Abbadi et al, 2019). However, to this day, family members, including children continue to play an important role in the sector (Baah, 2010).

Children's work in cocoa

Efforts to monitor children's work in cocoa production across West Africa commenced with the West Africa Cocoa and Commercial Agriculture Project (WACAP), which was launched in 2002 by the ILOs' International Programme on the Elimination of Child Labour (IPEC) (ILO-IPEC, 2007a). Implemented in Cameroon, Côte d'Ivoire, Ghana, Guinea and Nigeria, WACAP included fact-finding and awareness-raising about what work was acceptable for children of different ages (ILO-IPEC, 2007b). Under the project the Ghana Ministry of Manpower, Youth and Employment carried out comprehensive surveys (Ministry of Manpower, Youth and Employment, 2008) and explored which activities were potentially harmful (Amoo, 2008). Since this pioneering work, the US Department of Labor (USDoL) financed three large studies of children's participation in cocoa production in Ghana and Côte d'Ivoire in 2008–09, 2013–14 and 2018–19 as part of the implementation of the Harkin–Engel Protocol. In this section, we use the latest analysis (Sadhu et al, 2020), with a particular focus on labour requirements, harm and education.

In what follows, it is critical to bear in mind that the distinction between benign work and work that carries some risk of harm is often blurred, both conceptually and operationally (see Chapter 2, this volume, and Maconachie et al, 2021). As a result, it is exceptionally difficult to estimate and compare children's work across surveys and qualitative studies, particularly if the social characteristics of labour are not deconstructed to consider age-appropriate work as laid out in international or national labour standards, or as understood in rural communities. Studies use either ILO or Ghanaian national standards to distinguish between work that is 'permitted' from work that is not (Table 10.1). The Ghanaian labour standards set out daily limits for permitted work that are closely aligned with the national education strategy and distinguish between school days and non-school days. These standards also apply to children over 15 years, the minimum age for admission to employment or work (cf ILO C138, ratified June 2011).

Both sets of standards stipulate that no individual under the age of 18 should carry out work defined as hazardous (Amoo, 2008, 2016; Sadhu et al, 2020), yet they delineate hazardous work differently (Table 10.2). The ILO labels any work exceeding the permitted working hours as hazardous, as well as any involvement in specific activities including land clearing, the carrying of heavy loads, exposure to agrochemicals, the use of sharp tools and night work. In contrast, the national standards consider it unfavourable for children to work more hours than permitted, but these longer hours are only considered as hazardous if they impede schooling. They also emphasize

Table 10.1: Labour standards for permitted work for different age groups

Permitted work	ILO standard	Ghanaian national standard
No work	5–11-year-olds	5–12-year-olds
Light work <14 hrs/week	12–14-year-olds	13–14-year-olds – limited to less than two hours on school days and less than three hours on non-school days
Medium work <18 hrs/week	N/A	15–17-year-olds enrolled in school – limited to less than three hours per day on school days
Full-time work <43 hrs/week	15–17-year-olds	15–17-year-olds who are not enrolled in school

Source: Adapted from Amoo (2016) and Sadhu et al (2020)

Table 10.2: Activities defined as hazardous for children aged 5–17 years

ILO standard	Ghanaian national standard
Working more hours than permitted	Working full time and not attending school
Land clearing	Land clearing
Carrying heavy loads	Carrying heavy loads
Exposure to agrochemicals	Exposure to agrochemicals
Using sharp tools	Using sharp tools
Night work	Night work
	Climbing trees
	Working without protective clothing
	Working during cocoa harvest season that necessitates withdrawal from school
	Working in isolation

Source: Adapted from Amoo (2016) and Sadhu et al (2020)

Table 10.3: Average labour requirements on cocoa farms

Task	Person days per year
Clearing & weeding	36–84
Applying pesticides	36
Harvesting	39
Breaking cocoa pods	13
Field transport	15
Fermentation	Mix every 48 hours
Drying	15

Source: Abenyega and Gockowski (2003)

some social conditions of work and deem as hazardous any work done outside the normal social context (such as working in isolation).

The major demand for labour in cocoa production occurs during the harvest season, from October to December. Cocoa pods are harvested, then carried to points where they are broken open and the wet beans removed and allowed to ferment for four to seven days. The beans are then transported to the homestead and sundried for 5 to 14 days (Table 10.3). The other labour demanding tasks in the production cycle involve clearing and weeding in May/June and just before the main harvest in September/October, and pesticide application (in principle, fungicides are applied two to three times annually and insecticides three to four times).

Tasks

In 2018–19, 83 per cent of the children aged between 5 and 17 years in sampled agricultural households in cocoa-growing regions in Ghana had been economically active in the previous twelve months: 73 per cent had participated in agricultural work, and 60 per cent in cocoa production (Sadhu et al, 2020, pp 55–62).

In ethnographies of children's work in cocoa in Ghana and Côte d'Ivoire, Buono observes that very young children can be found alongside parents on both new and mature farms, regardless of whether the farms are in the hands of farm owners or sharecroppers. Schoolchildren will also work, especially, but not only, during peak harvesting periods when neighbours and relatives might work together. For the younger ones, their 'work' involves caring for younger siblings, play and gradually learning farming skills. Children under 10 years are rarely allowed to use cutlasses, as they are considered at risk of harming themselves or the trees. Older children, including those attending school, are expected to do more work, combining farm work with other work, and not always working under close adult supervision (Buono, 2010; Buono and Babo, 2013).

Access to labour is gendered and while men can rely on the labour of a wife or wives, female farmers depend on their children, relatives, and hired workers (Asare, 1995; Barrientos, 2014). In the Ghanaian cocoa belt, one-fourth of the farming households were headed by women in 2018–19 (Sadhu et al, 2020, p 40), and this can be an important determinant of children's work on cocoa farms (Berlan, 2013).

The activities that children working in cocoa most frequently undertook over a 12-month period in 2018–19 were gathering and heaping pods (53 per cent of children), maintenance activities such as weeding (28 per cent), breaking the pods and preparing the seeds for fermenting (27 per cent), carting fermented cocoa beans (25 per cent) and drying them (24 per cent), carrying water for applying agrochemicals (24 per cent) and harvest activities including plucking pods (16 per cent) (Sadhu et al, 2020, pp 181–2).

While boys and girls participate in many of the same activities, a survey undertaken in 2007–08 revealed that boys participated significantly more than girls in pesticides application, mistletoe control (mistletoe is a parasitic weed), and tree felling and burning, all of which had a male/female participation ratio over five (Ministry of Manpower, Youth and Employment, 2008). Age also shapes the work done by children, with the youngest children, aged 5–12 years, mainly engaging in weeding, and gathering and carrying cocoa pods over short distances. It was also reported that they are involved in carrying water for spraying, and turning the beans during drying. Children in the 15–17-year-old cohort harvest and break pods, and cut mistletoe. The surveyed

Table 10.4: Percentage of children involved in different types of work in the past 12 months (all agricultural households)

Type of work	2008–09	2018–19	Significance
All work	78	83	
Work in agriculture	73	73	
Work in cocoa	46	60	***

Significance: *** = probability p<0.01

Source: Adapted from Sadhu et al (2020, pp 56–86)

communities agreed that these activities were all within the capabilities of children (Ministry of Manpower, Youth and Employment, 2008).

Sadhu et al (2020) provide an analysis of the changing nature of children's work in cocoa farming households. Table 10.4 shows three important shifts over the ten-year period between 2008–09 and 2018–19. First, there was a small but statistically insignificant increase in the proportion of children who were economically active. Second, the proportion of children engaged in agricultural work did not change. Third, within agriculture, children's work apparently moved from other crops towards cocoa, which Sadhu et al (2020, p 50) link to the 36 per cent increase in cocoa production over the same period. This highlights the need to understand children's work in cocoa in the context of their broader economic activities.

Child labour

In the 2018–19 survey, children were considered to be in child labour either because they worked in cocoa more than the number of hours permitted by the ILO standards or because they undertook hazardous activities (hazardous child labour) (Sadhu et al, 2020). Table 10.5 shows that the majority of children worked fewer hours in cocoa than what is permitted for their age cohort, and that the proportion of children who worked more than the permitted hours was highest for the youngest cohort (who, according to both the ILO and Ghanaian labour standards, are too young to work at all). While by this criterion around a third of children under 11 are classed as in child labour, a much smaller proportion of children older than 11 work more than the permitted number of hours.

Engagement in hazardous activity is shown in Table 10.6. Children over 11 are nearly twice as likely to undertake these activities, and boys are more likely than girls. Carrying heavy loads, exposure to agrochemicals and using sharp tools are the hazardous activities most frequently undertaken by children.

Table 10.5: Working hours in cocoa production by age and gender, 2018–19 (cocoa growing households)

	Average hours worked per week		**% exceeding permitted hours**	
Age group (permitted work hours)	**Boys**	**Girls**	**Boys**	**Girls**
5–11 years **(<1 hour per week)**	5.1	5.2	34	32
12–14 year **(<14 hours per week)**	7.0	6.0	11	7
15–17 years **(<43 hours per week)**	10.4	7.3	2	1

Source: Adapted from Sadhu et al (2020, p 179)

Table 10.6: Percentage of children in cocoa-growing households exposed to hazardous activities in cocoa, 2018–19

	Gender		**Age (years)**		
Activity	**Boys**	**Girls**	**5–11**	**12–14**	**15–17**
Land clearing	19	8	6	22	31
Carrying heavy loads	34	30	22	45	50
Exposure to agrochemicals	36	27	20	45	57
Using sharp tools	50	35	27	64	72
Long working hours	1	0	0	0	2
Night work	4	2	1	5	6
Exposed to one or more hazardous tasks	57	45	37	71	77

Source: Adapted from Sadhu et al (2020, pp 185–6)

In combining the hours of work and hazardous activities criteria, Sadhu et al (2020, p 179) concluded that 83 per cent of children surveyed had worked in the past 12 months, 55 per cent were in child labour in cocoa production, and the vast majority of these were in hazardous labour. These data suggest that the majority of those who worked were in child labour, and the vast majority of those in child labour were also in hazardous child labour. The latter outcome is a logical consequence of the way hazardous work has been defined – indeed, few activities can be carried out on a cocoa farm without a sharp tool, carrying loads or exposure to agrochemicals. In effect, all work is, at least by definition, hazardous work.

Work and school

The theme of education, and in particular schooling, has been prominent in debates about child labour, both because schooling is one of the pillars in the universalized notion of childhood and because the need, or lure, of work is perceived to hinder educational achievement (Boyden, 1997; Bass, 2004; Chapter 4, this volume).

School enrolment in cocoa-growing areas in Ghana is generally high. A study carried out in 2007 revealed that household heads had been to school for an average of eight years (Abenyega and Gockowski, 2003, p 7). Further, 88, 95.5 and 83.9 per cent of children aged 5–12, 13–14 and 15–17, respectively, were enrolled in school. The 2018–19 survey found that 96 per cent of children in cocoa producing households had attended school within the previous twelve months (increased from 91 per cent in 2008–09) (Sadhu et al, 2020, pp 93–98). Significantly, there was no discernible difference in school attendance between working children, children considered to be in child labour or children in hazardous child labour in any of the three age cohorts.

However, these educational data are seriously flawed. They indicate whether a child ever attended school over the 12-month recall period but say nothing about the frequency of school attendance. It is thus impossible to examine whether children's work (or child labour) impacts on learning and performance at school or whether there are differences between households producing cocoa and those that do not.

It is also the case that many children in cocoa areas also work as part of their schooling (Ministry of Manpower, Youth and Employment, 2008; also see Chapter 4, this volume). In the 2006–07 farming season, 13.3 per cent of the surveyed school children worked for teachers and 11.5 per cent for a school contract farm (Ministry of Manpower, Youth and Employment, 2008, p 11). Berlan's (2009) 15-month study in the Ashanti Region further documents how children were required to do farm work for their teachers at least once a week, typically being allocated the task of clearing or weeding school plots with machetes with limited supervision. Children noted that this was heavier work than what they did on their family farms: work carried out on family cocoa farms was reported to be both safer and less strenuous.

The reality is more complex

The picture of children's work on Ghana's cocoa farms that emerges from the large-scale surveys conducted following the Harkin–Engel protocol, including Sadhu et al (2020), is problematic for several reasons.

First, and perhaps most importantly, the indicators of child labour and hazardous work are flawed (see Chapter 7, this volume, for a discussion of problems with flawed indicators). For example, a child needs to report using a sharp tool, or carrying a heavy load only once in a year, for even the shortest time period, to be considered in hazardous child labour. The use of sharp tools is the most frequently reported hazardous activity undertaken by children and includes using machetes for weeding, harvesting with a machete or sickle, plucking pods with a harvesting hook, breaking cocoa pods with a knife or other sharp object, handling motorized equipment or machines, and using knapsack sprayers and chainsaws (Sadhu et al, 2020, p 34). However, children in rural households are socialized into a variety of tasks, both on the farm and in the domestic sphere, that require the use of machetes, sickles and knives. Both boys and girls therefore become skilled in using sharp tools from a relatively young age and are proud of their work and skills (Berlan, 2009). In relation to heavy loads, neither the frequency nor the distance travelled are part of the criterion of hazardous work. Again, there is a tension between the criterion and rural children's broader experience – carrying is an integral part of domestic work throughout rural Ghana, and girls frequently carry water, crops and firewood over long distances. There are strong norms concerning gender and age-appropriate work; adults call on their children to do specific tasks, and children do them to demonstrate their maturity and inclination to work.

Second, the surveys, by accepting the ILO or national definitions, conflate the notions hazardous work and harmful work. It should go without saying that while all work carries some risk of harm, not all work actually results in harm. Similarly, not all hazardous work actually results in harm. As noted previously, children are trained to use a machete safely or gradually to carry loads and do other tasks on the cocoa farm (that is, do 'hazardous' work). Different surveys have shown that children experience physical injuries such as machete wounds,[7] tree stump injuries, slips and falls, thorn pricks, snake bites, leg/neck pains, small objects entering the eyes, skin rashes and itchy backs. However, they do not judge these afflictions to have long-term effects on their health or wellbeing (Ministry of Manpower, Youth and Employment, 2008; Sadhu et al, 2020). Sadhu et al (2020, p 80) suggest that there was not much difference in the physical injuries experienced by children working in cocoa production compared with other crops. Hazardous work related to pesticides has become more prevalent in the past decade because their use has increased over this period (Sadhu et al, 2020, pp 33–4). But children are not exposed uniformly. Girls and the youngest cohort of children predominantly carry water to the cocoa farm and/or are present in the vicinity of the farm during or shortly after spraying. Boys aged 12 years and above help preparing and cleaning the spraying equipment, while adults and children over 15 years of age do the spraying (Ministry of Manpower, Youth and Employment, 2008). Data enumerating days of hazardous work without unpacking the type and length of exposure are insufficient to assess the potential harm to children.

Third, in the determination of which children are in child labour, no account is taken of the conditions of work. For example, available research does not generally indicate whether children primarily work with one or both parents; whether they help out a relative or someone else; or whether they do casual work in their community or elsewhere for a wage. Yet, understanding the specific conditions and social relations that surround the work being undertaken is important. Indeed, research in other contexts has shown that whether or not work is experienced as hazardous or harmful may be more closely connected to the social context in which it takes place and to the relationships involved, than to the nature of the work itself (Bourdillon et al, 2010). The vast majority of children who work in cocoa in Ghana live with one or both parents and work on the family's farm(s). While their ability to exercise agency and make meaningful choices in their lives will be constrained by structural poverty and household dynamics (Bøås and Huser, 2006; Chapter 7 in Bourdillon et al, 2010; Berlan, 2013), it can be expected that their conditions of work will be different from children who have migrated to work outside their network of kin. Migrant children are the ones who are frequently reported as victims of trafficking (for example, Ould et al, 2004), but it is worth noting that the vast majority are working with or for relatives from earlier cohorts of migrants (Buono, 2011; Thorsen, 2012).

Fourth, the surveys fail to put children's work in the cocoa sector within the context of their broader engagement in work, both domestic and paid (as discussed in Chapter 4, this volume). For example, given the study's origin in the Harkin–Engel Protocol, Sadhu et al (2020) are concerned with child labour 'in cocoa'. Thus, their calculations of whether the hours worked are above the hours permitted, indicating child labour, relate only to cocoa. No account is taken of the hours that particularly girl children work at home or that boys and girls work on other crops or livestock. So, even if one accepts the definitions and indicators, the resulting picture of the prevalence of children's labour is partial at best, and potentially grossly misleading.

Drivers of children's work

In many cocoa farming communities in Ghana, the predominant view among adults is that children work to learn the essential skills of farming but also because their labour is appreciated and needed. Yeboah (2019) argues that from parents' perspectives work in the household context imparts moral, cultural and social values to the younger generation. Children also learn practical skills, often through interactions with their siblings and peers. Systemic failure of schools in rural areas to provide quality teaching may also impact on how adults and children trade-off between work and school (Yeboah, 2019; Chapter 4, this volume).

Contributing to the wellbeing of the household and the broader family is ingrained in the habitus of rural childhoods. Farm and domestic work are seen as everyday activities carried out when not in school, and sometimes at the expense of revising at home and/or attending school.

From an institutional perspective, where the focus shifts from children's work to child labour, there is often a general assumption that poverty is the main driver of child labour. For example, according to the World Cocoa Foundation:

> We now know that child labour is both a symptom and a self-perpetuating cause of poverty. Households in cocoa growing areas face the realities of rural poverty, and some parents have little choice but to put their children to work, and keep them out of school, to reduce labour costs on family farms. This often, in turn, deprives children of the chance to develop and advance themselves, and so entrenches the household's impoverishment for subsequent generations. (McCoy, 2018)

Poverty is clearly an important factor shaping how much children work, and in many cases, rural children are faced with limited opportunities to contribute to their school fees or to save up for desired commodities or travel (Bourdillon et al, 2010; Hashim, 2007). In situations of desperate poverty, extra demands may be put on them to help, either on cocoa or food farms. The liberalization of the cocoa sector over recent decades, and moves toward more intensive production systems, have exacerbated poverty for many small cocoa farmers. Luckstead et al (2019) argue that the number of children doing hazardous work in cocoa production in West Africa has increased in recent years due to the introduction of high yield, disease-resistant varieties of cocoa that demand more labour to harvest and process. Likewise, Owusu and Kwarteye (2008) argue, the 'invisible labour' of children has become even more important, as cocoa farmers are forced to reduce labour costs.[8]

Studies of children's work in cocoa production, however, often straddle two different positions in the relationship between work and poverty. One, upheld by those in favour of banning child labour, argues that the inability of poor cocoa producers to pay adult wages results in a farm labour deficit, which is filled by the employment of children. The second, argues from a child- and family-centred perspective, that farmers who lack money to hire workers need to balance their desire to increase production with their desire for children attaining school education (Thorsen, 2012). This balancing act reflects the perceived quality of schooling and children's academic performance.

Discourses and policy

The Harkin–Engel Protocol is emblematic of interventions to abolish child labour in cocoa production. Initiated in 2001 and with a new private–public partnership pledged in 2011, the protocol has encouraged the kind of child protection work started by the ILO's International Programme on the Elimination of Child Labour (IPEC). International policies in the late 1990s and early 2000s were based on the assumption that children working in cocoa were either family labour and not really in need of protection or migrant labour – trafficked, exploited and exposed to hazardous work (Dottridge, 2002; ILO-IPEC, 2007c). This perspective on children's work was informed by studies and media reports capturing the negative experiences of child and youth migrants in Côte d'Ivoire (Ould et al, 2004; Sackett, 2008), sometimes without due attention to country-specific data.[9] Moreover, it did not take into consideration the many children who migrated to work on cocoa farms without being deceived by recruiters or exploited by farm owners (Dottridge, 2011).

Research with Ghanaian cocoa producers did not find substantial evidence of child labour migrants, hence early policy discourses focused primarily on hazardous work and the work–school nexus (Mull and Kirkhorn, 2005; Ministry of Manpower, Youth and Employment, 2008) which was already stipulated in the Children's Act of 1998. The Harkin–Engel Protocol instigated a cocoa certification process in 2001, coordinated by the Cocoa Verification Board (CVB), which aimed to stamp out the worst forms of child labour. However, the CVB failed because it could not unite the various stakeholders. Simultaneously, certification programmes led by Fairtrade, Rainforest Alliance and others proliferated and invested in training and sensitization programmes for producers (Clark and Gow, 2011).

Interventions involved both 'upstream' and 'downstream' actions to create awareness of the kinds of work considered hazardous. Upstream actions targeted government at both district and central levels to encourage a change in attitude toward the enforcement of regulations. Moreover, early upstream actions built institutional capacity to prepare the ground for child labour monitoring systems as part of the certification of cocoa (Baah, 2010; also see Chapter 6, this volume). This process prompted rigorous fact-finding and mapping of the use of child labour in cocoa production (Tulane University, 2015; Sadhu et al, 2020).

Downstream actions were mainly aimed at creating awareness about child labour and hazardous work among cocoa producers, trade unions and non-governmental organizations (NGOs). WACAP established community child labour committees, whose members received training and were actively involved in sensitization activities (ILO-IPEC, 2007c). Although the approach was framed in terms of stakeholder consultation, due to time constraints the process was one of sensitizing the stakeholders about universalized notions of what was right and wrong for children (Thorsen, 2012). At the same time, ICI worked to raise awareness among radio and television broadcasters, which in turn stimulated call-in discussions on air (ILO-IPEC, 2007b).

The mobilization of villagers to monitor children's work and disseminate information was perceived by programme leaders as a sign of changing attitudes among cocoa producers. A labour survey in 2007/08 suggested that sensitization programmes had revealed that 76 per cent of the people sampled in six cocoa producing regions of Ghana were aware of the prohibition of the worst forms of child labour. Awareness was generally higher in relation to the application of pesticides and the dangers of transporting heavy loads (Ministry of Manpower, Youth and Employment, 2008). In 2011, the establishment of village child protection committees was driven by NGOs funded by international cocoa buyers, but an in-depth study of the implementation reveals cracks in the effectiveness of such programmes. The cracks develop around fundamentally different perceptions of childhood. While NGO field officers depicted children's work in cocoa farms as detrimental to schooling and as illegal in accordance with a globalized notion of childhood and the standards outlined in the CRC, parents upheld the importance of training children in the norms and customs of their culture, including practical and social skills that would earn them success in their community. Thus, parents emphasized the social integration of children over the individualized rights advocated in the CRC (Yeboah, 2019, pp 190–4). This disconnect between different notions of childhood rendered the committees ineffective and points to the need for in-depth research with parents and village leaders to understand their concerns and viewpoints (also see Chapter 8, this volume). What is particularly concerning in interventions like the one analysed by Yeboah (2019), is that the distinction between benign work and work that carries some risk of harm is erased. Instead of narrowly targeting occupational health issues and how they differ for children and adults, interventions turn into a critique of rural parenting. Given the plethora of reports of monitoring programmes run by Fairtrade and Rainforest Alliance, a detailed analysis of their evaluations should also be undertaken (see Chapter 3, this volume).

The emphasis on the work-education nexus often results in programmes focusing on education or technical training to draw children away from hazardous work, and success is measured in the number of children removed from such work (Ministry of Manpower, Youth and Employment, 2007; Tulane University, 2010). However, an important lesson learned from early WACAP interventions was the need to carefully assess available educational resources at the outset. Lack of access to formal education in rural areas, due to inadequate infrastructure, absence of teachers or the inability of parents to pay formal and informal fees, implies that education does not always constitute an alternative to agricultural work (Thorsen, 2012; also see Chapter 4, this volume).

Sadhu et al (2020) show that improved accessibility and affordability of schools facilitated the enrolment of children and reduced the time they work in cocoa production, whereas assistance with the provision of school materials and uniforms had no significant effect on children's exposure to child labour or hazardous work. Local vocational training programmes for children who were no longer in school were mostly pursued by girls, because they provide a foundation for economic activities outside farming. The most effective means to address exposure to hazardous work appeared to be occupational safety and health training, which children and youth appreciated. It was most effective when parents were also trained (Sadhu et al, 2020, p 9).

Conclusion

Over the past two decades, with the rise of traceability and ethical sourcing agendas, considerable debate has emerged over what role, if any, children should be allowed in cocoa supply chains. At the heart of this debate has been the issue of how hazardous and harmful work are defined and understood, and by whom. A clear-cut division exists between those who view all children's work as harmful and unacceptable, and those who favour a more nuanced and textured understanding of work in children's lives. However, in cocoa production, and agriculture in Africa more broadly, the distinction between the two is difficult to discern, as the hazards, risks and benefits of work are often intertwined. Children and their families find themselves weighing up both costs and benefits, making trade-offs, and situating this assessment within the realistic alternatives that exist.

This chapter highlights the fact that while numerous research projects and large-scale surveys have been undertaken over the last three decades, our understanding of children's work in cocoa production remains sketchy at best. Little progress has been made in illuminating the forms, prevalence, effects and drivers of children's work, to say nothing of the trade-offs that children and their families navigate between work and school, hazard and harm. Different standards and criteria are used to assess child labour and hazardous work, making comparison difficult. In some cases, studies have lacked sensitivity to both age and gender. But perhaps more serious is that many 'objective' criteria, and resulting data, lack any understanding of the context in which children contribute to cocoa production.

What is clear is that children's work in cocoa is widespread, and the need now is to understand it in the cultural context of rural Ghana, where contributing to family labour is a fundamental part of childhood. Work in cocoa also provides a means by which children can gradually become economically active (Baah, 2010; Hashim and Thorsen, 2011; Berlan, 2013).

The consideration of labour practices and judgements about the role that children play in cocoa production, in isolation from their wider social, cultural and economic contexts, is highly problematic. While poverty may be a driver of children's work, in cocoa communities there are numerous other reasons why children work – and choose to work – on farms. This may be to attend school, gain practical skills or build social capital. In many cases, it is also clear that children understand and experience the work they do as part of a process of maturation that allows them to gain self-esteem and social responsibility before entering adulthood.

An understanding of the specific conditions or social relations that surround children's work in cocoa is crucial. Ultimately, whether or not children's work on cocoa farms is experienced as hazardous or harmful may be more closely connected to its social context and the relationships in which it takes place, than to the work itself.

Notes

1 According to standards set out by the ILO, all work is considered harmful for children under the age of 12 years; work in excess of 13 hours per week or work considered hazardous is seen as harmful for children aged 12–14 years; and work in excess of 42 hours per week or engaging in hazardous activities is considered harmful for children aged 15–17 years (Sadhu et al, 2020).

2 The ILO Convention No. 182 *Concerning the Prohibition and Immediate Action for the Elimination of the Worst Forms of Child Labour* targets all forms of slavery or practices similar to slavery; the use, procuring or offering of a child for prostitution and pornography; the use, procuring or offering of a child for illicit activities; and work that by its nature or the circumstances in which it is carried out is likely to cause harm to the child's health, safety or moral (article 3).

3 Some reports suggest that between 1894 and 1908 a Ghanaian farmer could earn as much as ten times more income from cocoa than palm oil (Acquaah, 1999).

4 In the early 19th century, the main source of cocoa for British manufacturers was the islands of Sao Tomé and Principe, where it was grown on European plantations using various forms of unfree labour. Public pressure on Britain's leading chocolate manufacturer, Cadbury, forced the company to look for alternative sources of cocoa, with the Gold Coast becoming the preferred country for production (Amanor, 2019).

5 During this period, there was an influx of migrants from Upper Volta (now Burkina Faso), Niger, and Mali, who were attracted by the relatively high wages that cocoa production offered in southern Ghana.

6 Most migrants lacked sufficient capital to purchase land, so they sharecropped with earlier settlers under a system called *abusa*, in which labourers were paid one third of the sales price of the cocoa they harvested (Kolavalli and Vigneri, 2011).

7 A survey in Côte d'Ivoire documented that the proportion of children sustaining machete (cutlass) injuries grew with age: 9 per cent of children aged 6–12 years, 15 per cent aged 13–14 yeas, and 23 per cent aged 15–17-years reported injuring themselves using machetes (Hatløy and Aiello, 2008).

8 Early work by Polly Hill (1963) underscores this same point, arguing that entrepreneurial cocoa farmers were very hesitant to spend their capital on labour, preferring instead to invest it in land. There was therefore a preference for using family labour provided by their wives and children.

9 IITA (2002) points to different histories of labour mobility between the four main cocoa producers in West and Central Africa.

References

Abbadi, S. et al (2019) *Assessing the Employment Effects of Processing Cocoa in Ghana*. Geneva: International Labour Organization.

Abdul-Korah, G.B. (2007) '"Where is not home?": Dagaaba migrants in the Brong Ahafo Region, 1980 to the present', *African Affairs*, 106(422), pp 71–94.

Abenyega, O. and Gockowski, J. (2003) *Labor Practices in the Cocoa Sector of Ghana with a Special Focus on the Role of Children*. Kumasi: KNUST and IITA.

Acquaah, B. (1999) *Cocoa Development in West Africa: The Early Period with Particular Reference to Ghana*. Accra: Ghana Universities Press.

Amanor, K. (2019) *Cocoa Commercialisation in Ghana: History and Social Values. Future Agricultures*. Brighton: Future Agricultures Consortium.

Amoo, P. (2008) *Hazardous Child Labour Activity Framework for the Cocoa Sector in Ghana*. Accra: Child Labour Unit, Labour Department, Ministry of Employment and Social Welfare.

Amoo, P. (2016) *Hazardous Child Labour Activity Framework for Ghana (HAF)*. Accra: Child Labour Unit, Labour Department, Ministry of Employment and Social Welfare.

Asare, B. (1995) 'Women in commercial agriculture: the cocoa economy of southern Ghana', in *Women and Sustainable Development in Africa*. Westport, CT and London: Praeger, pp 101–112. Available at: https://books.google.co.uk/books?id=HK7Z6Wm3XDIC.

Baah, F. (2010) 'Use of children and the issue of child labour in Ghanaian cocoa farm activities', *Journal of Agricultural Extension and Rural Development*, 2(9), pp 198–204.

Barrientos, S. (2014) 'Gendered global production networks: analysis of cocoa–chocolate sourcing', *Regional Studies*, 48(5), pp 791–803.

Bass, L.E. (2004) *Child Labor in sub-Saharan Africa*. Boulder: Lynne Rienner Publishers.

Berlan, A. (2009) 'Child labour and cocoa: whose voices prevail?', *International Journal of Sociology and Social Policy*, 29(3/4), pp 141–51.

Berlan, A. (2013) 'Social sustainability in agriculture: an anthropological perspective on child labour in cocoa production in Ghana', *The Journal of Development Studies*, 49(8), pp 1088–100.

Bertrand, W. and de Buhr, E. (2015) 'Trade, development and child labor: regulation and law in the case of child labor in the cocoa industry', *Law and Development Review*, 8(2), pp 503–21.

Blowfield, M. (2003) 'Ethical supply chains in the cocoa, coffee and tea industries', *Greener Management International*, (43), pp 15–24.

Bøås, M. and Huser, A. (2006) *Child Labour and Cocoa Production in West Africa: The Case of Cote d'Ivoire and Ghana*. Fafo Report 522. Oslo: Fafo Institute for Applied International Studies.

Bourdillon, M. et al (2010) *Rights and Wrongs of Children's Work*. New Brunswick, New Jersey and London: Rutgers University Press.

Boyden, J. (1997) 'Childhood and the policy makers: a comparative perspective on the globalization of childhood', in James, A. and Prout, A. (eds) *Constructing and Reconstructing Childhood: Contemporary Issues in the Sociological Study of Childhood*. London: Falmer Press, pp 190–229.

Bulíř, A. (2002) 'Can price incentive to smuggle explain the contraction of the cocoa supply in Ghana?', *Journal of African Economies*, 11(3), pp 413–39.

Buono, C. (2010) *Vie quotidienne, normes sociales et travail des enfants dans les communautés productrices de cacao*. Geneva: International Cocoa Initiative. Available at: https://cocoainitiative.org/fr/knowledge-centre-post/vie-quotidienne-normes-sociales-et-travail-des-enfants-dans-les-communautes-productrices-de-cacao/ (Accessed 16 April 2020).

Buono, C. (2011) *Daily Life, Social Norms and Child Labour in the Cocoa-Producing Communities in Ghana*. Geneva: International Cocoa Initiative. Available at: https://cocoainitiative.org/knowledge-centre-post/daily-life-social-norms-and-child-labour-in-the-cocoa-producing-communities-in-ghana/ (Accessed 16 April 2020).

Buono, C. and Babo, A. (2013) 'Travail des enfants dans les exploitations de cacao en Côte d'Ivoire. Pour une réconciliation entre normes locales et normes internationales autour du "bic", du balai et de la machette', *Mondes en Développement*, 41(163), pp 69–84.

Clark, A. and Gow, H. (2011) *Public and Private Institutional Responses to Advocacy Attacks: The Case of the Global Cocoa Industry and Child Labour Abuse*. Paper presented at 2011 AAEA & NAREA Joint Annual Meeting, 24–26 July 2011, Pittsburgh and Philadelphia.

Dottridge, M. (2002) 'Trafficking in children in West and Central Africa', *Gender & Development*, 10(1), pp 38–42.

Dottridge, M. (2011) *Exploring Methods to Protect Children on the Move: A Handbook for Organisations Wanting to Prevent Child Trafficking, Exploitation and the Worst Forms of Child Labour*. Lausanne: Terre des Hommes International Federation.

Government of Ghana (1998) *The Children's Act*. Accra: Government of Ghana.

Green, R.H. and Hymer, S.H. (1966) 'Cocoa in the Gold Coast: a study in the relations between African farmers and agricultural experts', *The Journal of Economic History*, 26(3), pp 299–319.

Hashim, I.M. (2007) 'Independent child migration and education in Ghana', *Development and Change*, 38(5), pp 911–31.

Hashim, I. and Thorsen, D. (2011) *Child Migrants in Africa*. London: Zed Books.

Hatløy, A. and Aiello, H. (2008) *Vérification des Activités de certification dans le Secteur Cacaoyer d'Afrique de l'Ouest. Rapport de Vérification Finale: Côte d'Ivoire*. Oslo and Parktown North: Fafo Institute for Applied International Studies and Khulisa Management Services (Pty) Ltd.

Hill, P. (1963) *Migrant Cocoa Farmers of Southern Ghana: A Study in Rural Capitalism*. Cambridge: Cambridge University Press.

IITA (2002) *Child Labor in the Cocoa Sector of West Africa: A Synthesis of Findings in Cameroon, Côte D'Ivoire*, Ghana, and Nigeria. Ibadan, Nigeria: Sustainable Tree Crops Program (STCP).

ILO-IPEC (2007a) *Rooting Out Child Labour from Cocoa Farms. Paper No. 1, A Synthesis Report of Five Rapid Assessments*. Geneva: International Labour Organization – IPEC.

ILO-IPEC (2007b) *Rooting Out Child Labour from Cocoa Farms. Paper No. 2, Safety and Health Hazards*. Geneva: International Labour Organization – IPEC.

ILO-IPEC (2007c) *Rooting Out Child Labour from Cocoa Farms: Paper No. 3, Sharing Experiences*. Geneva: International Labour Organization – IPEC.

Kolavalli, S. and Vigneri, M. (2011) 'Cocoa in Ghana: shaping the success of an economy', in Chuhan-Pole, P. and Manka, A. (eds) *Yes Africa Can: Success Stories from a Dynamic Continent*. Washington, DC: World Bank, pp 201–17.

Lowe, A. (2017) *Creating Opportunities for Young People in Ghana's Cocoa Sector*. ODI Working Paper 511. London: Overseas Development Institute (ODI).

Luckstead, J., Tsiboe, F. and Nalley, L.L. (2019) 'Estimating the economic incentives necessary for eliminating child labor in Ghanaian cocoa production', *PLOS One*, 14(6), Article e0217230. doi: 10.1371/journal.pone.0217230

Maconachie, R., Howard, N. and Bock, R. (2021) 'Re-thinking "harm" in relation to children's work: a "situated," multi-disciplinary perspective', *Oxford Development Studies*, 50(3), pp 259–71.

McCoy, T. (2018) *Tackling Child Labor in the Cocoa Sector: An Industry Viewpoint of a Work in Progress*, World Cocoa Foundation blog, 13 February. Available at: https://www.worldcocoafoundation.org/blog/tackling-child-labor-in-the-cocoa-sector-an-industry-viewpoint-of-a-work-in-progress/ (Accessed 26 November 2022).

Ministry of Manpower, Youth and Employment (2007) *Labour Practices in Cocoa Production in Ghana*. Accra, Ghana: Ministry of Manpower, Youth & Employment.

Ministry of Manpower, Youth and Employment (2008) *Cocoa Labour Survey in Ghana – 2007/2008, National Programme for the Elimination of Worst Forms of Child Labour in Cocoa (NPECLC)*. Accra, Ghana: Ministry of Manpower, Youth & Employment.

Mull, L.D. and Kirkhorn, S.R. (2005) 'Child labor in Ghana cocoa production: focus upon agricultural tasks, ergonomic exposures, and associated injuries and illnesses', *Public Health Reports*, 120(6), pp 649–56.

NPECLC (2007) *Labour Practices in Cocoa Production in Ghana (Pilot Survey)*. Accra, Ghana: Ministry of Manpower, Youth & Employment.

Ould, D. et al (2004) *The Cocoa Industry in West Africa: A History of Exploitation*. London: Anti-Slavery International.

Owusu, V. and Kwarteye, A. (2008) 'An empirical analysis on the determinants of child labor in cocoa production in Ghana', in *PEGNet Conference 2008, Assessing Development Impact – Learning from Experience, 11–12 September 2008*, Accra, Ghana.

Sackett, M. (2008) 'Forced child labor and cocoa production in West Africa', *Topical Research Digest: Human Rights and Contemporary Slavery*, pp 84–99.

Sadhu, S. et al (2020) *Assessing Progress in Reducing Child Labor in Cocoa Production in Cocoa Growing Areas of Côte d'Ivoire and Ghana*. Chicago: NORC, University of Chicago.

Thorsen, D. (2012) *Children Working in Commercial Agriculture, Evidence from West and Central Africa*. Briefing paper No. 2. Dakar: UNICEF West and Central Africa Regional Office.

Tulane University (2010) *Fourth Annual Report: Oversight of Public and Private Initiatives to Eliminate the Worst Forms of Child Labour in the Cocoa Sector in Côte d'Ivoire and Ghana*. New Orleans: School of Public Health and Tropical Medicine, Tulane University.

Tulane University (2015) *Final Report: 2013/14 Survey Research on Child Labor in West African Cocoa-Growing Areas*. New Orleans: School of Public Health and Tropical Medicine, Tulane University.

Van Hear, N. (1982) 'Child labour and the development of capitalist agriculture in Ghana', *Development and Change*, 13(4), pp 499–514.

Yeboah, S.A. (2019) *Childhoods in Ghana: Understanding the Work of NGOs as Cultural Brokers and Translators in Childhood Construction*. Unpublished PhD thesis. Hong Kong: The Hong Kong Polytechnic University.

11

Children's Harmful Work in Ghana's Lake Volta Fishery: Beyond Discourses of Child Trafficking

Imogen Bellwood-Howard and Abdulai Abubakari

Introduction

Children's work in Ghana's Lake Volta fishery, as in the cocoa sector and the extractive industries, has a long history, takes various forms and provokes controversy. Such work can be helpful, harmful, or both for a given child or household. Considering the history of children's work-related mobility in West Africa, some academic sources have problematized a discourse on children's work in fisheries largely focused on trafficking (Koomson et al, 2021; Golo, 2005; Iversen, 2006). Nevertheless, this remains the dominant presentation of children's work in the Lake Volta fishery, embraced by local stakeholders as well as the popular media, many academics and advocacy organizations. This discourse obscures other dimensions of children's work in these fisheries, including motivations and trade-offs, and the exposure of migrant and home-working children to hazards and harm.

Some contemporary children's work in the Lake Volta fishery is part of long-established patterns of mobility. Some children have indeed been trafficked, but it is hard to say what proportion because many work with parents, neighbours, strangers or foster carers under a range of different terms and conditions. Some children work for cash or in-kind payment, and access new opportunities through their work. At the same time, they may be exposed to reversible or irreversible harms – ranging from light injuries to psychological and emotional damage, to death by drowning. Some may be forced to work against their will, while others choose to join the fishery.

Alternatively, their work may be the result of a household decision related to a perceived greater good: the wellbeing of their family.

Some aspects of children's work in the fishery are clearer than others. For example, the gender associations of harvesting, processing and marketing tasks are well established (Iversen, 2006; Torell et al, 2015). And, it is likely that poverty of parents and fishers motivates them to supply and use the relatively inexpensive labour of children (Golo, 2005). But other details are far less clear. The proportions of child workers who are fostered, migrants, trafficked or home-working have not been established, nor has their actual exposure to different forms of hazard or the actual experience of harm. Little is known about the decision-making processes that lead to these different categories of children working in the fishery, or about different perspectives of the relative costs and benefits of such work compared to schooling or other forms of work. Furthermore, there is a disconnect between the literature on children's work in the Lake Volta fishery and their work in other sectors. What explains the fact that the apparently strong link between migration and trafficking in the fishery (Tengey and Oguaah, 2002; Iversen, 2006) is not seen in other sectors?

In this chapter we argue that greater awareness of the historical and structural dimensions of child mobility and children's work is required to address these gaps and questions. To date, however, much research and policy has been framed by the overly simplistic trafficking discourse. The chapter proceeds as follows. The next section provides a general introduction to fishing on Lake Volta. This is followed by a note on the dominant focus on trafficking in the literature, and sections on the prevalence, implications and drivers of children's work. A section on current policy and interventions precedes the conclusion that outlines appropriate focuses for future research.

Historical, economic and labour context of the Lake Volta fishery

At independence, most of Ghana's economic wealth came from the export of cocoa, gold and timber. These industries had long shaped a pattern of labour migration from the North to the South of the country, supported by policy that fostered underdevelopment in the North (Plange 1979; Songsore and Denkabe 1995; Songsore et al, 2001). Independence leader Kwame Nkrumah instituted a programme of industrialization aimed at import substitution and reduced dependency on the export of raw materials. This programme included the construction of the Akosombo Hydroelectric Dam, which, between 1962 and 1966, created Lake Volta. As the lake filled, 80,000 people were forced to relocate (Raschid-Sally et al, 2008). Simultaneously, migrants, many with ethnic affiliations to fishing including the Ewe, Fante and Ga, migrated to the new lakeshore to fish. They eventually created a largely artisanal industry, which by 2004–05 was estimated to include approximately 80,000 fishers and 20,000 processors and traders (ILO-IPEC, 2013). Currently, the lake also provides irrigation, transportation and recreational services.

Akosombo Hydroelectric Power Plant continues to make an important contribution to Ghana's energy mix, although a decreasing one as fossil fuels have been used to meet rising demand for electricity since 1997.[1] However, construction of the dam was a factor contributing to Ghana's high external debt in the 1960s and forced those around the lake to relocate (Miescher, 2014). Following Nkrumah's overthrow in 1966, Ghana went through a succession of military and civilian rulers and experienced general macroeconomic decline (Fosu and Aryeetey, 2008). In the early 1980s, Jerry Rawlings accepted a package of structural adjustment measures and austerity policies promoted by the World Bank and International Monetary Fund (IMF). This, and the transition to democracy in 1992, led Ghana to be noted internationally as an example of economic growth, though poverty among farmers and fishers improved little (Ayelazuno 2014). Since the turn of the century, governments have followed international development accords and trends, notably the continent-wide calls for a 'New Green Revolution' comprising modernization and commercialization of the agriculture, livestock and fishing sectors (Kansanga et al, 2019). Ghana reached middle income status in 2011. Following the discovery of offshore oil in 2013, hydrocarbon profits contributed up to approximately 5 per cent to GDP annually, but did not precipitate significant economic growth.[2]

Despite political stability, continuing inequalities mean that people inhabiting less well-connected areas of the country, such as the shores of Lake Volta, continue with diversified, semi-subsistence livelihoods largely based on natural resources. The poverty in these areas is underpinned by the structural factors outlined earlier, including structural adjustment, historical labour migration and the legacy of the creation of the lake itself (ILO-IPEC, 2013; Okyere, 2017).

Fishing on Lake Volta

Fishing as practised on Lake Volta is arduous and time intensive. It is occasionally undertaken for subsistence purposes but is generally linked to local and national value chains. Fishers use a variety of gear and techniques, but the use of various types of nets dominates. Gill nets are hung in the water, cast nets are thrown and immediately retrieved, and seine nets are cast in a circle from a canoe and pulled in from the shore. Traps are also used, including, more recently, ones made from bamboo (Zdunnek et al, 2008).

Many of those currently engaged in fishing still perceive themselves as migrants, even though they or their parents may have been born in the villages and localities surrounding the lake (Zdunnek et al, 2008; ILO-IPEC, 2013). Members of such communities retain links to their 'hometowns', often in more southerly locations, and may travel there for festivals and funerals (Singleton et al, 2016). It is claimed that many of today's lakeside settlements started as seasonal fishing camps before the 1970s, and have gradually become more permanent (Chisholm, 1983).

Fishing in Ghana was traditionally governed by semi-formal structures including associations of fishers[3] (largely men) and of fish marketers (who are largely women) (Torell et al, 2015). Chief fishermen and market women played important roles, for example limiting offtake by enforcing 'taboo days' on which fishing or fish sales were prohibited. Some of these organizations and structures are still active today in lakeside communities. However, the associations are also likely to be involved in political or advocacy activities, for example advocating for subsidized premixed fuel or boat engines. Some are linked to national level organizations, such as the Ghana National Women Fish Processors and Traders Association (Torell et al, 2015). By no means are all those working in the fishery connected to these organizations. Employees and members of fishing crews, for example, are poorly organized, and there is no major representative body for children working in the sector. Golo (2005) points out that the ethnic orientation of many fishing organizations means more recent migrant fishers, including those displaced by conflicts elsewhere in West Africa, may not be welcomed as members or may operate outside their jurisdiction and rules. Fishers, whether in an association or not, tend to operate independently (ILO-IPEC, 2013).

Children's work in the Lake Volta fishery

Dominant focus on trafficking

Many children work in Lake Volta's fishing sector, and do so in a variety of ways, which will be explored in detail shortly. However, little is known about how many children are engaged in which tasks, under which circumstances. Much research and advocacy work on the sector has tended to focus on trafficking and conflated this with children's work, at least to some extent. It is therefore very difficult to extricate statistics or other insights on children's work in general. Therefore, we will discuss the perceptions and discourses associated with trafficking first, before moving on to present data available from the literature.

Because media, public, academic and policy discourses are almost exclusively focussed on trafficking and its associated harms, 'child rescue' has been highlighted as the main response. Rescue efforts by government, NGOs and others feature in the press,[4] and 'rescued' children are typically sent to children's homes (sometimes staying for several years) before being returned to their communities.

Huijsmans and Baker (2012) and Okyere (2017) describe how NGOs, in particular, have vested interests in promoting these discourses, as opposed to foregrounding structural and historical drivers of labour migration. Fundamentally, financial support for their activities depends on the proposition that child trafficking is a widespread and recurrent problem.

Despite some recognition that rescue is only a partial response, the focus on trafficking precludes an explicit problematization of harmful work, beyond its association with trafficking. Situations where children engage in hazardous work for their parents or kin are either ignored or seen as unavoidable. There is no recognition that children's engagement in hard, hazardous and harmful work prefigures their adult working lives. As the major problem is perceived to be trafficking, notions of rescue, rehabilitation and return to 'home' dominate the proposed responses. This pushes into the background important economic aspects of the fishery, such as labour costs and the consequences of declining fish stocks. It also downplays children's exposure to hazardous work across the whole edu-workscape, including at home (Chapter 4, this volume), and the fact that some migrants may have access to a more limited range of opportunities than indigenes, even when placed with kin (that is, as a classificatory parent) (Golo, 2005).

Equally important is the focus on trafficking, which essentially conflates movement and harm, and obscures the role and importance in children's lives of other forms of mobility. Work on children's migration elsewhere in West Africa shows that older children and youth often migrate alone or in groups for work, with or without the consent or assistance of their parents. In Ghana, children's autonomous seasonal migration has been reported for decades, particularly from North to South to work as head porters (Huijsmans, 2012; Giese and Thiel, 2015; Agyei et al, 2016). While child placement and fostering are referred to in the literature about the Lake Volta fishery (often framed as an unfortunate historical precedent for trafficking), the prevalence of autonomous migration is not reported. Within the dominant discourse, child trafficking overrides even the possibility of children's agency expressed as autonomous migration for work.

Prevalence of children's work

Partly due to this preoccupation with trafficking, there are limited data on the prevalence of children of different ages working in the fishery and on their engagement with various tasks, some of which entail hazardous work. Although it is very likely that a majority of fishers and fish marketers have children helping them in some capacity, it is currently impossible to say (1) what proportion of the labour force comprises children; (2) what proportion of children are involved; (3) the age and other characteristics of the children involved, including their migration status; and (4) under what terms and conditions they work.

Nevertheless, a few studies have attempted to estimate the proportion of children working who are trafficked or working away from their parents. In 2013, the ILO International Programme on the Elimination of Child Labour (ILO-IPEC) reported results of a survey of 350 children working in fishing across ten districts, and reported that 52 per cent were in their home communities, with the remainder from elsewhere in Ghana (ILO-IPEC, 2013). This latter group included children who had moved with one or both parents to the fishing community: 75 per cent of children lived with one or both parents, 17 per cent with other family members and only 8 per cent with their employer or another non-family member. The same study surveyed 90 fishers who employed children, 350 parents and 264 community members. Overall, they reported that while 65 per cent of working children were not in their parental community,[5] most of these children live with family members.

Singleton et al (2016) surveyed the southern portion of the lake by approaching every fishing boat seen and interviewing each child aboard. A total of 768 boys and three girls from 982 boats were surveyed, and the authors concluded that 60 per cent of the children were trafficked. This statistic has been widely cited. The study defined trafficking to include all children who had moved from their birthplace for work purposes but without their parents. Unfortunately, this definition includes many types of child mobility described in the literature from West Africa, including some forms of placement with relatives and autonomous migration (Thorsen, 2006, 2009, 2014).[6] Indeed, only 20 per cent of children encountered confirmed that this definition described their situation. The 60 per cent figure arose because the researchers classed a further 37 per cent as 'suspected' as having been trafficked. In these cases, they were unable to interview the boat occupants fully but, problematically, decided that children who appeared scared, shy, unkempt or deferential to adults were likely to be have been trafficked. Nearly 75 per cent of the children were confirmed or estimated to be aged 12 or under.

In 2003, the Ghana Statistical Service (GSS) and ILO-IPEC carried out the Ghana Child Labour Survey, and found about 25 per cent of children in the fishing industry across the whole of Ghana were aged between 5 and 9 years, 40 per cent were aged between 10 and 14, and 34 per cent were aged between 15 and 17 (Ghana Statistical Service, 2003, p 64). Eighty-seven per cent of child workers in fish harvesting were boys.

It is important to note that these studies focused on children working in fish capture, and therefore ultimately described the situation of boys. There is very little information available on the prevalence of children's work in fish processing and trading where girls are known to be better represented.

Table 11.1: Common living and working arrangements

	Child works with				
Child lives with	**One or both parents**	**Family member**	**Community member**	**Foster carer**	**Stranger**
One or both parents	X	X	X		
Foster carer or family member (away from parents)			X	X	X
Stranger (away from parents)					X

This review supports the conclusion that trafficking is likely to be present to some extent but may not be as widespread as if often supposed.

Organization and terms of children's work

Children involved in the Lake Volta fishery live and work in a variety of situations (Table 11.1), only one of which (living and working with a stranger away from parents) might immediately suggest trafficking. While there is little reliable information about the children working in the fishery, literature that focuses on trafficking in fisheries and that on children's work in general in other sectors (Kwankye et al, 2009; Berlan, 2013; Adonteng-Kissi, 2018; Koomson et al, 2022) allows us to summarize as follows.

Children may arrive in each of the situations depicted in Table 11.1 in a variety of ways. Some children may autonomously decide to migrate to a new location to work, as head porters have been recorded doing in Ghana for decades (Baah-Ennumh and Adoma, 2012). This could be seasonal or longer term and may or may not be part of a more complex migration trajectory. Movement to a foster home may be arranged to facilitate work, but it may also be seen as a way to teach the child how to deal with life's difficulties, relieve the parent(s) of caring responsibility, or to facilitate access to school or vocational training (Serra, 2009; also see Chapter 8, this volume). Fostering arrangements are generally agreed between the parents and foster carer, although in some cases not all adult parties are in agreement (Frempong-Ainguah et al, 2009; Singleton et al, 2016). Fostering may be initiated by the child, especially with older children who are engaged in economic activities of their own (Hashim and Thorsen, 2011). Orphans and children who have lost one parent may have been sent to live with relatives or may move of their own volition (for example, to help their mother after the death of their father). Many fishing communities continue to perceive themselves as migrant and continue to visit their 'home' towns, sometimes hundreds of miles away, for festivals and social visits. This can be the means through which voluntary migrants come to hear of working opportunities and fostered and 'trafficked' children are sourced (Singleton et al, 2016).

It is likely that the primary objective of a migrant fisher who takes on a child is to access cheap labour. The motivation for the parent(s) may be to escape the financial burden of caring. In some cases, parents will have paid someone (an agent or family member) to facilitate the child's movement. This is what is termed 'trafficking' in much advocacy literature (for example, the aforementioned study of Singleton et al, 2016, which does not distinguish between trafficking and other migration) with the assumption that an element of exploitation is involved. Academic literature points to the complexity of these situations. Some agency may be exercised by the child involved, or there may be an assumption on the part of the agent or employer that they are helping the child and/or their parents, for example by providing access to an apprenticeship (Thorsen, 2019). Some children may be kidnapped and forced to work for strangers.

Children work under a variety of (potentially overlapping) terms and conditions (Kielland, 2008; ILO-IPEC, 2013; Sackey and Johannesen, 2015). For example, boat- and shore-based tasks may be performed in the company of (or supervised by) adults, but are also carried out by children, often with older children acting as supervisors. Some children work for family or others without being paid a wage, and such work may be framed as an apprenticeship. Alternatively, they may receive more or less regular payments in cash or kind from their employer or their parent(s) may receive a one-off or regular payment from the child's master. A child may be working to repay a debt incurred by his or her parents, and the child or the parents may have been tricked into believing that payments will be forthcoming in the future. After a given period, the child may have the option to either continue the arrangement or cease work.

ILO-IPEC (2013) found that 78 per cent of the 350 working children they surveyed worked more than 4 hours a day, with 44 per cent working 7 or more hours. Fifty-one per cent said they were not paid, while 64 per cent were fed. This study recorded that a small number of children and young people had worked for up to ten years with a single master. However, Singleton et al (2016) found 2–3 year apprenticeships to be the most common mode of employment. Adeborna and Johnson (2014) note that parents keen for their children to inherit the family fishing business may be particularly eager for them to train as apprentices, whether with themselves or another fisher or trader.

The parents of fostered, migrant and trafficked children may not be aware of their child's living or working conditions, or any associated risks. In one study in communities from which children were trafficked to work in the fishery, 33 per cent of parents indicated that they did not know the conditions under which their children were living and working (Adeborna and Johnson, 2014).

Tasks and harm

Children work in all aspects of the fishery, on the water and at the lakeside. The gender distribution of tasks is marked. Generally, boys produce and maintain equipment and gear including boats, traps and nets. They set and collect traps, and go out onto the lake in boats, rowing, bailing water, casting and retrieving nets. They are often obliged to dive to free trapped nets, and this is frequently cited as the most dangerous task they perform (Harrison, 2010; Adeborna and Johnson, 2014). They carry fish to shore. Girls are then mostly involved in processing (cleaning, salting, drying, frying and so on) and selling fisk (Zdunnek et al, 2008; Singleton et al, 2016). There are exceptions to gendered allocations of tasks, for example in households that have no sons. When girls and women do fish, it is generally close to shore (ILO-IPEC, 2013). Some tasks are considered to be especially well-suited to children: on boats these include menial tasks like stringing out nets, bailing water and sitting in the prow to direct. Although adults and older youths are more likely to perform heavier tasks such as drawing in nets, younger children are not entirely exempt.

Girls' involvement in fish marketing is not problematized in the literature in the same way as boy's involvement in fishing. There may be a perception that marketing is an appropriate, formative and less harmful activity, and/or that opportunity costs for girls are lower, so their economic activity deserves less attention. Alternatively, it may be that boys' work catching fish attracts particular attention because it is more physical and apparently more dangerous. Whatever the reason, there is certainly scope to better understand the nature and implications of girls' work in the fishery. Important questions relate to the extent to which boys and girls perform domestic chores in addition to or instead of productive work (see Singleton et al, 2016); whether boys' and girls' mobility patterns are similar; and the function of ethnic tropes in the social construction of gendered work roles.

In Ghana's 1998 Children's Act, work that is likely to interfere with a child's education, endanger their health, expose them to physical harm or negatively affect them mentally, spiritually, morally or socially is considered 'child labour'. This term carries a strong negative connotation, unlike the more ambiguous 'children's work' (Adeborna and Johnson, 2014). Children are potentially exposed to various forms of harm – physical, emotional and psychological – during their work in the Lake Volta fishery (Table 11.2).

The framework set out in this table provides a starting point for further consideration of how harm interacts with other aspects of children's work.

Table 11.2: Forms of harm potentially experienced by children working in the fishery

Reversibility	Specific harm to children	General harm to children (and adults)
Never	• Stunting	• Drowning
Possibly	• Opportunity costs of missing school at a young age • Physical abuse from masters, supervisors and other children • Psychological and emotional distress at being separated from parents • Psychological and emotional distress from hard work • Wasting	• Lack of adequate sleep – though what is 'adequate' varies for adults and children • Malnutrition • Accidental physical injuries, for example, cuts, broken limbs, stings from fish, burns from processing fish • Exposure to elements, for example, sun or cold • Noise induced hearing problems • Psychological and emotional distress from seeing friends suffer or die

Sources: ILO-IPEC (2013), Singleton et al (2016) and Zdunnek et al (2008)

Some of these harms are experienced by children working in the fishery but are not necessarily caused by their work. The interaction of these forms of potential harm with children's work and the circumstances under which they work are complex. For example, some children migrate to work in fishing communities to avoid harms such as malnutrition, neglect or domestic violence. Being separated from parents is not experienced as a harm equally by all children but depends on cultural norms about childhood and parenthood, and the reasons for their mobility. For many children, it is normal not to grow up with biological parents, and it is common in Ghana to move between relatives (Hashim and Thorsen, 2011).

Negative impacts of working in the fishery on schooling are a major component of the dominant discourse (Zdunnek et al, 2008; Sackey and Johannesen, 2015; Singleton et al, 2016). Early morning and afternoon fishing work causes some children to miss some or all school sessions. The 2013 ILO-IPEC survey of 90 employers reported that 75 per cent said their working children also attended school (ILO-IPEC, 2013). From the sample of 350 parents, 53 per cent said their children had dropped out of school, with 34 per cent of those citing fishing-related reasons. Nevertheless, interactions between work and school are complex. For example, schools are often weak or absent in fishing communities.[7] Teachers may be poorly supported or ill equipped to stay for extended periods in remote locations that lack infrastructure. Where the quality of learning is poor, working may be a more reasonable choice for children, with more tangible, immediate rewards (Iversen, 2006). When school opportunities are lacking in a child's home community, it may make sense for them to travel to another location to work and gain some access to school in the process (Zdunnek et al, 2008; Singleton et al, 2016). Literature also shows that there is often positive interaction between work and school when school fees are met by children through their own work. School feeding programmes can act as an incentive for parents and fishers to send their wards to school, and possibly even for parents to send their children to live in a community where they know there is a school feeding programme (Ofei-Aboagye, 2013; Awojobi, 2019).

ILO-IPEC (2013) examined the perception and occurrence of physical injuries and ill-health. When parents, employers, children and community members were surveyed about injuries and sicknesses that had occurred over a six-month period, the most frequently mentioned injury was bruising, but these data do not show the prevalence of injuries by type. Rather, being based on perception and recall, they demonstrate how hard it is to define and quantify 'harmful' work and point to the need to work closely with the children themselves.

Drivers of children's work in the Lake Volta fishery

The preceding sections have begun to show the complex interactions between the development of the fishing industry and the involvement of children in different types of work within it.

Historical and structural drivers

Some studies draw attention to the historical drivers of work in the fishery in general (Béné and Russell, 2007; ILO-IPEC, 2013; Okyere, 2017). The colonial and postcolonial context of North to South labour migration, the displacement of households during the creation of Lake Volta and Structural Adjustment Policies all form part of the background to the persistent impoverishment of fishing communities (ILO-IPEC, 2013; Okyere, 2017). Golo (2005) proposes that these drivers interact with the mismanagement of the fishing sector. Repeated economic downturns since the 1960s pushed many people into primary production, including fishing, which increased pressure on fish stocks and reduced off-take. Okyere (2017) also blames inadequate investment in infrastructure, the poor skills base that prevents fishers accessing alternative employment and poor access to financial services including credit. Béné and Russell (2007) note a lack of access to farmland for fishing communities around the lakeshore, including for those seen as migrants. The failure of both formal and traditional governance structures to manage these pressures has strengthened the dynamic between diminishing resources, poverty and demand for cheap labour. The latter has implications for children's work. Critically, their labour is cheaper than that of adults, so engaging them to perform at least some of the essential functions of a fishing crew lowers costs for the fishing operation. It is commonly said that demand for cheap labour in fishing communities reflects the general level of 'poverty' (Moreto et al, 2019): it is claimed that fishers cannot make a living if they pay full wages to adult crew members.

One media report speculated on the possible longer-term drivers of change. Boyle (2013) reports that the apprentices recruited into family fishing businesses in the decades after the formation of Lake Volta were adolescents who had already finished middle school. However, as young people's perceptions of attractive adult occupations changed, they turned away from fishing. As adult fishers found that adolescent labour was less available, they turned to younger, more obedient children to fill the gap.

Ecological factors

The demand for cheap labour interacts with, and may even partly be driven by, decrease in catch (for example, Zdunnek et al, 2008) linked to the decline of the traditional governance mechanisms including taboo days, and the increasing use of prohibited fishing methods such as closely woven nets and night fishing with lights. Apparently, even though prices have risen as fish have become scarcer, this is insufficient to make up for the lower catch (Teh et al, 2019).

Ecological realities of fishing also play a role in shaping children's involvement. Though fishing can be carried out throughout the year, children are often engaged during times when stocks are in abundance, to deal with, or in anticipation of, large catches (Iversen, 2006). Further, the nature of lake fishing is such that income is more directly related to the daily labour input than in activities like farming, animal rearing or aquaculture, where there is a set sequence of tasks to be performed, over an extended period of time, to bring a crop to harvest (Béné and Russell, 2007). In fishing, additional labour input has the potential to lead to a higher catch, even if there are diminishing marginal returns to labour. In other words, without putting in more labour there is no chance of further gain; and, the cheaper the labour, the greater the potential return. The fact that fishing can be practised on a daily rather than seasonal basis means that it can play a role as a supplemental activity in a diversified livelihood or even a way to finance other non-fishing enterprises. These realities promote the ad hoc involvement of children in fishing and not just those who may be brought to a community specifically to fish.

Household level drivers

At household level, parents' inability to provide adequate care is cited as contributing to decisions (by parents and/or children) leading children to move elsewhere to work in fishing (Tengey and Oguaah, 2002; Béné and Russell, 2007; Zdunnek et al, 2008; Adeborna and Johnson, 2014; Singleton et al, 2016). For some employers, accepting a child worker is a favour to the parents; they are relieving the family of a burden, and offering an opportunity to earn (Zdunnek et al, 2008; ILO-IPEC, 2013).

However, fostering and deciding to work in an extended family context may be prompted by other norms and expectations. Beyond alleviating the burden on parents or providing the child access to opportunities such as schooling that do not exist in the birth parent's home, sending a child from one arm of the family to another can reinforce social and familial bonds. The literature on child mobility in West Africa shows how child placement and fostering, as well as autonomous child migration, takes place in a context of extended family and ethnic relations, where a young person's upbringing can be translocal, and mobility between different branches of the family, clan or ethnic group may be seen as advantageous (Hashim and Thorsen, 2011; Boyden and Howard, 2013). Though fostering is recognized, the emphasis on child labour and trafficking in the discourse on the Lake Volta fishery means that the subtlety and reciprocal nature of most fostering arrangements are lost.

Some literature frames child trafficking as a subversion of traditional fostering, and suggests it is an increasingly prevalent and undesirable driver of children's harmful work (for example, Iversen, 2006). This sense of a shift in the nature of fostering has been linked to an increase in breakdown of parental relationships, single parenthood, unwanted children and the decline of family values (ILO-IPEC, 2013; Torell et al, 2015). Yet, as noted earlier, the relation between children's work, migration and fostering is much more nuanced (Golo, 2005).

Individual decisions

Children have some agency in decisions regarding work (Thorsen, 2006). Many wish to experience shorter- and longer-term advantages of working, including increased income or access to food, an opportunity to work towards a future vocation as an apprentice, or a sense that they are developing an adult persona. The latter may be strongly associated with fishing for members of ethnic groups who have such historical ethno-professional links. Mobile children may also seek to travel to live with extended family, as they can then make claims upon kin and peers as they negotiate entry into work, for example by seeking accommodation, work experience or introductions to employers.

Many children also feel a responsibility to contribute to their parental household, shaped by norms to do with household responsibilities and community expectations (see Chapter 8, this volume). Such norms may prompt them to work with their parents or migrate. Children appear to understand and appreciate the potential advantages of work, and even studies which are highly critical of children working and child trafficking show that many children working outside their home communities do not wish to return (Tengey and Oguaah, 2002).

Policy, key stakeholders and interventions

Ghana has formally recognized child labour and trafficking as problematic through both ratification of international conventions and enactment of national legislation (Table 11.3; also see Chapter 8, this volume). Nevertheless, children's harmful work in the fishing industry is not specifically recognized: it is not mentioned in either the Fisheries Act or the National Fisheries and Aquaculture Strategy.

One significant aspect of the legislation is that it defines children as people under 18 years of age, which does not always correspond to local understandings of social age or childhood (Golo, 2005). Certainly, some individuals below the age of 18 may need to perform potentially hazardous (that is, proscribed) work to support their families or their own children. To complicate matters, not all children know their age, even though birth certificates have been mandatory since 1965.

Despite the existing legislation and policies, implementation is weak (MOFAD, 2014). The focus on trafficking means that 'rescue' dominates as the perceived solution to the problem of trafficking, in isolation from considerations of child work more generally. Charities partner with the government Department for Social Welfare in removing supposedly trafficked children from the communities they work in and placing them in orphanages.

There are, however, some alternative mechanisms. In 2015, United States Agency for International Development (USAID), Netherlands Development Organization (SNV) and the Fisheries Commission, with the input of the Ghana Agricultural Workers' Union (GAWU), instigated the development of a Strategy on Anti-Child Labour and Trafficking in Fisheries. The Strategy is based on the 'Torkor Model', developed in the lakeshore village of Kpando Torkor, where community structures and informal labour groups took responsibility for addressing child labour, rather than relying on external agencies (MOFAD, 2014; ILO, 2016). The initial intervention lasted one year and led to the establishment of some structures, such as a special school for children leaving employment. Reports from the field describe how the

Table 11.3: Conventions, policies, strategies and plans relevant to children's work in Ghanaian fisheries

Year	Convention, policy, strategy or plan
1990	Ratification of the UN Convention on the Rights of the Child
1998	The Children's Act (Act 560) brought into law the recommendations of the 1973 ILO Minimum Age Convention for Admission to Employment (Convention No. 138). So, people of 13 years old can legally perform light work that does not threaten their health, safety or education; those of 15 may do other non-hazardous work; and those 18 and over hazardous work.
2000	Ghana ratified the 1999 ILO Worst Forms of Child Labour Convention (182)
2002	Fisheries Act (Act 625) – This contains no mention of child work
2003	Labour Act (Act 651) – Section 58 prohibits employment of people under 18 in hazardous work
2005	Human Trafficking Act (Act 694)
2007	Domestic Violence Act
2008	National Fisheries and Aquaculture Strategy – contains no mention of child work
2009	Human Trafficking Act (Act 694) amended
2010	National Plan of Action for the Elimination of Worst Forms of Child Labour in Ghana (2009–15)
2015	Child and Family Welfare Policy
2015	National Social Protection Policy
2016	National Plan of Action for the Elimination of Worst Forms of Child Labour in Ghana (2016–20)
2018	Strategy on Anti-Child Labour and Trafficking in Fisheries formalised

Source: MOFAD (2014)

model has become internationally renowned, continues to work and has been institutionalized to some degree, for example being included in the district assembly's medium- and long-term plans of action and drawn upon by other development initiatives, such as, the USAID/SNV Sustainable Fisheries Management Partnership (SFMP). However, many children continue to work due to drivers such as household poverty (Semordzi, 2018).

This approach emphasizes the importance of workers in the informal sector being organized, and of interconnections between stakeholders at different levels and with different interests. As shown in Table 11.4, this could involve quite a wide range of diverse actors. The Torkor Model experience, as that of the SFMP, shows that communication between different sectors is critical. However, it is often fraught: community leaders in Torkor thought that the police were not playing their full role in the

Table 11.4: Key actor and stakeholder groups and organizations

Grouping	Actors
Government	Ministry of Fisheries and Aquaculture; Fisheries Commission; Ministry of Employment and Labour Relations; Ministry of Education, Ghana Education Service; Ministry of Gender, Children and Social Protection, Labour Unit; Anti-Human Trafficking Unit of the Ghana Police Service; Local District Councils; Ghana Navy; Department of Community Development and Social Welfare; Members of Parliament; Assembly persons; Unit Committee Members
Industry	Ghana Canoe Fishermen Council; General Agricultural Workers Union of Trade Union Congress (TUC); Ghana Employers' Association; National Fisheries Association of Ghana; Ghana National Inshore Fisheries Association; National Inland Canoe Fishermen Council; local fishery associations; National Fish Processors and Traders' Association
Community	Chief fishermen and market women; chiefs; religious bodies; parents; children; youth
NGOs	Free the Slaves; Parent and Child Foundation; Challenging Heights; International Needs; Engage Now Africa; Friends of the Nation; Partners in community Development Programme; Savannah Signatures
International agencies	ILO; UNICEF; SNV; USAID; University of Rhode Island (under the Sustainable Fisheries Management Partnership)

Source: ILO-IPEC (2013)

process thus undermining the efforts of others. Additionally, members of the armed forces cited inconsistent communication between their service, the municipal authorities, and traditional leaders.

Another example is the Ghana Child Labour Strategic Initiative, a three-year project funded by the private philanthropy organization The Legatum Foundation in 2007 to deal with child labour and trafficking in the fishing communities of Lake Volta. The project focused partly on rescues, but, like the Torkor Model and SFMP, recognized some of the wider drivers of child work and undertook initiatives to introduce parents to alternative income-generating activities (Adeborna and Johnson, 2014).

Perhaps reflecting a recognition that elimination of children's work may not be realistic, attempts have been made to address the conflict between work and school, reflected in lateness, inability to concentrate and absenteeism. For example, ILO-IPEC (2013) suggests school hours could be changed to take account of morning and evening fishing, and school holidays could similarly be organized around the fishing season.

Besides discourses of trafficking and rescue, policy focussed work, such as that carried out by ILO-IPEC (2013), has advocated market-based or value-chain approaches informed by the now dominant agricultural development frameworks, which promote marketization and commercialization. These approaches focus on giving fishers business training to improve their profits and reduce demand for cheap child labour.

Consumer willingness to pay more for fish has been mentioned in the literature as a solution to the demand for cheap labour. The willingness to pay for other desirable attributes, such as sustainability, is mobilized in value chains around the world, for example the Fairtrade system (McClenachan et al, 2016). Still, it must be borne in mind that the fish value chains in question are largely domestic; any changes in price, therefore, have food and nutrition security implications, particularly for the poor.

In a national analysis of Ghana's fisheries, Failler et al (2014) proposed tilapia aquaculture as a way to change the relationship between labour, inputs and profit, considered to feed demand for cheap child labour. It has also been suggested that a shift from nets to traps would have a similar effect. Smoking fish for export is seen by some as way to raise the value of fish products and, thus, the amount that can be spent on adult rather than child labour. However, the regulatory requirements are currently beyond most fishers (Failler et al, 2014). Finally, it has been proposed that business training can reduce demand for cheaper labour by raising profits.

Human rights discourse has been used in relation to harmful children's work in fisheries, though it has been far more widely used to examine access to resources such as fishing grounds (Ratner et al, 2014). In such frameworks, children's rights would be situated in the context of workers' rights in general (Ratner et al, 2014), and authors like Teh et al (2019) suggest that human rights frameworks can only be instituted in a setting where legal pluralism is recognized.

Conclusion

Aside from distribution of tasks by gender, few aspects of children's work in the Lake Volta fishery are well understood: the current knowledge base is insufficient to support robust policymaking and implementation. Four areas warrant particular attention.

First, the prevalence of children's work, children's harmful work and different forms of children's mobility. It is not currently possible to speak with any certainty about the proportion of working children who are with parents, relatives or strangers; the importance of children's work in different aspects of the fishery; or the prevalence of harm of various types among working girls and boys.

Second, the preoccupation with child trafficking. It is critically important to understand why the trafficking discourse continues to dominate; why the hazardous nature of work is not seen as a problem for all children (or all workers more broadly); and why there has been so much focus on fishing, and so little on processing and marketing.

Third, the historical, ecological and cultural factors that shape children's work, perceptions of hazardous work and children's experience of harm. Here it will be particularly important to take full account of dynamics driven by, for example, declines in catch, the cost of labour, changes in technology, and increasing public awareness of child labour and trafficking.

And finally, children's agency. The focus here must be on how children in different socio-economic positions make choices to do with school and work; and what work to do, under what conditions. It is extremely important that research does not fetishize children's agency but rather understands it in the context of the other forces and factors, many of which are outside their control, affecting children's lives.

Notes

1 https://www.iea.org/countries/ghana

2 https://data.worldbank.org/indicator/NY.GDP.PETR.RT.ZS?end=2020&locations=GH&start=1961&view=chart; https://data.worldbank.org/indicator/NY.GDP.MKTP.PP.KD?end=2020&locations=GH&start=1961&view=chart

3 The following terms will be used: Fishers: people who fish. Fisherfolk: people in fishing communities, including inhabitants ethnically associated with fishing, fishers and fish marketers.

4 For example: https://www.ghanaweb.com/GhanaHomePage/regional/Challenging-Heights-rescues-23-more-children-from-slavery-1493615 and https://www.ghanaweb.com/GhanaHomePage/features/Challenging-Heights-rescued-153-children-in-2021-1448539. Also see Okali, Frimpong Boamah and Sumberg (2022).

5 This assumption that all data sources were combined to give the later sets of results seems the easiest way to reconcile the finding that 65 per cent of children are working in communities other than their parental community, while 52 per cent were in their home communities. Another apparent discrepancy is that 75 per cent of children are reported as living with parents, but also 65 per cent as working outside their parental community. It may be that the study defined 'parental' and 'home' communities differently. In general, this points to a still unfulfilled need to be more explicit about such terms.

6 Nor does this definition refer to the notion of exploitation, central to most understandings of trafficking. Although a definition referring to a unique set of legislation may be overly rigid, there is at least a need to understand what constitutes trafficking in relation to who sees which type of labour as exploitative.

7 The continued tendency of different ethnic groups with ethno-professional fishing identities to perceive themselves as migrants is reflected in the lack of investment (for example, in housing) in some lakeshore communities, even when they have existed for a several generations. The temporary appearance of those communities is said to have discouraged local government from building permanent facilities such as schools and community centres, and instilling electricity (ILO-IPEC, 2013). This reinforces the link between poverty, children's work and limited schooling.

References

Adeborna, D. and Johnson, K. (2014) *Child Labour Literature Review and Scoping Study Report: Ghana*. Narragansett, RI: USAID/Ghana Sustainable Fisheries Management Project. Available at: www.crc.uri.edu.

Adonteng-Kissi, O. (2018) 'Causes of child labour: perceptions of rural and urban parents in Ghana', *Children and Youth Services Review*, 91, pp 55–65.

Agyei, Y.A., Kumi, E. and Yeboah, T. (2016) 'Is better to be a kayayei than to be unemployed: reflecting on the role of head portering in Ghana's informal economy', *GeoJournal*, 81(2), pp 293–318.

Awojobi, O. (2019) 'A systematic review of the impact of Ghana's school feeding programme on educational and nutritional outcomes', *Agro-Science*, 18(2), pp 42–50.

Ayelazuno, J. A. (2014) 'Neoliberalism and growth without development in Ghana: a case for state-led industrialization', *Journal of Asian and African Studies*, 49(1), pp 80–99.

Baah-Ennumh, T.Y. and Adoma, M.O. (2012) 'The living conditions of female head porters in the Kumasi metropolis, Ghana', *Journal of Social and Development Sciences*, 3(7), pp 229–44.

Béné, C. and Russell, A.J. (2007) *Diagnostic Study of the Volta Basin Fisheries: Part 2 Livelihoods and Poverty Analysis, Current Trends and Projections*. Volta Basin Project Report 7. Cairo: WorldFish Centre.

Berlan, A. (2013) 'Social sustainability in agriculture: an anthropological perspective on child labour in cocoa production in Ghana', *The Journal of Development Studies*, 49(8), pp 1088–1100.

Boyden, J. and Howard, N. (2013) 'Why does child trafficking policy need to be reformed? The moral economy of children's movement in Benin and Ethiopia', *Children's Geographies*, 11(3), pp 354–68.

Boyle, L. (2013) 'Child trafficking: a symbol of poverty and vulnerability', 20 December. Available at: https://www.graphic.com.gh/features/opinion/child-trafficking-a-symbol-of-poverty-and-vulnerability.html (Accessed 16 April 2020).

Chisholm, N.G. (1983) *Response of Some Rural Communities in South-East Ghana to Economic Recession 1982*. Cambridge: African Studies Centre, Cambridge University.

Failler, P., Beyens, Y. and Asiedu, B. (2014) *Value Chain Analysis of the Fishery Sector in Ghana, with Focus on Quality, Environmental, Social, Sustainable, Food Safety, Organic Requirements and Its Compliance Infrastructure, Us/Gha/06/005 – Contract No. 3000018889*. Draft Final Report – 17/06/2014. Accra: Aets Apave.

Fosu, A. K. and Aryeetey, E. (2008) 'Ghana's post-independence economic growth 1960–2000', in Aryeetey, E. and Kanbur, R. (eds) *Economy of Ghana: Analytical Perspectives on Stability, Growth and Poverty*. Martlesham: Boydell & Brewer, pp 36–77. Available at: https://www.cambridge.org/core/books/economy-of-ghana/ghanas-postindependence-economic-growth-19602000/27A6E56BE39A0D30E37498BAEA361DBA.

Frempong-Ainguah, F., Badasu, D. and Codjoe, S.N.A. (2009) 'North–south independent child migration in Ghana: the push and pull factors', in Anarfi, J.K. and Kwankye, S.O. (eds) *Independent Migration of Children in Ghana*. Legon, Ghana: Institute of Statistical, Social and Economic Research (ISSER).

Ghana Statistical Service (2003) *Ghana Child Labour Survey*. Geneva and Accra: ILO and Ghana Statistical Service. Available at: https://www.ilo.org/ipec/Informationresources/WCMS_IPEC_PUB_690/lang--en/index.htm.

Giese, K. and Thiel, A. (2015) 'Chinese factor in the space, place and agency of female head porters in urban Ghana', *Social & Cultural Geography*, 16(4), pp 444–64.

Golo, H.K. (2005) *Poverty and Child Trafficking in Ghana: A Study of the Fishing Sector. Unpublished Masters Dissertation*. The Hague: Institute of Social Sciences.

Harrison, M.W. (2010) 'Child labour in the Ghanaian fishing industry: a review of situational reports from 1996–2010 for some selected fishing communities', *Distance Forum Journal*, 3, pp 226–36.

Hashim, I. and Thorsen, D. (2011) *Child Migrants in Africa*. London: Zed Books.

Huijsmans, R. (2012) *Background Paper on Young Migrants in Urban Ghana, Focusing Particularly on Young Female Head Porters (kayayei)*. The Hague: Institute of Social Sciences.

Huijsmans, R. and Baker, S. (2012) 'Child trafficking: "worst form" of child labour, or worst approach to young migrants?', *Development and Change*, 43(4), pp 919–46.

ILO (2016) *Child Labor in the Fish Supply Chain on Lake Volta: The Torkor Model*. Geneva: International Labour Organization.

ILO-IPEC (2013) *Analytical Study on Child Labour in Volta Lake fishing in Ghana*. Geneva: International Labour Organization – IPEC.

Iversen, V. (2006) *Children's Work in Fisheries: A Cause for Alarm?* Accra, Ghana: Sustainable Fisheries Livelihoods Programme.

Kansanga, M. et al (2019) 'Traditional agriculture in transition: examining the impacts of agricultural modernization on smallholder farming in Ghana under the new Green Revolution', *International Journal of Sustainable Development & World Ecology*, 26(1), pp 11–24.

Kielland, A. (2008) *Child Labor Migration in Benin: Incentive, Constraint or Agency? A Multinomial Logistic Regression*. Riga: VDM Publishing.

Koomson, B. et al (2022) 'I agreed to go because … examining the agency of children within a phenomenon conceptualised as trafficking in Ghana', *Children & Society*, 36(1), pp 101–17.

Kwankye, S.O. et al (2009) *Independent North–South Child Migration in Ghana: The Decision Making Process*. Working Paper T-29. Brighton: Development Research Centre on Migration, Globalisation and Poverty.

McClenachan, L., Dissanayake, S.T.M. and Chen, X.J. (2016) 'Fair trade fish: consumer support for broader seafood sustainability', *Fish and Fisheries*, 17(3), pp 825–38.

Miescher, S.F. (2014) '"Nkrumah's Baby": the Akosombo Dam and the dream of development in Ghana, 1952–1966', *Water History*, 6(4), pp 341–66.

MOFAD (2014) *Strategy on Anti-Child Labour and Trafficking in Fisheries. Towards the Eradication of Child Labour and Trafficking in Ghanaian Fishing Communities*. Accra: Fisheries Commission, Ministry of Fisheries and Aquaculture Development.

Moreto, W. D. et al (2019) 'The convergence of CAPTURED fish and people: examining the symbiotic nature of labor trafficking and illegal, unreported and unregulated fishing', *Deviant Behavior*, 41(6), pp 733–49.

Ofei-Aboagye, E. (2013) *Advancing Social Accountability in Social Protection and Socio-Economic Interventions: The Ghana School Feeding Programme*. Accra: Institute of Local Government Studies.

Okali, K., Frimpong Boamah, E. and Sumberg, J. (2022) 'The quantification of child labour by Ghana's mass media: a missed opportunity?', *Africa Spectrum*, 57(2), pp155–77.

Okyere, S. (2017) '"Shock and awe": a critique of the Ghana-centric child trafficking discourse', *Anti-Trafficking Review*, (9), pp 92–105.

Plange, N. (1979) 'Underdevelopment in Northern Ghana: natural causes or colonial capitalism?', *Review of African Political Economy*, 6(15–16), pp 4–14.

Raschid-Sally, L. et al (2008) *The Resettlement Experience of Ghana Analyzed via Case Studies of the Akosombo and Kpong Dams*. Paper presented at the 9th Annual Symposium on Poverty Research in Sri Lanka, Exploring Experiences of Resettlement.

Ratner, B.D., Asgard, B. and Allison, E.H. (2014) 'Fishing for justice: human rights, development, and fisheries sector reform', *Global Environmental Change – Human and Policy Dimensions*, 27, pp 120–30.

Sackey, E.T. and Johannesen, B.O. (2015) 'Earning identity and respect through work: A study of children involved in fishing and farming practices in Cape Coast, Ghana', *Childhood – a Global Journal of Child Research*, 22(4), pp 447–59.

Semordzi, E. (2018) *Report on Learning Tour to Torkor for SFMP Partners and Selected Stakeholders. The USAID/Ghana Sustainable Fisheries Management Project (SFMP).* Narragansett, RI: Coastal Resources Center, Graduate School of Oceanography, University of Rhode Island and SNV Netherlands Development Organisation.

Serra, R. (2009) 'Child fostering in Africa: when labor and schooling motives may coexist', *Journal of Development Economics*, 88(1), pp 157–70.

Singleton, K., Stone, K.B. and Stricker, J. (2016) *Child Trafficking into Forced Labor on Lake Volta, Ghana. A Mixed-Methods Assessment.* Washington, DC: International Justice Mission.

Songsore, J. et al (2001) 'Challenges of education in Northern Ghana: a case for Northern Ghana Education Trust Fund (netfund)', in Saaka, Y. (ed) *Regionalism and Public Policy in Northern Ghana.* New York: Peter Lang, pp 223–39.

Songsore, J. and Denkabe, A. (1995) *Challenging Rural Poverty in Northern Ghana: The Case of the Upper-West Region.* Trondheim: Centre for Environment and Development, University of Trondheim.

Teh, L.C.L. et al (2019) 'The role of human rights in implementing socially responsible seafood', *PLOS One*, 14(1), Article e0210241.

Tengey, W. and Oguaah, E. (2002) *The Little Ghanaian Slaves Cry for Help, A Report on Child Trafficking in Ghana.* Accra, Ghana: ACHD.

Thorsen, D. (2006) 'Child migrants in transit: strategies to become adult in rural Burkina Faso', in Utas, M. and Vigh, H.E. (eds) *Navigating Youth, Generating Adulthood: Social Becoming in an African Context.* Uppsala: Nordic African Institute, pp 88–114.

Thorsen, D. (2009) 'From shackles to links in the chain: theorising adolescent boys' relocation in Burkina Faso', *Forum for Development Studies*, 36(2), pp 81–107.

Thorsen, D. (2014) 'Jeans, bicycles and mobile phones: adolescent migrants' material consumption in Burkina Faso', in Veale, A. and Dona, G. (eds) *Child and Youth Migration: Mobility-in-Migration in an Era of Globalization.* Basingstoke: Palgrave MacMillan, pp 67–90.

Thorsen, D. (2019) 'Work opportunities and frictions for rural child migrants in West African cities', in Bourdillon, M. and Mulumbwa, G.M. (eds) *The Place of Work in African Childhoods.* Dakar: CODESRIA (Conseil pour le Developpement de la Recherche Economique et Sociale en Afrique), pp 93–106.

Torell, E., Owusu, A. and Okyere Nyako, A. (2015) *Ghana Fisheries Gender Analysis.* Narragansett, RI: USAID/Ghana Sustainable Fisheries Management Project.

Zdunnek, G. et al (2008) *Child Labour and Children's Economic Activities in Agriculture in Ghana. SLE Publication Series – S233*. Berlin: Centre for Advanced Training in Rural Development (SLE), Humbolt University, on behalf the Food and Agriculture Organization of the United Nations (FAO).

12

Children's Work in African Agriculture: Ways Forward

James Sumberg and Rachel Sabates-Wheeler

We sat down to draft this final chapter in the run up to Easter 2022, at a moment when shops across the UK were promoting a bewildering variety of seasonal chocolate eggs – small and large; solid and hollow; white, milk and dark; economy and top-of-the-line. At this same time, *The Observer* newspaper ran a story about an upcoming Channel 4 *Dispatches* programme[1] with the headline: 'Cadbury faces fresh accusations of child labour on cocoa farms in Ghana. A new TV documentary alleges that children as young as 10 are using machetes to harvest pods.'[2] And on Saturday 16th (the last day before Easter to buy chocolate eggs), *The Guardian* newspaper carried a full-page advertisement for *Tony's Chocolonely* – a self-proclaimed '100% slave free' chocolate producer – with a vivid, colourful accusation to readers, spanning two-thirds of the page, that 'there's child labour in your Easter chocolate.'

The beat goes on, and there is little sign that the debate around children, work, school, harm and agriculture in rural Africa will be disappearing anytime soon.

Despite children's work in African agriculture most often being portrayed as a 'bad', pure and simple, the preceding chapters confirm the fact that there is nothing simple or straightforward about this longstanding conundrum. Understandings of harm are not universal, but contingent – international norms and definitions can be irrelevant, if not harmful, at the local level. Complex definitions and assumptions about what is hazardous and/or harmful obscure the fact that there is little evidence that large numbers of children actually experience harm from work. School versus work is a false choice: many children work in order to go to school, and they work as part of the school day. Girls and boys can experience harm at home and in school, as well as when working; and through work children can learn, earn and increase their social status and self-esteem. The relationship between poverty and children's work is highly complex, such that well-intentioned interventions can negatively affect children. The governance mechanisms within domestic agricultural value chains offer few opportunities to address harm, while results from interventions in global value chains are at best mixed.

None of this is meant to downplay or dismiss the need to be cognizant of and address harm experienced by children in rural Africa, wherever it arises. Rather, it is to highlight the need to think again about how this might be accomplished.

A critical insight is that the experience of work-based harm by children in rural SSA is embedded in deeply entwined economic, political and socio-cultural systems that interact across multiple scales. The implication is clear: addressing children's harmful work as essentially an agriculture sector problem, or a poverty problem, or a school-quality problem, or a cultural problem, will certainly fail.

In this light, we need to think again about the existing framework of international conventions, instruments and organizational mandates, and how it can be made more reflective of and relevant to national and local worldviews, traditions, norms and circumstances. Specifically, the challenge here is to reimagine and reinvigorate global social policy around child labour and children's work (and childhood more generally) so that it is characterized by bottom-up inclusivity rather than top-down hegemony. This is about institutional power, and decolonization.

We need to think again about the framing of policy and public debate relating to children and work. Language – child labour, acceptable work, hazardous and harmful work, trafficking, slavery – matters, as does the portrayal of working children as helpless victims (or unconstrained free agents) of local communities as backward and so on. This is about discursive power.

We need to think again about the re-shaping of agrarian relations and livelihoods that is on-going in Africa. How will these changes affect gendered access to land, gendered engagement in local, national and international agricultural value chains, and ways that these chains are governed? Will they increase the influence of African producers and the returns to agriculture – for larger land owners, for male and female small-scale producers, or for male and female farm labourers? This is about economic power.

We need to think again about economic and political geography and specifically the left-behind rural areas and the poor quality of rural services – including education – with which their populations live. The focus here must be on policy priorities, policy processes and the dynamics of electoral politics, and how they maintain – and could potentially address – gendered deficits of economic opportunity, in agriculture and beyond, in rural areas. This is about political power.

We need to think again about broader shifts in state-society relations in SSA, about citizenship and meaningful political participation. Only then will the rallying cry of working children's movements – 'nothing about us without us' – begin to come to life for children (disabled and able-bodied), for parents, and for all rural people. This is about people power.

And we need to think again about how all of these complex relations manifest themselves in children's gendered experience – and their families' and the broader rural population's gendered understandings – of the trade-offs around work, school and potential harm. Of particular interest here are views about the costs and benefits (broadly conceived) of various interventions, from enforced prohibition through to price premiums and local monitoring committees. This is about the power of voice.

It should be clear that the continued existence of children's harmful work in African agriculture is an expression of multiple, interacting forms of power. As such, we can expect little from policies, strategies and interventions that are not rooted in a systemic understanding, and that do not focus in on, disrupt and re-align these power relations and their resulting inequalities. For example, what benefit will arise from improving the quality of rural schools if local farmers (and parents) – whether producing for international or local markets (and probably both) – don't have enough income to pay school fees? What will be the benefit of community-based child labour monitoring committees if local views on the importance and value of children's work are subordinated to universal definitions of child labour developed in Geneva or New York? Or, what will be the benefit of a cash transfer intervention if continual pressure to squeeze cost from the value chains keeps returns to agricultural labour artificially low?

Is this to say that addressing children's harmful work in African agriculture is just too complicated? Is it to suggest that for African children, harm arising from work in agriculture is the unfortunate but acceptable price of living with poverty in rural areas?

Absolutely not!

Rather, it is to insist that the time has now come for fundamental change in the organizations, frameworks, strategies, programmes and interventions that seek to tackle children's harmful work. Such change must certainly include:

- Grounding analysis of children's harmful work in a critical perspective on power in its various forms – economic, social, political, inter-generational, discursive, market and so on. All of these forms affect the room to manoeuvre available to communities, households and children in rural SSA, and are therefore integral to the forms, prevalence and experience of work-related harm. Interventions to address children's harmful work are also power-laden, and must be evaluated as such.

- Taking the variety of local understandings of childhood much more seriously, including traditions and practices that highlight the importance of children learning to work. These understandings, traditions and practices should not be lost to the seductive power of universal, decontextualized concepts and approaches.
- Problematizing the notion of harm so that associated terms like risk, hazard, hazardous, harmful and harmed have enhanced analytical purchase. Insights are on offer from multiple academic disciplines, but the challenge is to integrate these with the gendered and grounded perspectives of children, parents and others (including, for example, religious and political authorities).
- Foregrounding the critically important distinction between work and harmful work. This implies loosening the stranglehold of 'child labour' discourse on policy, research, corporate branding and marketing, the media and public debate. This will surely be a struggle, as interests are deeply entrenched, but without movement on this front there will be limited opportunity for progress.
- Bringing the notion of trade-off to centre stage as a way to interrogate simplistic assumptions that, for example, school is always better (and safer) than work, or that education and work are always antithetical.
- Finding a realistic middle ground between the trope of working children as helpless victims in need of protection and rescue, and the trope of children as economic and social agents who are in control of their lives. Children's agency is real, but its reification represents a significant retrograde step. Child-centred theories must give ground to relational understandings of the positionality of children in connection to both structure and voice.
- Reimagining research methods beyond the quantitative–qualitative divide. Further progress in the development and use of innovative, mixed-methods and participatory approaches will be particularly important, especially as regards the experiences and perspectives of children and their families, and how they understand and navigate complex trade-offs. Non-traditional sources of data (for example, data generated through certification schemes and child labour monitoring schemes) also have much to offer, but their inherent bias toward particular commodities and value chains must be clearly acknowledged.
- Bringing the state back in as the essential actor in addressing children's harmful work across all commodities and agricultural value chains – simple or complex, local, national or global. Responsibility for the wellbeing of African children should no longer be off-shored to the US Congress, northern consumers, global food corporations, certification agencies and international advocacy groups. Neither can the artificial split between global commodities and value chains on the one hand, and crops and

livestock for domestic consumption on the other, be sustained. The state has a vital role to play, but its willingness and ability to play this role brings us right back to the top of this list, where an analysis of power takes centre stage.

There is much to be done.

Notes

1 'Cadbury Exposed' aired on 4 April 2022 (https://www.channel4.com/programmes/cadbury-exposed-dispatches)

2 https://www.theguardian.com/law/2022/apr/03/cadbury-faces-fresh-accusations-of-child-labour-on-cocoa-farms-in-ghana

Index

References to figures appear in *italic* type; those in **bold** type refer to tables